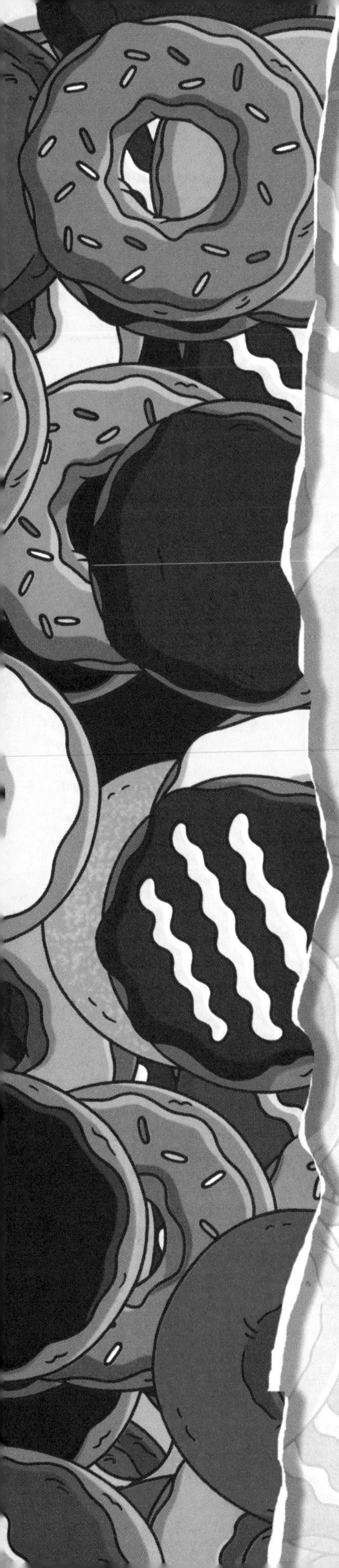

# Table of Contents

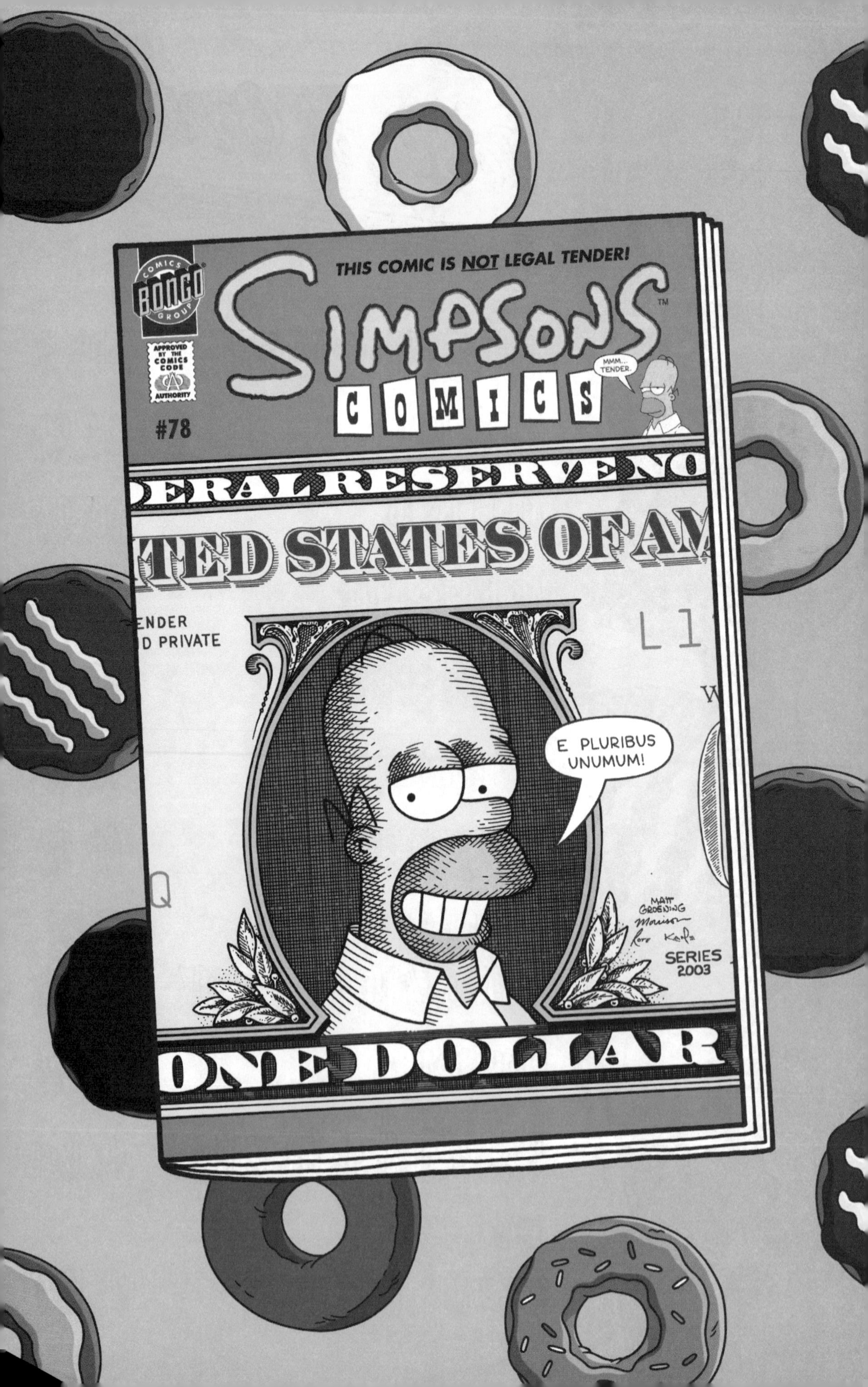

THIS COMIC IS NOT LEGAL TENDER!
SIMPSONS
COMICS
#78
MMM... TENDER.
DERAL RESERVE NO
TED STATES OF AM
ENDER
D PRIVATE
E PLURIBUS UNUMUM!
MATT GROENING
SERIES 2003
ONE DOLLAR

# SIMPSONS™ COMICS DOLLAR$ TO DONUTS

**TITAN BOOKS**

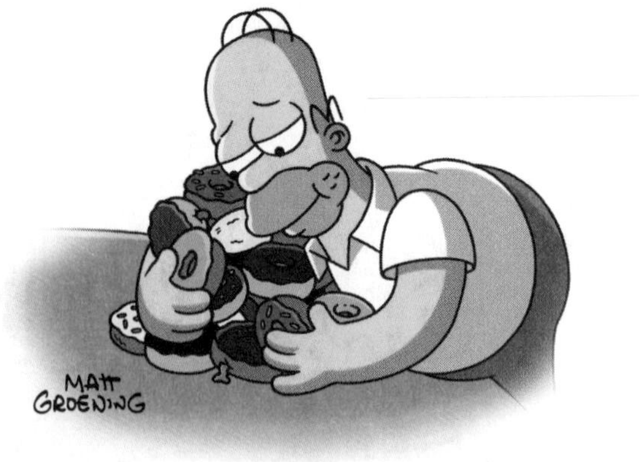
MATT
GROENING



SIMPSONS COMICS DOLLARS TO DONUTS



Published in the UK by Titan Books, a division of Titan Publishing Group,
144 Southwark St., London SE1 0UP, under licence from Bongo Entertainment, Inc.



FIRST EDITION: JANUARY 2008

ISBN-10: 1-84576-751-9
ISBN-13: 9781845767518

2 4 6 8 10 9 7 5 3 1

Publisher: Matt Groening
Creative Director: Bill Morrison
Managing Editor: Terry Delegeane
Director of Operations: Robert Zaugh
Art Director: Nathan Kane
Art Director Special Projects: Serban Cristescu
Production Manager: Christopher Ungar
Legal Guardian: Susan A. Grode

Trade Paperback Concepts and Design: Serban Cristescu

Contributing Artists:
Karen Bates, Tim Bavington, John Costanza, Dan DeCarlo, Mike DeCarlo, Luis Escobar,
Chia-Hsien Jason Ho, Nathan Kane, Scott McRae, Bill Morrison, Kevin M. Newman, Phyllis Novin,
Phil Ortiz, Patrick Owsley, Mike Rote, Howard Shum, Chris Ungar, Art Villanueva

Contributing Writers:
Ian Boothby, Dan Fybel, Earl Kress, Jesse Leon McCann, David McKean, Gail Simone, David Slack

PRINTED IN CANADA

# THE BUCK STOPS EVERYWHERE

1865...

HOLD ON A MINUTE! I THINK I *BLINKED!*

| IAN BOOTHBY | PHIL ORTIZ | MIKE DECARLO | ART VILLANUEVA | KAREN BATES | BILL MORRISON | MATT GROENING |
|---|---|---|---|---|---|---|
| Script | Pencils | Inks | Colors | Letters | Editor | The Great Anticipator |

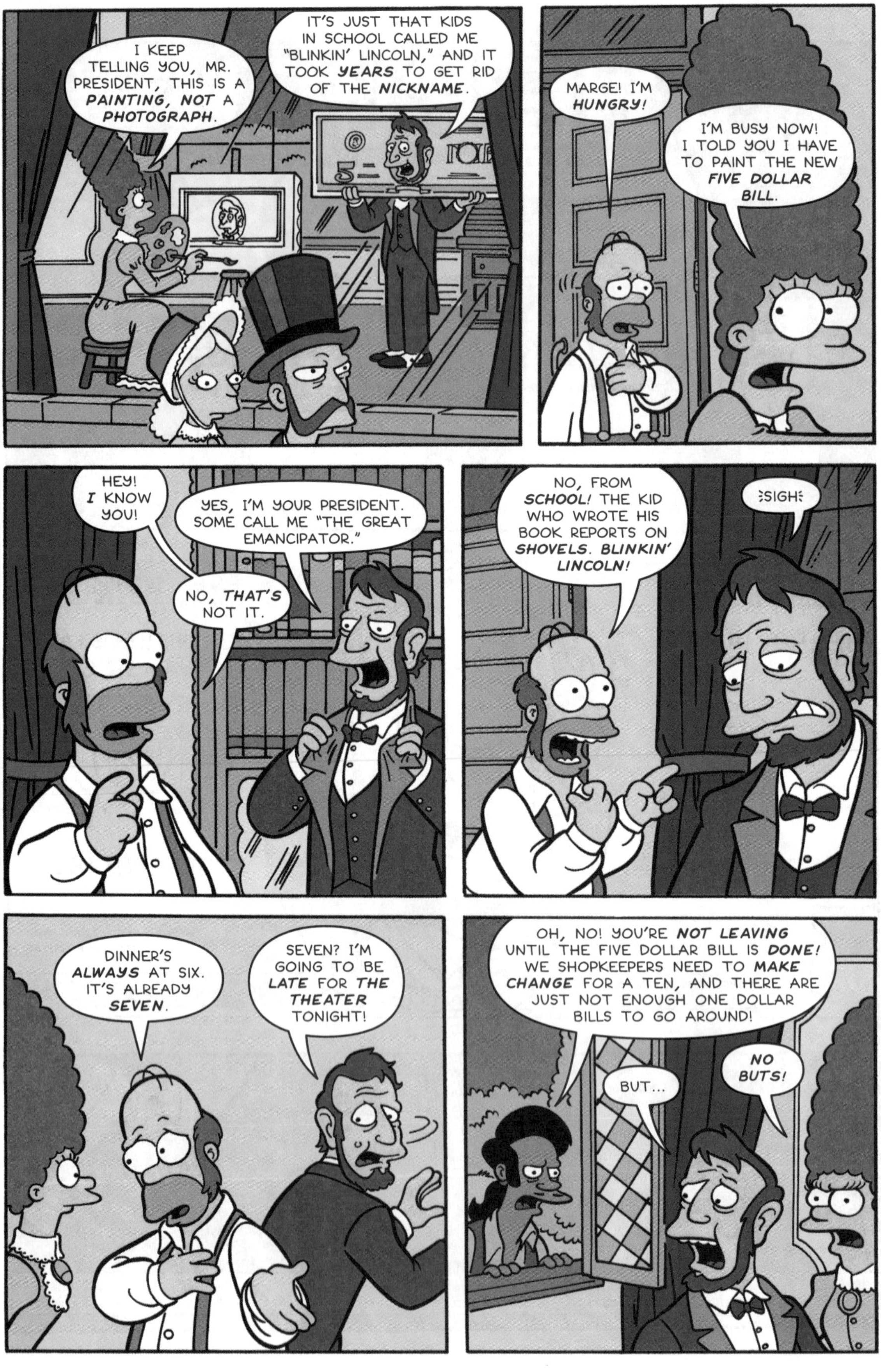
I KEEP TELLING YOU, MR. PRESIDENT, THIS IS A *PAINTING, NOT* A *PHOTOGRAPH*.
IT'S JUST THAT KIDS IN SCHOOL CALLED ME "BLINKIN' LINCOLN," AND IT TOOK *YEARS* TO GET RID OF THE *NICKNAME*.
MARGE! I'M *HUNGRY!*
I'M BUSY NOW! I TOLD YOU I HAVE TO PAINT THE NEW *FIVE DOLLAR BILL*.
HEY! *I* KNOW YOU!
YES, I'M YOUR PRESIDENT. SOME CALL ME "THE GREAT EMANCIPATOR."
NO, *THAT'S* NOT IT.
NO, FROM *SCHOOL!* THE KID WHO WROTE HIS BOOK REPORTS ON *SHOVELS. BLINKIN' LINCOLN!*
SIGH
DINNER'S *ALWAYS* AT SIX. IT'S ALREADY *SEVEN*.
SEVEN? I'M GOING TO BE *LATE* FOR *THE THEATER* TONIGHT!
OH, NO! YOU'RE *NOT LEAVING* UNTIL THE FIVE DOLLAR BILL IS *DONE!* WE SHOPKEEPERS NEED TO *MAKE CHANGE* FOR A TEN, AND THERE ARE JUST NOT ENOUGH ONE DOLLAR BILLS TO GO AROUND!
BUT...
*NO BUTS!*

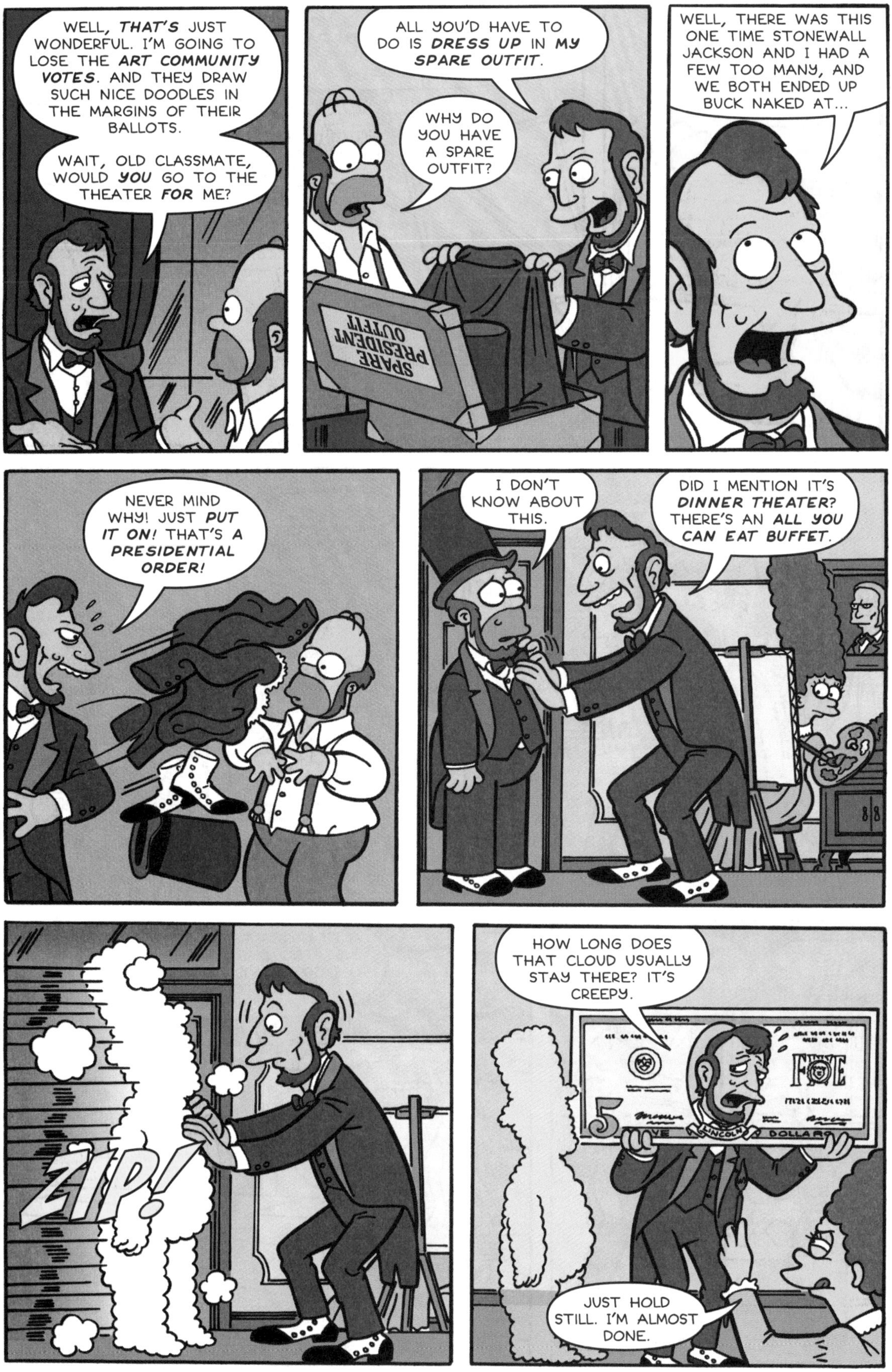

WELL, THAT'S JUST WONDERFUL. I'M GOING TO LOSE THE ART COMMUNITY VOTES. AND THEY DRAW SUCH NICE DOODLES IN THE MARGINS OF THEIR BALLOTS.
WAIT, OLD CLASSMATE, WOULD YOU GO TO THE THEATER FOR ME?
ALL YOU'D HAVE TO DO IS DRESS UP IN MY SPARE OUTFIT.
WHY DO YOU HAVE A SPARE OUTFIT?
SPARE PRESIDENT OUTFIT
WELL, THERE WAS THIS ONE TIME STONEWALL JACKSON AND I HAD A FEW TOO MANY, AND WE BOTH ENDED UP BUCK NAKED AT...
NEVER MIND WHY! JUST PUT IT ON! THAT'S A PRESIDENTIAL ORDER!
I DON'T KNOW ABOUT THIS.
DID I MENTION IT'S DINNER THEATER? THERE'S AN ALL YOU CAN EAT BUFFET.
ZIP!
HOW LONG DOES THAT CLOUD USUALLY STAY THERE? IT'S CREEPY.
FIVE
5
LINCOLN
DOLLARS
JUST HOLD STILL. I'M ALMOST DONE.

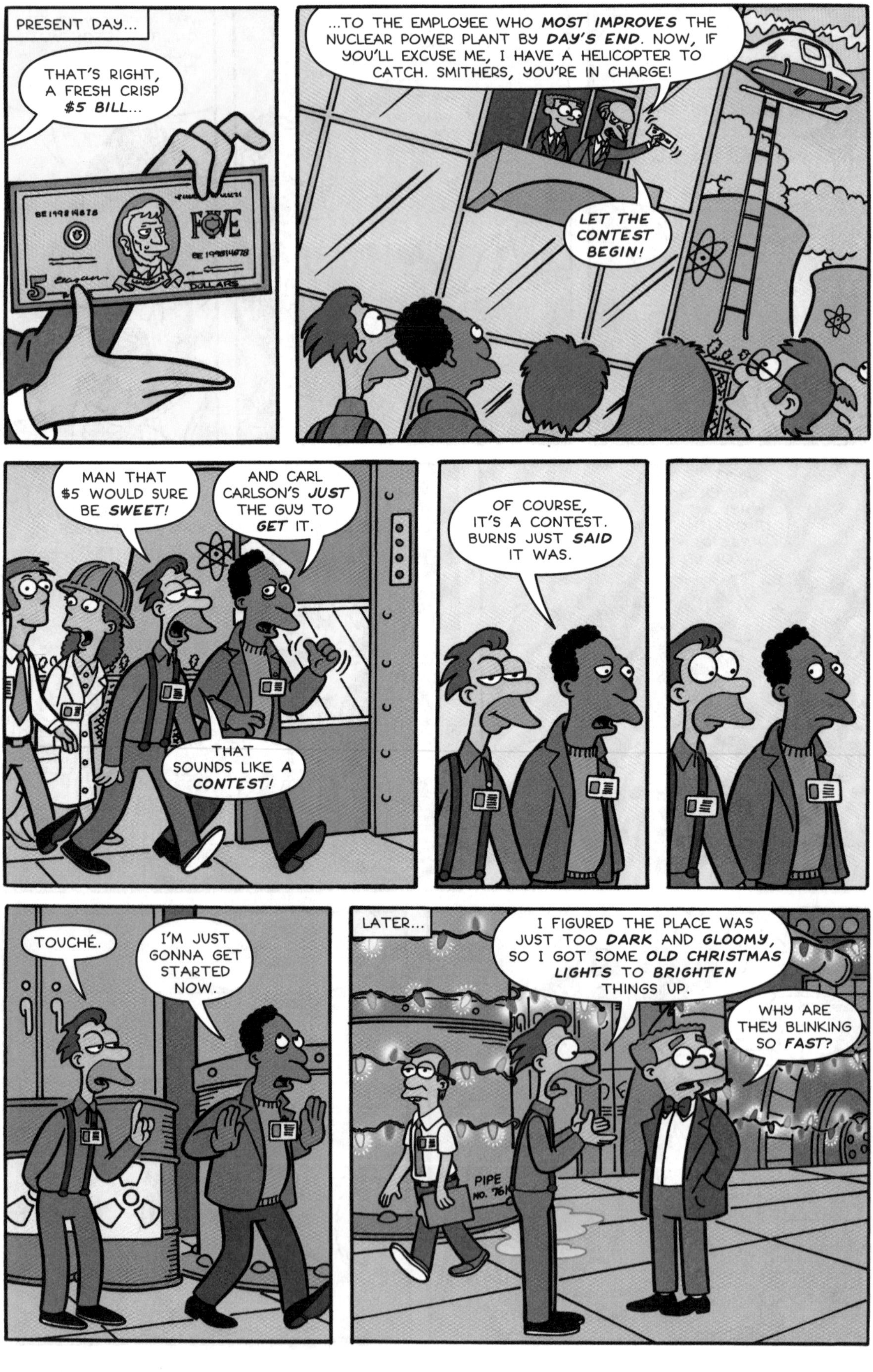
PRESENT DAY...
THAT'S RIGHT, A FRESH CRISP $5 BILL...
FIVE
DOLLARS
...TO THE EMPLOYEE WHO MOST IMPROVES THE NUCLEAR POWER PLANT BY DAY'S END. NOW, IF YOU'LL EXCUSE ME, I HAVE A HELICOPTER TO CATCH. SMITHERS, YOU'RE IN CHARGE!
LET THE CONTEST BEGIN!
MAN THAT $5 WOULD SURE BE SWEET!
AND CARL CARLSON'S JUST THE GUY TO GET IT.
THAT SOUNDS LIKE A CONTEST!
OF COURSE, IT'S A CONTEST. BURNS JUST SAID IT WAS.
TOUCHÉ.
I'M JUST GONNA GET STARTED NOW.
LATER...
I FIGURED THE PLACE WAS JUST TOO DARK AND GLOOMY, SO I GOT SOME OLD CHRISTMAS LIGHTS TO BRIGHTEN THINGS UP.
WHY ARE THEY BLINKING SO FAST?
PIPE NO. 761

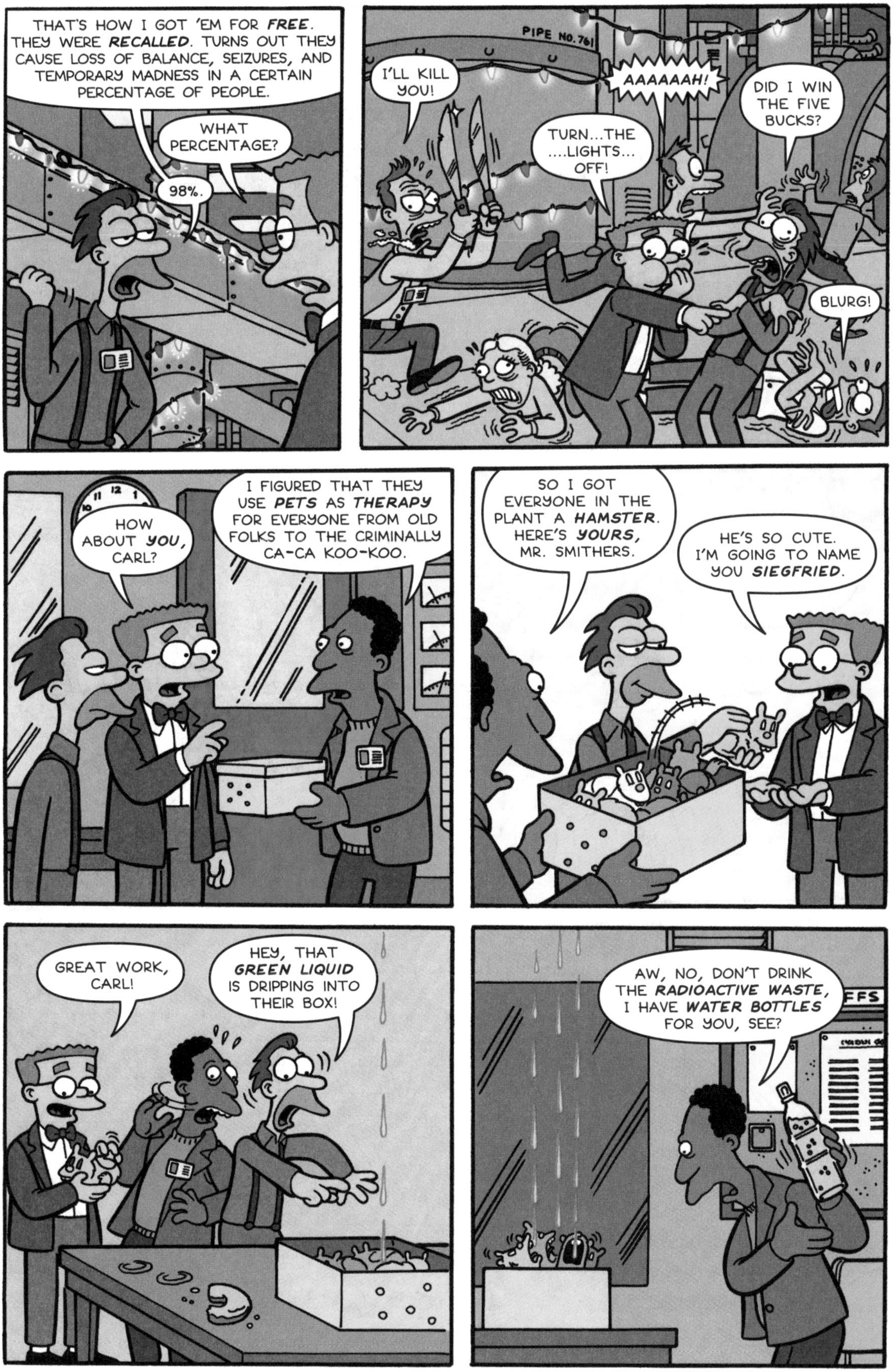
THAT'S HOW I GOT 'EM FOR FREE. THEY WERE RECALLED. TURNS OUT THEY CAUSE LOSS OF BALANCE, SEIZURES, AND TEMPORARY MADNESS IN A CERTAIN PERCENTAGE OF PEOPLE.
WHAT PERCENTAGE?
98%.
PIPE NO. 761
I'LL KILL YOU!
AAAAAAH!
TURN...THE ....LIGHTS... OFF!
DID I WIN THE FIVE BUCKS?
BLURG!
HOW ABOUT YOU, CARL?
I FIGURED THAT THEY USE PETS AS THERAPY FOR EVERYONE FROM OLD FOLKS TO THE CRIMINALLY CA-CA KOO-KOO.
SO I GOT EVERYONE IN THE PLANT A HAMSTER. HERE'S YOURS, MR. SMITHERS.
HE'S SO CUTE. I'M GOING TO NAME YOU SIEGFRIED.
GREAT WORK, CARL!
HEY, THAT GREEN LIQUID IS DRIPPING INTO THEIR BOX!
AW, NO, DON'T DRINK THE RADIOACTIVE WASTE, I HAVE WATER BOTTLES FOR YOU, SEE?

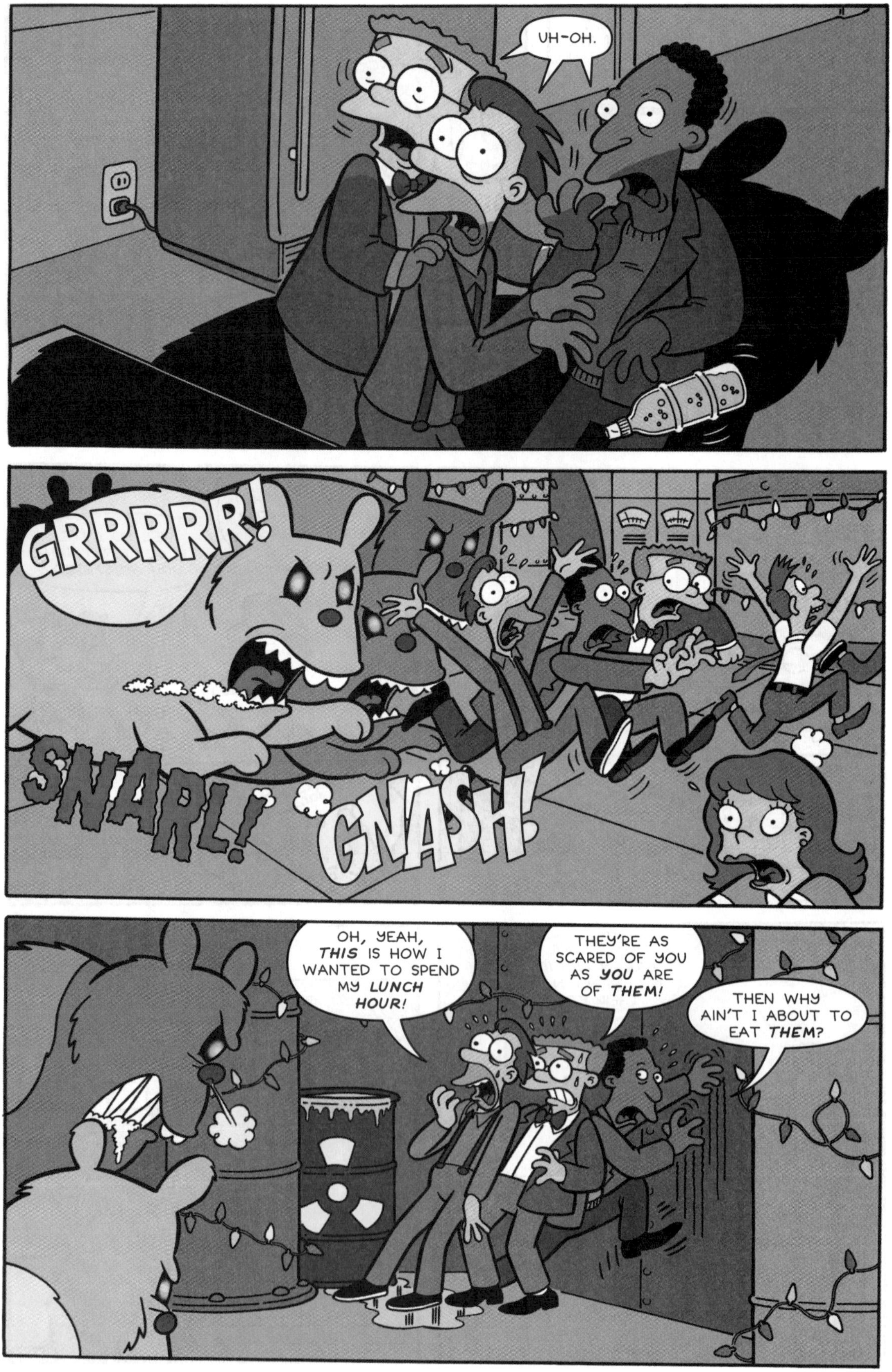
UH-OH.
GRRRRR!
SNARL!
GNASH!
OH, YEAH, THIS IS HOW I WANTED TO SPEND MY LUNCH HOUR!
THEY'RE AS SCARED OF YOU AS YOU ARE OF THEM!
THEN WHY AIN'T I ABOUT TO EAT THEM?

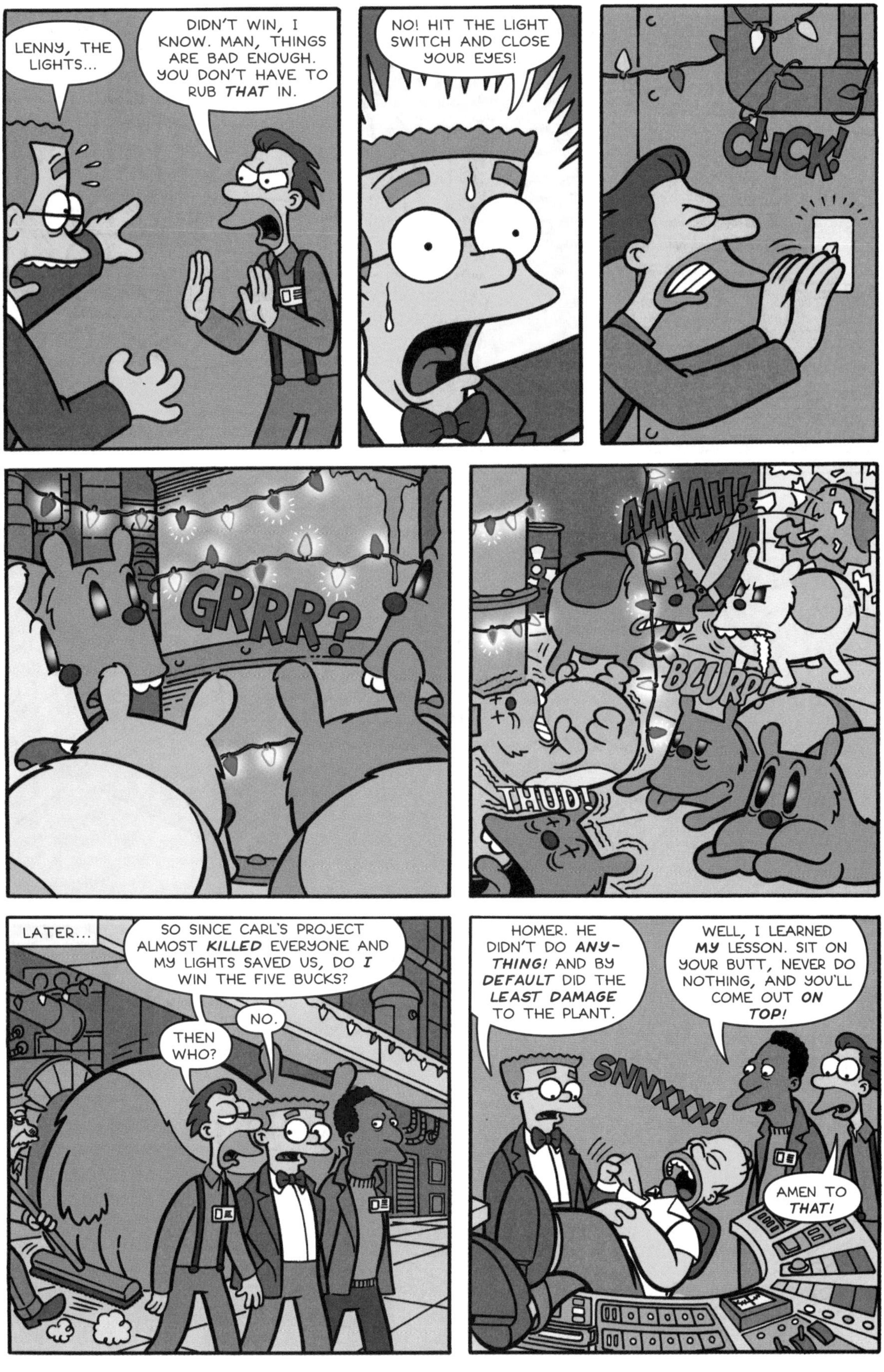
LENNY, THE LIGHTS...
DIDN'T WIN, I KNOW. MAN, THINGS ARE BAD ENOUGH. YOU DON'T HAVE TO RUB *THAT* IN.
NO! HIT THE LIGHT SWITCH AND CLOSE YOUR EYES!
CLICK!
GRRR?
AAAAH!
BLURP!
THUD!
LATER...
SO SINCE CARL'S PROJECT ALMOST ***KILLED*** EVERYONE AND MY LIGHTS SAVED US, DO ***I*** WIN THE FIVE BUCKS?
NO.
THEN WHO?
HOMER. HE DIDN'T DO ***ANY-THING!*** AND BY ***DEFAULT*** DID THE ***LEAST DAMAGE*** TO THE PLANT.
WELL, I LEARNED ***MY*** LESSON. SIT ON YOUR BUTT, NEVER DO NOTHING, AND YOU'LL COME OUT ***ON TOP!***
SNNXXX!
AMEN TO ***THAT!***

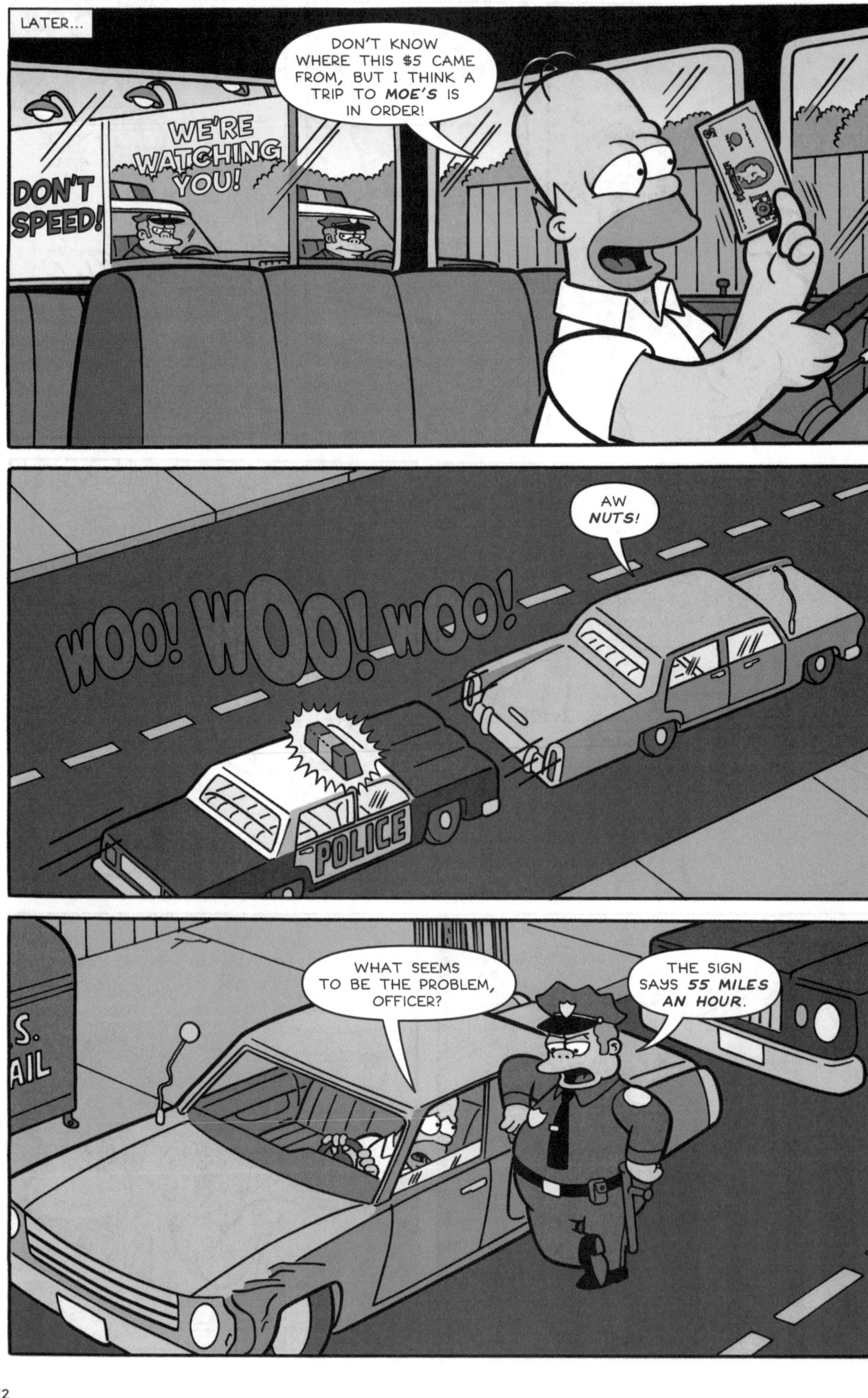
LATER...
WE'RE WATCHING YOU!
DON'T SPEED!
DON'T KNOW WHERE THIS $5 CAME FROM, BUT I THINK A TRIP TO **MOE'S** IS IN ORDER!
AW **NUTS!**
WOO! WOO! WOO!
POLICE
WHAT SEEMS TO BE THE PROBLEM, OFFICER?
THE SIGN SAYS **55 MILES AN HOUR**.

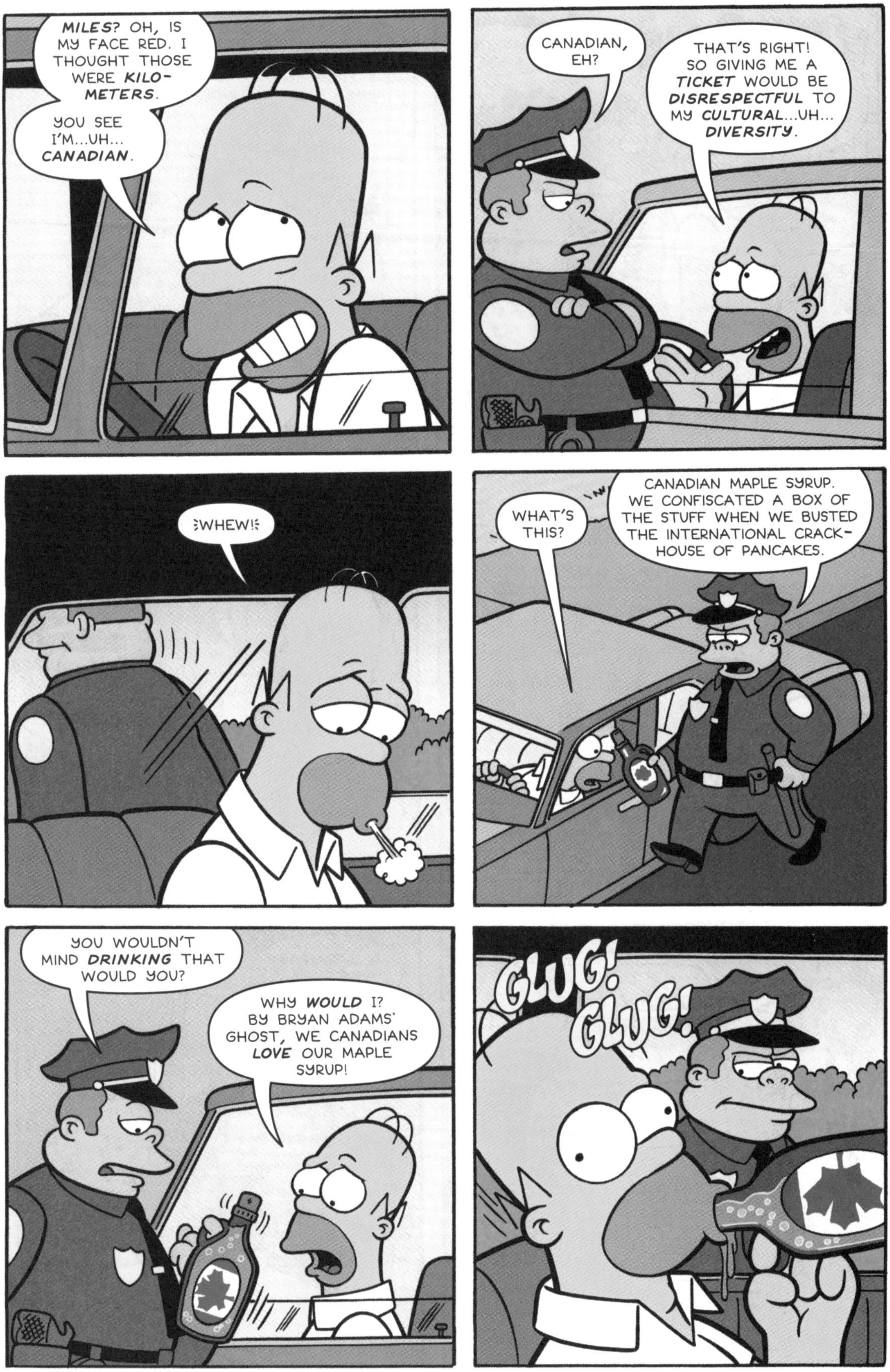
MILES? OH, IS MY FACE RED. I THOUGHT THOSE WERE KILO-METERS.
YOU SEE I'M...UH... CANADIAN.
CANADIAN, EH?
THAT'S RIGHT! SO GIVING ME A TICKET WOULD BE DISRESPECTFUL TO MY CULTURAL...UH... DIVERSITY.
WHEW!
WHAT'S THIS?
CANADIAN MAPLE SYRUP. WE CONFISCATED A BOX OF THE STUFF WHEN WE BUSTED THE INTERNATIONAL CRACK-HOUSE OF PANCAKES.
YOU WOULDN'T MIND DRINKING THAT WOULD YOU?
WHY WOULD I? BY BRYAN ADAMS' GHOST, WE CANADIANS LOVE OUR MAPLE SYRUP!
GLUG! GLUG!

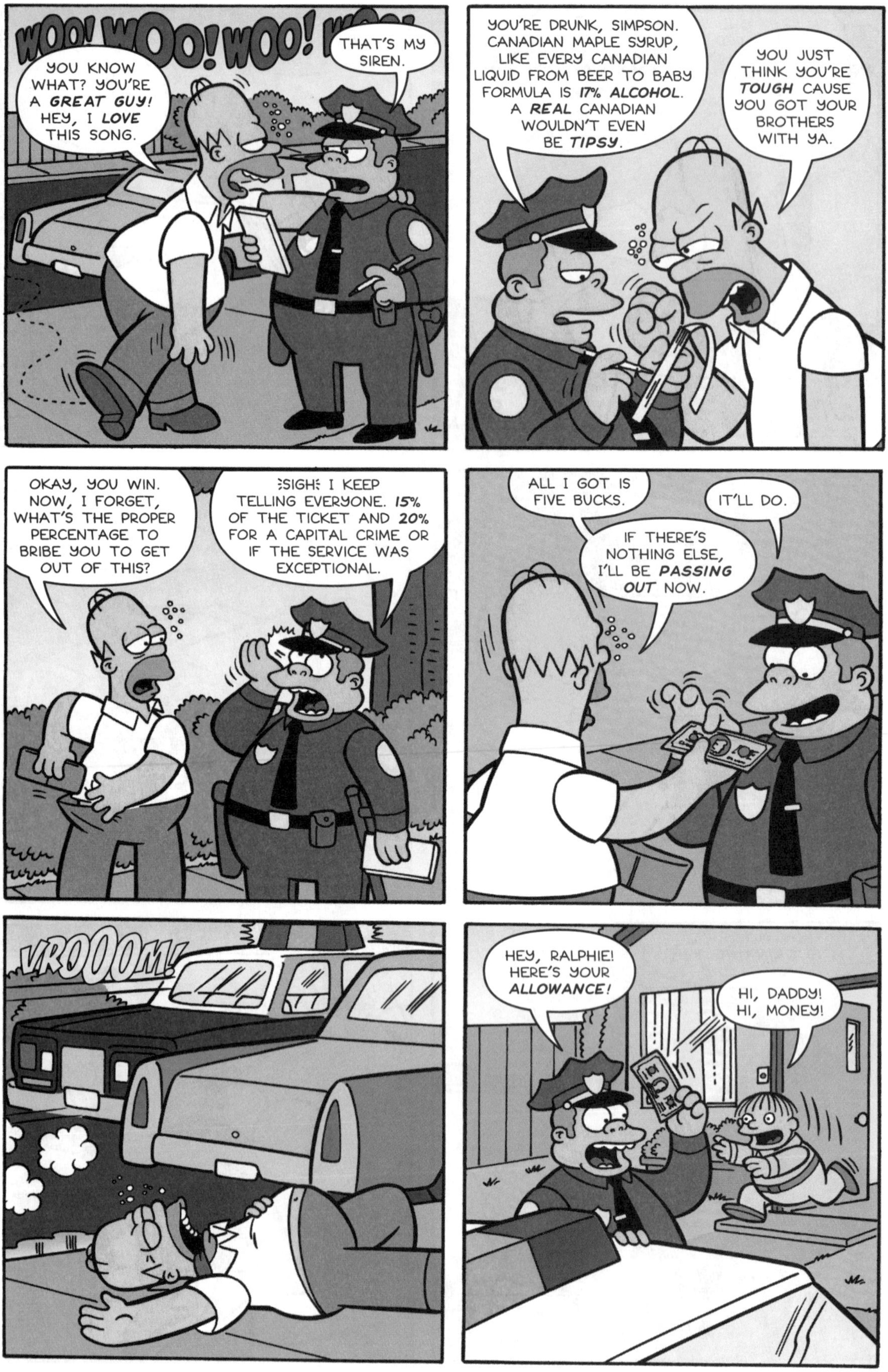
WOO! WOO! WOO!
YOU KNOW WHAT? YOU'RE A **GREAT GUY**! HEY, I **LOVE** THIS SONG.
THAT'S MY SIREN.
YOU'RE DRUNK, SIMPSON. CANADIAN MAPLE SYRUP, LIKE EVERY CANADIAN LIQUID FROM BEER TO BABY FORMULA IS **17% ALCOHOL**. A **REAL** CANADIAN WOULDN'T EVEN BE **TIPSY**.
YOU JUST THINK YOU'RE **TOUGH** CAUSE YOU GOT YOUR BROTHERS WITH YA.
OKAY, YOU WIN. NOW, I FORGET, WHAT'S THE PROPER PERCENTAGE TO BRIBE YOU TO GET OUT OF THIS?
:SIGH: I KEEP TELLING EVERYONE. **15%** OF THE TICKET AND **20%** FOR A CAPITAL CRIME OR IF THE SERVICE WAS EXCEPTIONAL.
ALL I GOT IS FIVE BUCKS.
IT'LL DO.
IF THERE'S NOTHING ELSE, I'LL BE **PASSING OUT** NOW.
VROOOM!
HEY, RALPHIE! HERE'S YOUR **ALLOWANCE**!
HI, DADDY! HI, MONEY!

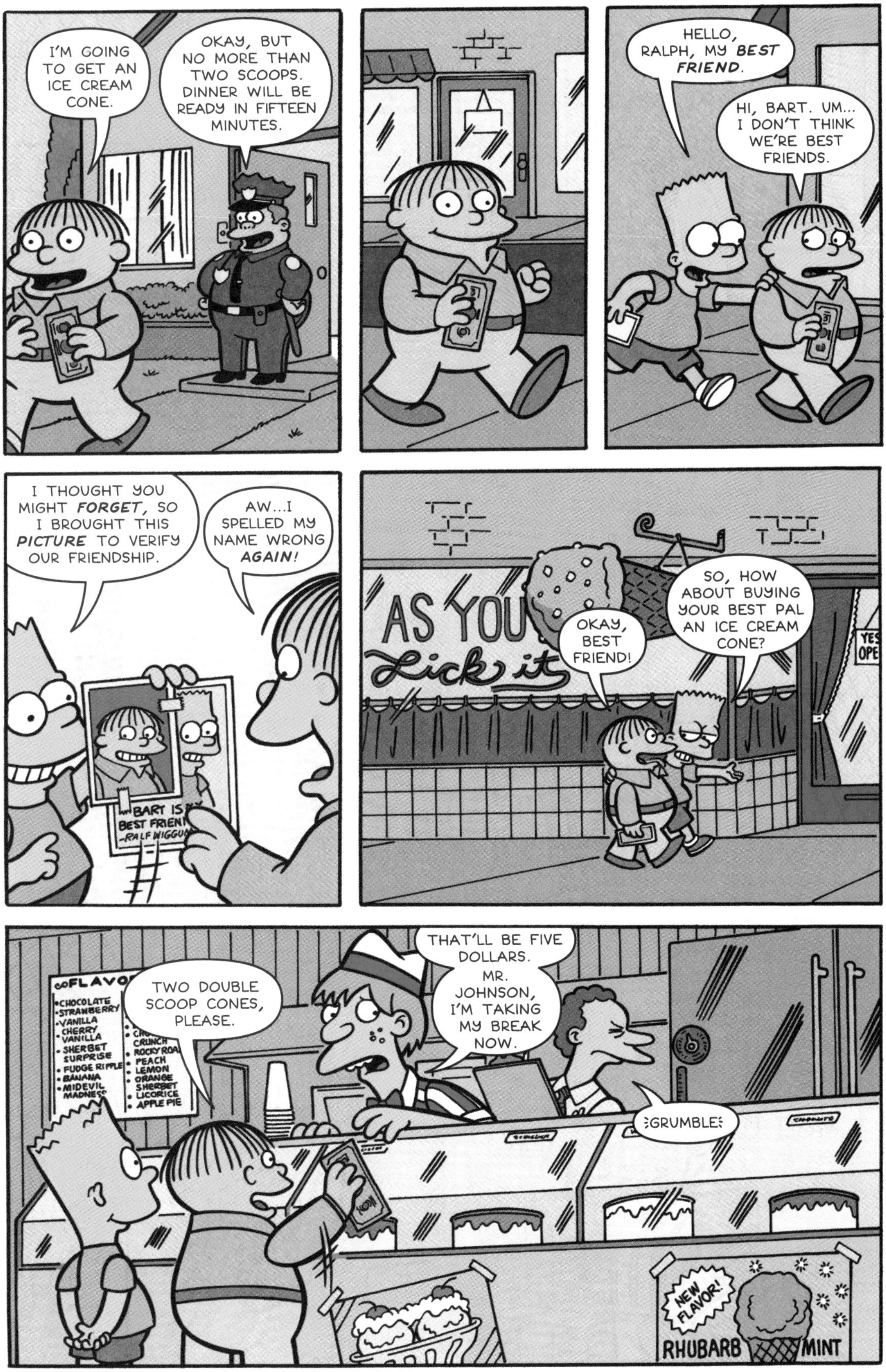
I'M GOING TO GET AN ICE CREAM CONE.
OKAY, BUT NO MORE THAN TWO SCOOPS. DINNER WILL BE READY IN FIFTEEN MINUTES.
HELLO, RALPH, MY *BEST FRIEND*.
HI, BART. UM... I DON'T THINK WE'RE BEST FRIENDS.
I THOUGHT YOU MIGHT *FORGET*, SO I BROUGHT THIS *PICTURE* TO VERIFY OUR FRIENDSHIP.
AW...I SPELLED MY NAME WRONG *AGAIN*!
Lick it
SO, HOW ABOUT BUYING YOUR BEST PAL AN ICE CREAM CONE?
OKAY, BEST FRIEND!
CHOCOLATE
STRAWBERRY
VANILLA
CHERRY VANILLA
SHERBET SURPRISE
FUDGE RIPPLE
BANANA
CRUNCH
PEACH
LEMON
ORANGE SHERBET
LICORICE
APPLE PIE
TWO DOUBLE SCOOP CONES, PLEASE.
THAT'LL BE FIVE DOLLARS.
MR. JOHNSON, I'M TAKING MY BREAK NOW.
GRUMBLE
NEW FLAVOR!
RHUBARB MINT

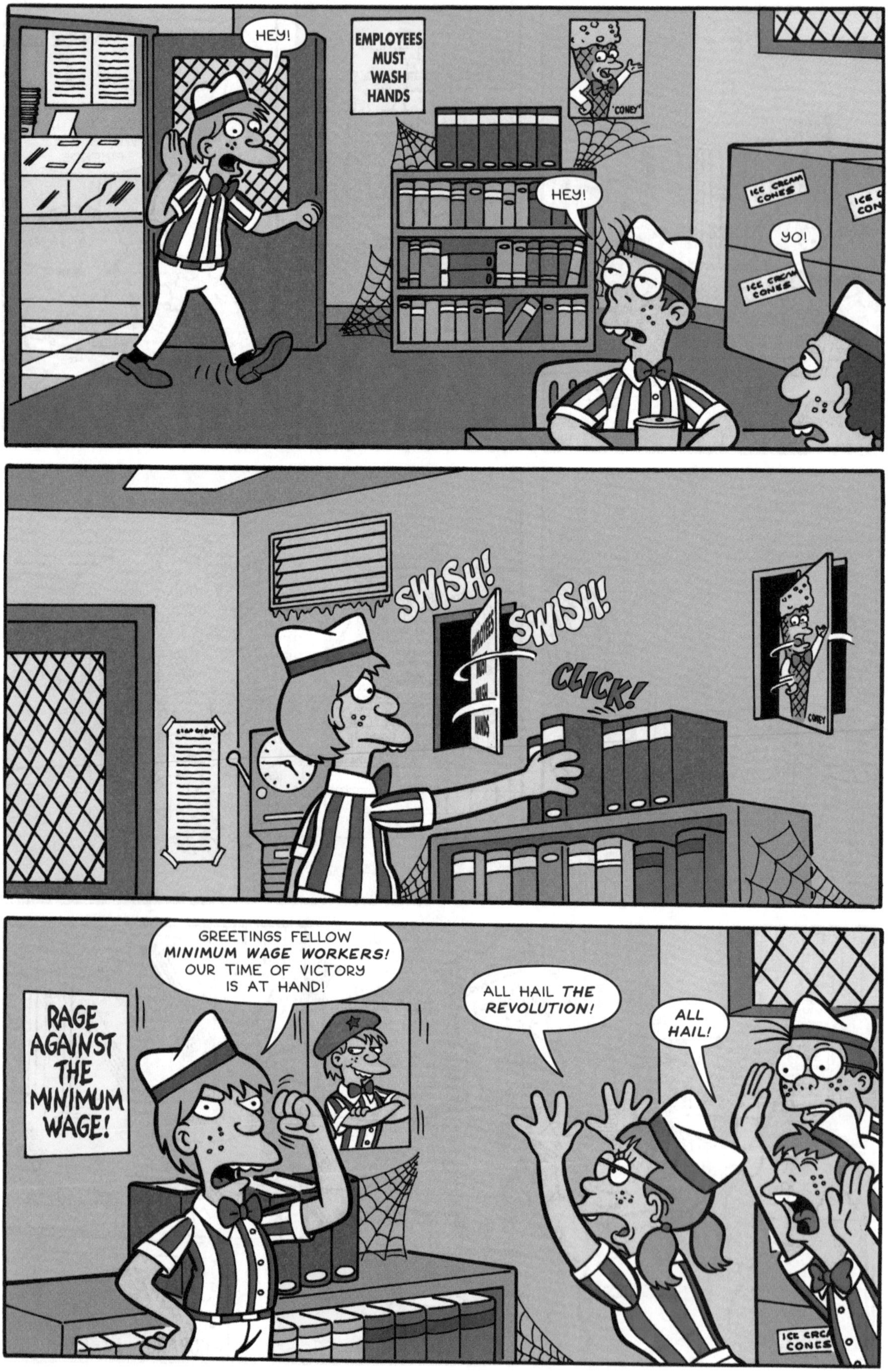
HEY!
EMPLOYEES MUST WASH HANDS
"CONEY"
HEY!
ICE CREAM CONES
YO!
ICE CREAM CONES
SWISH!
SWISH!
CLICK!
RAGE AGAINST THE MINIMUM WAGE!
GREETINGS FELLOW *MINIMUM WAGE WORKERS!* OUR TIME OF VICTORY IS AT HAND!
ALL HAIL *THE REVOLUTION!*
ALL HAIL!
ICE CREAM CONES

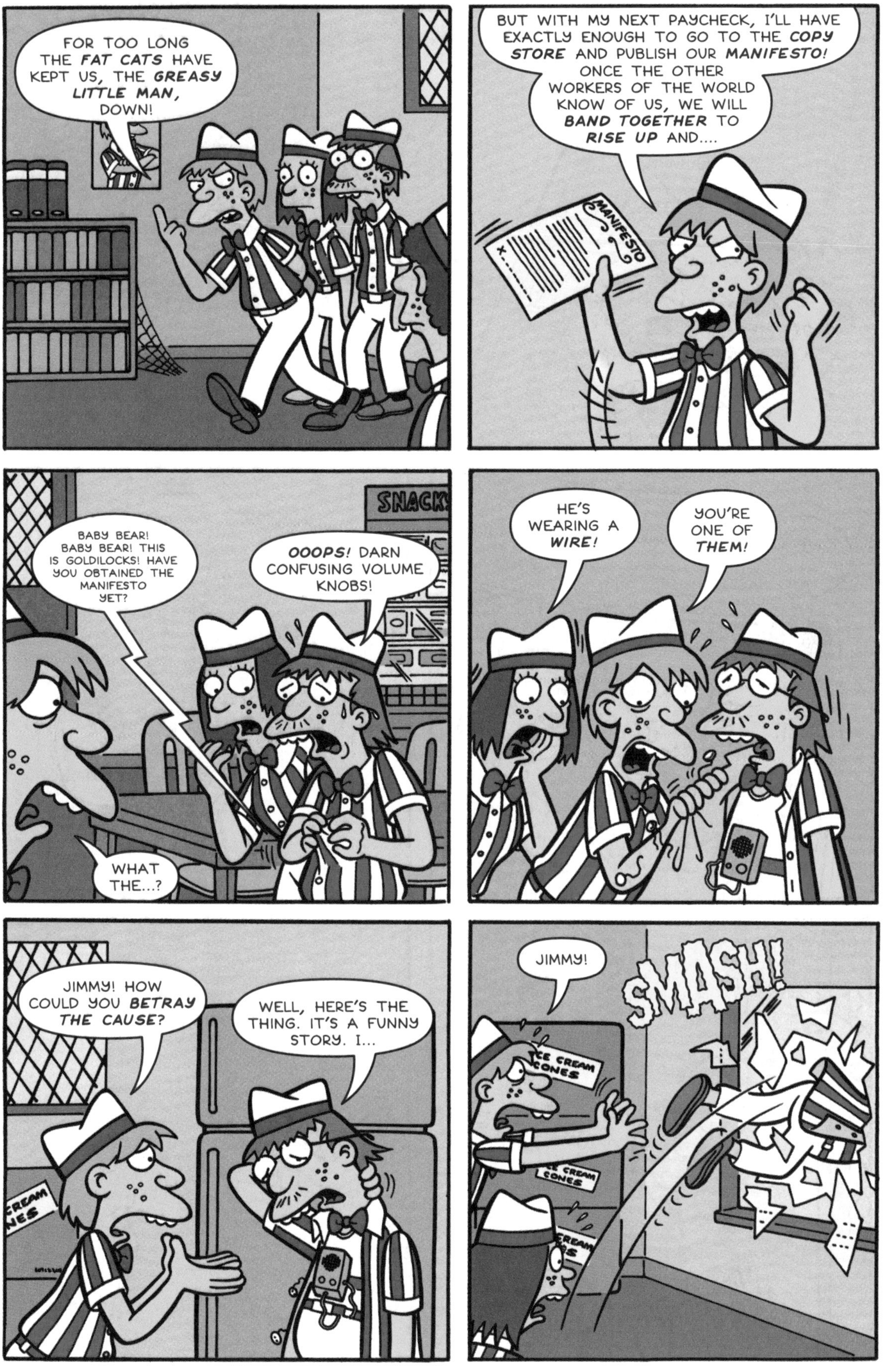

FOR TOO LONG THE FAT CATS HAVE KEPT US, THE GREASY LITTLE MAN, DOWN!
BUT WITH MY NEXT PAYCHECK, I'LL HAVE EXACTLY ENOUGH TO GO TO THE COPY STORE AND PUBLISH OUR MANIFESTO! ONCE THE OTHER WORKERS OF THE WORLD KNOW OF US, WE WILL BAND TOGETHER TO RISE UP AND....
MANIFESTO
SNACKS
BABY BEAR! BABY BEAR! THIS IS GOLDILOCKS! HAVE YOU OBTAINED THE MANIFESTO YET?
OOOPS! DARN CONFUSING VOLUME KNOBS!
WHAT THE...?
HE'S WEARING A WIRE!
YOU'RE ONE OF THEM!
JIMMY! HOW COULD YOU BETRAY THE CAUSE?
WELL, HERE'S THE THING. IT'S A FUNNY STORY. I...
JIMMY!
SMASH!
ICE CREAM CONES
ICE CREAM CONES

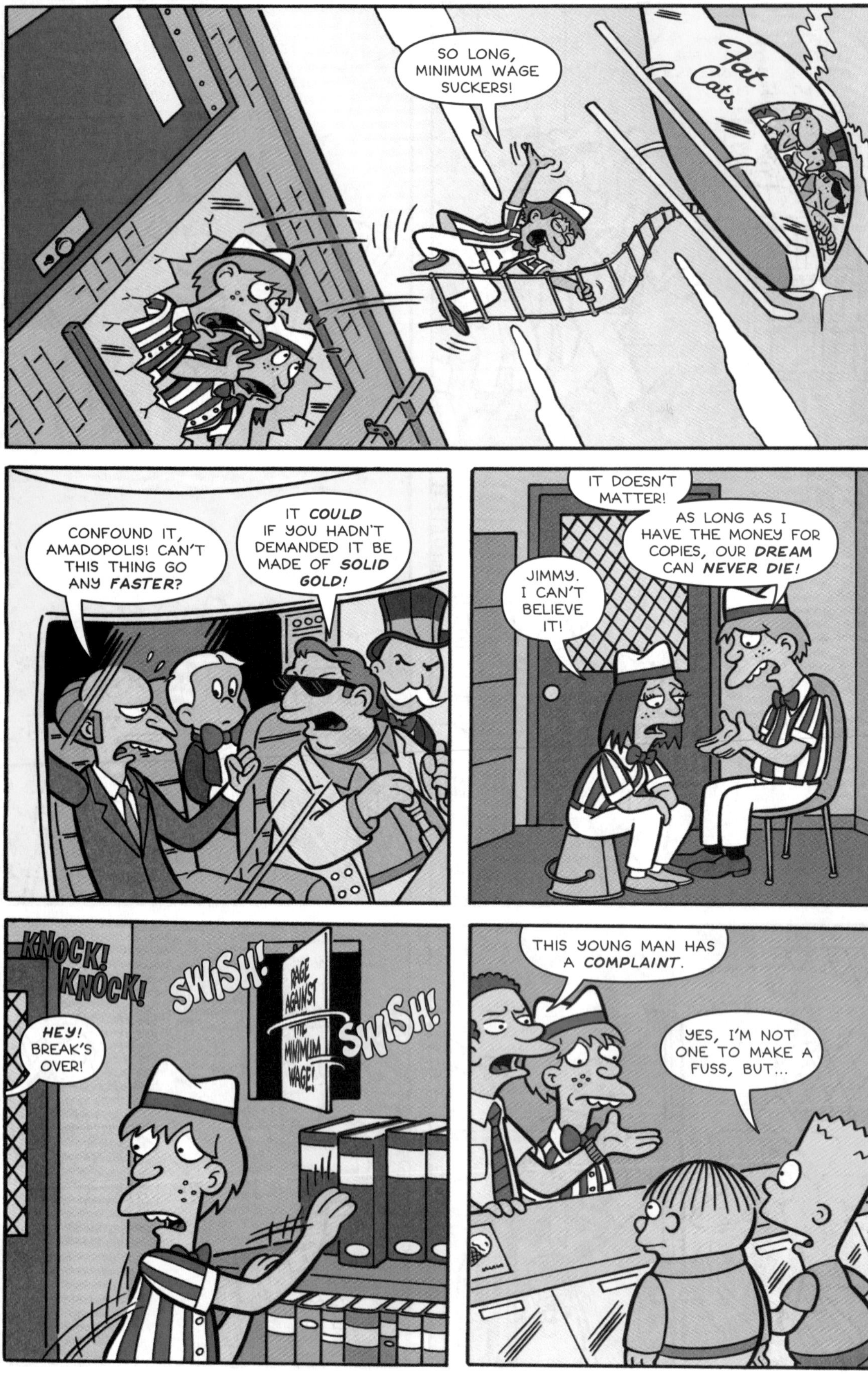
SO LONG, MINIMUM WAGE SUCKERS!
Fat Cats
CONFOUND IT, AMADOPOLIS! CAN'T THIS THING GO ANY *FASTER*?
IT *COULD* IF YOU HADN'T DEMANDED IT BE MADE OF *SOLID GOLD*!
JIMMY. I CAN'T BELIEVE IT!
IT DOESN'T MATTER!
AS LONG AS I HAVE THE MONEY FOR COPIES, OUR *DREAM* CAN *NEVER DIE*!
KNOCK! KNOCK!
HEY! BREAK'S OVER!
SWISH!
RAGE AGAINST THE MINIMUM WAGE!
SWISH!
THIS YOUNG MAN HAS A *COMPLAINT*.
YES, I'M NOT ONE TO MAKE A FUSS, BUT...

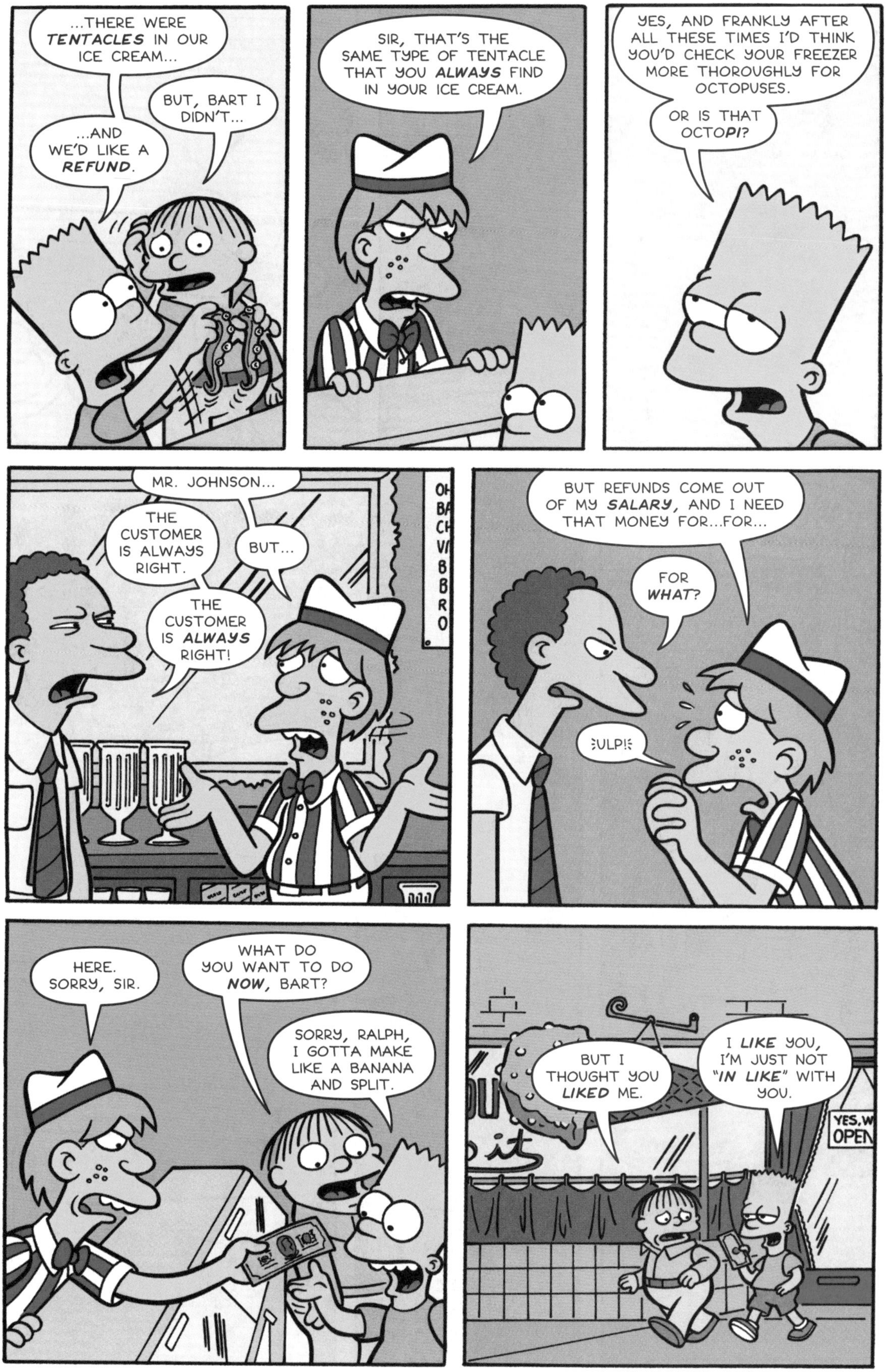
...THERE WERE TENTACLES IN OUR ICE CREAM...
...AND WE'D LIKE A REFUND.
BUT, BART I DIDN'T...
SIR, THAT'S THE SAME TYPE OF TENTACLE THAT YOU ALWAYS FIND IN YOUR ICE CREAM.
YES, AND FRANKLY AFTER ALL THESE TIMES I'D THINK YOU'D CHECK YOUR FREEZER MORE THOROUGHLY FOR OCTOPUSES.
OR IS THAT OCTOPI?
MR. JOHNSON...
THE CUSTOMER IS ALWAYS RIGHT.
BUT...
THE CUSTOMER IS ALWAYS RIGHT!
BUT REFUNDS COME OUT OF MY SALARY, AND I NEED THAT MONEY FOR...FOR...
FOR WHAT?
ULP!
HERE. SORRY, SIR.
WHAT DO YOU WANT TO DO NOW, BART?
SORRY, RALPH, I GOTTA MAKE LIKE A BANANA AND SPLIT.
BUT I THOUGHT YOU LIKED ME.
I LIKE YOU, I'M JUST NOT "IN LIKE" WITH YOU.
YES, W
OPEN

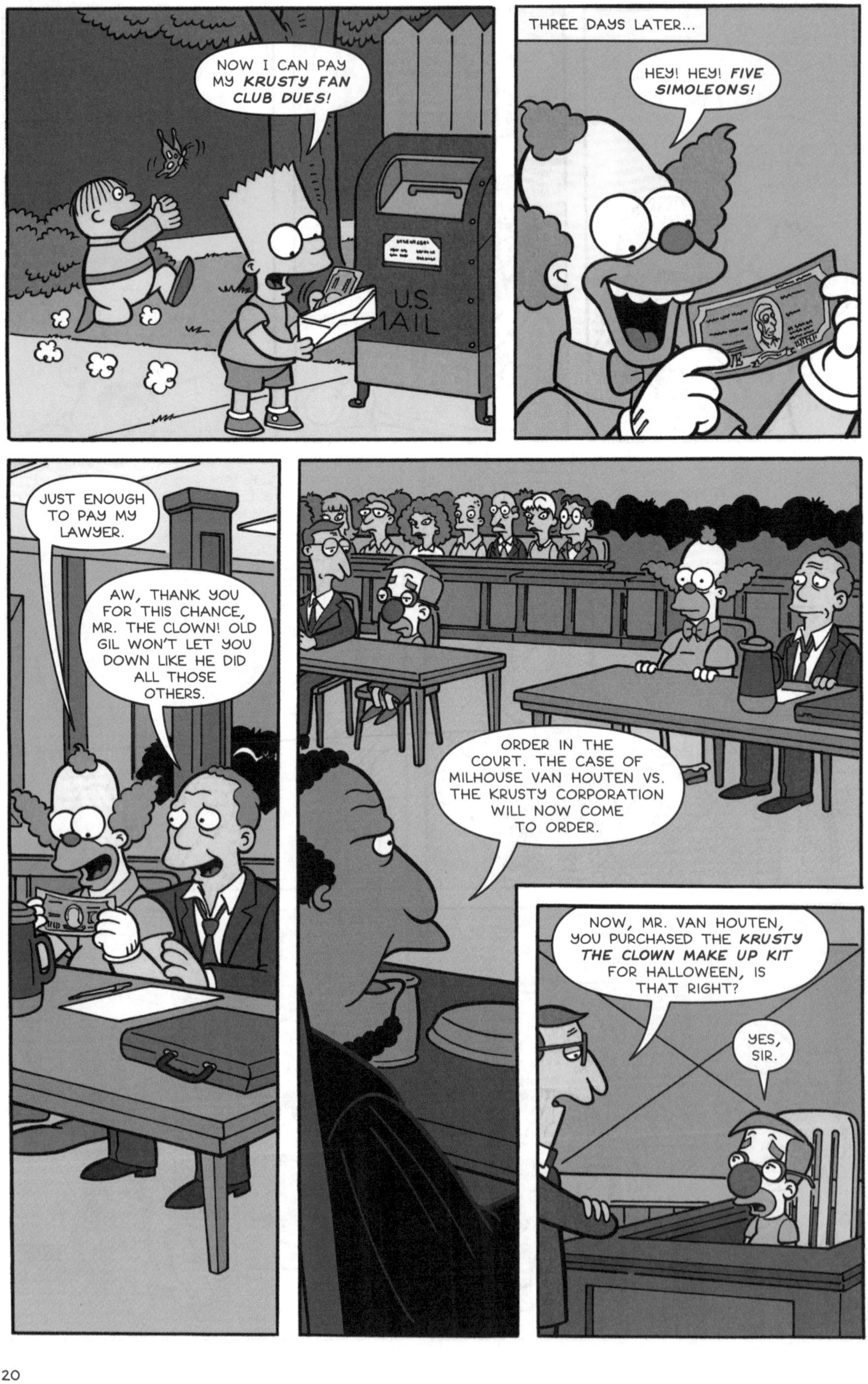

NOW I CAN PAY MY ***KRUSTY FAN CLUB DUES!***
THREE DAYS LATER...
HEY! HEY! ***FIVE SIMOLEONS!***
JUST ENOUGH TO PAY MY LAWYER.
AW, THANK YOU FOR THIS CHANCE, MR. THE CLOWN! OLD GIL WON'T LET YOU DOWN LIKE HE DID ALL THOSE OTHERS.
ORDER IN THE COURT. THE CASE OF MILHOUSE VAN HOUTEN VS. THE KRUSTY CORPORATION WILL NOW COME TO ORDER.
NOW, MR. VAN HOUTEN, YOU PURCHASED THE ***KRUSTY THE CLOWN MAKE UP KIT*** FOR HALLOWEEN, IS THAT RIGHT?
YES, SIR.

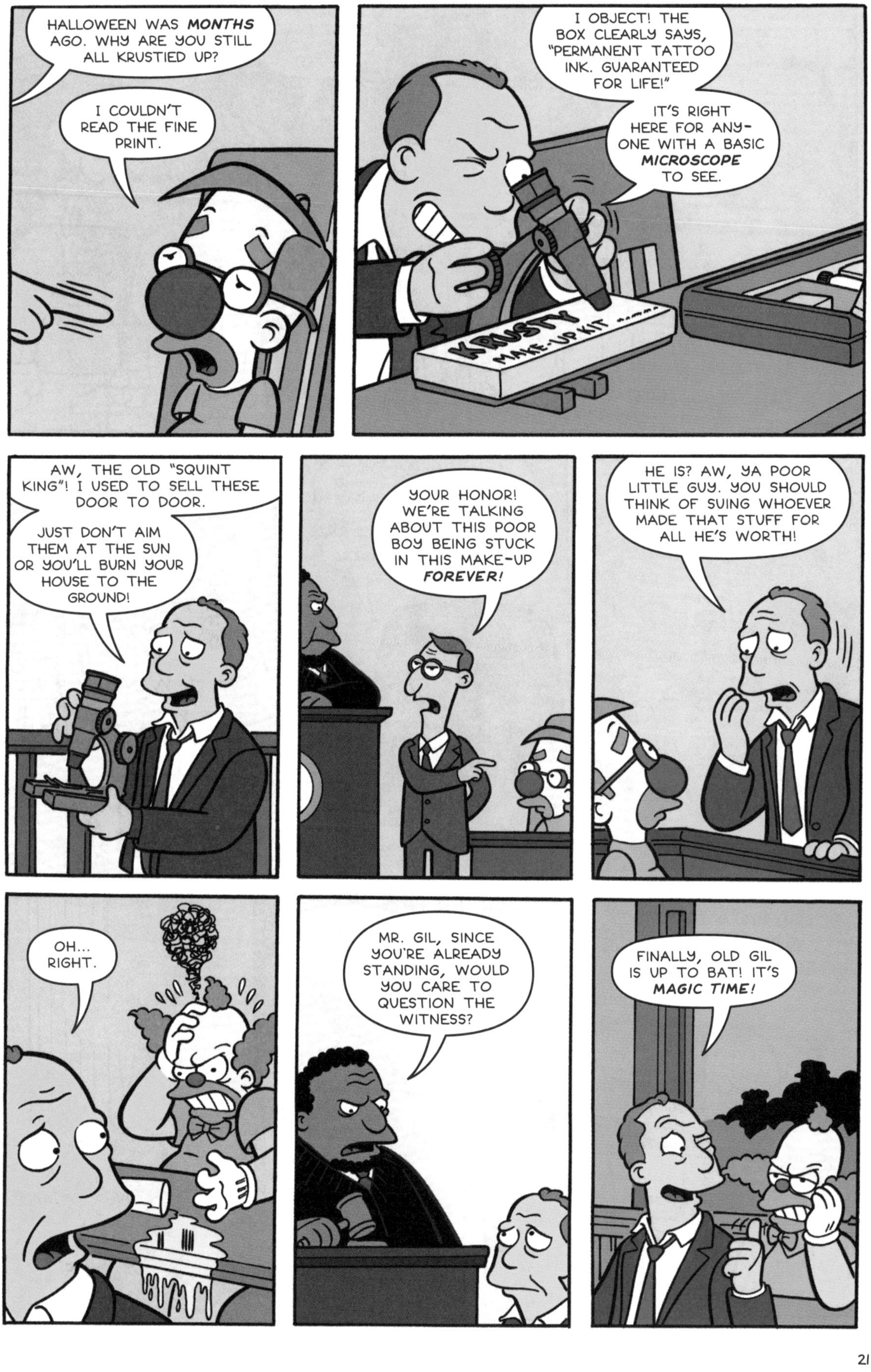
HALLOWEEN WAS **MONTHS** AGO. WHY ARE YOU STILL ALL KRUSTIED UP?
I COULDN'T READ THE FINE PRINT.
I OBJECT! THE BOX CLEARLY SAYS, "PERMANENT TATTOO INK. GUARANTEED FOR LIFE!"
IT'S RIGHT HERE FOR ANY-ONE WITH A BASIC **MICROSCOPE** TO SEE.
KRUSTY MAKE-UP KIT
AW, THE OLD "SQUINT KING"! I USED TO SELL THESE DOOR TO DOOR.
JUST DON'T AIM THEM AT THE SUN OR YOU'LL BURN YOUR HOUSE TO THE GROUND!
YOUR HONOR! WE'RE TALKING ABOUT THIS POOR BOY BEING STUCK IN THIS MAKE-UP ***FOREVER!***
HE IS? AW, YA POOR LITTLE GUY. YOU SHOULD THINK OF SUING WHOEVER MADE THAT STUFF FOR ALL HE'S WORTH!
OH... RIGHT.
MR. GIL, SINCE YOU'RE ALREADY STANDING, WOULD YOU CARE TO QUESTION THE WITNESS?
FINALLY, OLD GIL IS UP TO BAT! IT'S ***MAGIC TIME!***

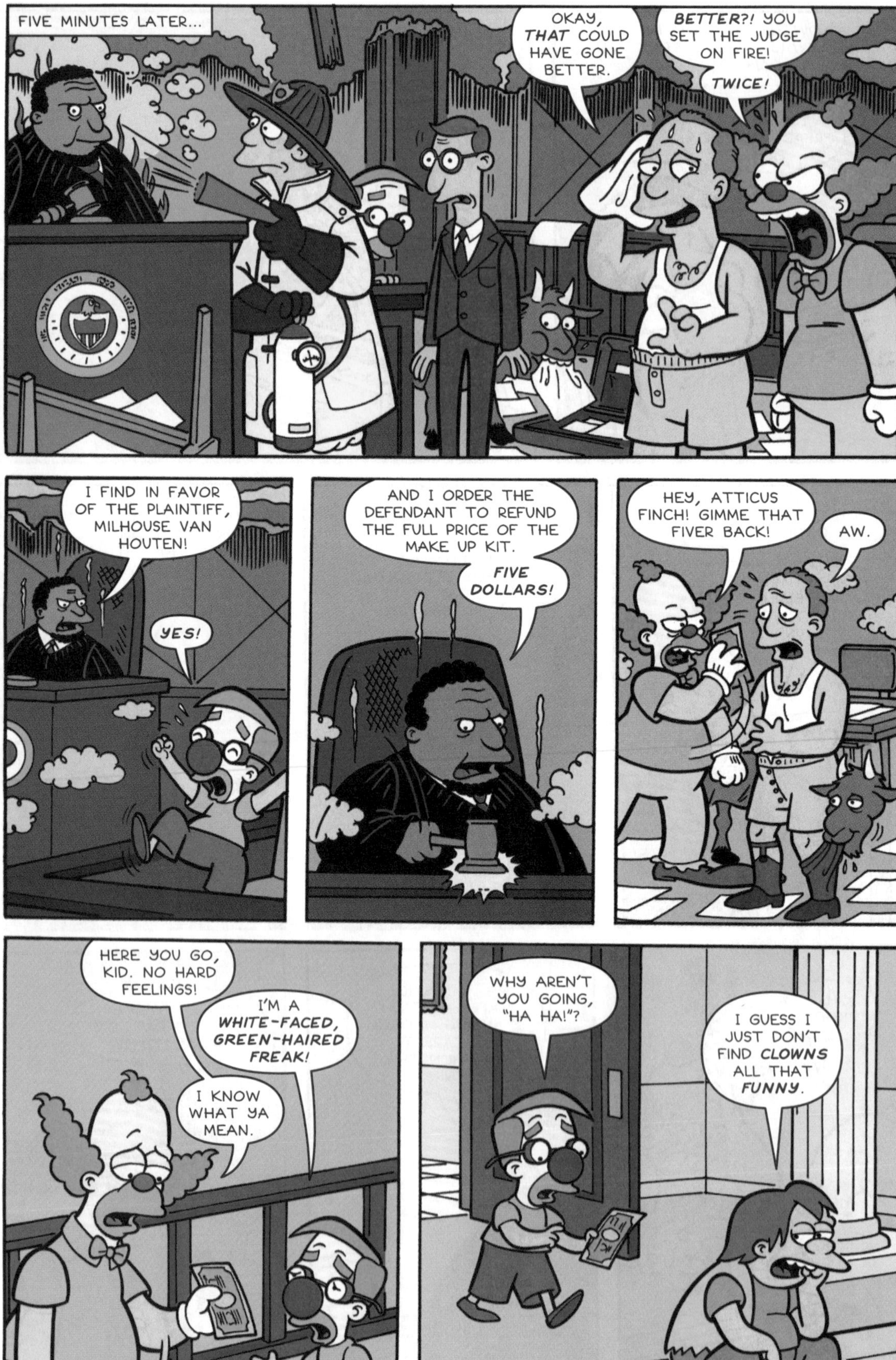

FIVE MINUTES LATER...
OKAY, THAT COULD HAVE GONE BETTER.
BETTER?! YOU SET THE JUDGE ON FIRE!
TWICE!
I FIND IN FAVOR OF THE PLAINTIFF, MILHOUSE VAN HOUTEN!
YES!
AND I ORDER THE DEFENDANT TO REFUND THE FULL PRICE OF THE MAKE UP KIT.
FIVE DOLLARS!
HEY, ATTICUS FINCH! GIMME THAT FIVER BACK!
AW.
HERE YOU GO, KID. NO HARD FEELINGS!
I'M A WHITE-FACED, GREEN-HAIRED FREAK!
I KNOW WHAT YA MEAN.
WHY AREN'T YOU GOING, "HA HA!"?
I GUESS I JUST DON'T FIND CLOWNS ALL THAT FUNNY.

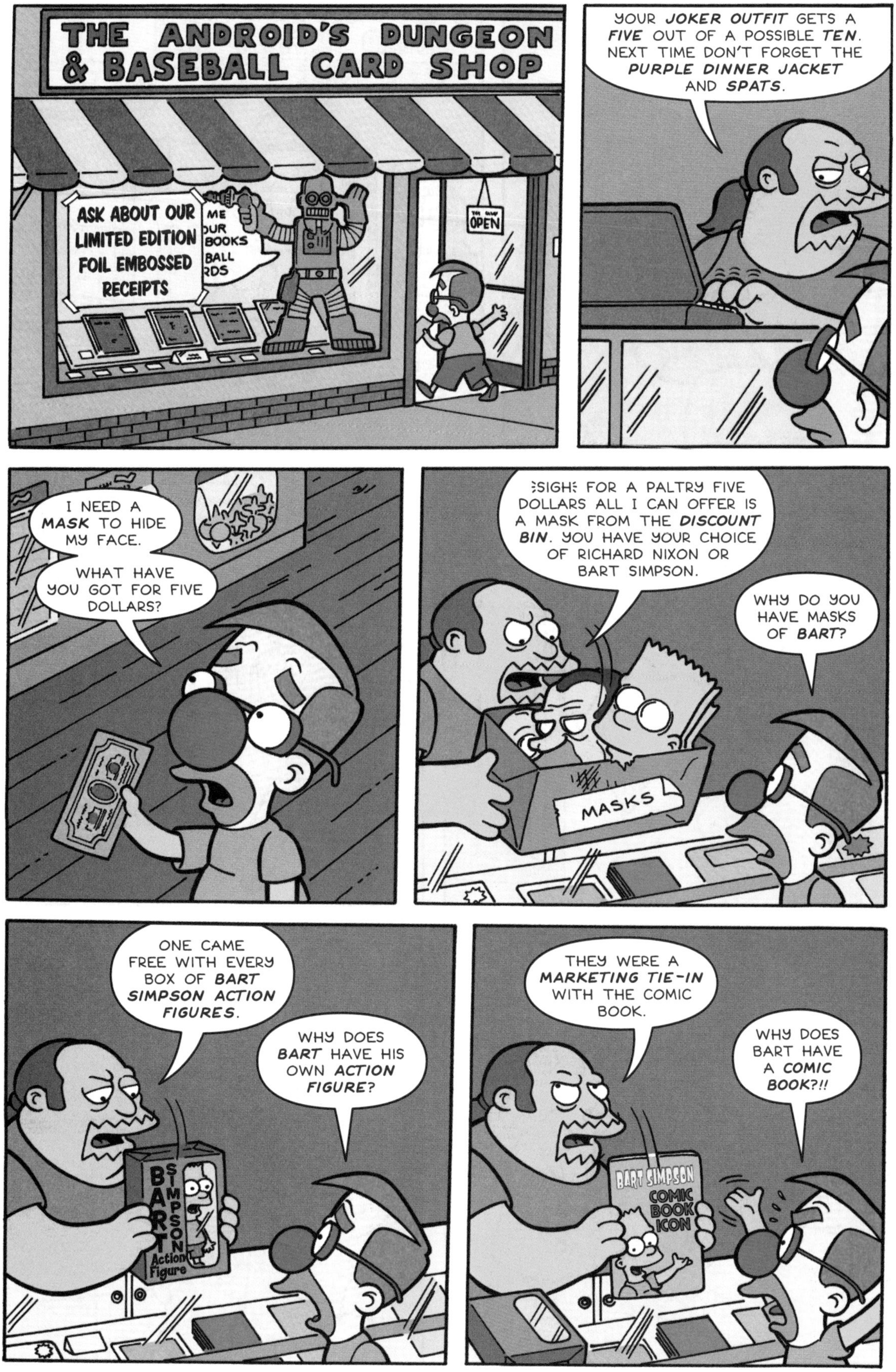
THE ANDROID'S DUNGEON & BASEBALL CARD SHOP
ASK ABOUT OUR LIMITED EDITION FOIL EMBOSSED RECEIPTS
OPEN
YOUR **JOKER OUTFIT** GETS A **FIVE** OUT OF A POSSIBLE **TEN**. NEXT TIME DON'T FORGET THE **PURPLE DINNER JACKET** AND **SPATS**.
I NEED A **MASK** TO HIDE MY FACE.
WHAT HAVE YOU GOT FOR FIVE DOLLARS?
:SIGH: FOR A PALTRY FIVE DOLLARS ALL I CAN OFFER IS A MASK FROM THE **DISCOUNT BIN**. YOU HAVE YOUR CHOICE OF RICHARD NIXON OR BART SIMPSON.
WHY DO YOU HAVE MASKS OF **BART**?
MASKS
ONE CAME FREE WITH EVERY BOX OF **BART SIMPSON ACTION FIGURES**.
WHY DOES **BART** HAVE HIS OWN **ACTION FIGURE**?
BART SIMPSON Action Figure
THEY WERE A **MARKETING TIE-IN** WITH THE COMIC BOOK.
WHY DOES BART HAVE A **COMIC BOOK**?!!
BART SIMPSON COMIC BOOK ICON

YOUR QUESTIONS HAVE BECOME MORE *REDUNDANT* AND ANNOYING THAN THE LAST THREE "HIGHLANDER" MOVIES.

BUT...

YONK!

ID'S DUNGEON CARD SHOP

BEGONE!

YES, WE'RE OPEN

BUT...

507

BUT...

YES, WE'RE OPEN

AH, BART SIMPSON! *THERE* YOU ARE!

TRYING TO SKIP OUT ON YOUR *DETENTION*, WERE YOU?

JUST FOR THAT, IT'S *DOUBLED!*

TALKING BACK? CONSIDER IT *TRIPLED!*

BUT...

TAKE M
TO YOUR
COMIC BOO
BASE

THIS STORE WOULD BE MY *PRIVATE PLEASURE PLANET* IF IT WEREN'T FOR ALL THE FREAKIN' *CUSTOMERS.*

NOW BACK TO MY *ONLINE BIDDING* FOR THE *BONES OF STAN LEE!*

ebuy!

BIG CHUG!

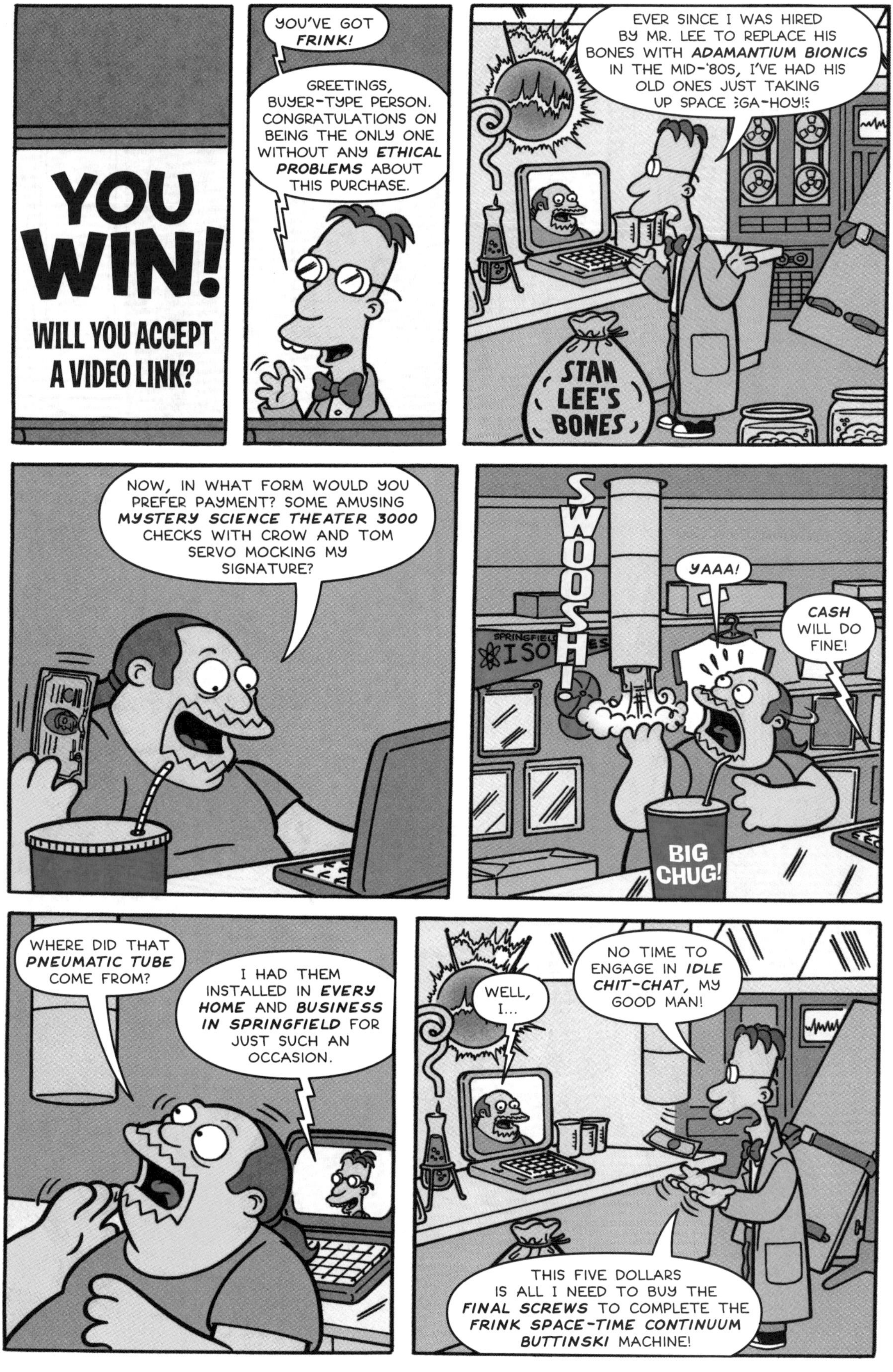
YOU WIN!
WILL YOU ACCEPT A VIDEO LINK?
YOU'VE GOT FRINK!
GREETINGS, BUYER-TYPE PERSON. CONGRATULATIONS ON BEING THE ONLY ONE WITHOUT ANY ETHICAL PROBLEMS ABOUT THIS PURCHASE.
EVER SINCE I WAS HIRED BY MR. LEE TO REPLACE HIS BONES WITH ADAMANTIUM BIONICS IN THE MID-'80S, I'VE HAD HIS OLD ONES JUST TAKING UP SPACE ;GA-HOY!;
STAN LEE'S BONES
NOW, IN WHAT FORM WOULD YOU PREFER PAYMENT? SOME AMUSING MYSTERY SCIENCE THEATER 3000 CHECKS WITH CROW AND TOM SERVO MOCKING MY SIGNATURE?
SWOOSH!
YAAA!
CASH WILL DO FINE!
BIG CHUG!
WHERE DID THAT PNEUMATIC TUBE COME FROM?
I HAD THEM INSTALLED IN EVERY HOME AND BUSINESS IN SPRINGFIELD FOR JUST SUCH AN OCCASION.
WELL, I...
NO TIME TO ENGAGE IN IDLE CHIT-CHAT, MY GOOD MAN!
THIS FIVE DOLLARS IS ALL I NEED TO BUY THE FINAL SCREWS TO COMPLETE THE FRINK SPACE-TIME CONTINUUM BUTTINSKI MACHINE!

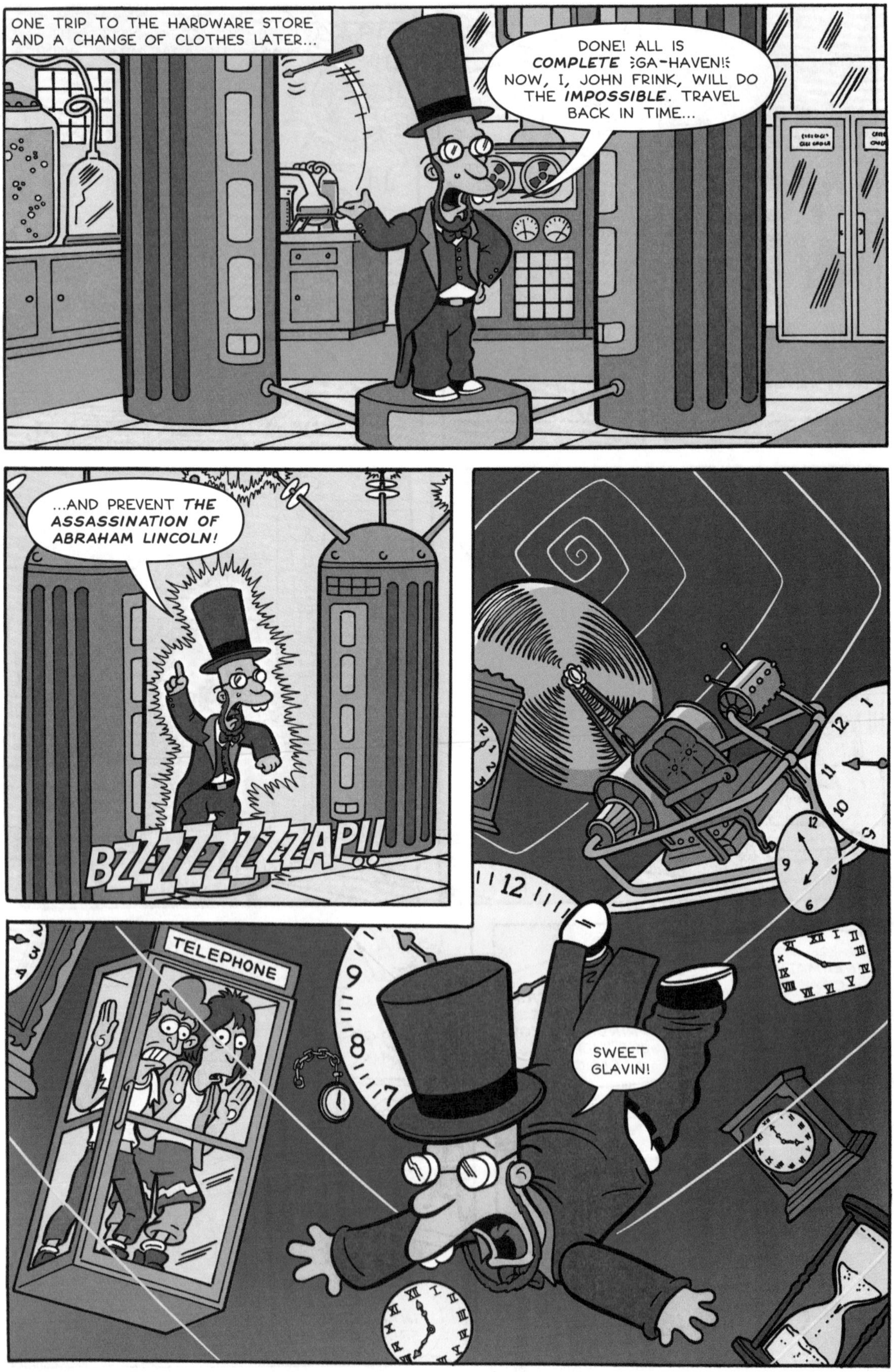
ONE TRIP TO THE HARDWARE STORE AND A CHANGE OF CLOTHES LATER...
DONE! ALL IS *COMPLETE* GA-HAVEN! NOW, I, JOHN FRINK, WILL DO THE *IMPOSSIBLE*. TRAVEL BACK IN TIME...
...AND PREVENT *THE ASSASSINATION OF ABRAHAM LINCOLN!*
BZZZZZZZZAP!!
TELEPHONE
SWEET GLAVIN!

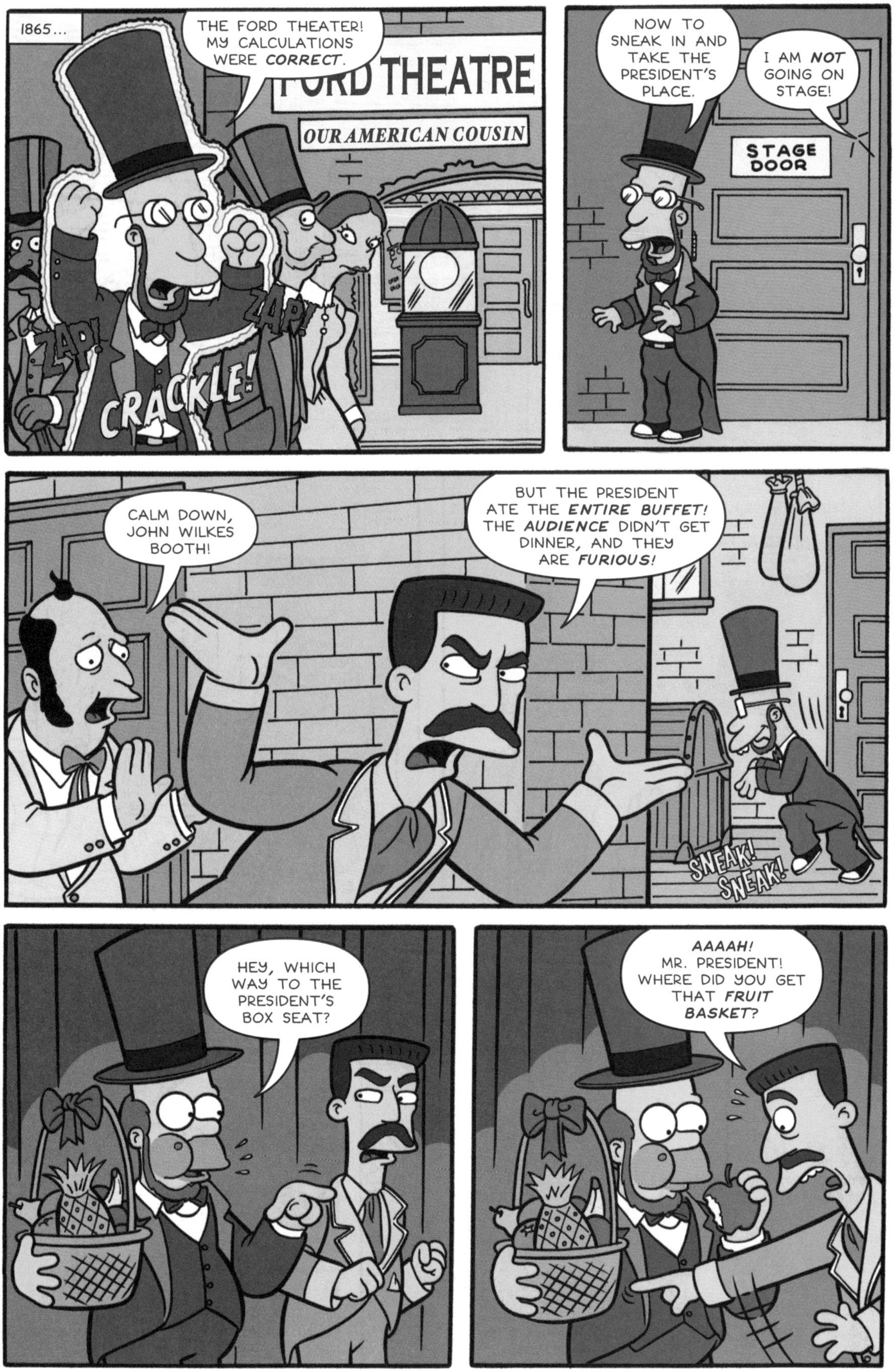
1865...
THE FORD THEATER! MY CALCULATIONS WERE CORRECT.
FORD THEATRE
OUR AMERICAN COUSIN
ZAP!
ZAP!
CRACKLE!
NOW TO SNEAK IN AND TAKE THE PRESIDENT'S PLACE.
I AM NOT GOING ON STAGE!
STAGE DOOR
CALM DOWN, JOHN WILKES BOOTH!
BUT THE PRESIDENT ATE THE ENTIRE BUFFET! THE AUDIENCE DIDN'T GET DINNER, AND THEY ARE FURIOUS!
SNEAK! SNEAK!
HEY, WHICH WAY TO THE PRESIDENT'S BOX SEAT?
AAAAH! MR. PRESIDENT! WHERE DID YOU GET THAT FRUIT BASKET?

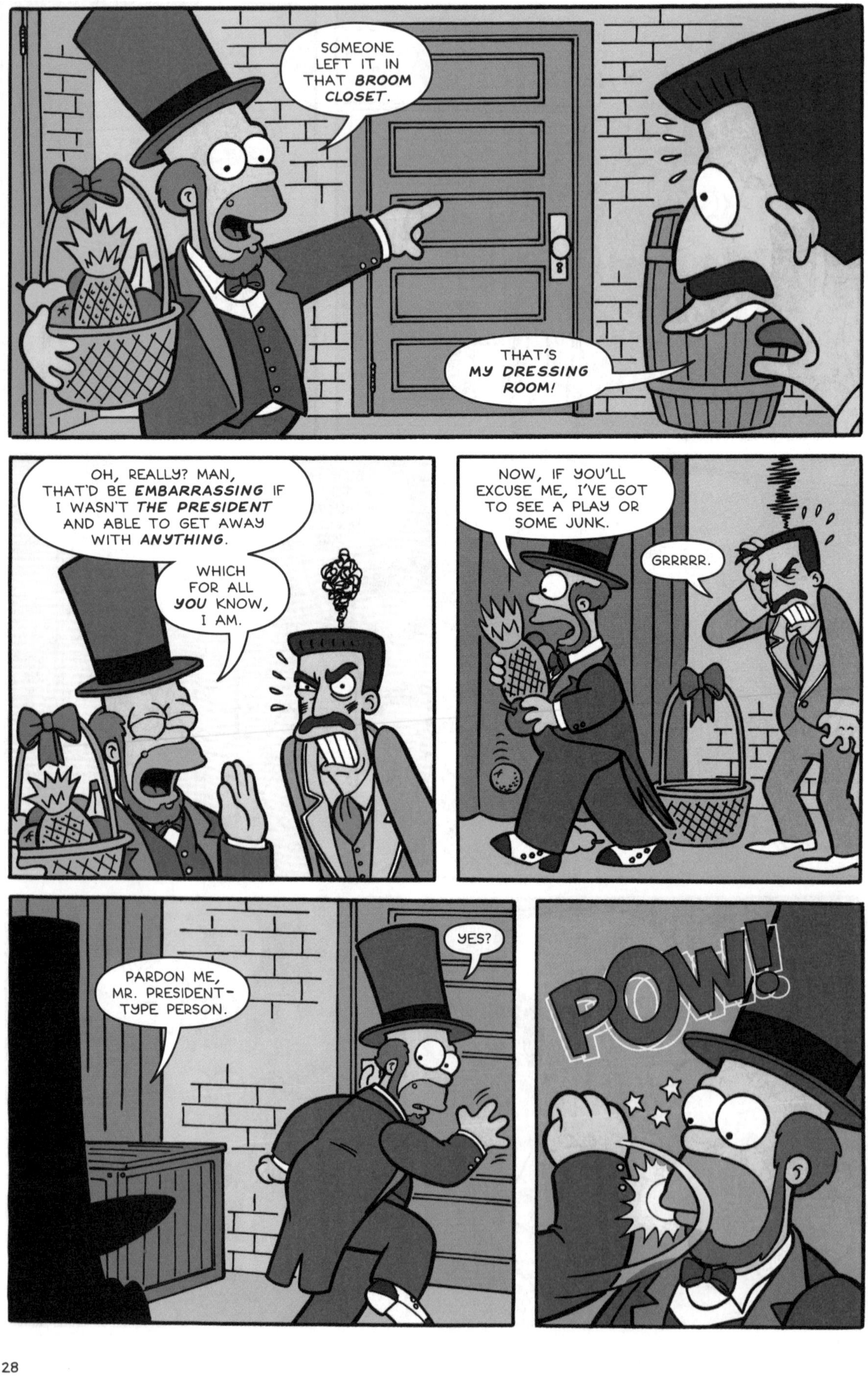
SOMEONE LEFT IT IN THAT BROOM CLOSET.
THAT'S MY DRESSING ROOM!
OH, REALLY? MAN, THAT'D BE EMBARRASSING IF I WASN'T THE PRESIDENT AND ABLE TO GET AWAY WITH ANYTHING.
WHICH FOR ALL YOU KNOW, I AM.
NOW, IF YOU'LL EXCUSE ME, I'VE GOT TO SEE A PLAY OR SOME JUNK.
GRRRRR.
PARDON ME, MR. PRESIDENT-TYPE PERSON.
YES?
POW!

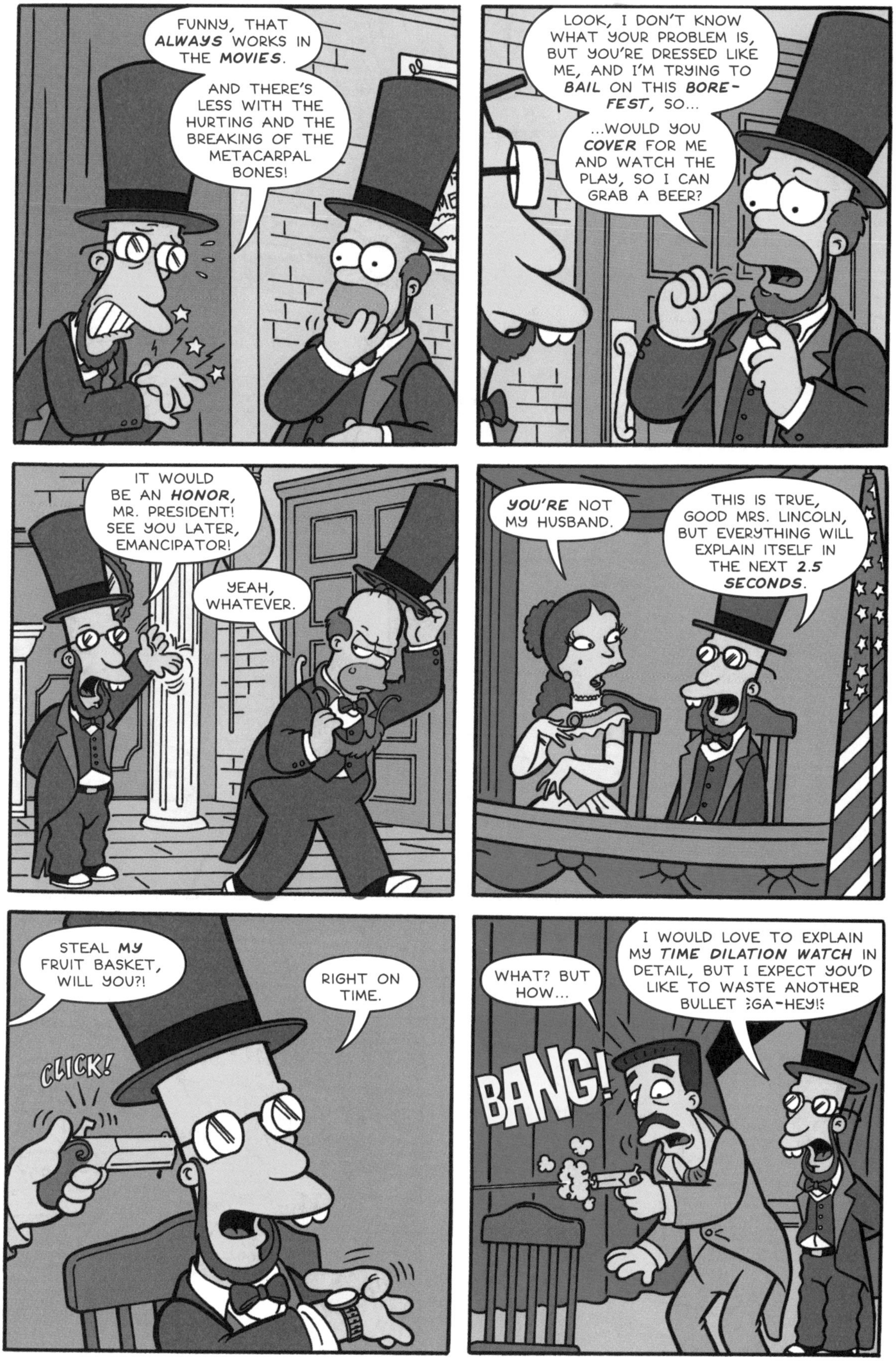
FUNNY, THAT ALWAYS WORKS IN THE MOVIES.
AND THERE'S LESS WITH THE HURTING AND THE BREAKING OF THE METACARPAL BONES!
LOOK, I DON'T KNOW WHAT YOUR PROBLEM IS, BUT YOU'RE DRESSED LIKE ME, AND I'M TRYING TO BAIL ON THIS BORE-FEST, SO...
...WOULD YOU COVER FOR ME AND WATCH THE PLAY, SO I CAN GRAB A BEER?
IT WOULD BE AN HONOR, MR. PRESIDENT! SEE YOU LATER, EMANCIPATOR!
YEAH, WHATEVER.
YOU'RE NOT MY HUSBAND.
THIS IS TRUE, GOOD MRS. LINCOLN, BUT EVERYTHING WILL EXPLAIN ITSELF IN THE NEXT 2.5 SECONDS.
STEAL MY FRUIT BASKET, WILL YOU?!
RIGHT ON TIME.
CLICK!
WHAT? BUT HOW...
I WOULD LOVE TO EXPLAIN MY TIME DILATION WATCH IN DETAIL, BUT I EXPECT YOU'D LIKE TO WASTE ANOTHER BULLET GA-HEY!
BANG!

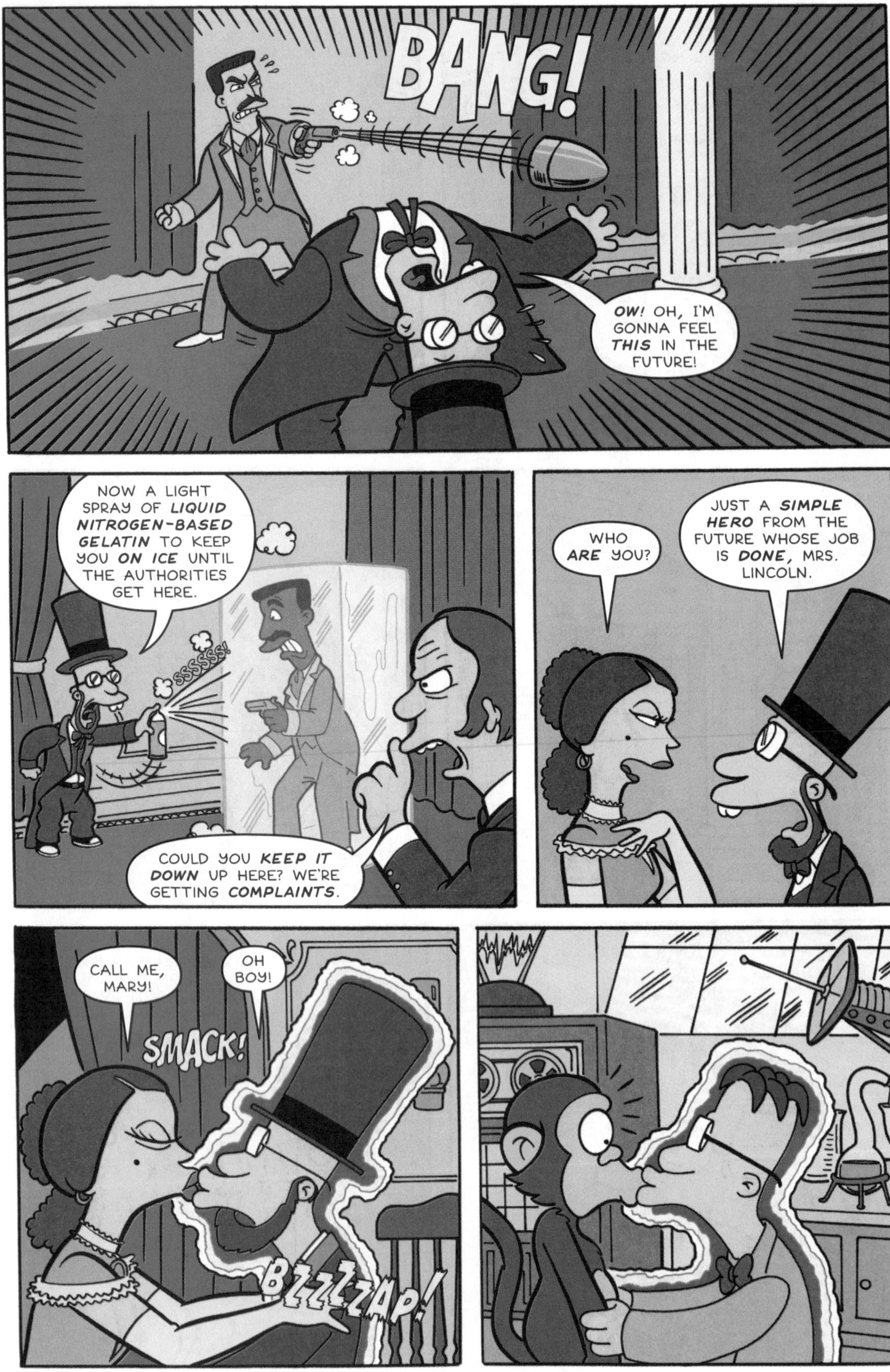
BANG!
OW! OH, I'M GONNA FEEL THIS IN THE FUTURE!
NOW A LIGHT SPRAY OF LIQUID NITROGEN-BASED GELATIN TO KEEP YOU ON ICE UNTIL THE AUTHORITIES GET HERE.
SSSSSS!
COULD YOU KEEP IT DOWN UP HERE? WE'RE GETTING COMPLAINTS.
WHO ARE YOU?
JUST A SIMPLE HERO FROM THE FUTURE WHOSE JOB IS DONE, MRS. LINCOLN.
CALL ME, MARY!
OH BOY!
SMACK!
BZZZZAP!

SWEET GLAVIN! NOW I HAVE BANANA AND FUR IN MY TEETH. THAT NEVER HAPPENED TO SCOTT BAKULA.

DING! DONG!

MOUTH WASH

AH, YES, THE *LUNCH* I ORDERED!

THAT'LL BE $4.95 FOR THE CHOPPED LIVER AND DILL PICKLE, PALLY!

I ONLY PRAY THAT MY *MEDDLING* IN THE *PAST* DOESN'T HAVE ANY *REPERCUSSIONS* IN THE *PRESENT*.

YEAH, THAT'D BE A *DRAG*. NOW MAKE WITH THE MONEY. IT'S HOT, AND I GOT *EGG SALAD* IN THE CAR WITH THE WINDOWS ROLLED UP.

KEEP THE *CHANGE*, MY GOOD FELLOW.

THAT *CHEAPSKATE* SURE LOOKED *FAMILIAR*.

RESERVE NOTE
THE UNITED STATES OF AMERICA
BE 198814808
1988
UNITED STATES
IN GLAVIN WE TRUST
FIVE
DOLL

THE MONUMENTAL END

31

SPRINGFIELD CONVENTION CENTER TONIGHT:
**SPRINGFIELD MEDIA AWARDS** FEATURING A TRIBUTE TO **KENT BROCKMAN**

A TRIBUTE TO *KENT BROCKMAN?* WHY ARE *WE* HERE AGAIN?

BECAUSE LISA IS *NOMINATED* FOR A *FREE BUFFET DINNER!*

AN *AWARD,* HOMER! LISA IS NOMINATED FOR AN AWARD!

FH2Z8

**KENT'S STATE**

MATT GROENING

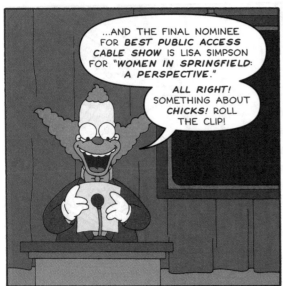

...AND THE FINAL NOMINEE FOR *BEST PUBLIC ACCESS CABLE SHOW* IS LISA SIMPSON FOR *"WOMEN IN SPRINGFIELD: A PERSPECTIVE."*

ALL RIGHT! SOMETHING ABOUT *CHICKS!* ROLL THE CLIP!

LUNCHLADY DORIS, AS A *MODERN CAREER WOMAN,* ARE YOU SUSTAINED BY THE MYTHS OF THOSE *VISIONARY WOMEN* WHO WENT BEFORE YOU, LIKE MADAME CURIE, AMELIA EARHART AND HELEN GURLEY BROWN?

I JUST MAKE SURE THE *GREASE TRAP* DOESN'T *OVERFLOW.*

DAVID MCKEAN
STORY

DAN DECARLO
LAYOUTS

MIKE ROTE
PENCILS

TIM BAVINGTON
INKS

KAREN BATES
COLORS & LETTERS

BILL MORRISON
EDITOR

MATT GROENING
TOASTMASTER

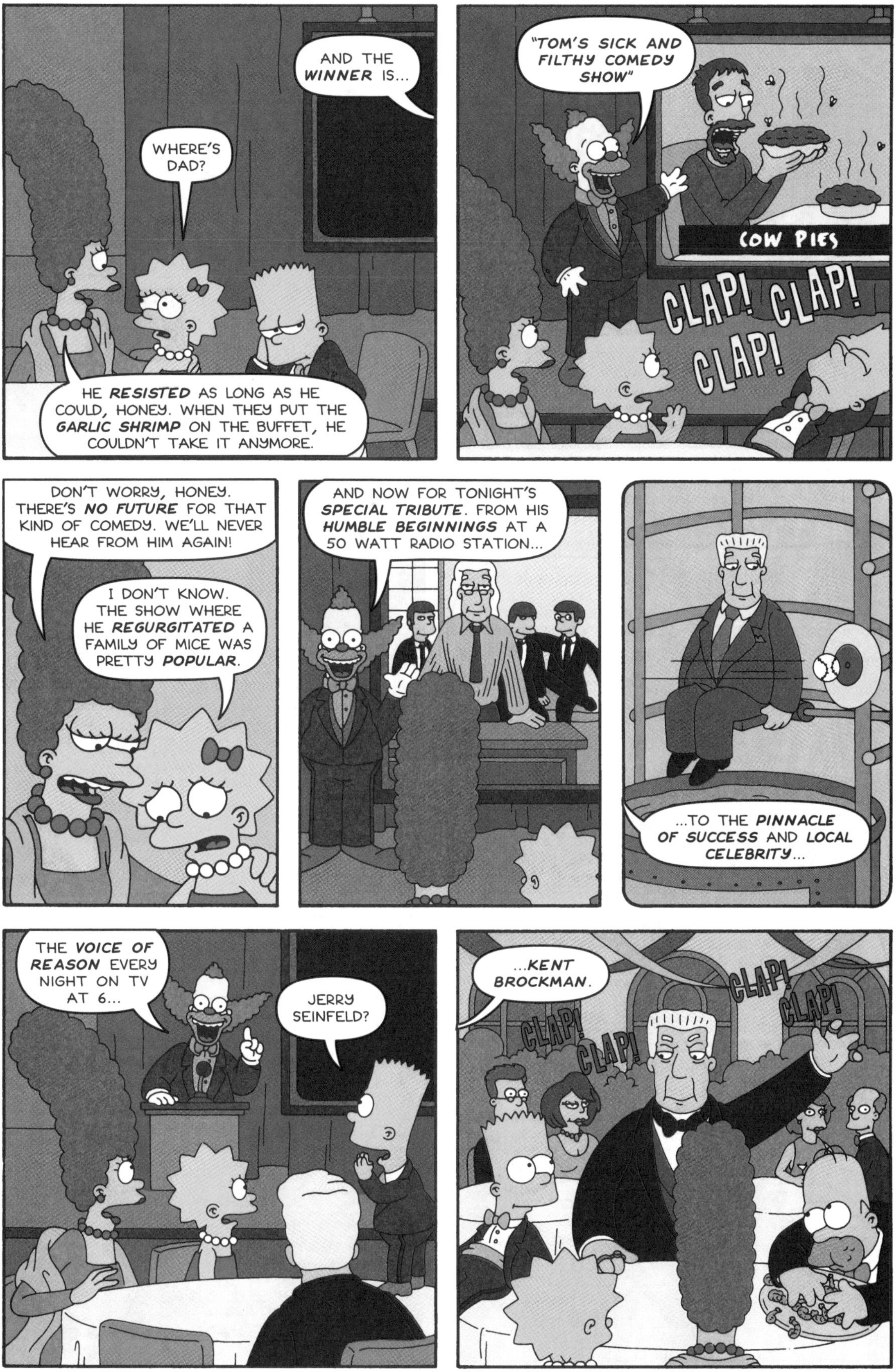
AND THE WINNER IS...
WHERE'S DAD?
HE RESISTED AS LONG AS HE COULD, HONEY. WHEN THEY PUT THE GARLIC SHRIMP ON THE BUFFET, HE COULDN'T TAKE IT ANYMORE.
"TOM'S SICK AND FILTHY COMEDY SHOW"
COW PIES
CLAP! CLAP! CLAP!
DON'T WORRY, HONEY. THERE'S NO FUTURE FOR THAT KIND OF COMEDY. WE'LL NEVER HEAR FROM HIM AGAIN!
I DON'T KNOW. THE SHOW WHERE HE REGURGITATED A FAMILY OF MICE WAS PRETTY POPULAR.
AND NOW FOR TONIGHT'S SPECIAL TRIBUTE. FROM HIS HUMBLE BEGINNINGS AT A 50 WATT RADIO STATION...
...TO THE PINNACLE OF SUCCESS AND LOCAL CELEBRITY...
THE VOICE OF REASON EVERY NIGHT ON TV AT 6...
JERRY SEINFELD?
...KENT BROCKMAN.
CLAP! CLAP! CLAP! CLAP!

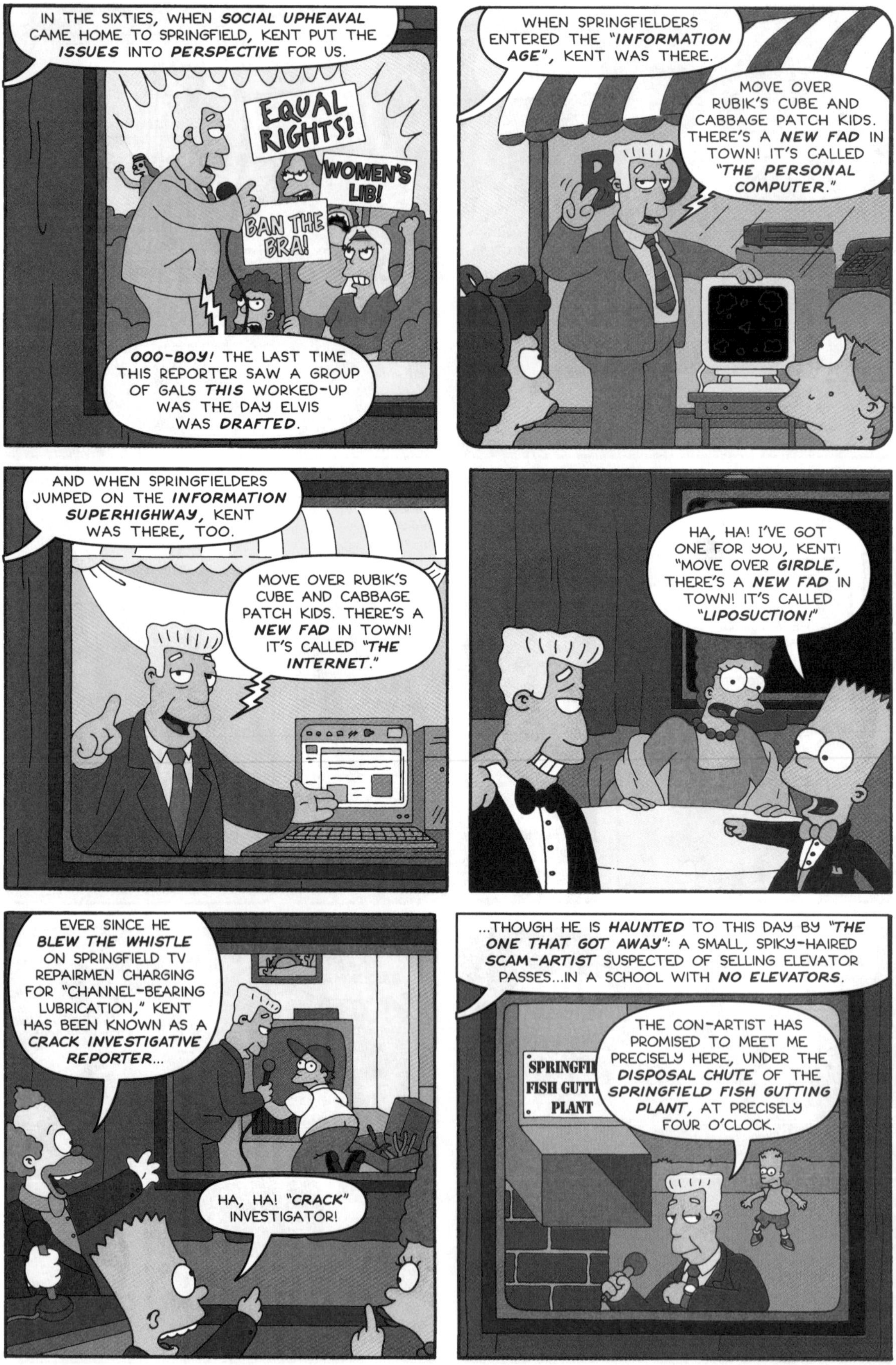
IN THE SIXTIES, WHEN SOCIAL UPHEAVAL CAME HOME TO SPRINGFIELD, KENT PUT THE ISSUES INTO PERSPECTIVE FOR US.
EQUAL RIGHTS!
WOMEN'S LIB!
BAN THE BRA!
OOO-BOY! THE LAST TIME THIS REPORTER SAW A GROUP OF GALS THIS WORKED-UP WAS THE DAY ELVIS WAS DRAFTED.
WHEN SPRINGFIELDERS ENTERED THE "INFORMATION AGE", KENT WAS THERE.
MOVE OVER RUBIK'S CUBE AND CABBAGE PATCH KIDS. THERE'S A NEW FAD IN TOWN! IT'S CALLED "THE PERSONAL COMPUTER."
AND WHEN SPRINGFIELDERS JUMPED ON THE INFORMATION SUPERHIGHWAY, KENT WAS THERE, TOO.
MOVE OVER RUBIK'S CUBE AND CABBAGE PATCH KIDS. THERE'S A NEW FAD IN TOWN! IT'S CALLED "THE INTERNET."
HA, HA! I'VE GOT ONE FOR YOU, KENT! "MOVE OVER GIRDLE, THERE'S A NEW FAD IN TOWN! IT'S CALLED "LIPOSUCTION!"
EVER SINCE HE BLEW THE WHISTLE ON SPRINGFIELD TV REPAIRMEN CHARGING FOR "CHANNEL-BEARING LUBRICATION," KENT HAS BEEN KNOWN AS A CRACK INVESTIGATIVE REPORTER...
HA, HA! "CRACK" INVESTIGATOR!
...THOUGH HE IS HAUNTED TO THIS DAY BY "THE ONE THAT GOT AWAY": A SMALL, SPIKY-HAIRED SCAM-ARTIST SUSPECTED OF SELLING ELEVATOR PASSES...IN A SCHOOL WITH NO ELEVATORS.
THE CON-ARTIST HAS PROMISED TO MEET ME PRECISELY HERE, UNDER THE DISPOSAL CHUTE OF THE SPRINGFIELD FISH GUTTING PLANT, AT PRECISELY FOUR O'CLOCK.

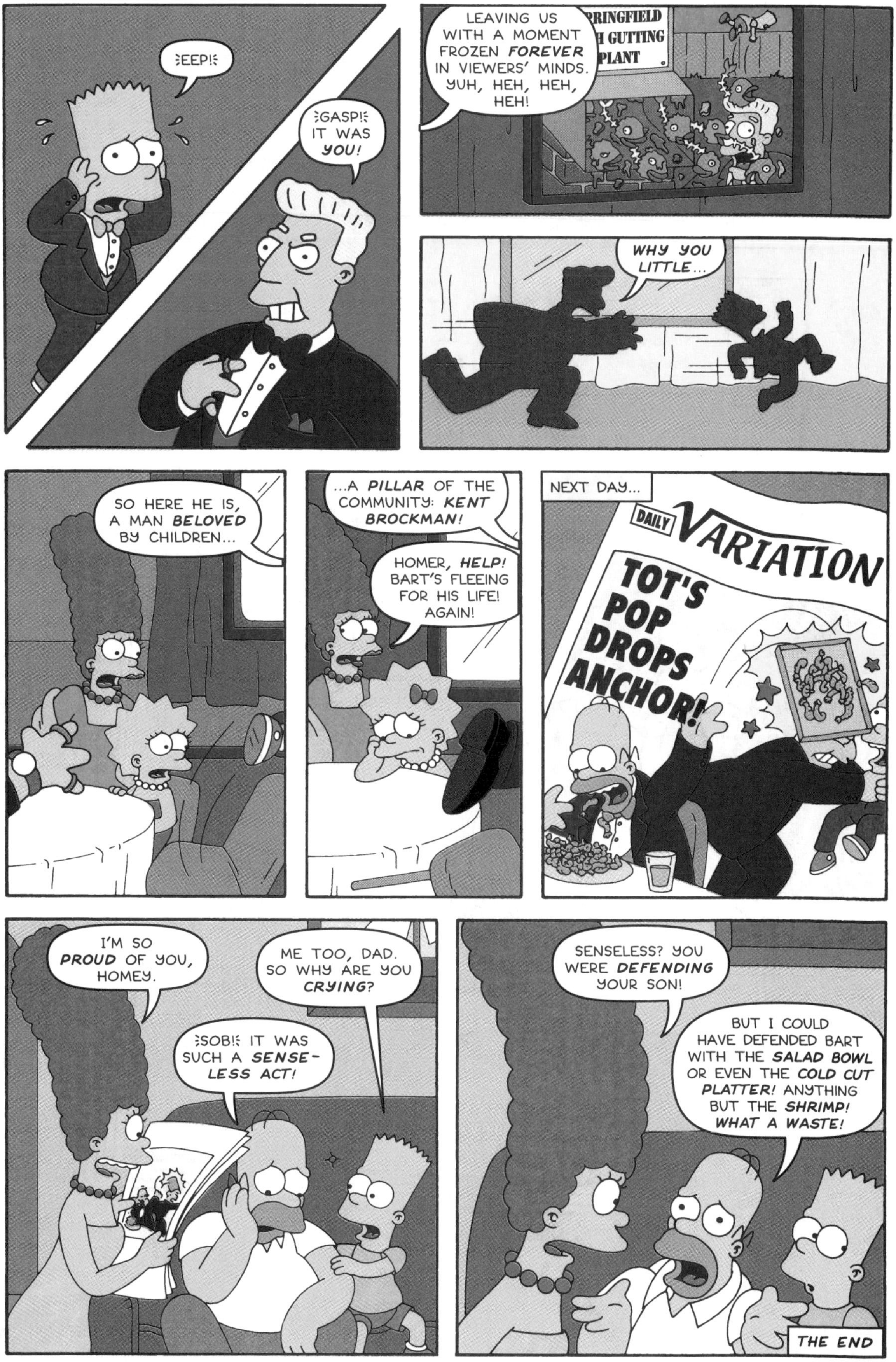
EEP!
GASP! IT WAS YOU!
LEAVING US WITH A MOMENT FROZEN FOREVER IN VIEWERS' MINDS. YUH, HEH, HEH, HEH!
SPRINGFIELD FISH GUTTING PLANT
WHY YOU LITTLE...
SO HERE HE IS, A MAN BELOVED BY CHILDREN...
...A PILLAR OF THE COMMUNITY: KENT BROCKMAN!
HOMER, HELP! BART'S FLEEING FOR HIS LIFE! AGAIN!
NEXT DAY...
DAILY VARIATION
TOT'S POP DROPS ANCHOR!
I'M SO PROUD OF YOU, HOMEY.
ME TOO, DAD. SO WHY ARE YOU CRYING?
SOB! IT WAS SUCH A SENSELESS ACT!
SENSELESS? YOU WERE DEFENDING YOUR SON!
BUT I COULD HAVE DEFENDED BART WITH THE SALAD BOWL OR EVEN THE COLD CUT PLATTER! ANYTHING BUT THE SHRIMP! WHAT A WASTE!
THE END

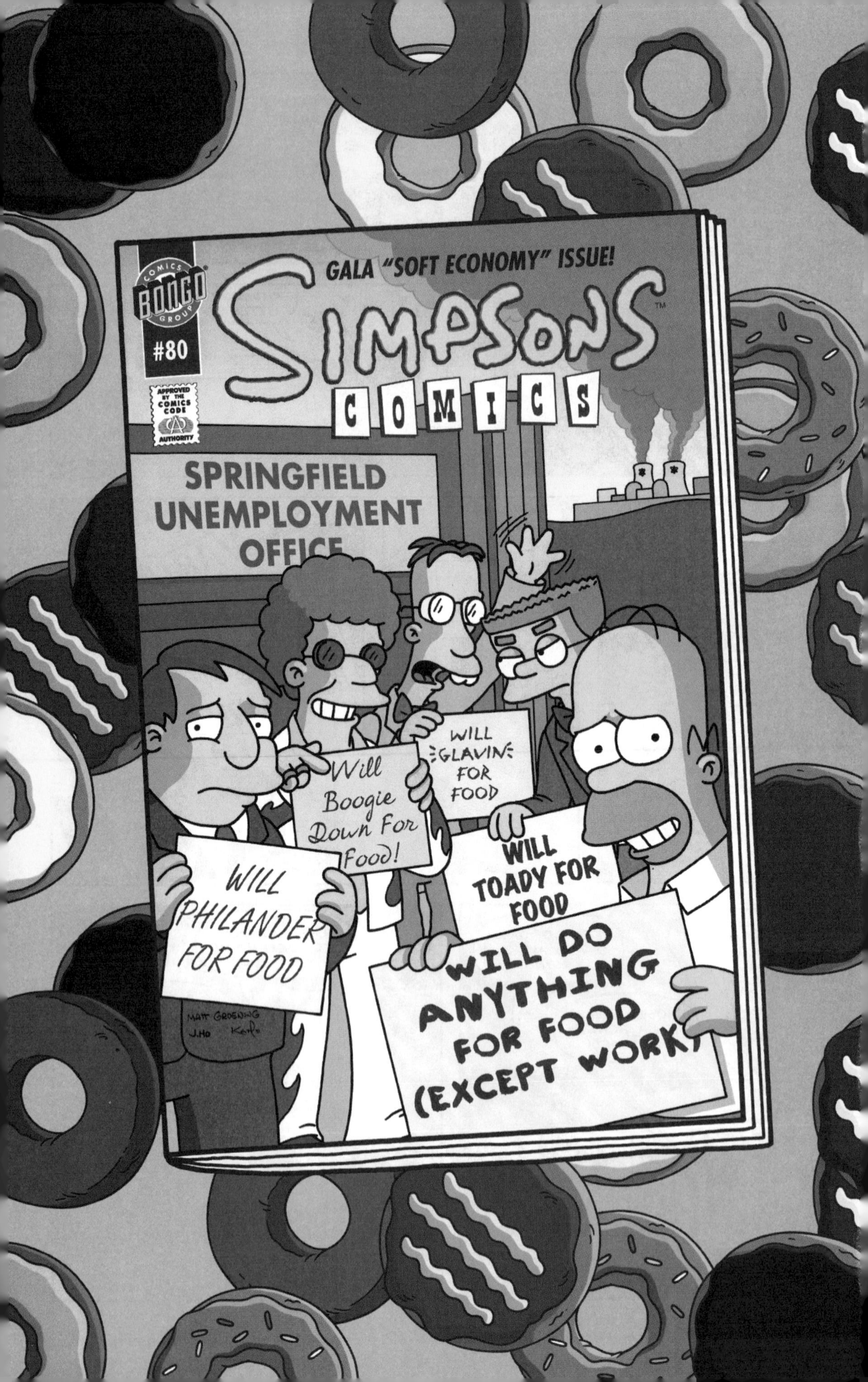

GALA "SOFT ECONOMY" ISSUE!
BONGO COMICS GROUP
#80
SIMPSONS COMICS
APPROVED BY THE COMICS CODE AUTHORITY
SPRINGFIELD UNEMPLOYMENT OFFICE
Will Boogie Down For Food!
WILL GLAVIN FOR FOOD
WILL TOADY FOR FOOD
WILL PHILANDER FOR FOOD
WILL DO ANYTHING FOR FOOD (EXCEPT WORK)
MATT GROENING

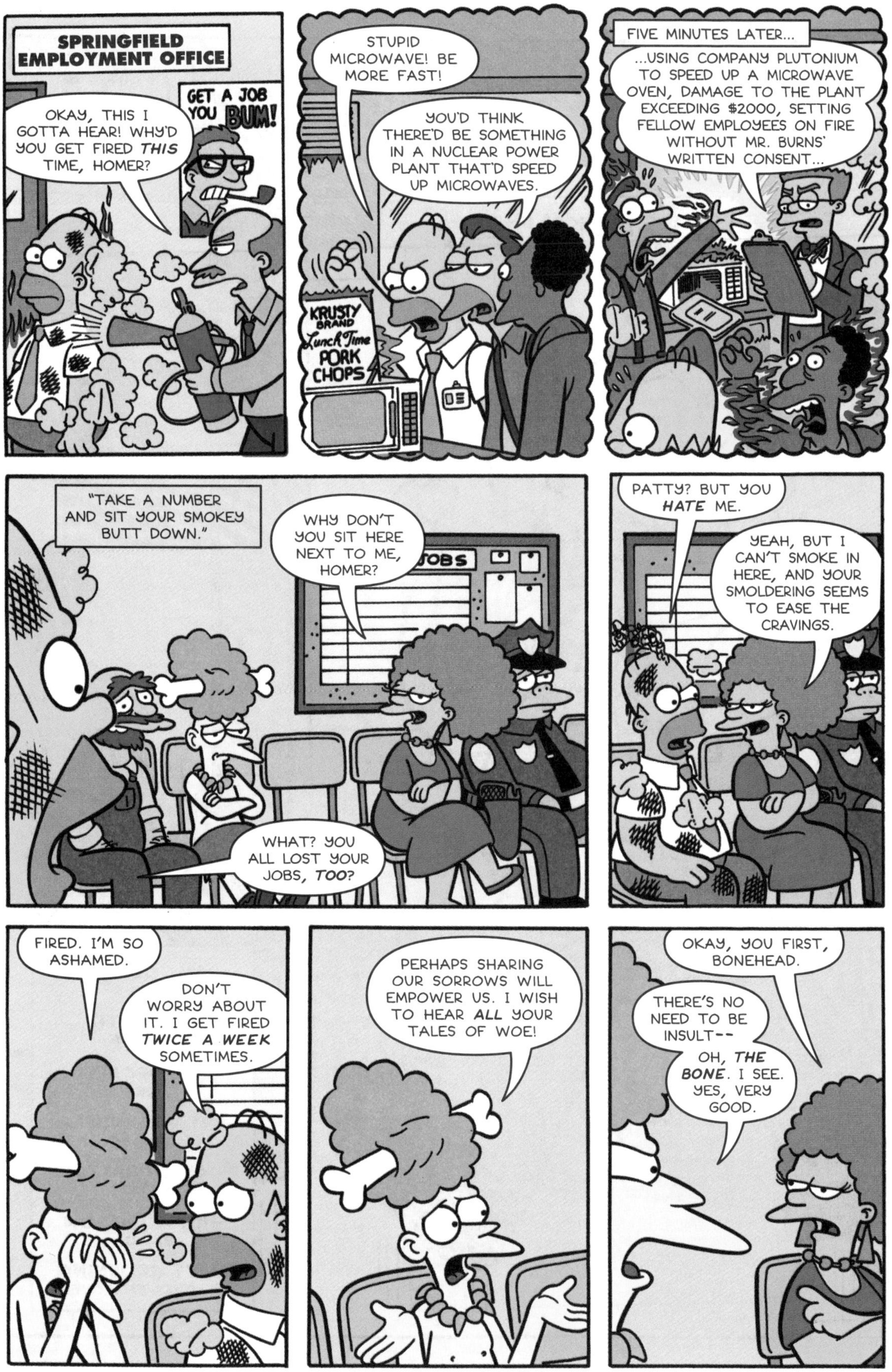
SPRINGFIELD EMPLOYMENT OFFICE
GET A JOB YOU BUM!
OKAY, THIS I GOTTA HEAR! WHY'D YOU GET FIRED *THIS* TIME, HOMER?
STUPID MICROWAVE! BE MORE FAST!
YOU'D THINK THERE'D BE SOMETHING IN A NUCLEAR POWER PLANT THAT'D SPEED UP MICROWAVES.
KRUSTY BRAND Lunch Time PORK CHOPS
FIVE MINUTES LATER...
...USING COMPANY PLUTONIUM TO SPEED UP A MICROWAVE OVEN, DAMAGE TO THE PLANT EXCEEDING $2000, SETTING FELLOW EMPLOYEES ON FIRE WITHOUT MR. BURNS' WRITTEN CONSENT...
"TAKE A NUMBER AND SIT YOUR SMOKEY BUTT DOWN."
WHY DON'T YOU SIT HERE NEXT TO ME, HOMER?
JOBS
WHAT? YOU ALL LOST YOUR JOBS, *TOO*?
PATTY? BUT YOU *HATE* ME.
YEAH, BUT I CAN'T SMOKE IN HERE, AND YOUR SMOLDERING SEEMS TO EASE THE CRAVINGS.
FIRED. I'M SO ASHAMED.
DON'T WORRY ABOUT IT. I GET FIRED *TWICE A WEEK* SOMETIMES.
PERHAPS SHARING OUR SORROWS WILL EMPOWER US. I WISH TO HEAR *ALL* YOUR TALES OF WOE!
OKAY, YOU FIRST, BONEHEAD.
THERE'S NO NEED TO BE INSULT--
OH, *THE BONE*. I SEE. YES, VERY GOOD.

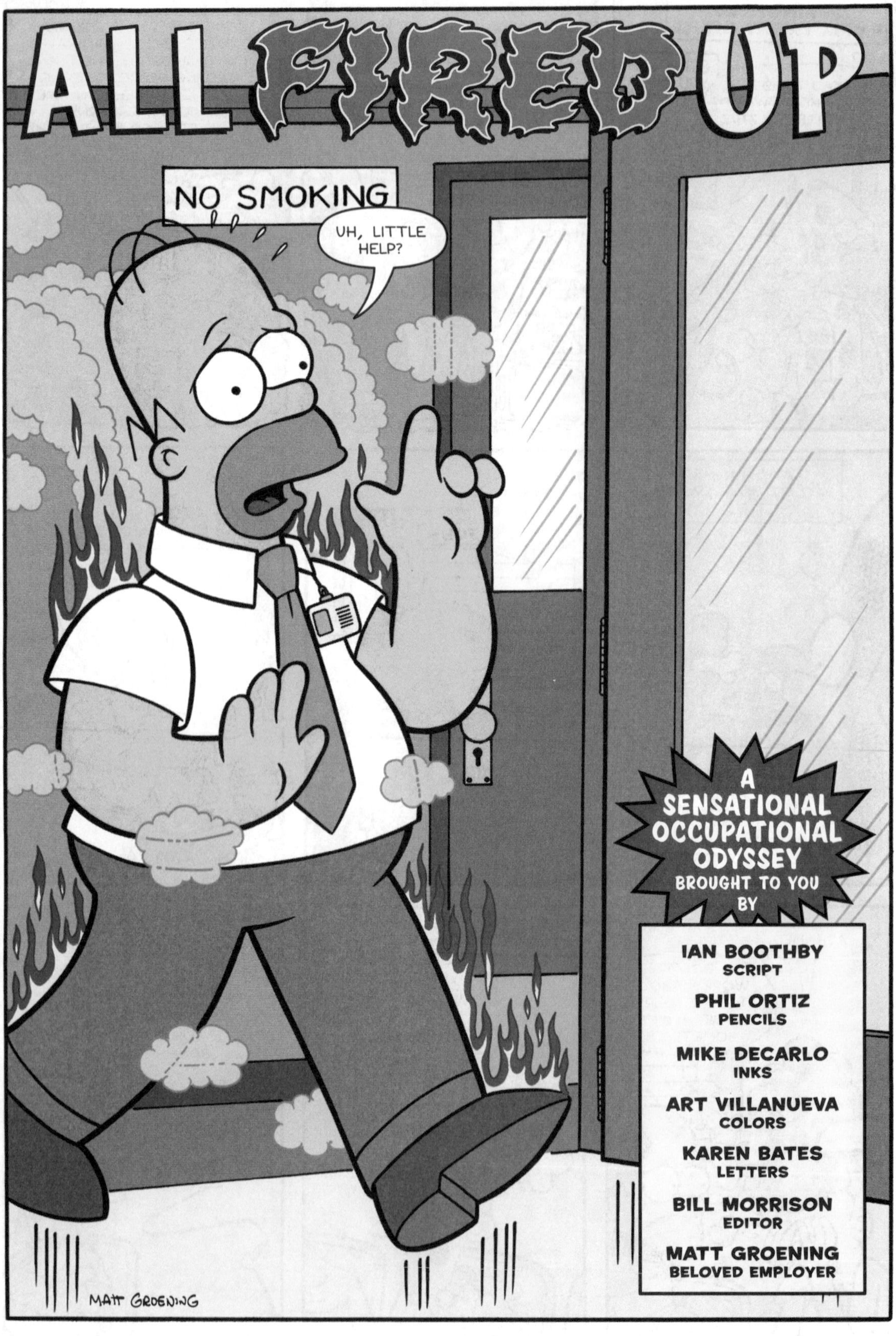
ALL FIRED UP
NO SMOKING
UH, LITTLE HELP?
A SENSATIONAL OCCUPATIONAL ODYSSEY BROUGHT TO YOU BY
IAN BOOTHBY SCRIPT
PHIL ORTIZ PENCILS
MIKE DECARLO INKS
ART VILLANUEVA COLORS
KAREN BATES LETTERS
BILL MORRISON EDITOR
MATT GROENING BELOVED EMPLOYER
MATT GROENING

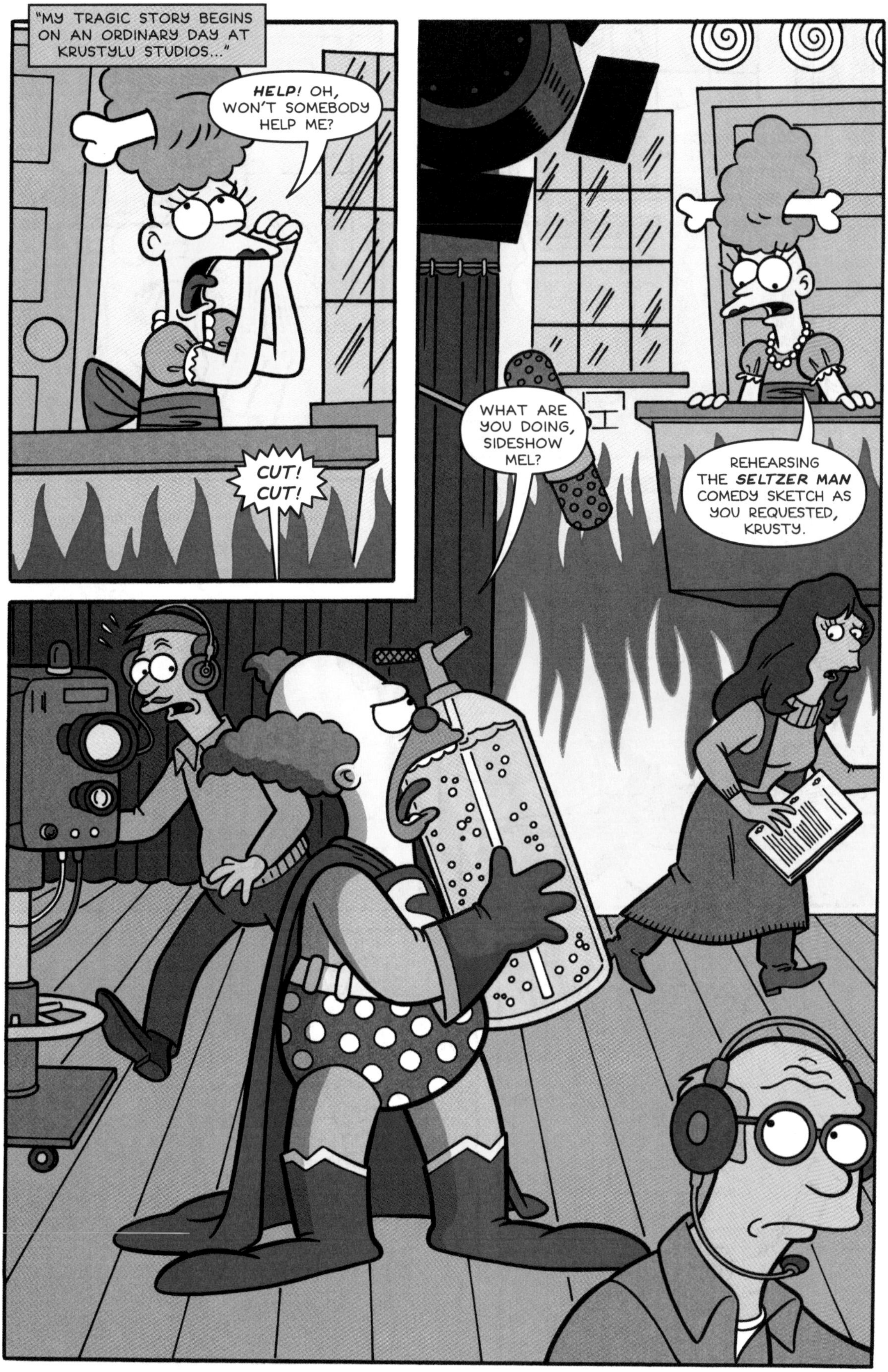
"MY TRAGIC STORY BEGINS ON AN ORDINARY DAY AT KRUSTYLU STUDIOS..."
HELP! OH, WON'T SOMEBODY HELP ME?
CUT! CUT!
WHAT ARE YOU DOING, SIDESHOW MEL?
REHEARSING THE SELTZER MAN COMEDY SKETCH AS YOU REQUESTED, KRUSTY.

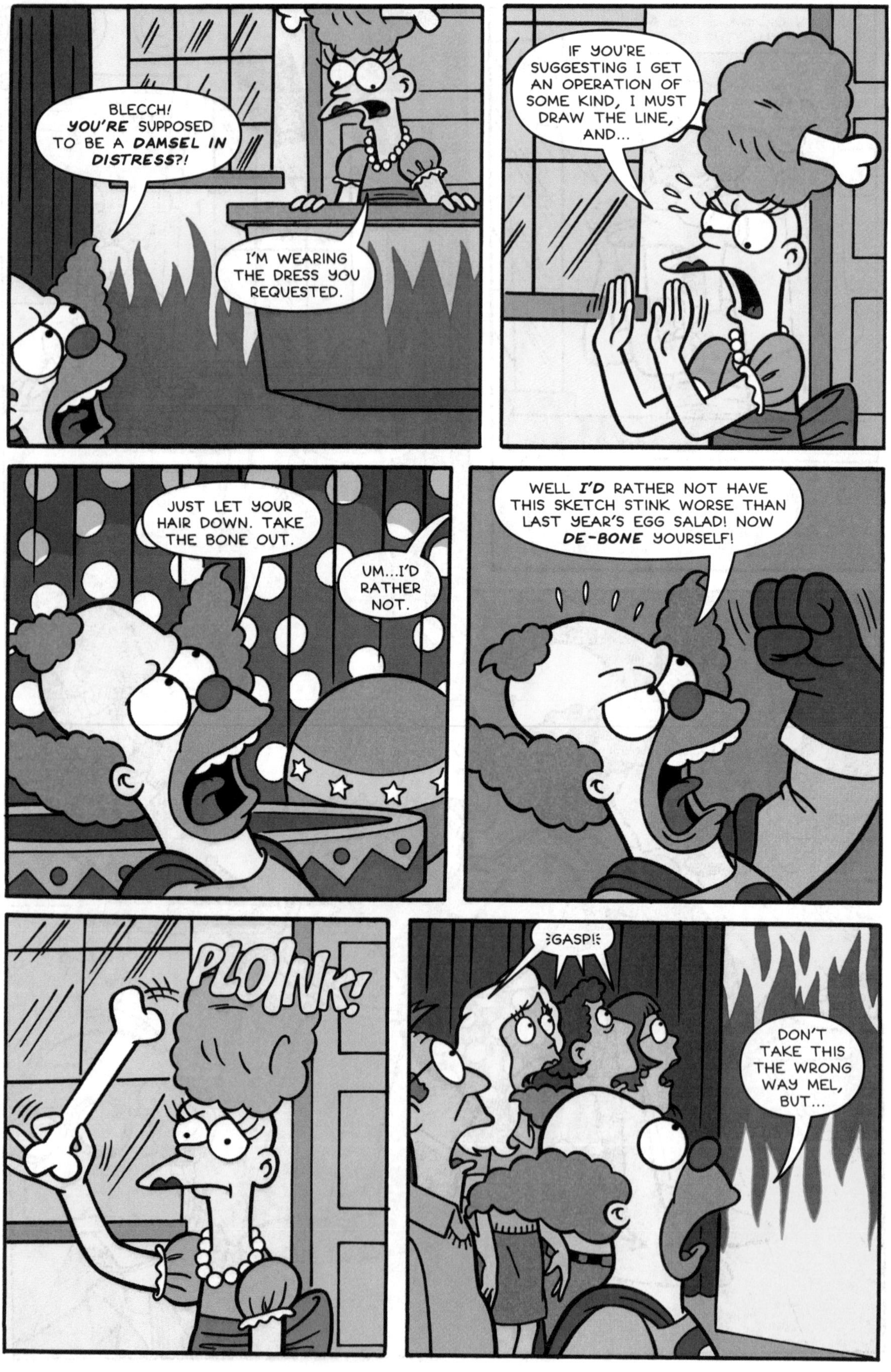
BLECCH! **YOU'RE** SUPPOSED TO BE A **DAMSEL IN DISTRESS?!**
I'M WEARING THE DRESS YOU REQUESTED.
IF YOU'RE SUGGESTING I GET AN OPERATION OF SOME KIND, I MUST DRAW THE LINE, AND...
JUST LET YOUR HAIR DOWN. TAKE THE BONE OUT.
UM...I'D RATHER NOT.
WELL **I'D** RATHER NOT HAVE THIS SKETCH STINK WORSE THAN LAST YEAR'S EGG SALAD! NOW **DE-BONE** YOURSELF!
PLOINK!
GASP!
DON'T TAKE THIS THE WRONG WAY MEL, BUT...

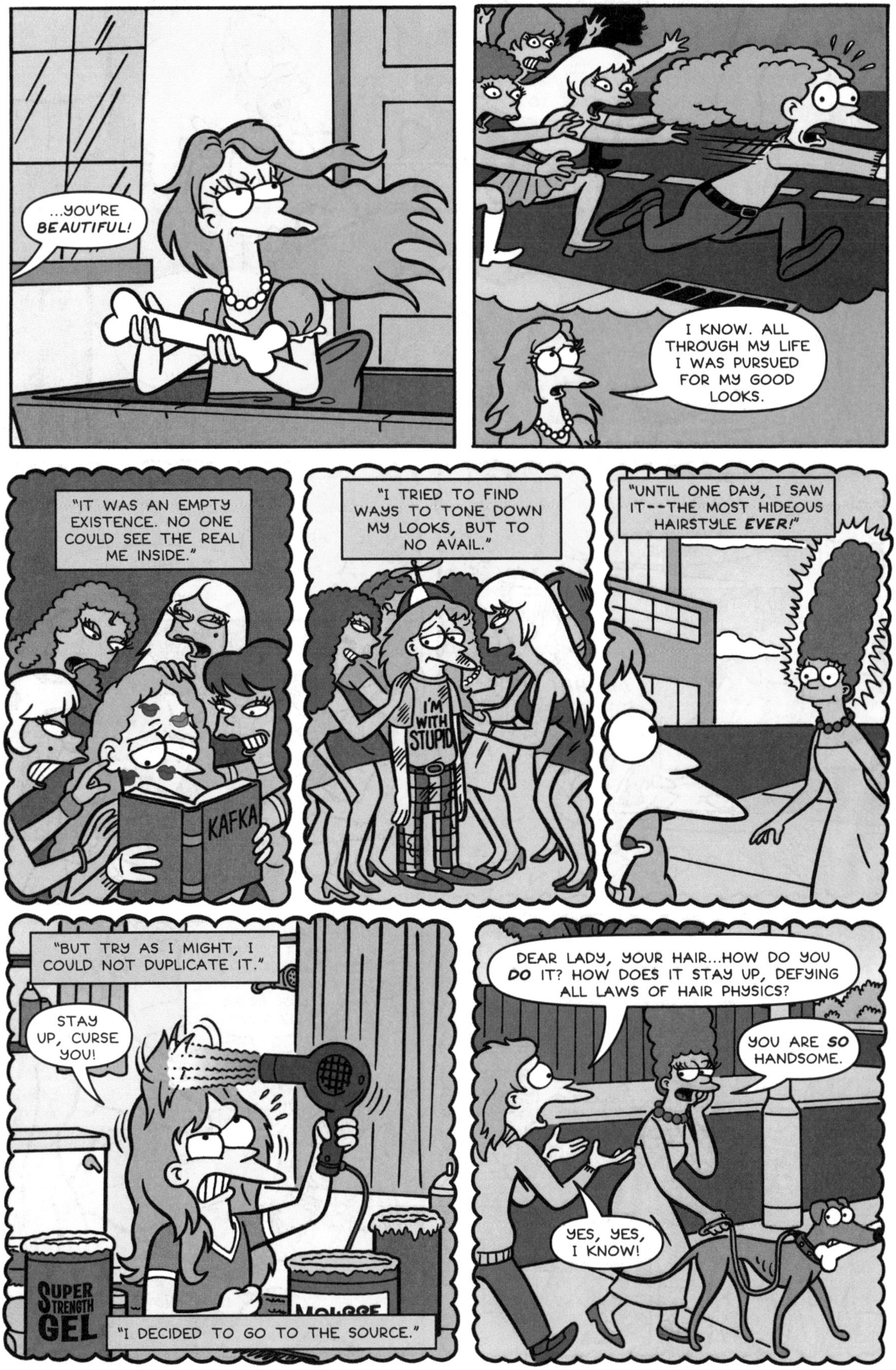
...YOU'RE BEAUTIFUL!
I KNOW. ALL THROUGH MY LIFE I WAS PURSUED FOR MY GOOD LOOKS.
"IT WAS AN EMPTY EXISTENCE. NO ONE COULD SEE THE REAL ME INSIDE."
KAFKA
"I TRIED TO FIND WAYS TO TONE DOWN MY LOOKS, BUT TO NO AVAIL."
I'M WITH STUPID
"UNTIL ONE DAY, I SAW IT--THE MOST HIDEOUS HAIRSTYLE EVER!"
"BUT TRY AS I MIGHT, I COULD NOT DUPLICATE IT."
STAY UP, CURSE YOU!
SUPER STRENGTH GEL
"I DECIDED TO GO TO THE SOURCE."
DEAR LADY, YOUR HAIR...HOW DO YOU DO IT? HOW DOES IT STAY UP, DEFYING ALL LAWS OF HAIR PHYSICS?
YOU ARE SO HANDSOME.
YES, YES, I KNOW!

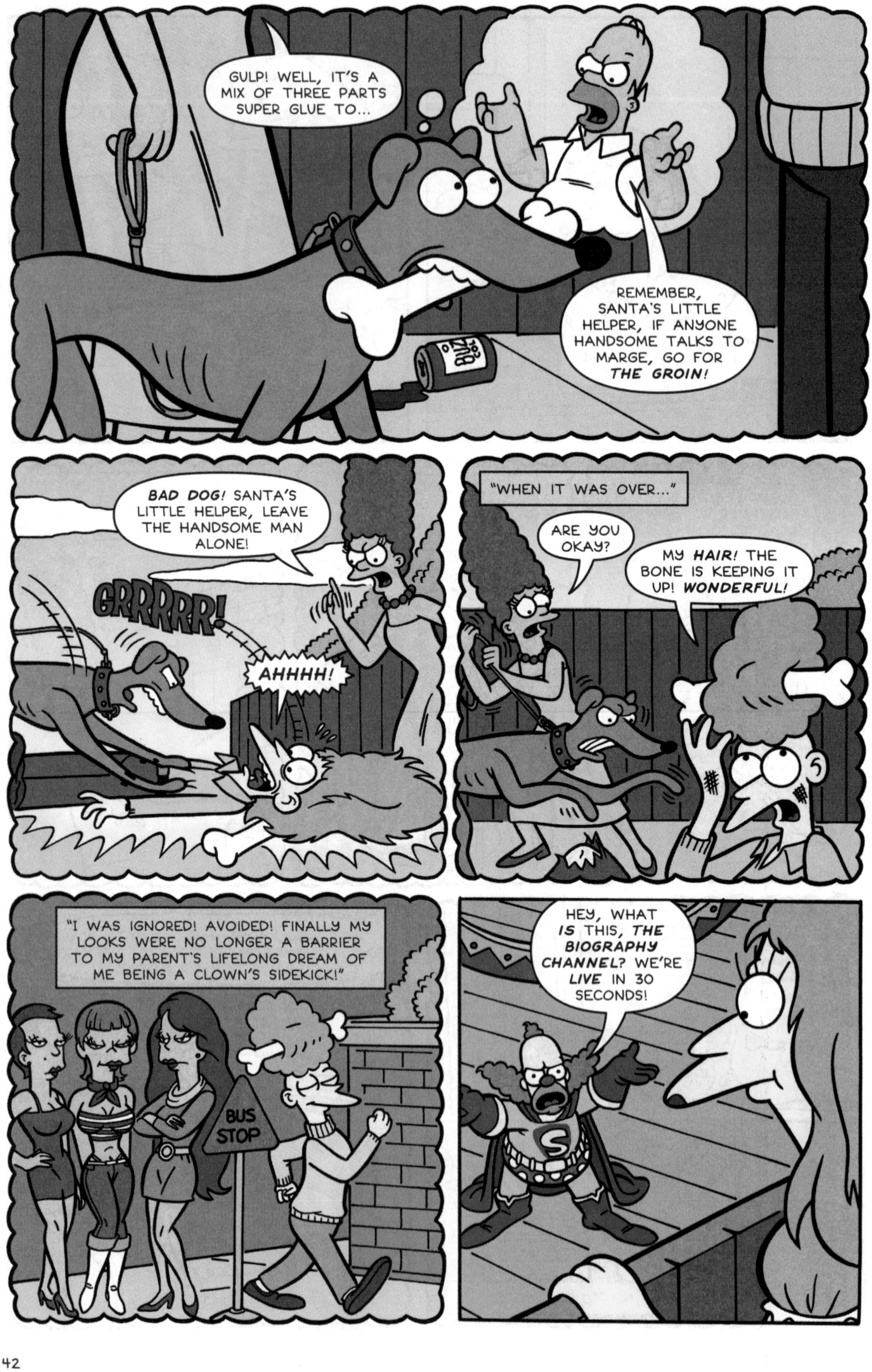
GULP! WELL, IT'S A MIX OF THREE PARTS SUPER GLUE TO...
REMEMBER, SANTA'S LITTLE HELPER, IF ANYONE HANDSOME TALKS TO MARGE, GO FOR **THE GROIN**!
**BAD DOG!** SANTA'S LITTLE HELPER, LEAVE THE HANDSOME MAN ALONE!
GRRRRR!
**AHHHH!**
"WHEN IT WAS OVER..."
ARE YOU OKAY?
MY **HAIR**! THE BONE IS KEEPING IT UP! **WONDERFUL!**
"I WAS IGNORED! AVOIDED! FINALLY MY LOOKS WERE NO LONGER A BARRIER TO MY PARENT'S LIFELONG DREAM OF ME BEING A CLOWN'S SIDEKICK!"
BUS STOP
HEY, WHAT ***IS*** THIS, ***THE BIOGRAPHY CHANNEL***? WE'RE ***LIVE*** IN 30 SECONDS!

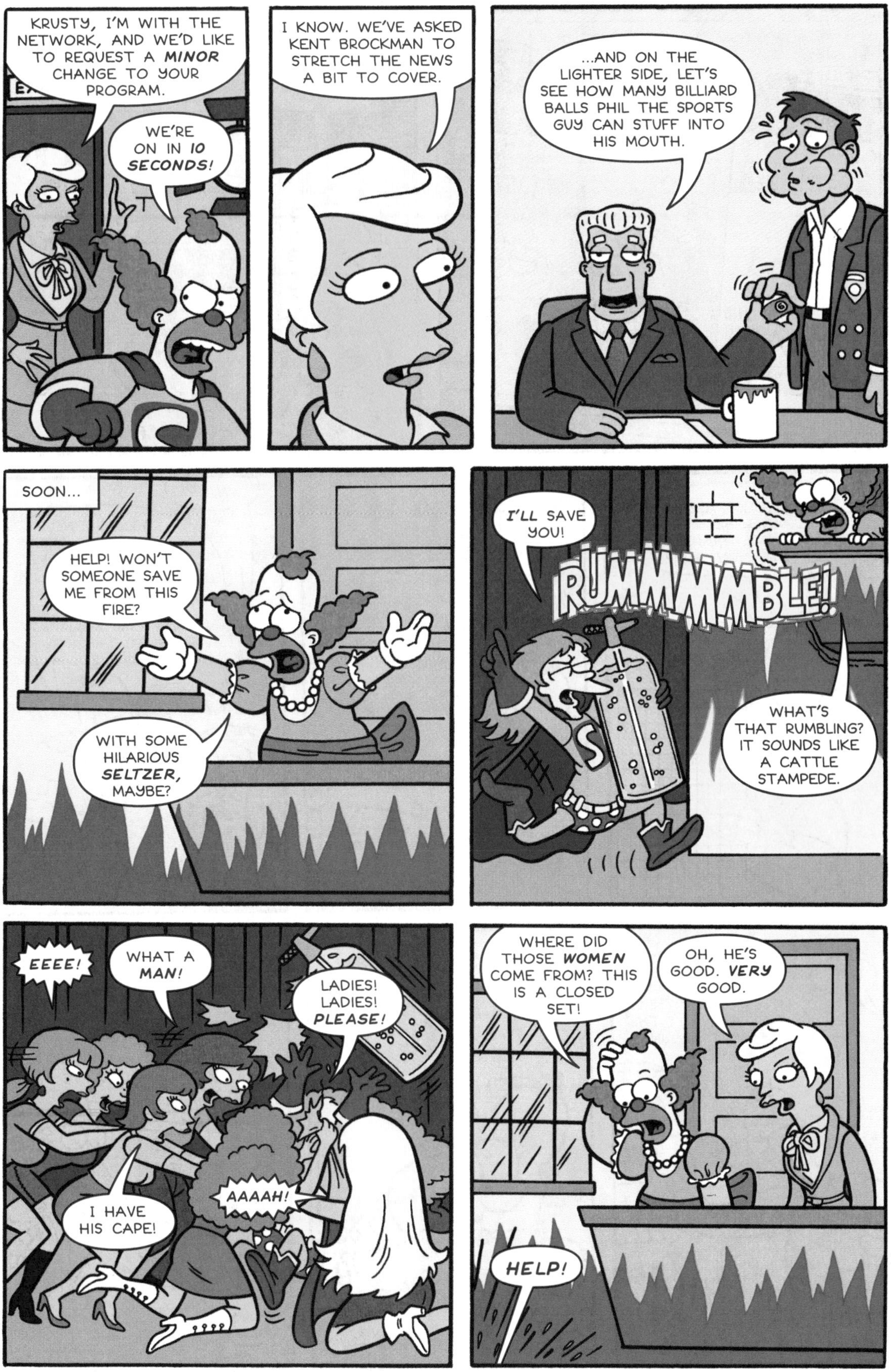
KRUSTY, I'M WITH THE NETWORK, AND WE'D LIKE TO REQUEST A MINOR CHANGE TO YOUR PROGRAM.
WE'RE ON IN 10 SECONDS!
I KNOW. WE'VE ASKED KENT BROCKMAN TO STRETCH THE NEWS A BIT TO COVER.
...AND ON THE LIGHTER SIDE, LET'S SEE HOW MANY BILLIARD BALLS PHIL THE SPORTS GUY CAN STUFF INTO HIS MOUTH.
SOON...
HELP! WON'T SOMEONE SAVE ME FROM THIS FIRE?
WITH SOME HILARIOUS SELTZER, MAYBE?
I'LL SAVE YOU!
RUMMMMBLE!
WHAT'S THAT RUMBLING? IT SOUNDS LIKE A CATTLE STAMPEDE.
EEEE!
WHAT A MAN!
LADIES! LADIES! PLEASE!
I HAVE HIS CAPE!
AAAAH!
WHERE DID THOSE WOMEN COME FROM? THIS IS A CLOSED SET!
OH, HE'S GOOD. VERY GOOD.
HELP!

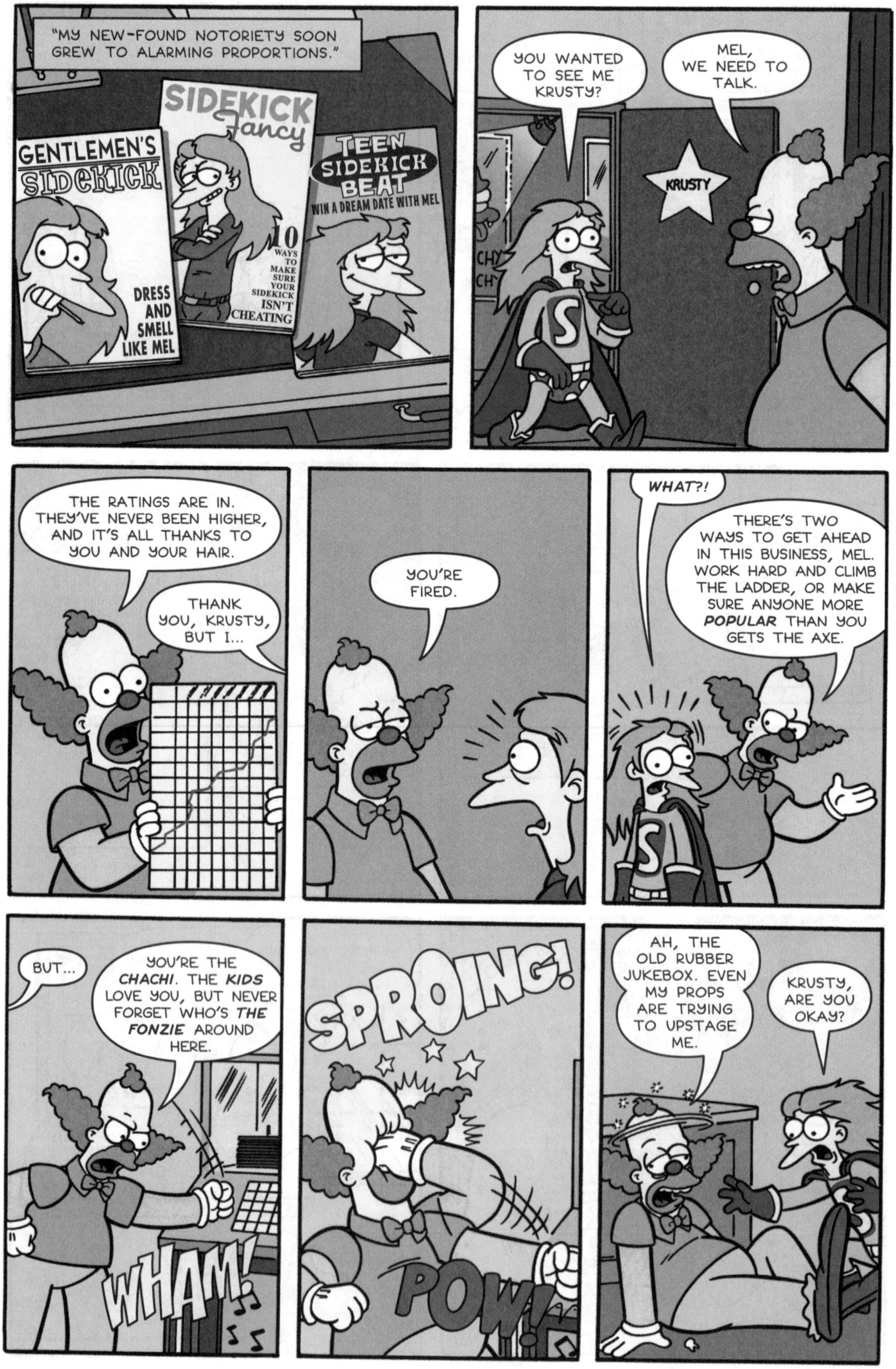
"MY NEW-FOUND NOTORIETY SOON GREW TO ALARMING PROPORTIONS."
GENTLEMEN'S SIDEKICK
DRESS AND SMELL LIKE MEL
SIDEKICK Fancy
10 WAYS TO MAKE SURE YOUR SIDEKICK ISN'T CHEATING
TEEN SIDEKICK BEAT
WIN A DREAM DATE WITH MEL
YOU WANTED TO SEE ME KRUSTY?
MEL, WE NEED TO TALK.
KRUSTY
THE RATINGS ARE IN. THEY'VE NEVER BEEN HIGHER, AND IT'S ALL THANKS TO YOU AND YOUR HAIR.
THANK YOU, KRUSTY, BUT I...
YOU'RE FIRED.
WHAT?!
THERE'S TWO WAYS TO GET AHEAD IN THIS BUSINESS, MEL. WORK HARD AND CLIMB THE LADDER, OR MAKE SURE ANYONE MORE POPULAR THAN YOU GETS THE AXE.
BUT...
YOU'RE THE CHACHI. THE KIDS LOVE YOU, BUT NEVER FORGET WHO'S THE FONZIE AROUND HERE.
WHAM!
SPROING!
POW!
AH, THE OLD RUBBER JUKEBOX. EVEN MY PROPS ARE TRYING TO UPSTAGE ME.
KRUSTY, ARE YOU OKAY?

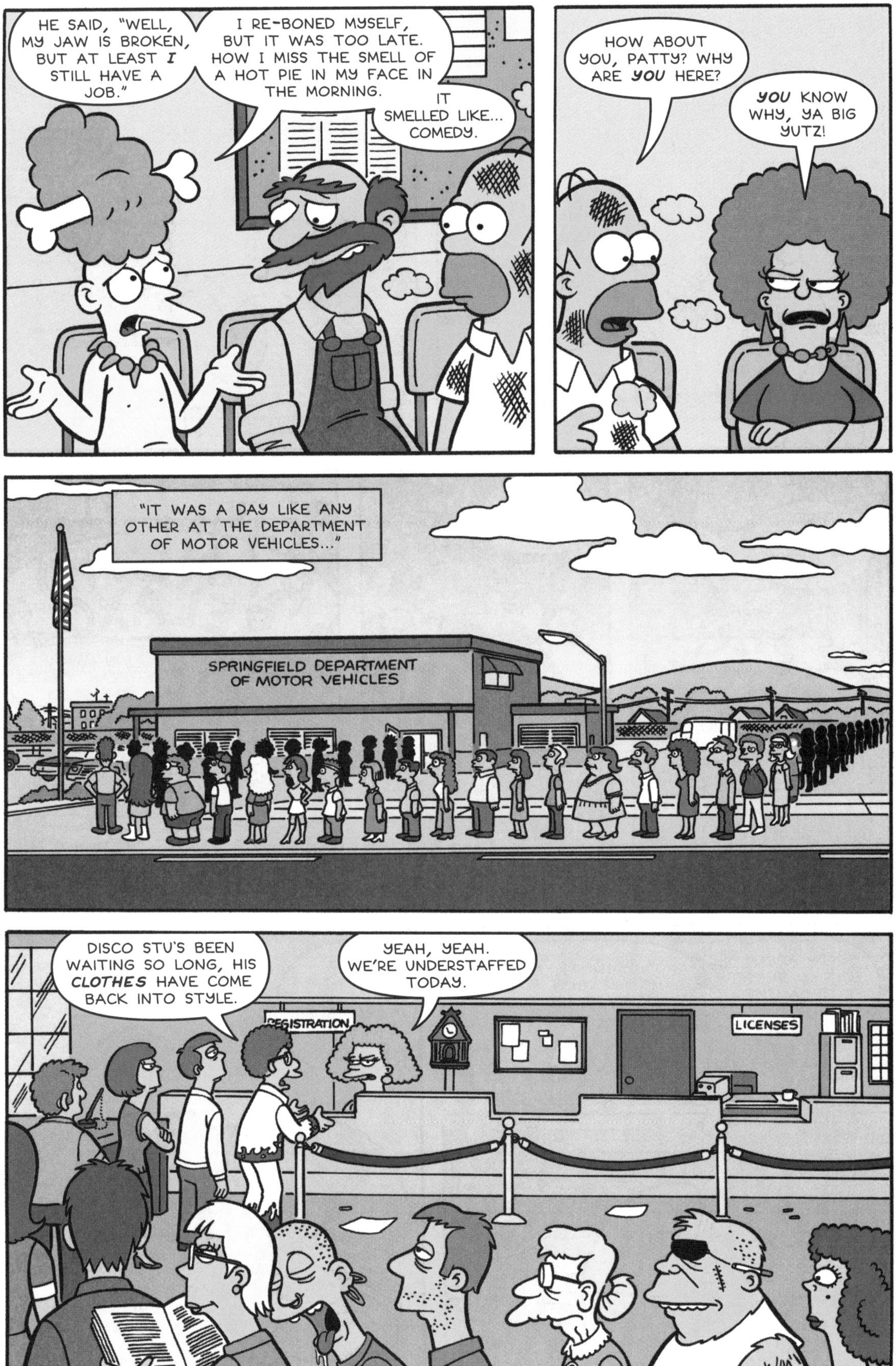
HE SAID, "WELL, MY JAW IS BROKEN, BUT AT LEAST I STILL HAVE A JOB."
I RE-BONED MYSELF, BUT IT WAS TOO LATE. HOW I MISS THE SMELL OF A HOT PIE IN MY FACE IN THE MORNING.
IT SMELLED LIKE... COMEDY.
HOW ABOUT YOU, PATTY? WHY ARE YOU HERE?
YOU KNOW WHY, YA BIG YUTZ!
"IT WAS A DAY LIKE ANY OTHER AT THE DEPARTMENT OF MOTOR VEHICLES..."
SPRINGFIELD DEPARTMENT OF MOTOR VEHICLES
DISCO STU'S BEEN WAITING SO LONG, HIS CLOTHES HAVE COME BACK INTO STYLE.
YEAH, YEAH. WE'RE UNDERSTAFFED TODAY.
REGISTRATION
LICENSES

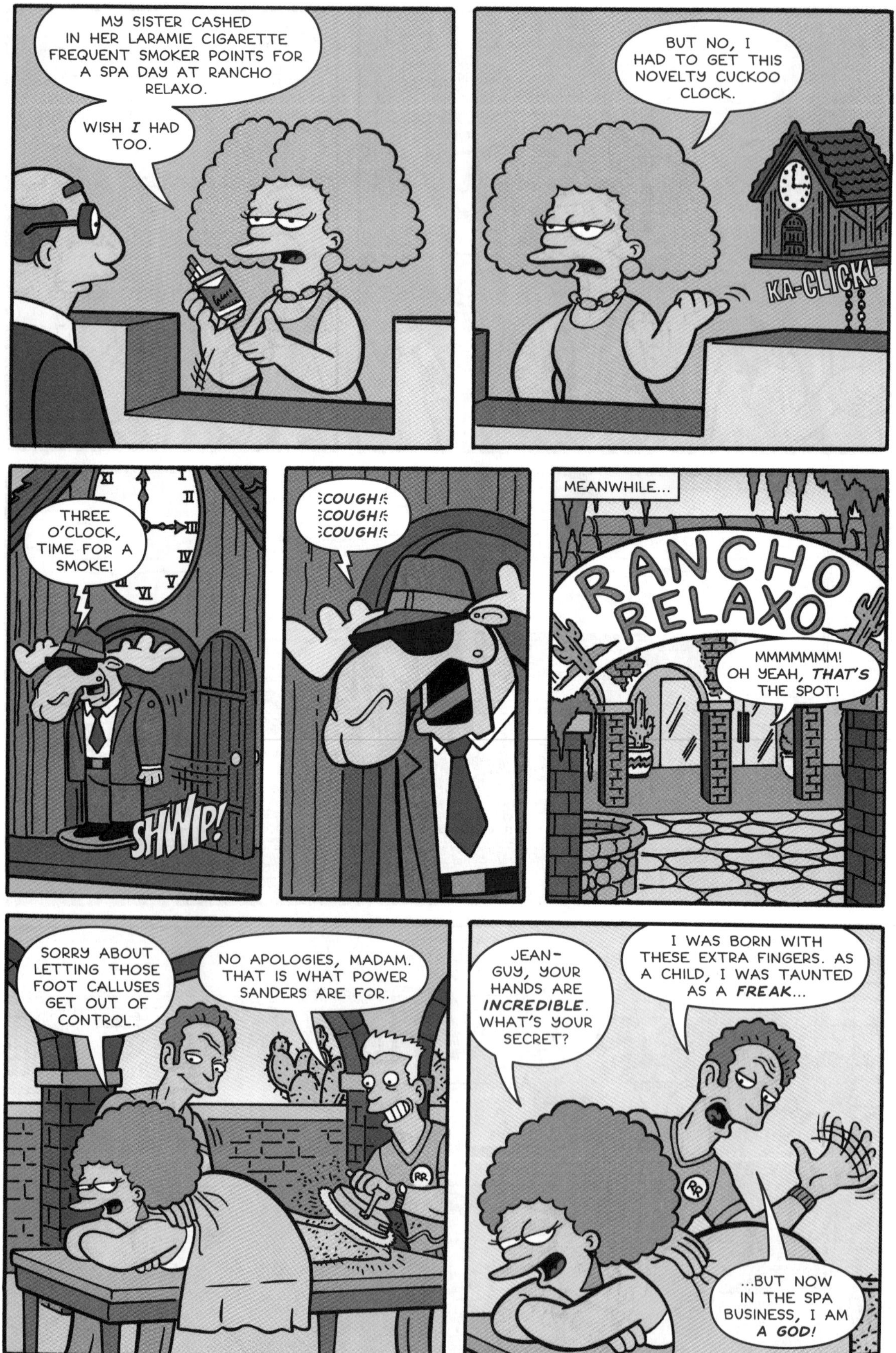
MY SISTER CASHED IN HER LARAMIE CIGARETTE FREQUENT SMOKER POINTS FOR A SPA DAY AT RANCHO RELAXO.
WISH I HAD TOO.
BUT NO, I HAD TO GET THIS NOVELTY CUCKOO CLOCK.
KA-CLICK!
THREE O'CLOCK, TIME FOR A SMOKE!
SHWIP!
COUGH! COUGH! COUGH!
MEANWHILE...
RANCHO RELAXO
MMMMMMM! OH YEAH, THAT'S THE SPOT!
SORRY ABOUT LETTING THOSE FOOT CALLUSES GET OUT OF CONTROL.
NO APOLOGIES, MADAM. THAT IS WHAT POWER SANDERS ARE FOR.
JEAN-GUY, YOUR HANDS ARE INCREDIBLE. WHAT'S YOUR SECRET?
I WAS BORN WITH THESE EXTRA FINGERS. AS A CHILD, I WAS TAUNTED AS A FREAK...
...BUT NOW IN THE SPA BUSINESS, I AM A GOD!

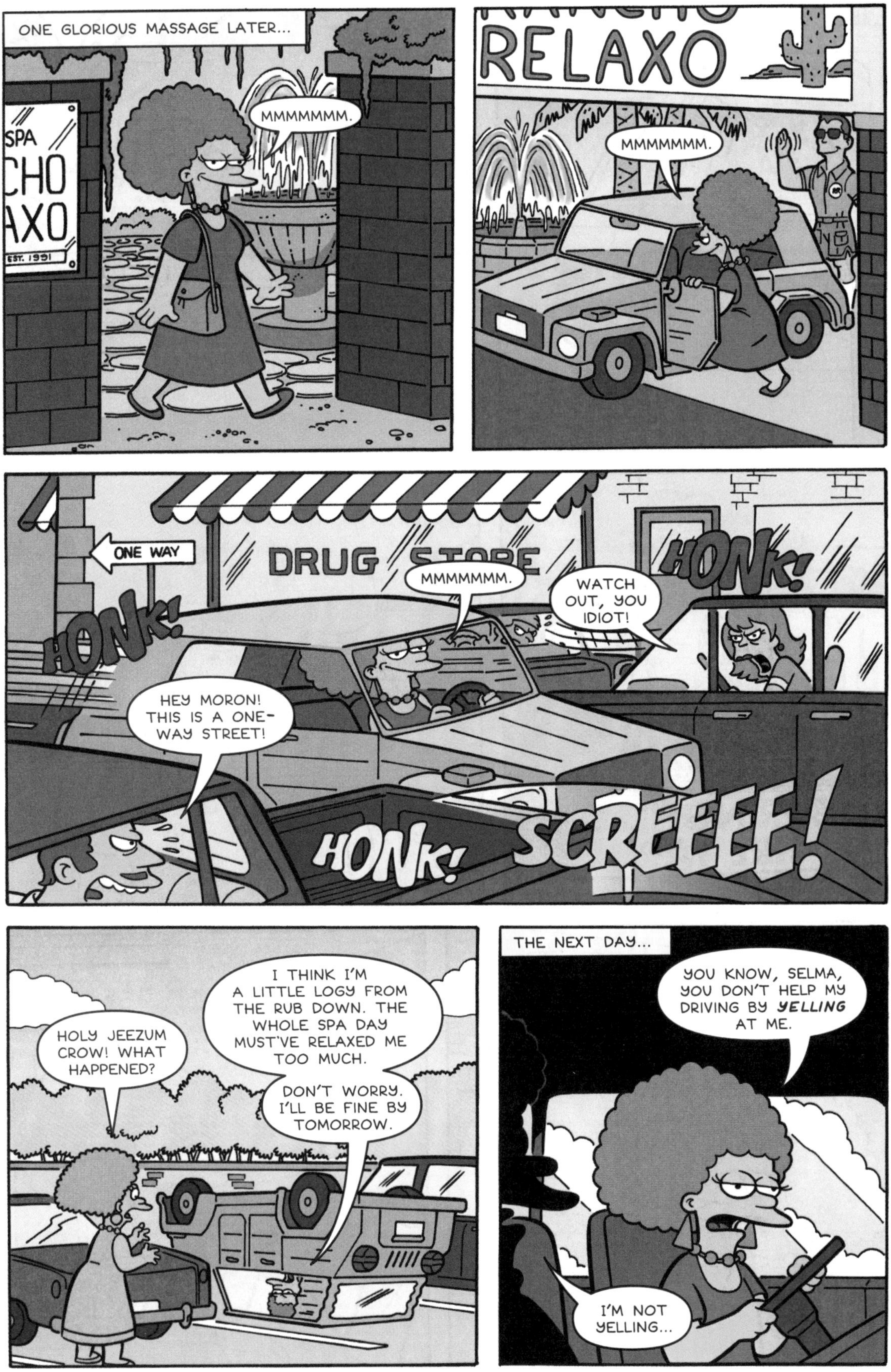
ONE GLORIOUS MASSAGE LATER...
SPA
CHO
AXO
EST. 1991
MMMMMMM.
RELAXO
MMMMMMM.
ONE WAY
DRUG
HONK!
MMMMMMM.
WATCH OUT, YOU IDIOT!
HONK!
HEY MORON! THIS IS A ONE-WAY STREET!
HONK!
SCREEEE!
HOLY JEEZUM CROW! WHAT HAPPENED?
I THINK I'M A LITTLE LOGY FROM THE RUB DOWN. THE WHOLE SPA DAY MUST'VE RELAXED ME TOO MUCH.
DON'T WORRY. I'LL BE FINE BY TOMORROW.
THE NEXT DAY...
YOU KNOW, SELMA, YOU DON'T HELP MY DRIVING BY *YELLING* AT ME.
I'M NOT YELLING...

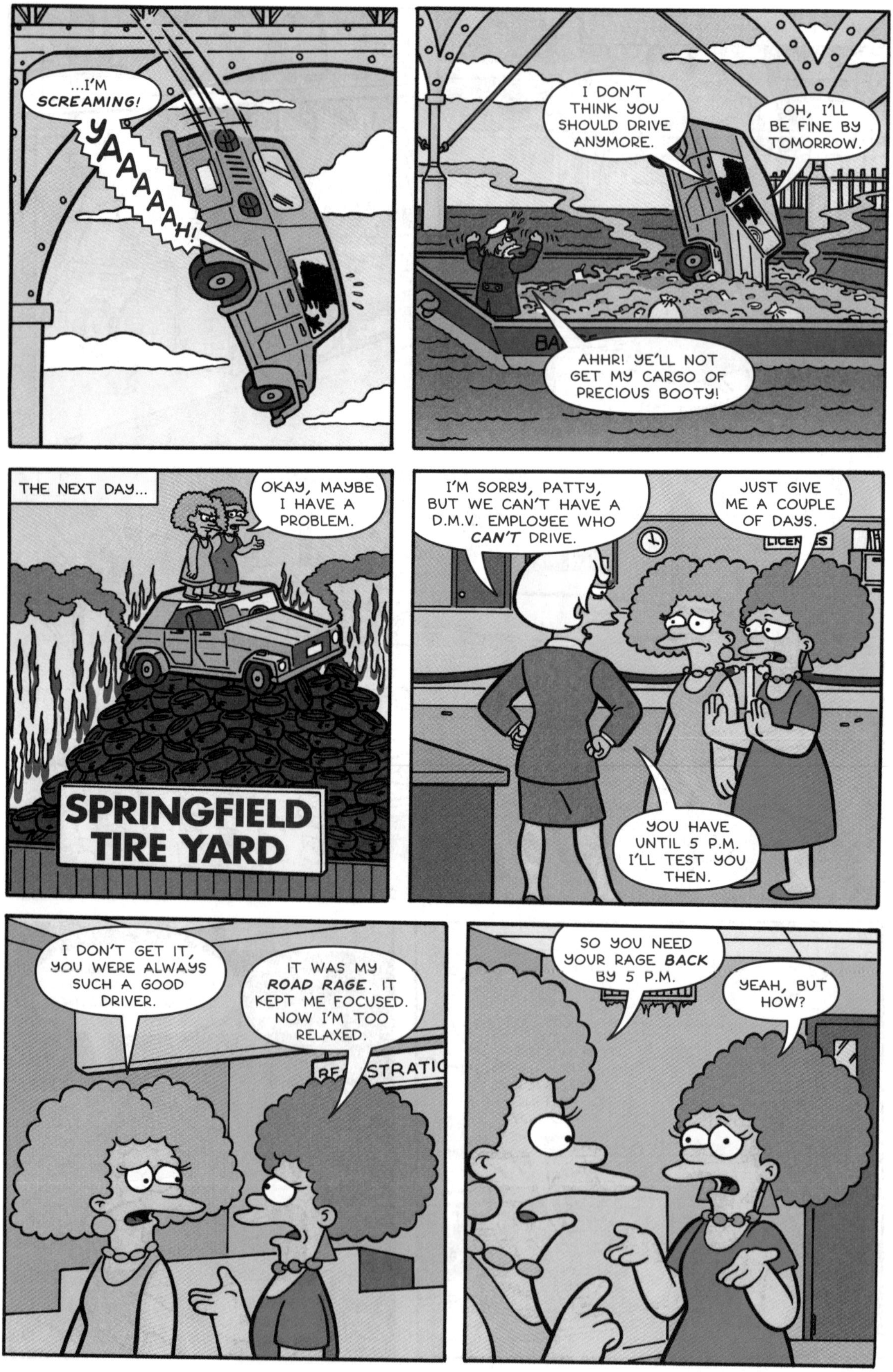
...I'M SCREAMING!
YAAAAAAH!
I DON'T THINK YOU SHOULD DRIVE ANYMORE.
OH, I'LL BE FINE BY TOMORROW.
AHHR! YE'LL NOT GET MY CARGO OF PRECIOUS BOOTY!
THE NEXT DAY...
OKAY, MAYBE I HAVE A PROBLEM.
SPRINGFIELD TIRE YARD
I'M SORRY, PATTY, BUT WE CAN'T HAVE A D.M.V. EMPLOYEE WHO CAN'T DRIVE.
JUST GIVE ME A COUPLE OF DAYS.
YOU HAVE UNTIL 5 P.M. I'LL TEST YOU THEN.
I DON'T GET IT, YOU WERE ALWAYS SUCH A GOOD DRIVER.
IT WAS MY ROAD RAGE. IT KEPT ME FOCUSED. NOW I'M TOO RELAXED.
SO YOU NEED YOUR RAGE BACK BY 5 P.M.
YEAH, BUT HOW?

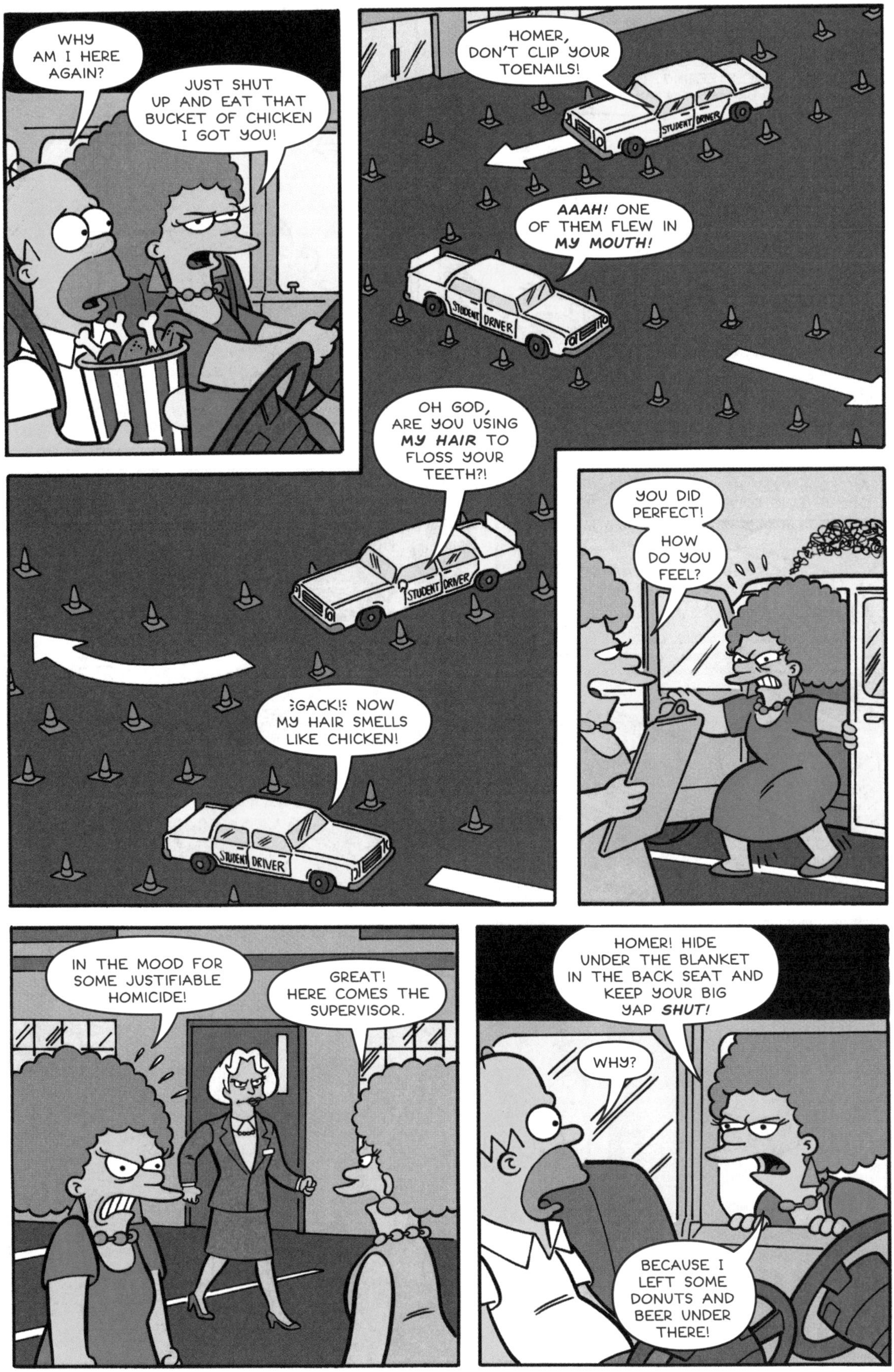
WHY AM I HERE AGAIN?
JUST SHUT UP AND EAT THAT BUCKET OF CHICKEN I GOT YOU!
HOMER, DON'T CLIP YOUR TOENAILS!
STUDENT DRIVER
AAAH! ONE OF THEM FLEW IN MY MOUTH!
STUDENT DRIVER
OH GOD, ARE YOU USING MY HAIR TO FLOSS YOUR TEETH?!
STUDENT DRIVER
GACK! NOW MY HAIR SMELLS LIKE CHICKEN!
STUDENT DRIVER
YOU DID PERFECT!
HOW DO YOU FEEL?
IN THE MOOD FOR SOME JUSTIFIABLE HOMICIDE!
GREAT! HERE COMES THE SUPERVISOR.
HOMER! HIDE UNDER THE BLANKET IN THE BACK SEAT AND KEEP YOUR BIG YAP SHUT!
WHY?
BECAUSE I LEFT SOME DONUTS AND BEER UNDER THERE!

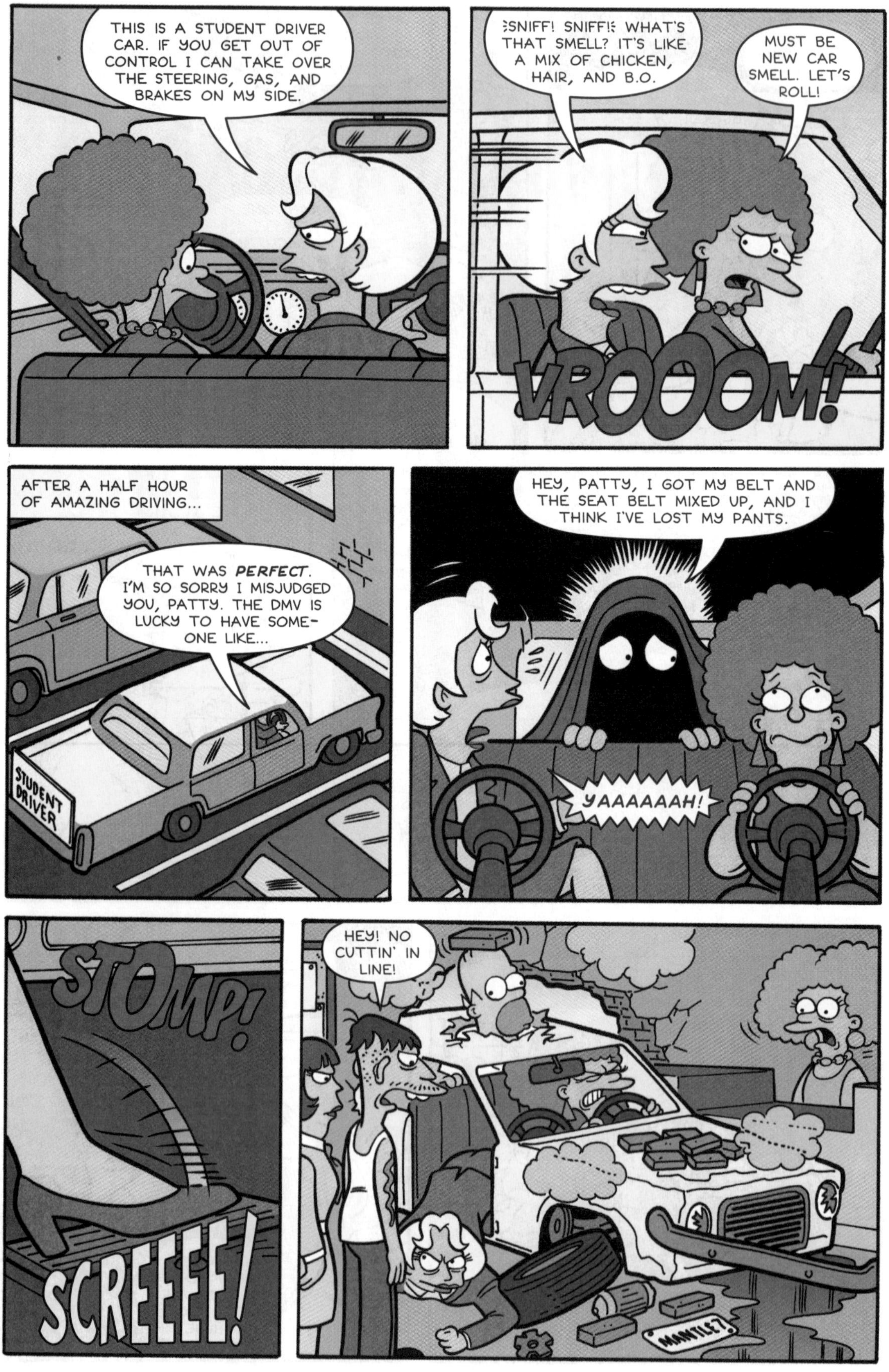
THIS IS A STUDENT DRIVER CAR. IF YOU GET OUT OF CONTROL I CAN TAKE OVER THE STEERING, GAS, AND BRAKES ON MY SIDE.
:SNIFF! SNIFF!: WHAT'S THAT SMELL? IT'S LIKE A MIX OF CHICKEN, HAIR, AND B.O.
MUST BE NEW CAR SMELL. LET'S ROLL!
VROOOOM!
AFTER A HALF HOUR OF AMAZING DRIVING...
THAT WAS PERFECT. I'M SO SORRY I MISJUDGED YOU, PATTY. THE DMV IS LUCKY TO HAVE SOME-ONE LIKE...
STUDENT DRIVER
HEY, PATTY, I GOT MY BELT AND THE SEAT BELT MIXED UP, AND I THINK I'VE LOST MY PANTS.
YAAAAAAH!
STOMP!
SCREEEE!
HEY! NO CUTTIN' IN LINE!
MANTLE7

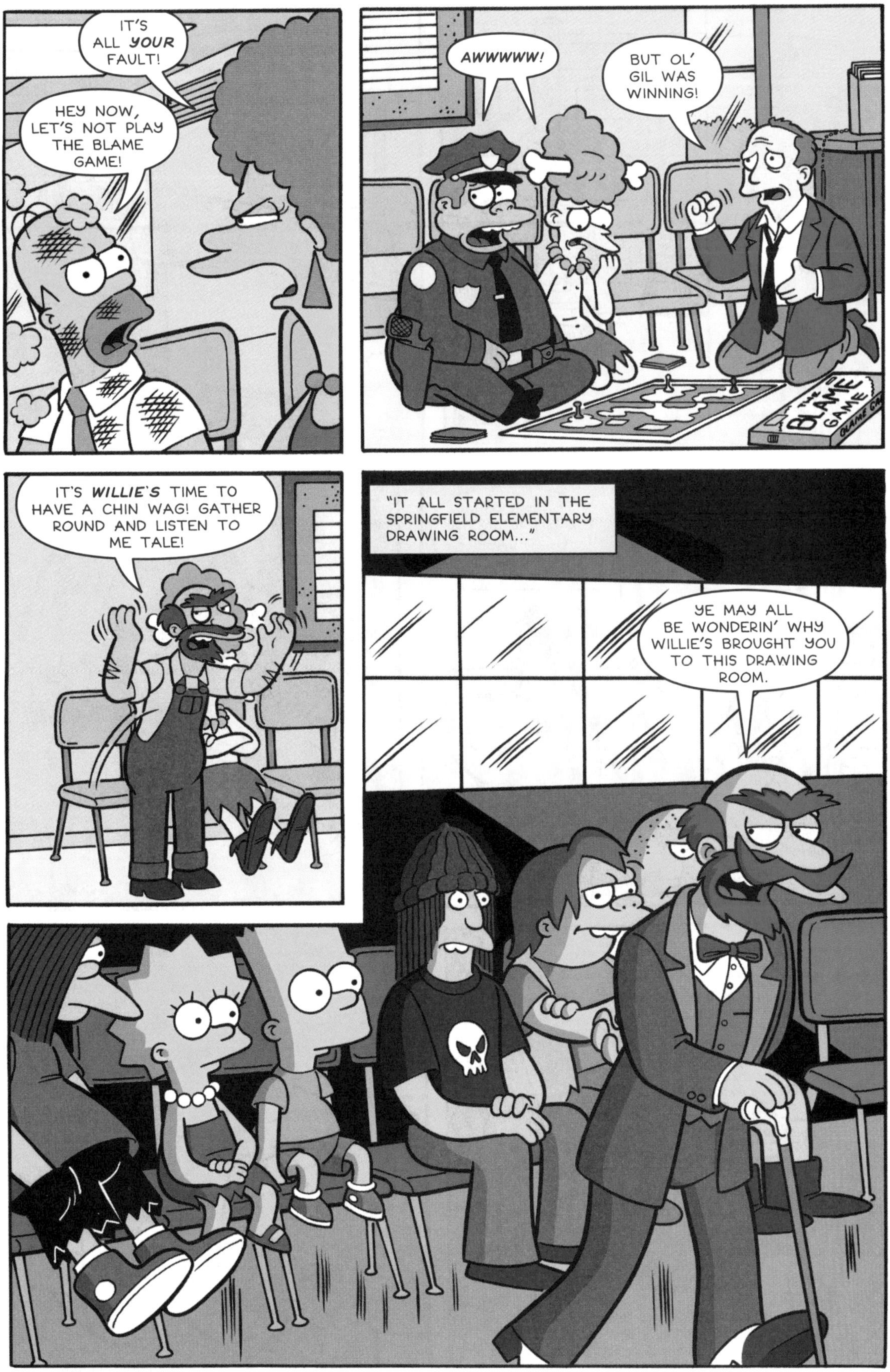
IT'S ALL *YOUR* FAULT!
HEY NOW, LET'S NOT PLAY THE BLAME GAME!
*AWWWWW!*
BUT OL' GIL WAS WINNING!
THE BLAME GAME
IT'S *WILLIE'S* TIME TO HAVE A CHIN WAG! GATHER ROUND AND LISTEN TO ME TALE!
"IT ALL STARTED IN THE SPRINGFIELD ELEMENTARY DRAWING ROOM..."
YE MAY ALL BE WONDERIN' WHY WILLIE'S BROUGHT YOU TO THIS DRAWING ROOM.

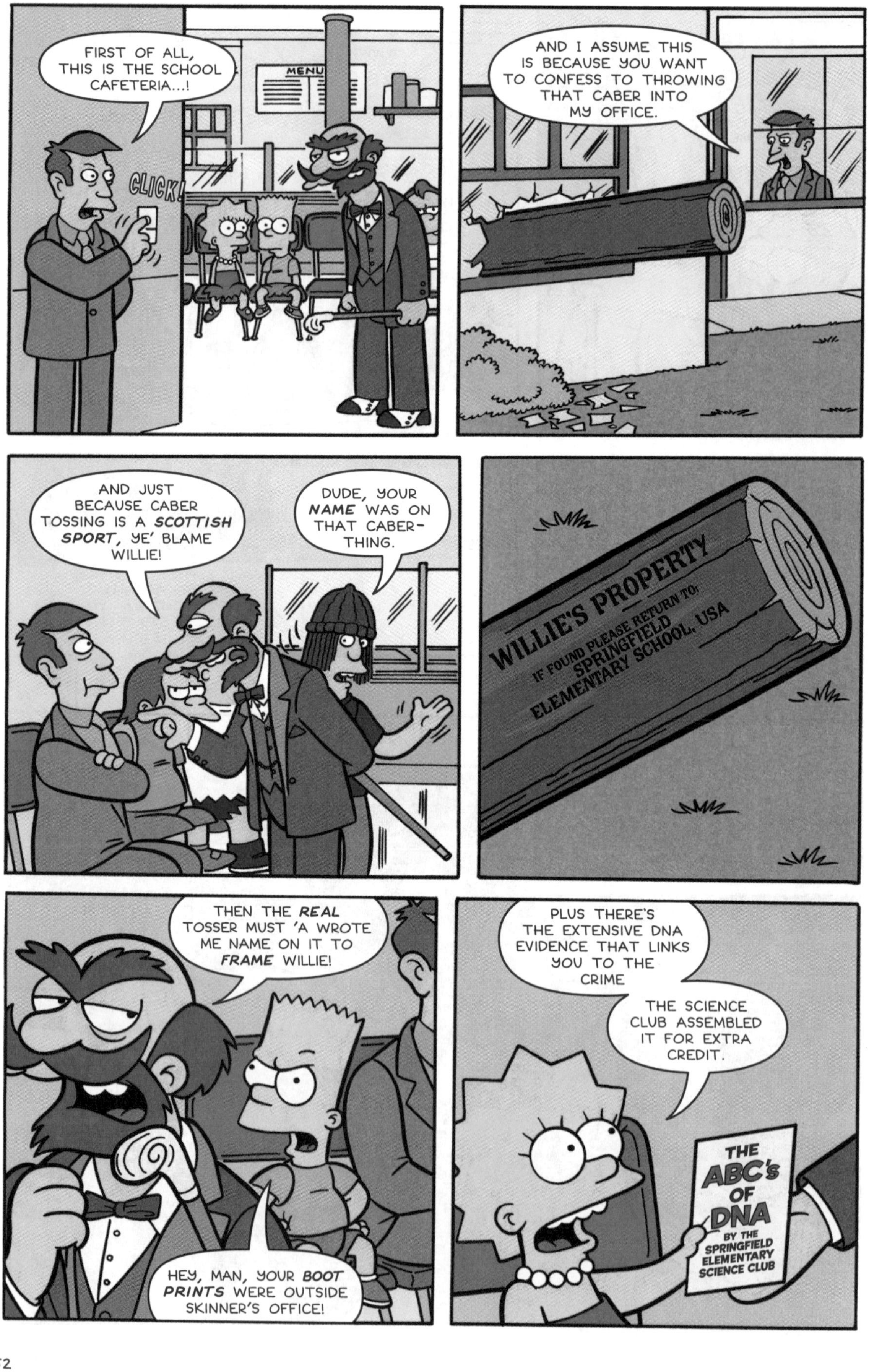
FIRST OF ALL, THIS IS THE SCHOOL CAFETERIA...!
CLICK!
MENU
AND I ASSUME THIS IS BECAUSE YOU WANT TO CONFESS TO THROWING THAT CABER INTO MY OFFICE.
AND JUST BECAUSE CABER TOSSING IS A *SCOTTISH SPORT,* YE' BLAME WILLIE!
DUDE, YOUR *NAME* WAS ON THAT CABER-THING.
WILLIE'S PROPERTY
IF FOUND PLEASE RETURN TO: SPRINGFIELD ELEMENTARY SCHOOL, USA
THEN THE *REAL* TOSSER MUST 'A WROTE ME NAME ON IT TO *FRAME* WILLIE!
HEY, MAN, YOUR *BOOT PRINTS* WERE OUTSIDE SKINNER'S OFFICE!
PLUS THERE'S THE EXTENSIVE DNA EVIDENCE THAT LINKS YOU TO THE CRIME
THE SCIENCE CLUB ASSEMBLED IT FOR EXTRA CREDIT.
THE ABC's OF DNA
BY THE SPRINGFIELD ELEMENTARY SCIENCE CLUB

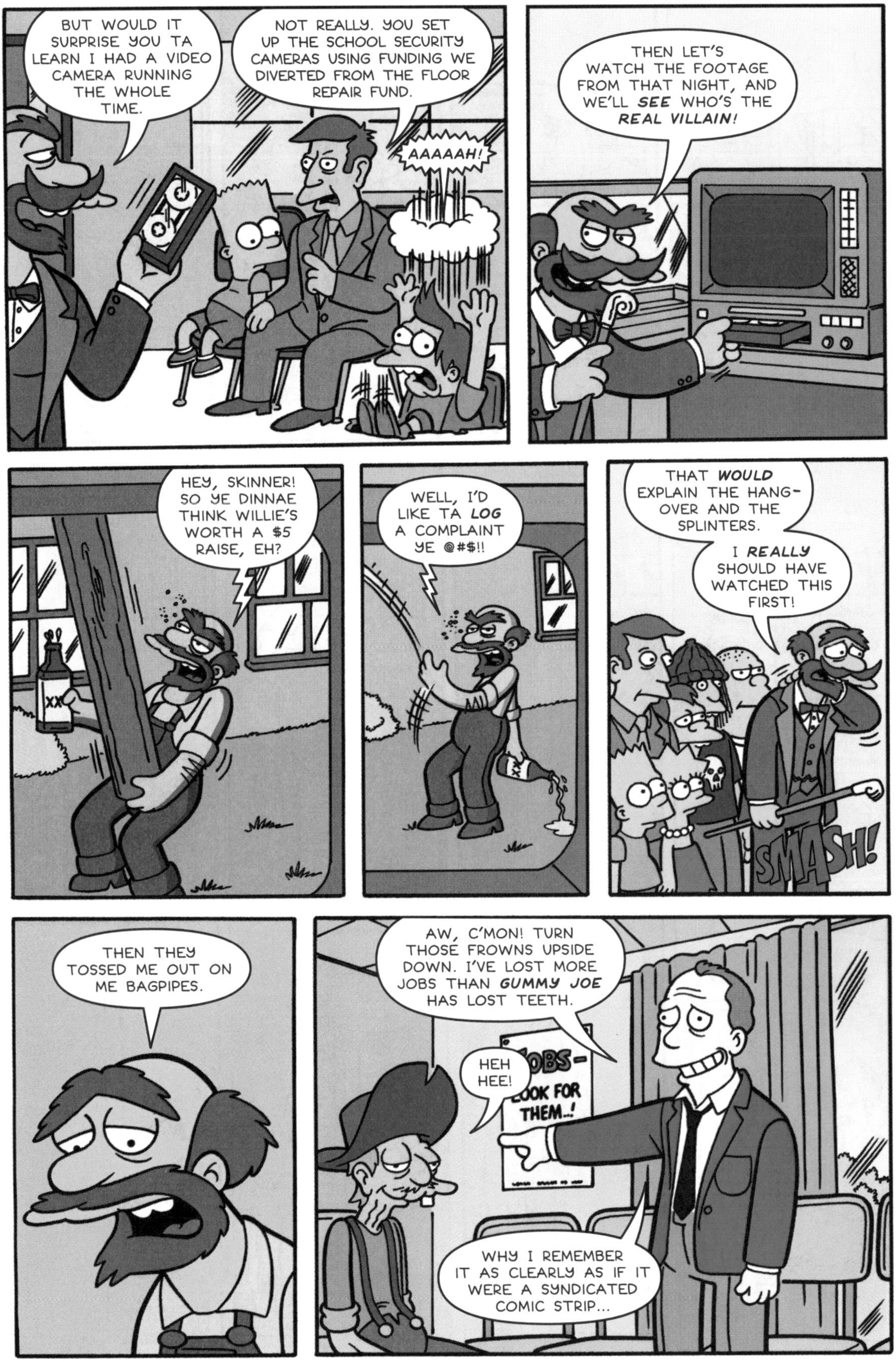
BUT WOULD IT SURPRISE YOU TA LEARN I HAD A VIDEO CAMERA RUNNING THE WHOLE TIME.
NOT REALLY. YOU SET UP THE SCHOOL SECURITY CAMERAS USING FUNDING WE DIVERTED FROM THE FLOOR REPAIR FUND.
AAAAAH!
THEN LET'S WATCH THE FOOTAGE FROM THAT NIGHT, AND WE'LL **SEE** WHO'S THE **REAL VILLAIN**!
HEY, SKINNER! SO YE DINNAE THINK WILLIE'S WORTH A $5 RAISE, EH?
WELL, I'D LIKE TA **LOG** A COMPLAINT YE @#$!!
THAT **WOULD** EXPLAIN THE HANG-OVER AND THE SPLINTERS.
I **REALLY** SHOULD HAVE WATCHED THIS FIRST!
SMASH!
THEN THEY TOSSED ME OUT ON ME BAGPIPES.
AW, C'MON! TURN THOSE FROWNS UPSIDE DOWN. I'VE LOST MORE JOBS THAN **GUMMY JOE** HAS LOST TEETH.
HEH HEE!
LOOK FOR THEM..!
WHY I REMEMBER IT AS CLEARLY AS IF IT WERE A SYNDICATED COMIC STRIP...

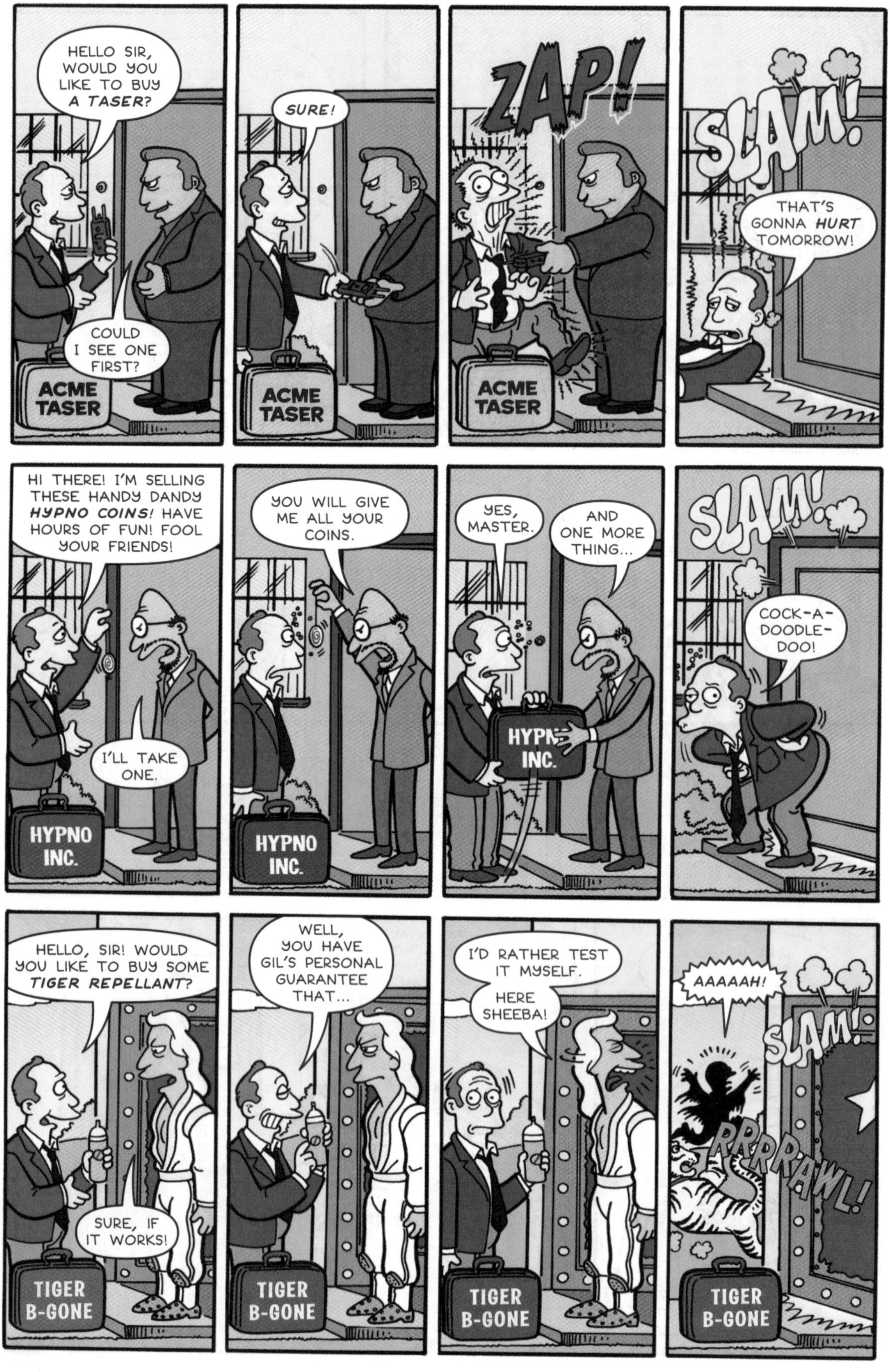
HELLO SIR, WOULD YOU LIKE TO BUY A TASER?
COULD I SEE ONE FIRST?
ACME TASER
SURE!
ACME TASER
ZAP!
ACME TASER
SLAM!
THAT'S GONNA HURT TOMORROW!
HI THERE! I'M SELLING THESE HANDY DANDY HYPNO COINS! HAVE HOURS OF FUN! FOOL YOUR FRIENDS!
I'LL TAKE ONE.
HYPNO INC.
YOU WILL GIVE ME ALL YOUR COINS.
HYPNO INC.
YES, MASTER.
AND ONE MORE THING...
HYPNO INC.
SLAM!
COCK-A-DOODLE-DOO!
HELLO, SIR! WOULD YOU LIKE TO BUY SOME TIGER REPELLANT?
SURE, IF IT WORKS!
TIGER B-GONE
WELL, YOU HAVE GIL'S PERSONAL GUARANTEE THAT...
TIGER B-GONE
I'D RATHER TEST IT MYSELF.
HERE SHEEBA!
TIGER B-GONE
AAAAAH!
SLAM!
RRRRAWL!
TIGER B-GONE

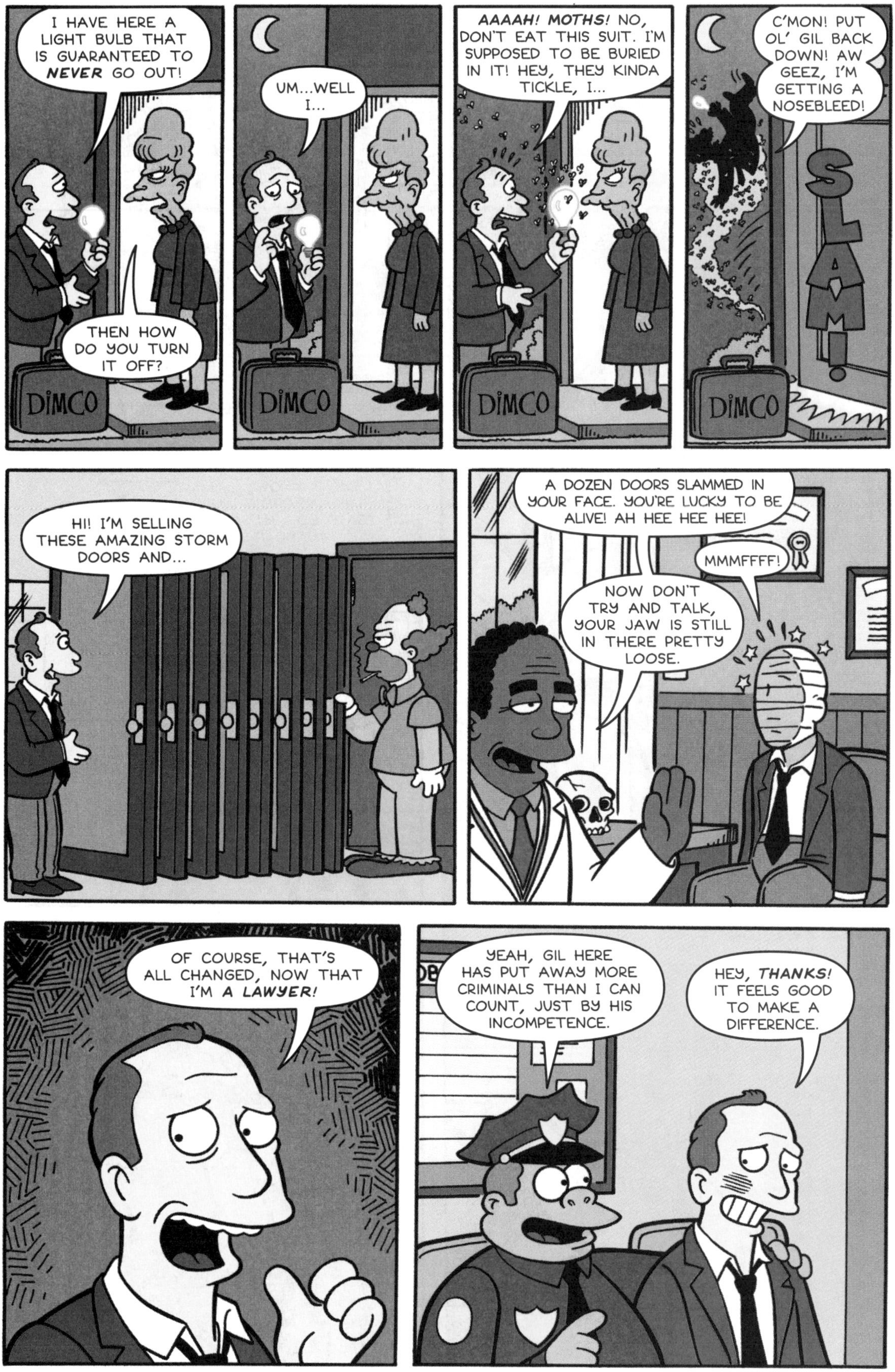
I HAVE HERE A LIGHT BULB THAT IS GUARANTEED TO NEVER GO OUT!
THEN HOW DO YOU TURN IT OFF?
DIMCO
UM...WELL I...
DIMCO
AAAAH! MOTHS! NO, DON'T EAT THIS SUIT. I'M SUPPOSED TO BE BURIED IN IT! HEY, THEY KINDA TICKLE, I...
DIMCO
C'MON! PUT OL' GIL BACK DOWN! AW GEEZ, I'M GETTING A NOSEBLEED!
SLAM!
DIMCO
HI! I'M SELLING THESE AMAZING STORM DOORS AND...
A DOZEN DOORS SLAMMED IN YOUR FACE. YOU'RE LUCKY TO BE ALIVE! AH HEE HEE HEE!
MMMFFFF!
NOW DON'T TRY AND TALK, YOUR JAW IS STILL IN THERE PRETTY LOOSE.
OF COURSE, THAT'S ALL CHANGED, NOW THAT I'M A LAWYER!
YEAH, GIL HERE HAS PUT AWAY MORE CRIMINALS THAN I CAN COUNT, JUST BY HIS INCOMPETENCE.
HEY, THANKS! IT FEELS GOOD TO MAKE A DIFFERENCE.

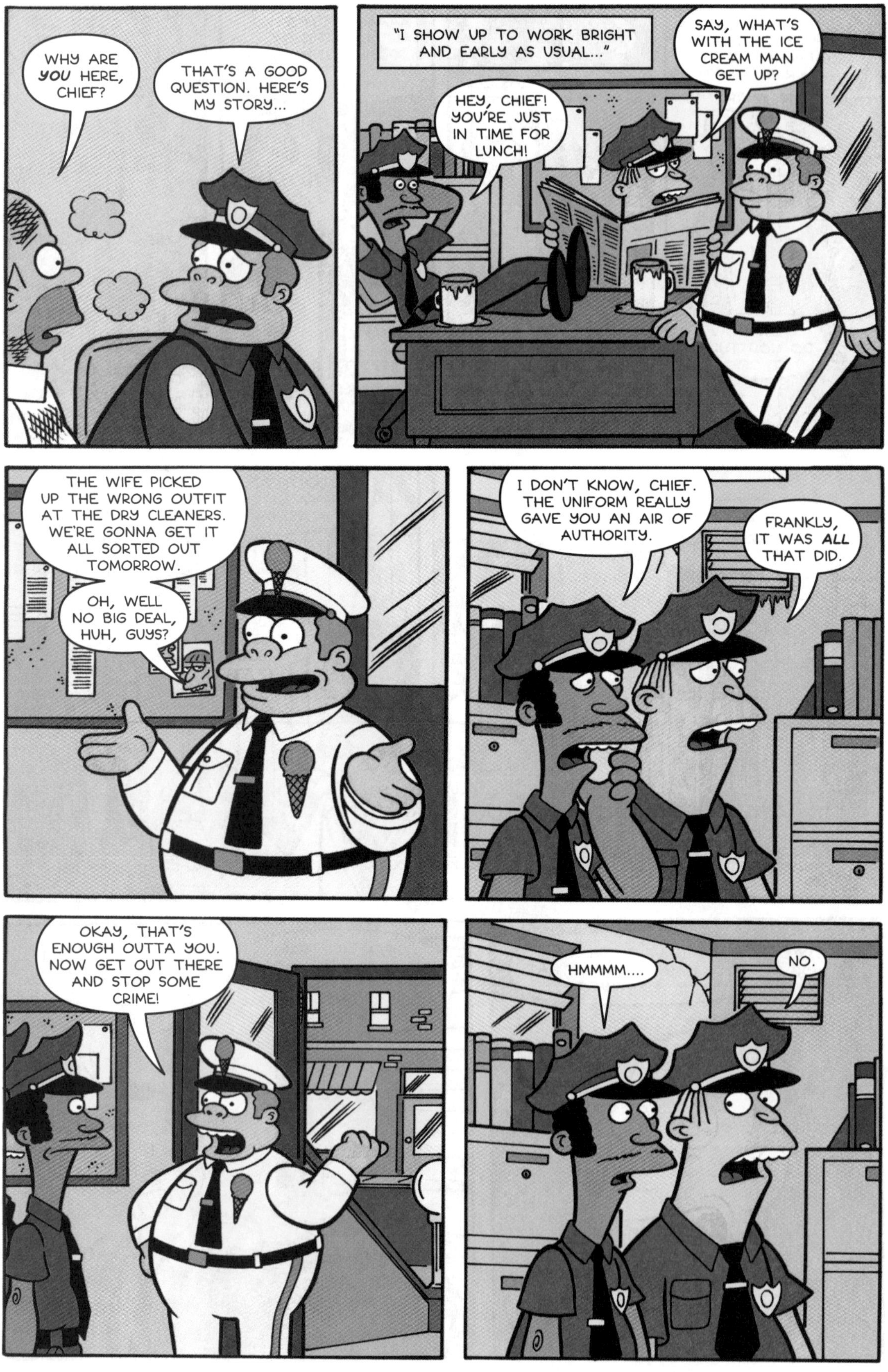
WHY ARE YOU HERE, CHIEF?
THAT'S A GOOD QUESTION. HERE'S MY STORY...
"I SHOW UP TO WORK BRIGHT AND EARLY AS USUAL..."
HEY, CHIEF! YOU'RE JUST IN TIME FOR LUNCH!
SAY, WHAT'S WITH THE ICE CREAM MAN GET UP?
THE WIFE PICKED UP THE WRONG OUTFIT AT THE DRY CLEANERS. WE'RE GONNA GET IT ALL SORTED OUT TOMORROW.
OH, WELL NO BIG DEAL, HUH, GUYS?
I DON'T KNOW, CHIEF. THE UNIFORM REALLY GAVE YOU AN AIR OF AUTHORITY.
FRANKLY, IT WAS ALL THAT DID.
OKAY, THAT'S ENOUGH OUTTA YOU. NOW GET OUT THERE AND STOP SOME CRIME!
HMMMM....
NO.

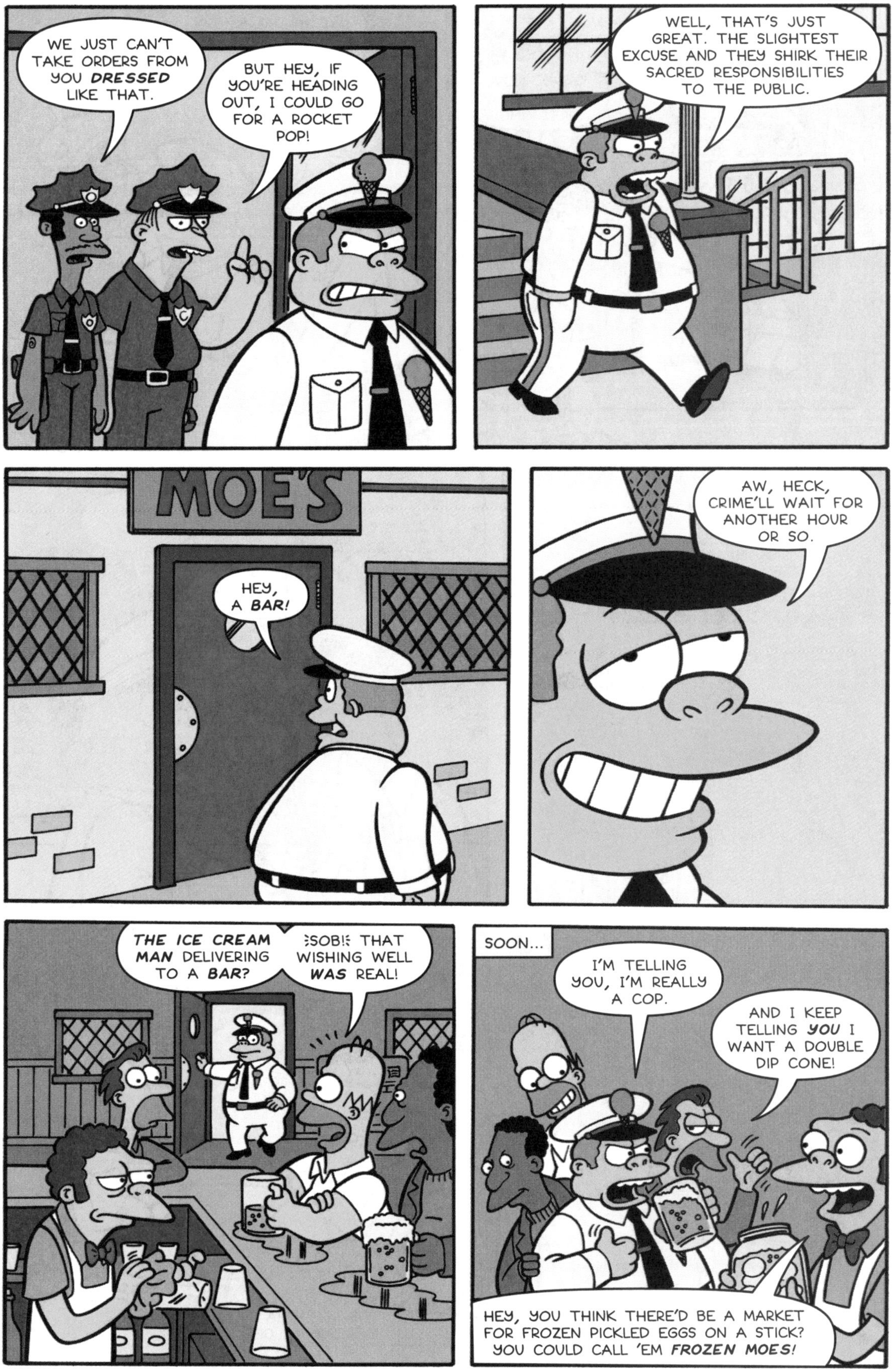

WE JUST CAN'T TAKE ORDERS FROM YOU DRESSED LIKE THAT.
BUT HEY, IF YOU'RE HEADING OUT, I COULD GO FOR A ROCKET POP!
WELL, THAT'S JUST GREAT. THE SLIGHTEST EXCUSE AND THEY SHIRK THEIR SACRED RESPONSIBILITIES TO THE PUBLIC.
MOE'S
HEY, A BAR!
AW, HECK, CRIME'LL WAIT FOR ANOTHER HOUR OR SO.
THE ICE CREAM MAN DELIVERING TO A BAR?
SOB! THAT WISHING WELL WAS REAL!
SOON...
I'M TELLING YOU, I'M REALLY A COP.
AND I KEEP TELLING YOU I WANT A DOUBLE DIP CONE!
HEY, YOU THINK THERE'D BE A MARKET FOR FROZEN PICKLED EGGS ON A STICK? YOU COULD CALL 'EM FROZEN MOES!

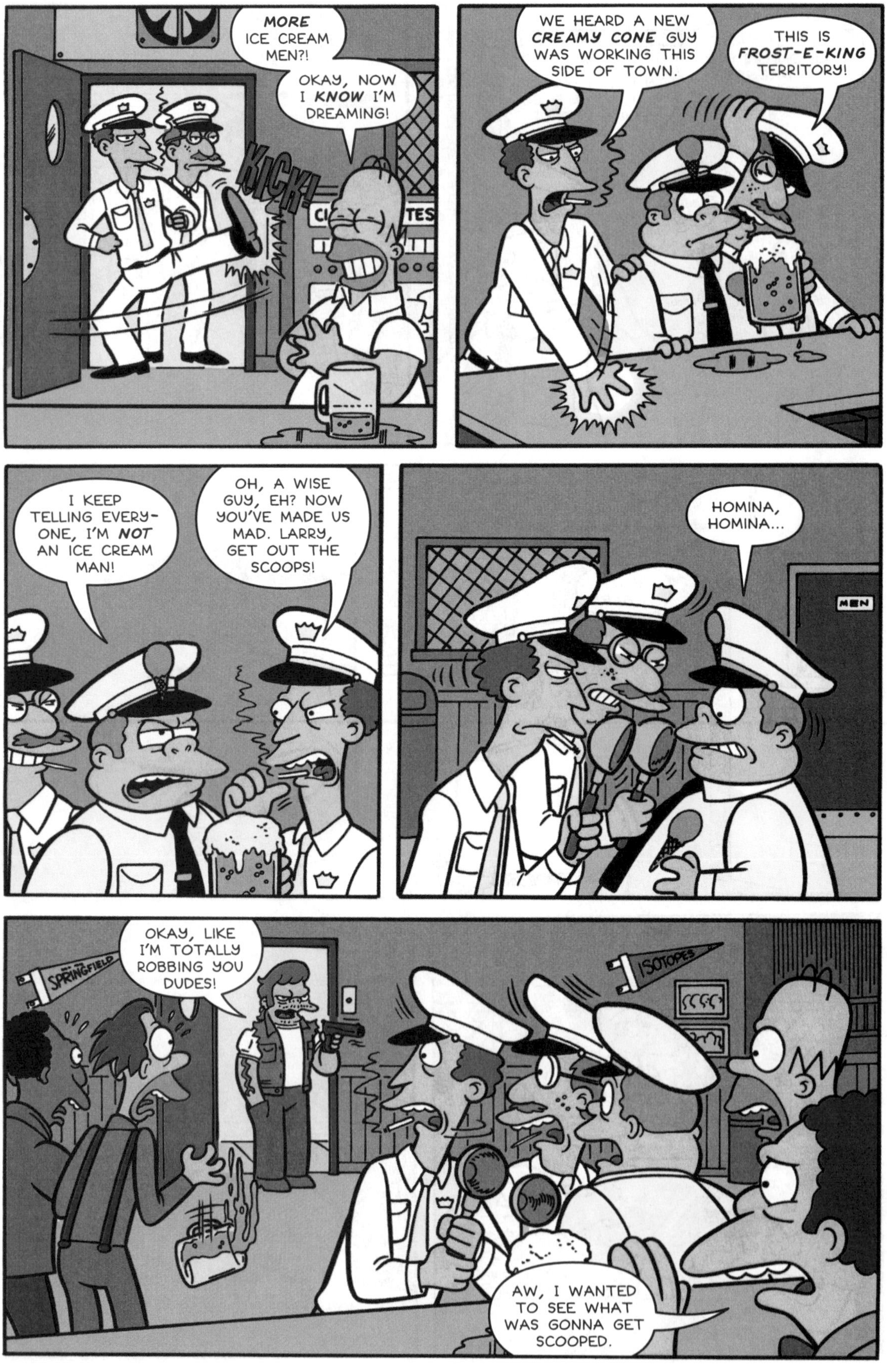
MORE ICE CREAM MEN?!
OKAY, NOW I KNOW I'M DREAMING!
KICK!
CI TES
WE HEARD A NEW CREAMY CONE GUY WAS WORKING THIS SIDE OF TOWN.
THIS IS FROST-E-KING TERRITORY!
I KEEP TELLING EVERY-ONE, I'M NOT AN ICE CREAM MAN!
OH, A WISE GUY, EH? NOW YOU'VE MADE US MAD. LARRY, GET OUT THE SCOOPS!
HOMINA, HOMINA...
MEN
OKAY, LIKE I'M TOTALLY ROBBING YOU DUDES!
SPRINGFIELD
ISOTOPES
AW, I WANTED TO SEE WHAT WAS GONNA GET SCOOPED.

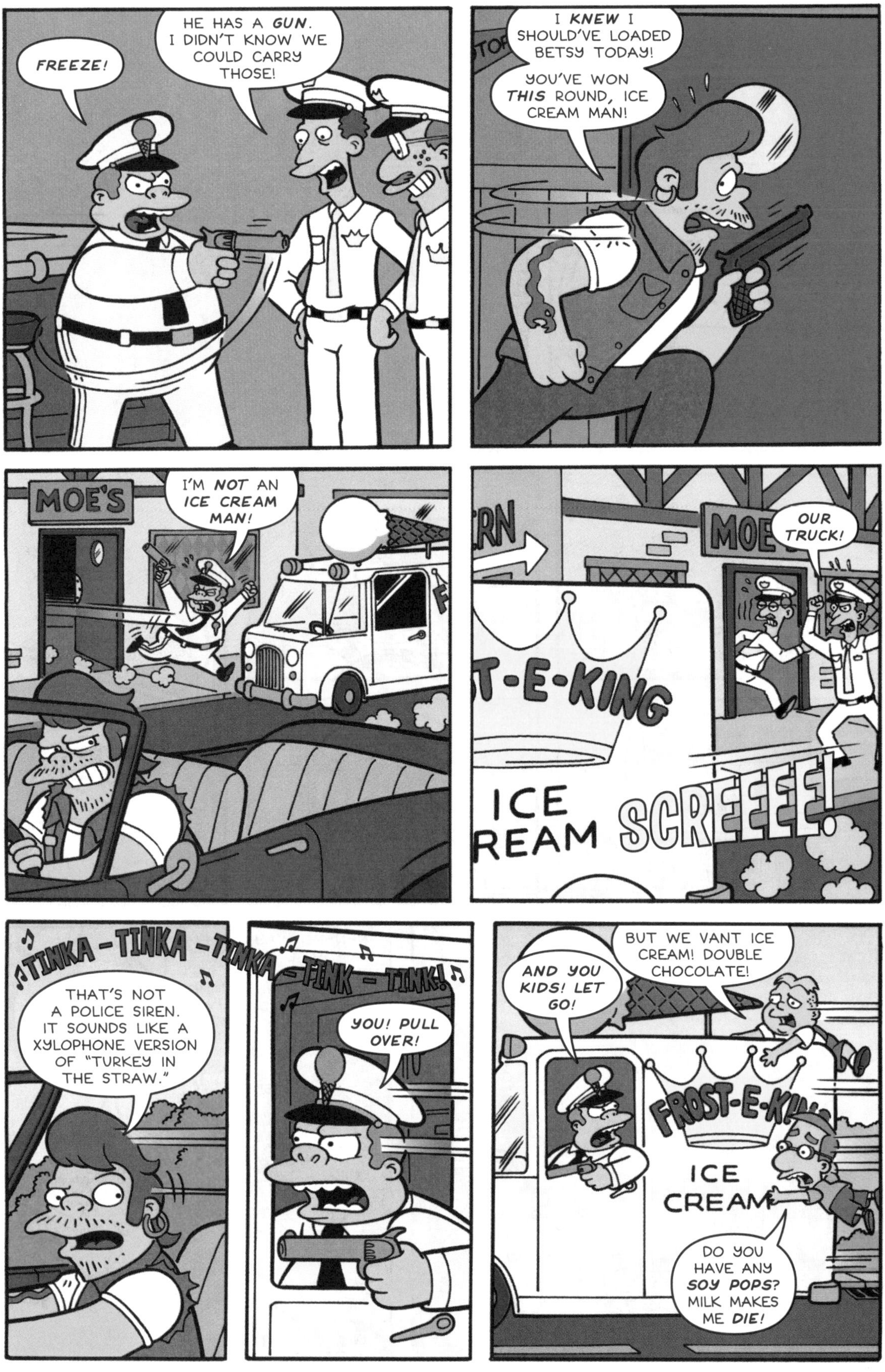
FREEZE!
HE HAS A GUN. I DIDN'T KNOW WE COULD CARRY THOSE!
I KNEW I SHOULD'VE LOADED BETSY TODAY!
YOU'VE WON THIS ROUND, ICE CREAM MAN!
MOE'S
I'M NOT AN ICE CREAM MAN!
MOE
OUR TRUCK!
ICE
REAM
SCREEEE!
TINKA-TINKA-TINKA-TINK-TINK!
THAT'S NOT A POLICE SIREN. IT SOUNDS LIKE A XYLOPHONE VERSION OF "TURKEY IN THE STRAW."
YOU! PULL OVER!
AND YOU KIDS! LET GO!
BUT WE VANT ICE CREAM! DOUBLE CHOCOLATE!
ICE
CREAM
DO YOU HAVE ANY SOY POPS? MILK MAKES ME DIE!

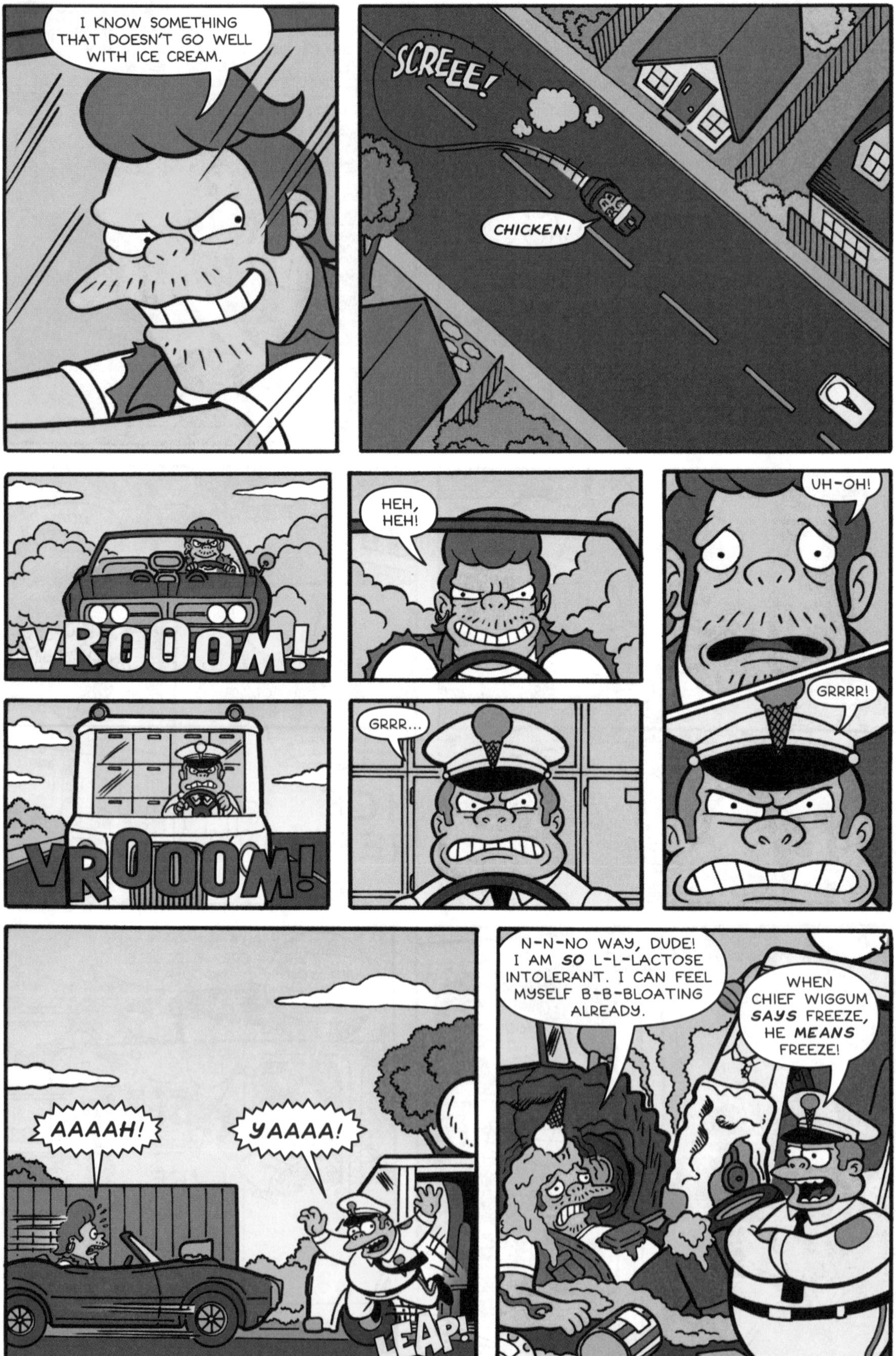
I KNOW SOMETHING THAT DOESN'T GO WELL WITH ICE CREAM.
SCREEEE!
CHICKEN!
VROOOM!
HEH, HEH!
UH-OH!
VROOOM!
GRRR...
GRRRR!
AAAAH!
YAAAA!
LEAP!
N-N-NO WAY, DUDE! I AM SO L-L-LACTOSE INTOLERANT. I CAN FEEL MYSELF B-B-BLOATING ALREADY.
WHEN CHIEF WIGGUM SAYS FREEZE, HE MEANS FREEZE!

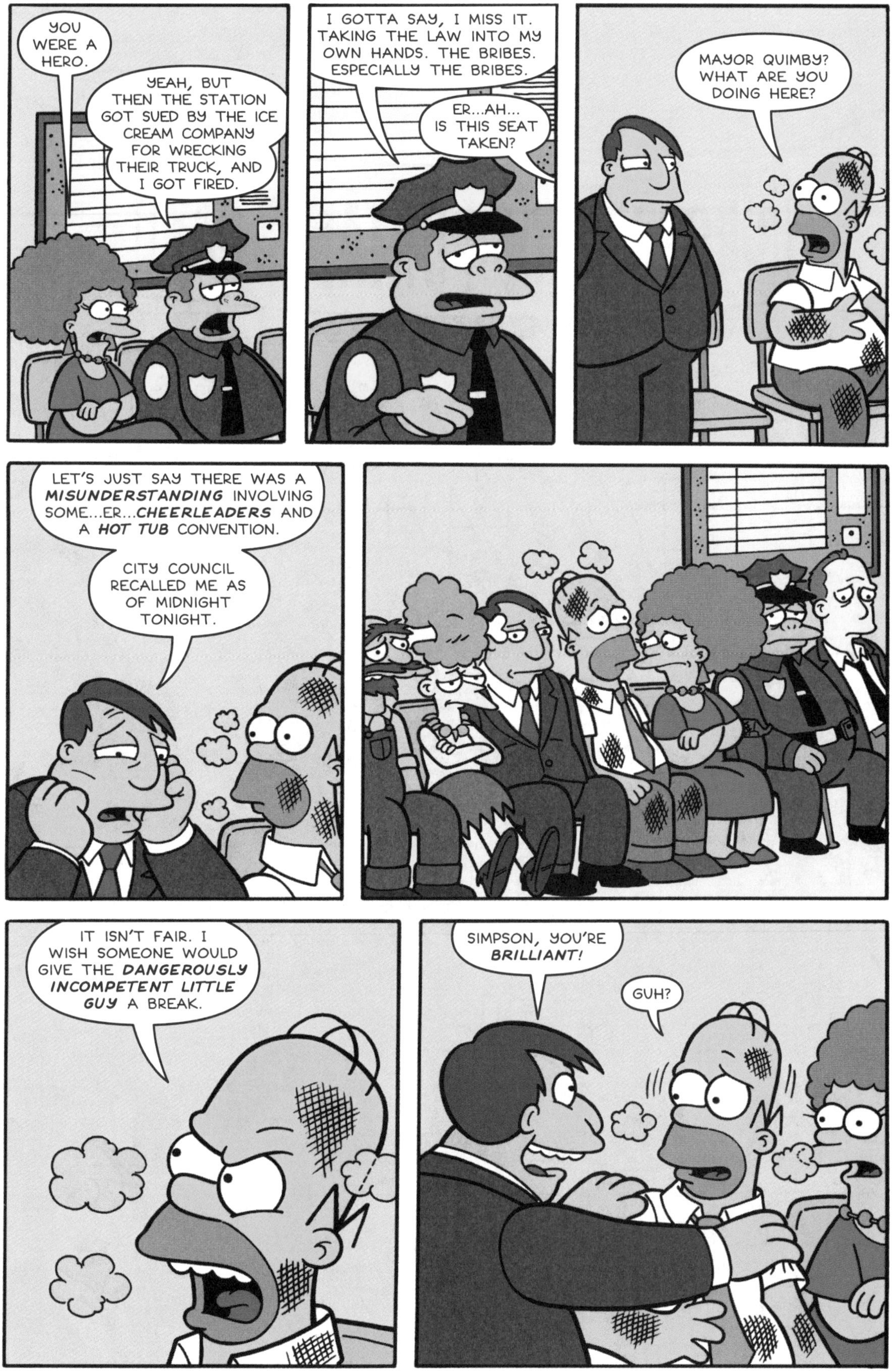
YOU WERE A HERO.
YEAH, BUT THEN THE STATION GOT SUED BY THE ICE CREAM COMPANY FOR WRECKING THEIR TRUCK, AND I GOT FIRED.
I GOTTA SAY, I MISS IT. TAKING THE LAW INTO MY OWN HANDS. THE BRIBES. ESPECIALLY THE BRIBES.
ER...AH... IS THIS SEAT TAKEN?
MAYOR QUIMBY? WHAT ARE YOU DOING HERE?
LET'S JUST SAY THERE WAS A *MISUNDERSTANDING* INVOLVING SOME...ER...*CHEERLEADERS* AND A *HOT TUB* CONVENTION.
CITY COUNCIL RECALLED ME AS OF MIDNIGHT TONIGHT.
IT ISN'T FAIR. I WISH SOMEONE WOULD GIVE THE *DANGEROUSLY INCOMPETENT LITTLE GUY* A BREAK.
SIMPSON, YOU'RE *BRILLIANT*!
GUH?

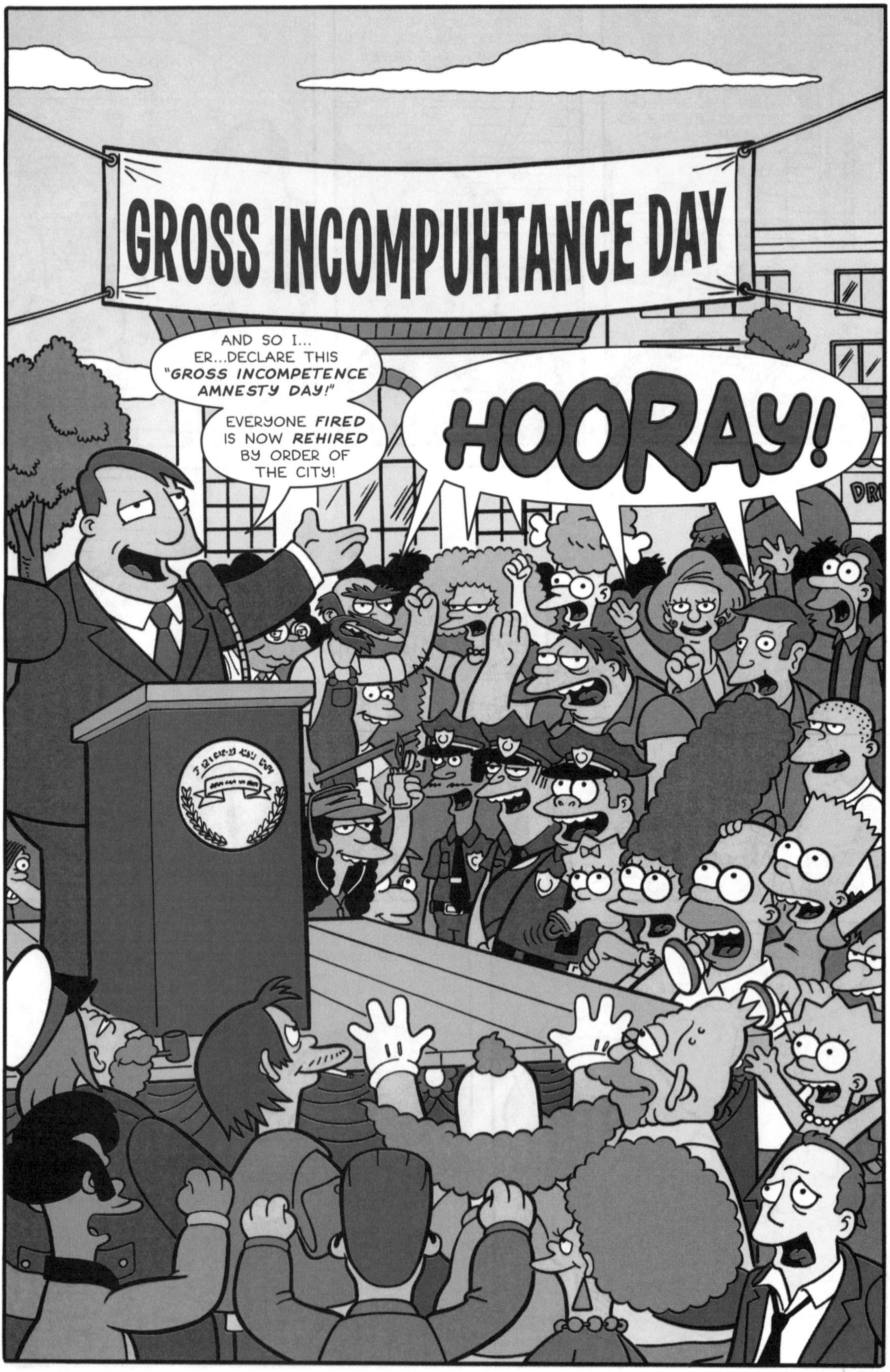
GROSS INCOMPUHTANCE DAY
AND SO I... ER...DECLARE THIS "GROSS INCOMPETENCE AMNESTY DAY!"
EVERYONE FIRED IS NOW REHIRED BY ORDER OF THE CITY!
HOORAY!

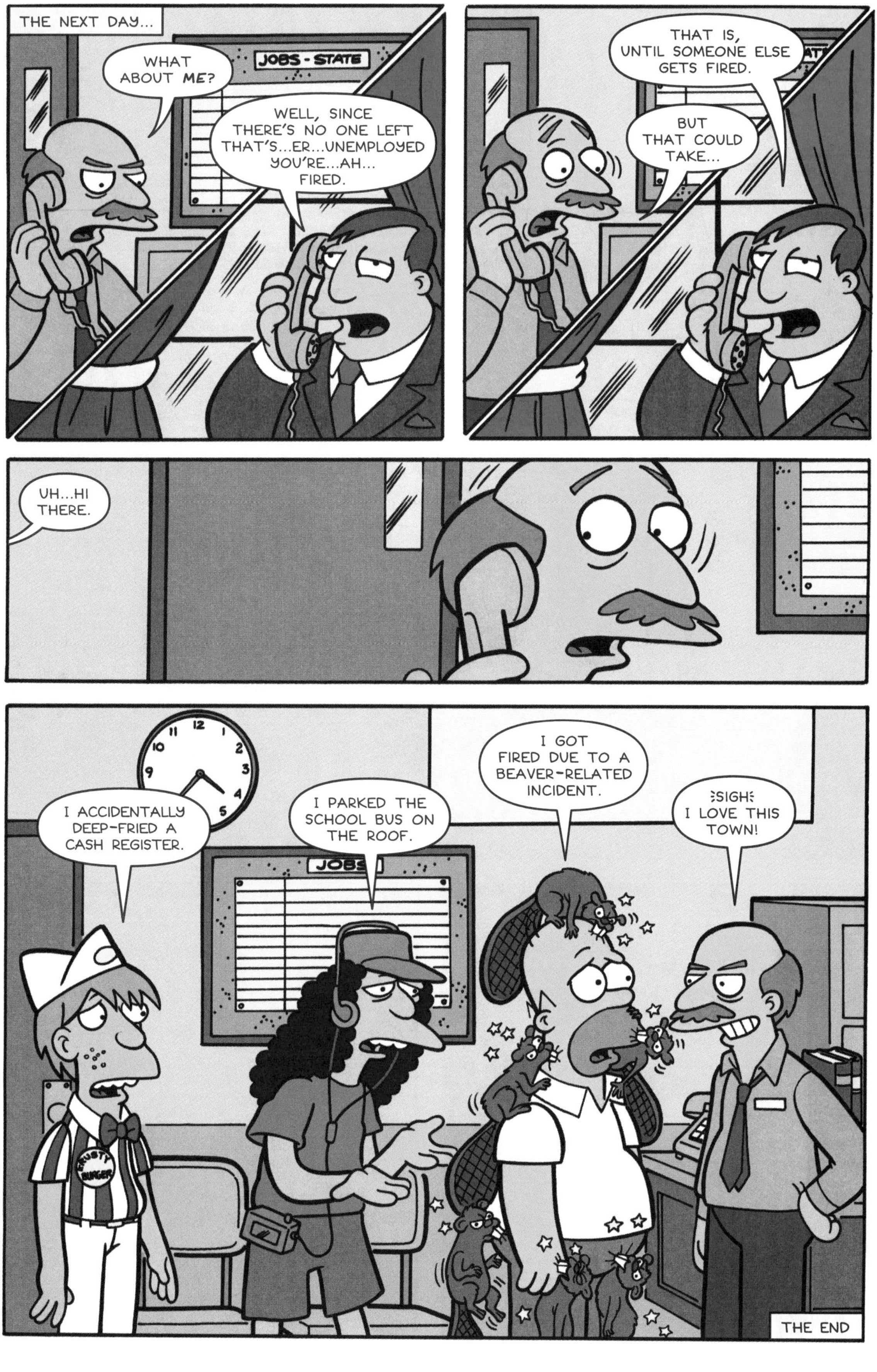
THE NEXT DAY...
JOBS - STATE
WHAT ABOUT ME?
WELL, SINCE THERE'S NO ONE LEFT THAT'S...ER...UNEMPLOYED YOU'RE...AH... FIRED.
THAT IS, UNTIL SOMEONE ELSE GETS FIRED.
BUT THAT COULD TAKE...
UH...HI THERE.
I ACCIDENTALLY DEEP-FRIED A CASH REGISTER.
I PARKED THE SCHOOL BUS ON THE ROOF.
I GOT FIRED DUE TO A BEAVER-RELATED INCIDENT.
⁝SIGH⁝ I LOVE THIS TOWN!
THE END

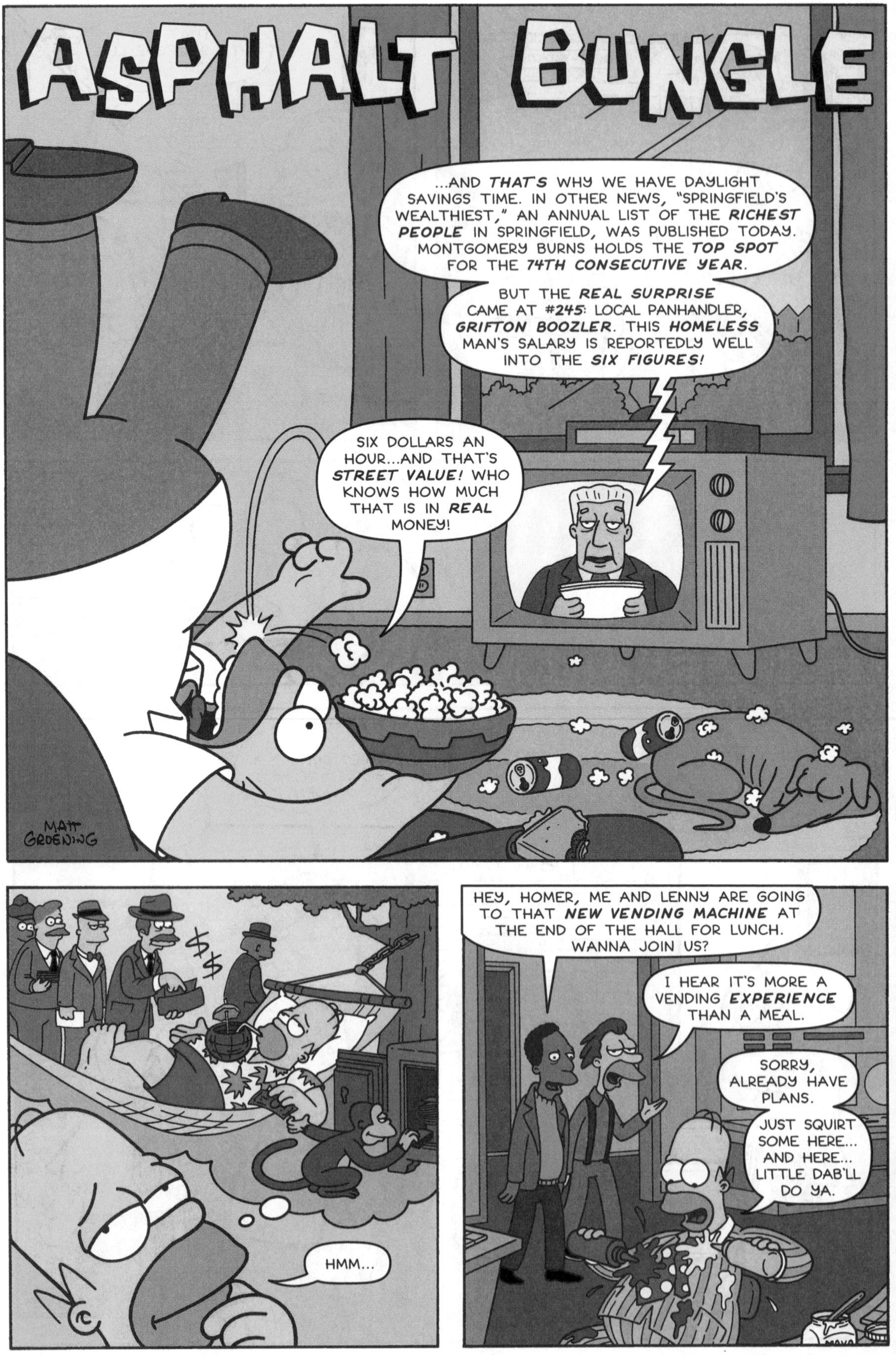
ASPHALT BUNGLE
...AND THAT'S WHY WE HAVE DAYLIGHT SAVINGS TIME. IN OTHER NEWS, "SPRINGFIELD'S WEALTHIEST," AN ANNUAL LIST OF THE RICHEST PEOPLE IN SPRINGFIELD, WAS PUBLISHED TODAY. MONTGOMERY BURNS HOLDS THE TOP SPOT FOR THE 74TH CONSECUTIVE YEAR.
BUT THE REAL SURPRISE CAME AT #245: LOCAL PANHANDLER, GRIFTON BOOZLER. THIS HOMELESS MAN'S SALARY IS REPORTEDLY WELL INTO THE SIX FIGURES!
SIX DOLLARS AN HOUR...AND THAT'S STREET VALUE! WHO KNOWS HOW MUCH THAT IS IN REAL MONEY!
MATT GROENING
$$
HMM...
HEY, HOMER, ME AND LENNY ARE GOING TO THAT NEW VENDING MACHINE AT THE END OF THE HALL FOR LUNCH. WANNA JOIN US?
I HEAR IT'S MORE A VENDING EXPERIENCE THAN A MEAL.
SORRY, ALREADY HAVE PLANS.
JUST SQUIRT SOME HERE... AND HERE... LITTLE DAB'LL DO YA.
MAYO

DAN FYBEL SCRIPT | JOHN COSTANZA PENCILS | MIKE ROTE INKS | CHRIS UNGAR COLORS | KAREN BATES LETTERS | MATT GROENING PAVEMENT POUNDER

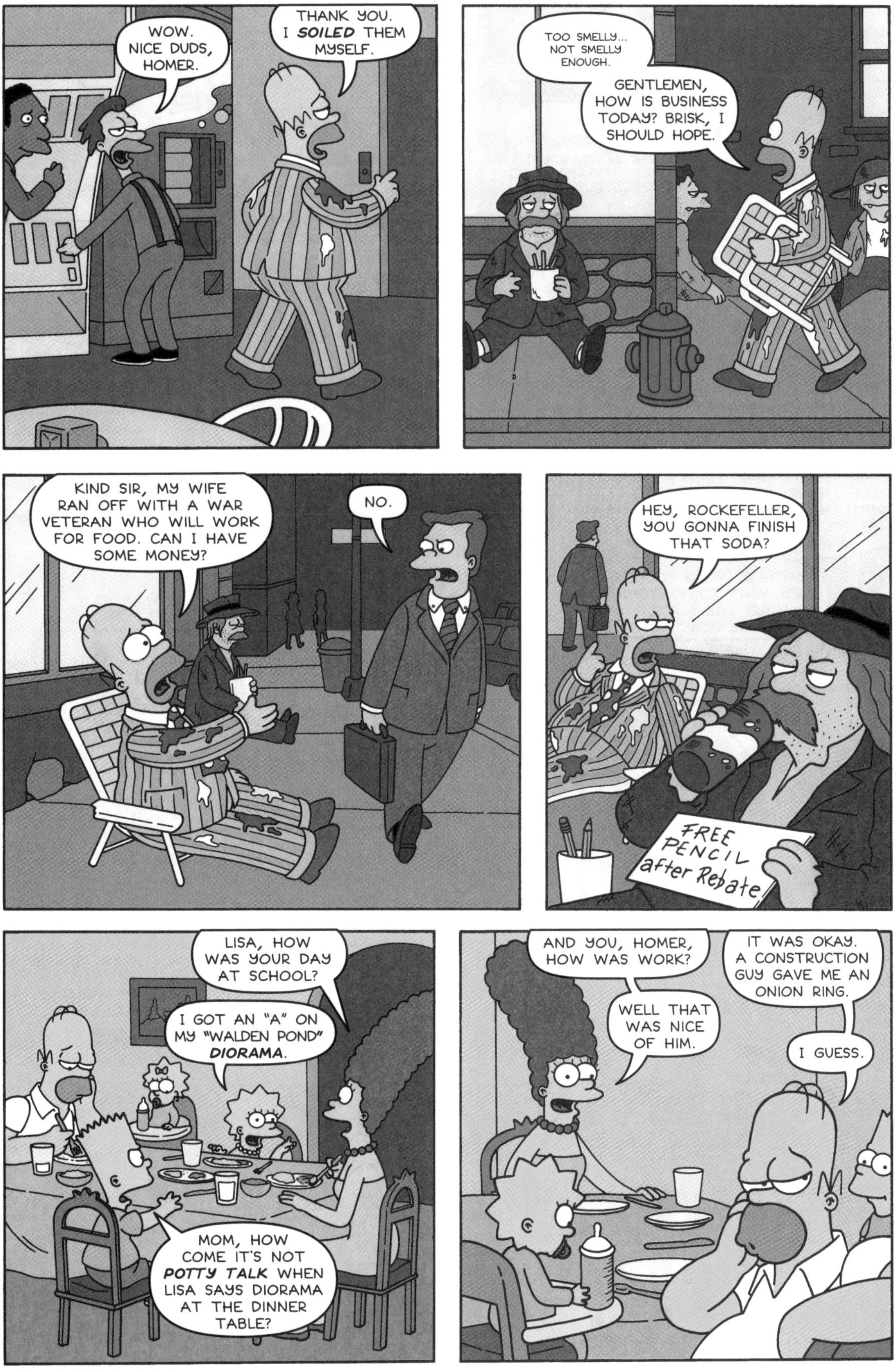
WOW. NICE DUDS, HOMER.
THANK YOU. I **SOILED** THEM MYSELF.
TOO SMELLY... NOT SMELLY ENOUGH.
GENTLEMEN, HOW IS BUSINESS TODAY? BRISK, I SHOULD HOPE.
KIND SIR, MY WIFE RAN OFF WITH A WAR VETERAN WHO WILL WORK FOR FOOD. CAN I HAVE SOME MONEY?
NO.
HEY, ROCKEFELLER, YOU GONNA FINISH THAT SODA?
FREE PENCIL after Rebate
LISA, HOW WAS YOUR DAY AT SCHOOL?
I GOT AN "A" ON MY "WALDEN POND" **DIORAMA**.
MOM, HOW COME IT'S NOT **POTTY TALK** WHEN LISA SAYS DIORAMA AT THE DINNER TABLE?
AND YOU, HOMER, HOW WAS WORK?
IT WAS OKAY. A CONSTRUCTION GUY GAVE ME AN ONION RING.
WELL THAT WAS NICE OF HIM.
I GUESS.

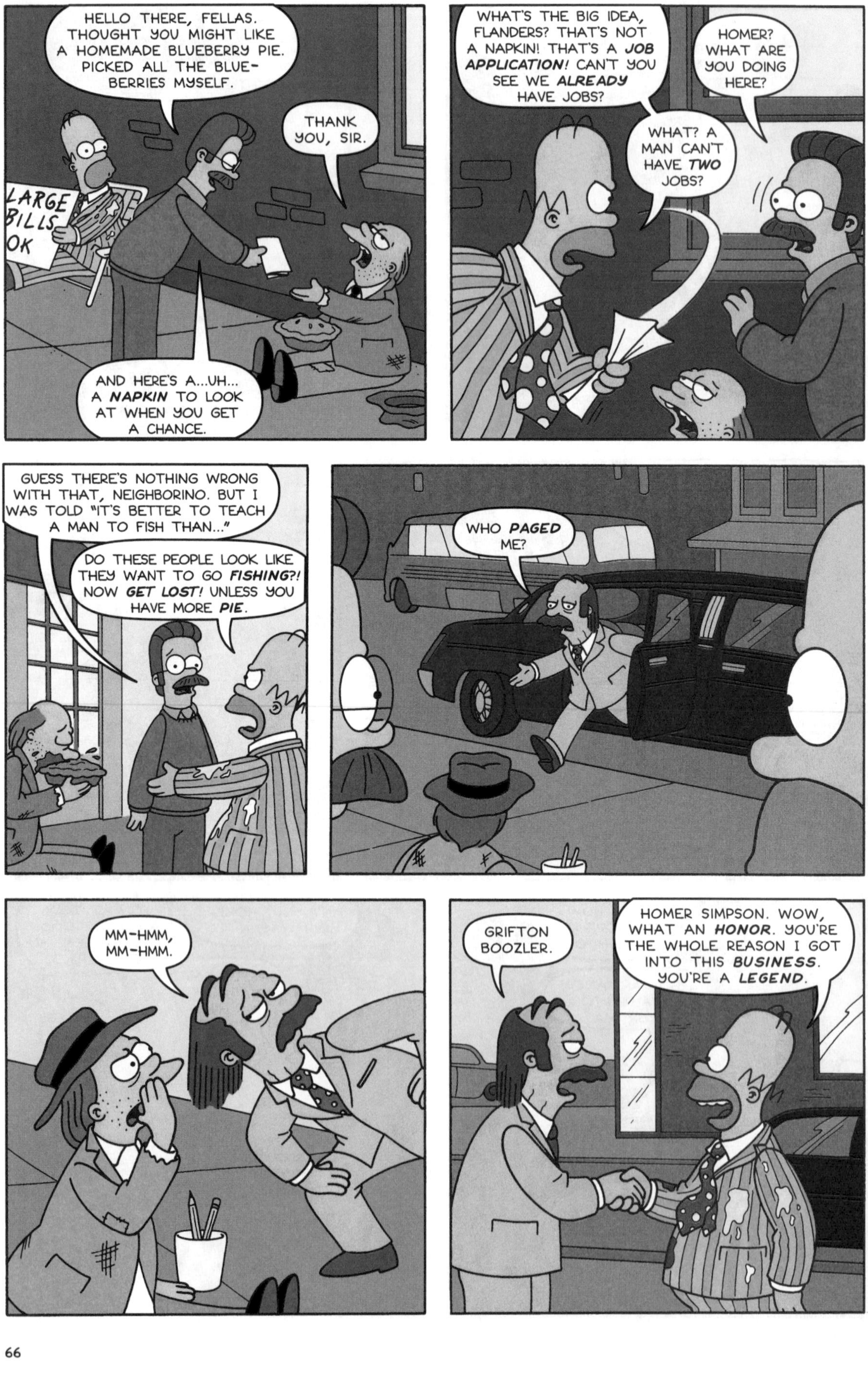
HELLO THERE, FELLAS. THOUGHT YOU MIGHT LIKE A HOMEMADE BLUEBERRY PIE. PICKED ALL THE BLUE-BERRIES MYSELF.
LARGE BILLS OK
THANK YOU, SIR.
AND HERE'S A...UH... A **NAPKIN** TO LOOK AT WHEN YOU GET A CHANCE.
HOMER? WHAT ARE YOU DOING HERE?
WHAT'S THE BIG IDEA, FLANDERS? THAT'S NOT A NAPKIN! THAT'S A **JOB APPLICATION**! CAN'T YOU SEE WE **ALREADY** HAVE JOBS?
WHAT? A MAN CAN'T HAVE **TWO** JOBS?
GUESS THERE'S NOTHING WRONG WITH THAT, NEIGHBORINO. BUT I WAS TOLD "IT'S BETTER TO TEACH A MAN TO FISH THAN..."
DO THESE PEOPLE LOOK LIKE THEY WANT TO GO **FISHING**?! NOW **GET LOST**! UNLESS YOU HAVE MORE **PIE**.
WHO **PAGED** ME?
MM-HMM, MM-HMM.
GRIFTON BOOZLER.
HOMER SIMPSON. WOW, WHAT AN **HONOR**. YOU'RE THE WHOLE REASON I GOT INTO THIS **BUSINESS**. YOU'RE A **LEGEND**.

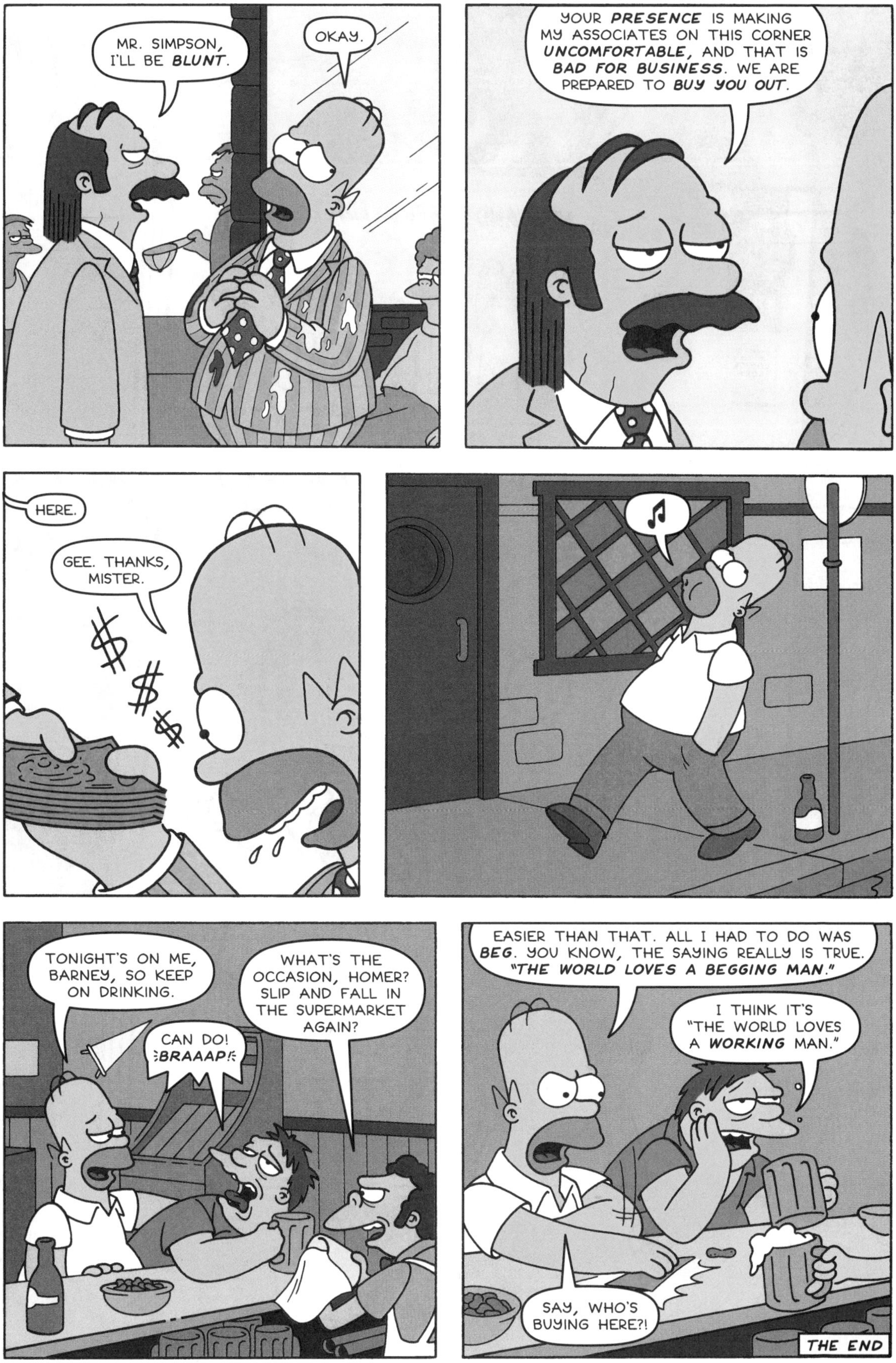
MR. SIMPSON, I'LL BE BLUNT.
OKAY.
YOUR PRESENCE IS MAKING MY ASSOCIATES ON THIS CORNER UNCOMFORTABLE, AND THAT IS BAD FOR BUSINESS. WE ARE PREPARED TO BUY YOU OUT.
HERE.
GEE. THANKS, MISTER.
TONIGHT'S ON ME, BARNEY, SO KEEP ON DRINKING.
CAN DO! BRAAAP!
WHAT'S THE OCCASION, HOMER? SLIP AND FALL IN THE SUPERMARKET AGAIN?
EASIER THAN THAT. ALL I HAD TO DO WAS BEG. YOU KNOW, THE SAYING REALLY IS TRUE. "THE WORLD LOVES A BEGGING MAN."
I THINK IT'S "THE WORLD LOVES A WORKING MAN."
SAY, WHO'S BUYING HERE?!
THE END

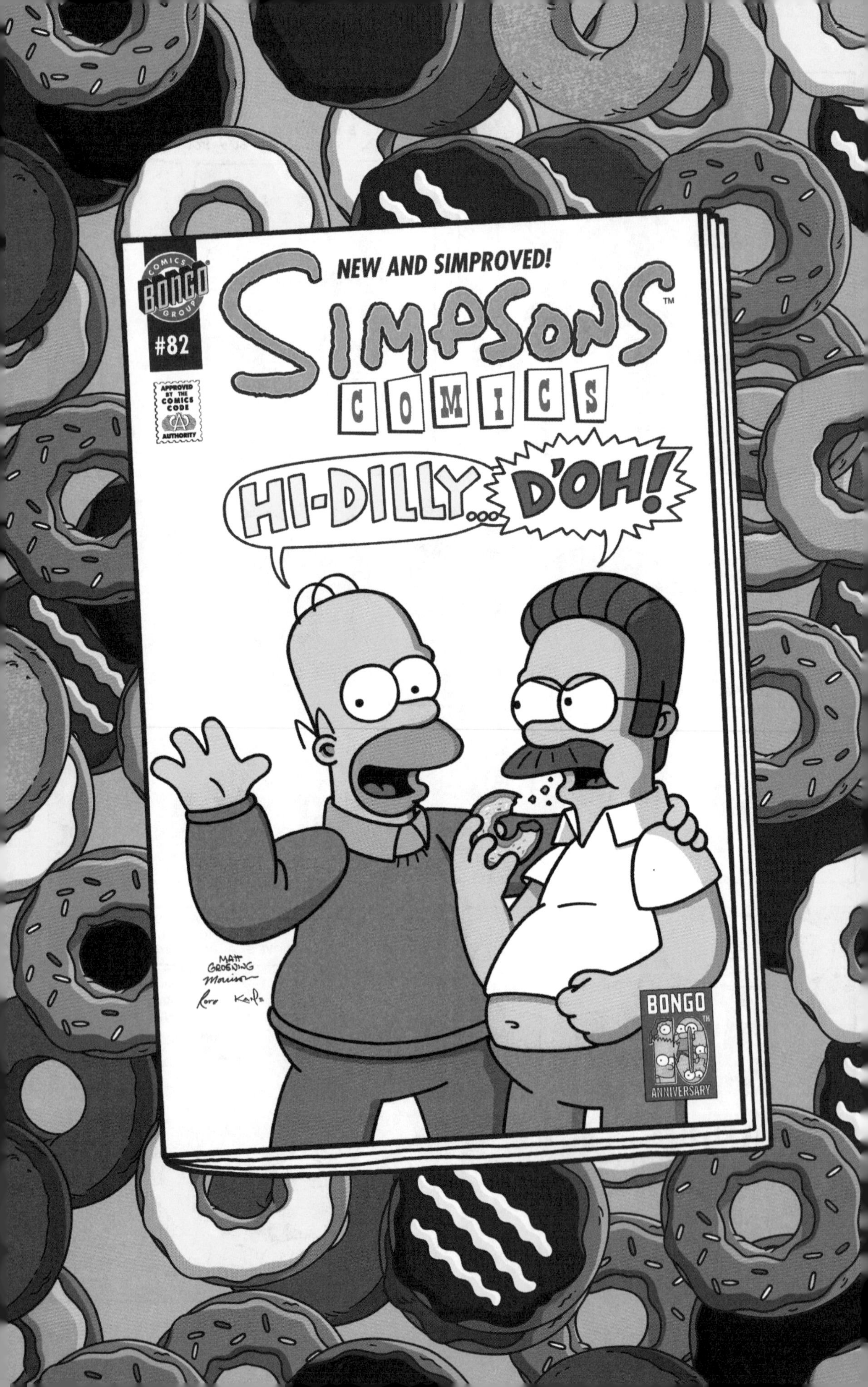
NEW AND SIMPROVED!
SIMPSONS COMICS
#82
HI-DILLY...
D'OH!
BONGO 10TH ANNIVERSARY

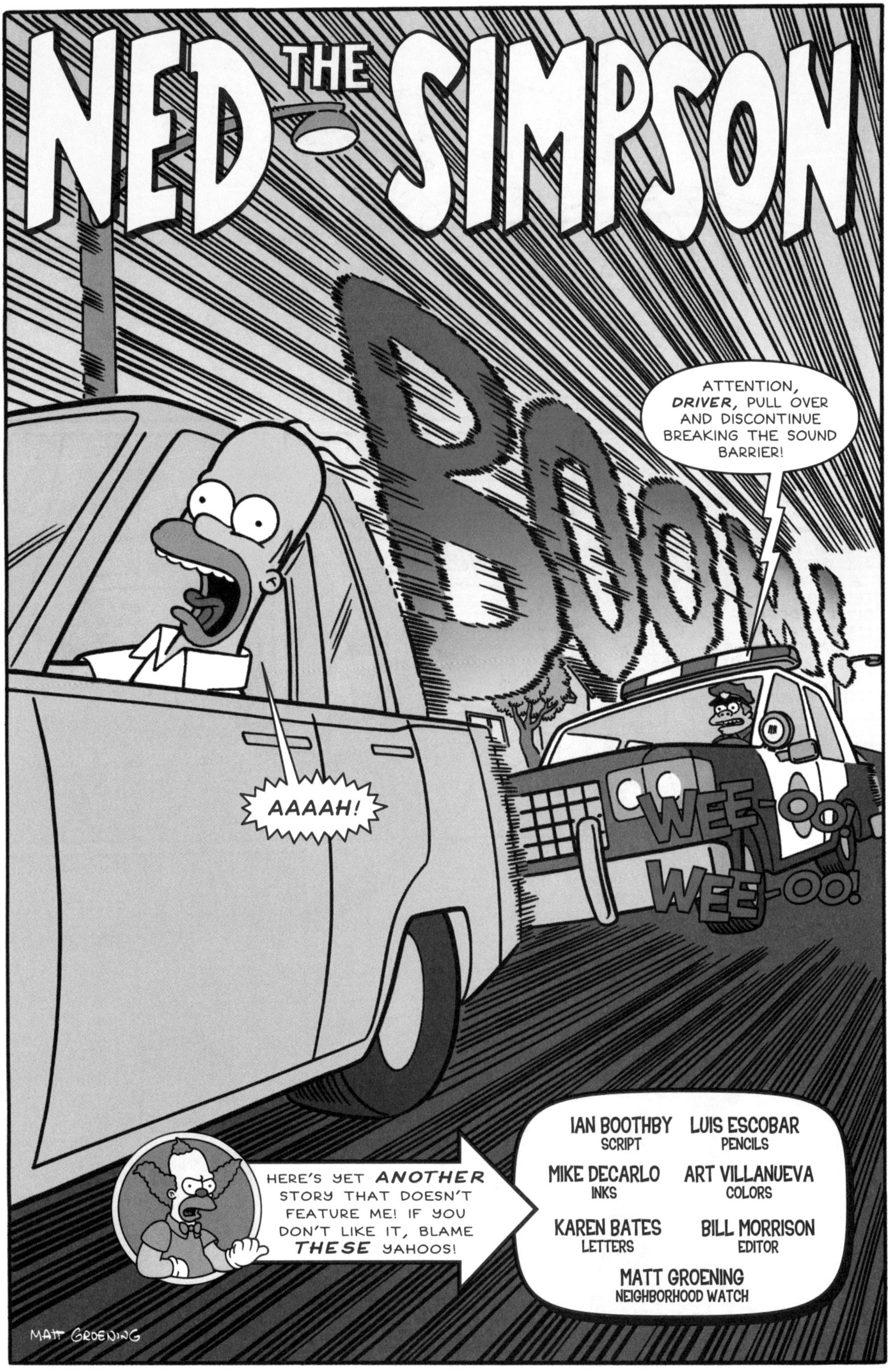

NED THE SIMPSON
BOOOM!
ATTENTION, DRIVER, PULL OVER AND DISCONTINUE BREAKING THE SOUND BARRIER!
AAAAH!
WEE-OO! WEE-OO!
HERE'S YET ANOTHER STORY THAT DOESN'T FEATURE ME! IF YOU DON'T LIKE IT, BLAME THESE YAHOOS!
IAN BOOTHBY SCRIPT
LUIS ESCOBAR PENCILS
MIKE DECARLO INKS
ART VILLANUEVA COLORS
KAREN BATES LETTERS
BILL MORRISON EDITOR
MATT GROENING NEIGHBORHOOD WATCH
MATT GROENING

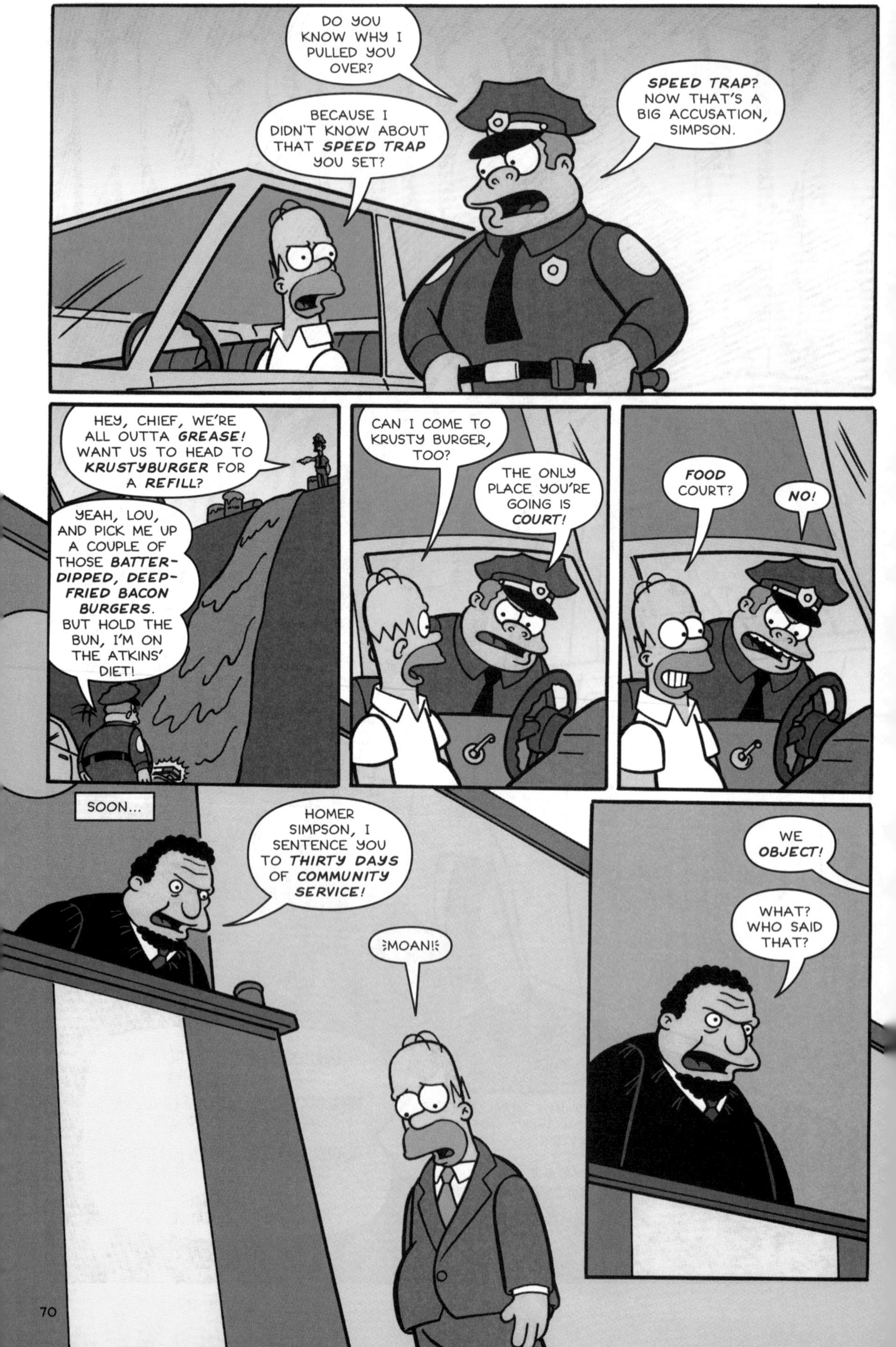
DO YOU KNOW WHY I PULLED YOU OVER?
BECAUSE I DIDN'T KNOW ABOUT THAT SPEED TRAP YOU SET?
SPEED TRAP? NOW THAT'S A BIG ACCUSATION, SIMPSON.
HEY, CHIEF, WE'RE ALL OUTTA GREASE! WANT US TO HEAD TO KRUSTYBURGER FOR A REFILL?
YEAH, LOU, AND PICK ME UP A COUPLE OF THOSE BATTER-DIPPED, DEEP-FRIED BACON BURGERS. BUT HOLD THE BUN, I'M ON THE ATKINS' DIET!
CAN I COME TO KRUSTY BURGER, TOO?
THE ONLY PLACE YOU'RE GOING IS COURT!
FOOD COURT?
NO!
SOON...
HOMER SIMPSON, I SENTENCE YOU TO THIRTY DAYS OF COMMUNITY SERVICE!
MOAN!
WE OBJECT!
WHAT? WHO SAID THAT?

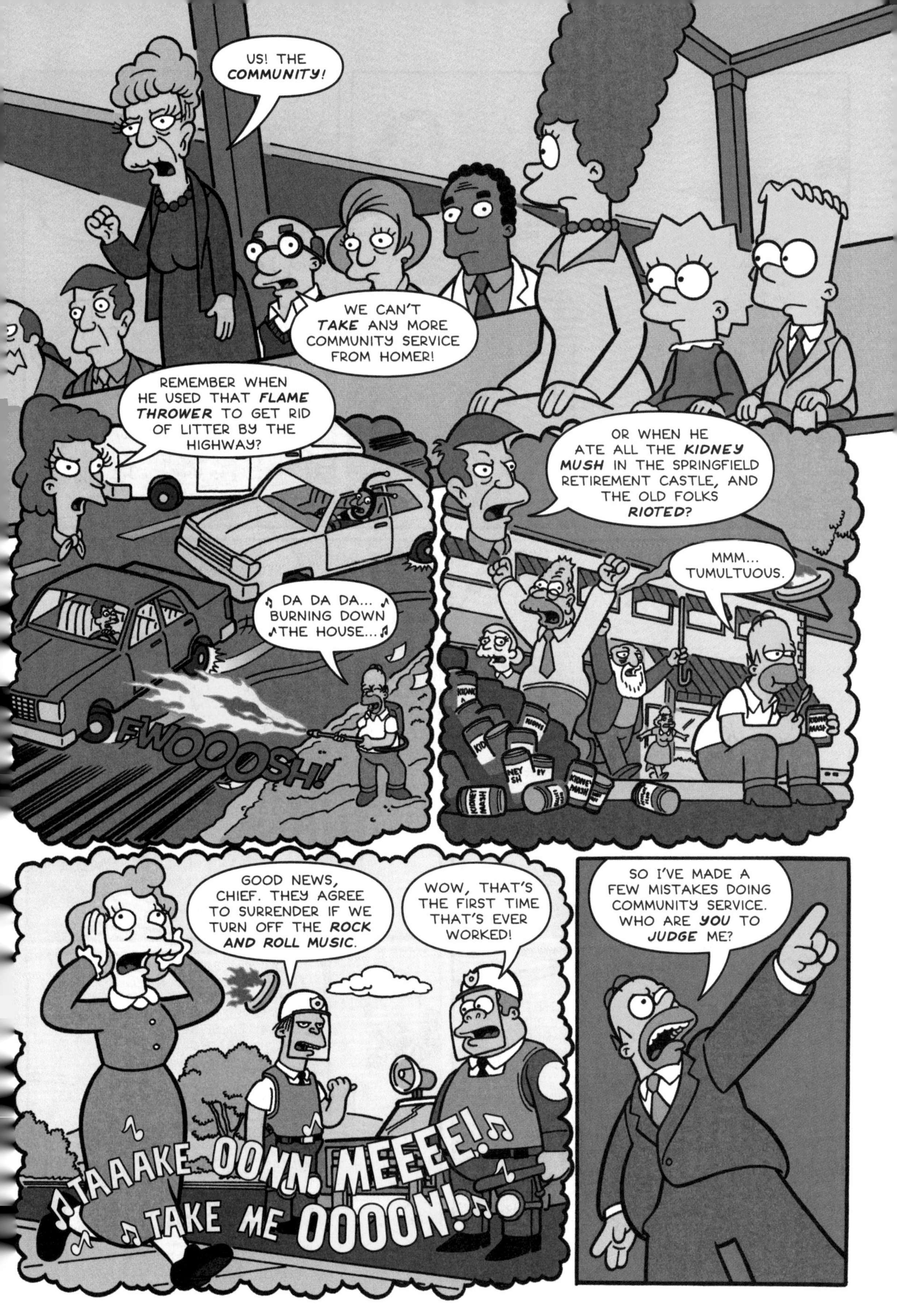

US! THE COMMUNITY!
WE CAN'T TAKE ANY MORE COMMUNITY SERVICE FROM HOMER!
REMEMBER WHEN HE USED THAT FLAME THROWER TO GET RID OF LITTER BY THE HIGHWAY?
DA DA DA... BURNING DOWN THE HOUSE...
FWOOOSH!
OR WHEN HE ATE ALL THE KIDNEY MUSH IN THE SPRINGFIELD RETIREMENT CASTLE, AND THE OLD FOLKS RIOTED?
MMM... TUMULTUOUS.
GOOD NEWS, CHIEF. THEY AGREE TO SURRENDER IF WE TURN OFF THE ROCK AND ROLL MUSIC.
WOW, THAT'S THE FIRST TIME THAT'S EVER WORKED!
TAAAKE OONN. MEEEE!
TAKE ME OOOON!
SO I'VE MADE A FEW MISTAKES DOING COMMUNITY SERVICE. WHO ARE YOU TO JUDGE ME?

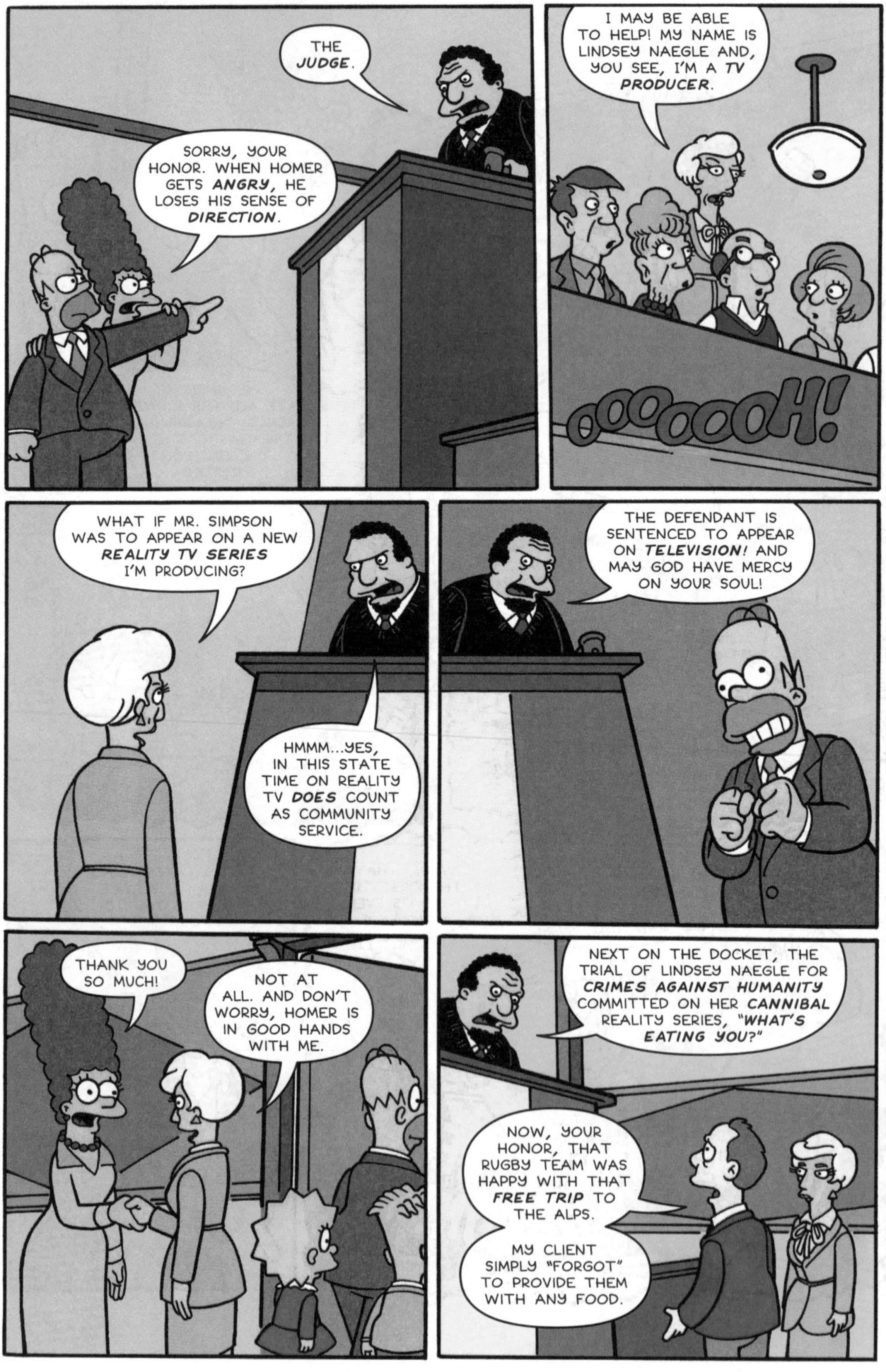
THE JUDGE.
SORRY, YOUR HONOR. WHEN HOMER GETS ANGRY, HE LOSES HIS SENSE OF DIRECTION.
I MAY BE ABLE TO HELP! MY NAME IS LINDSEY NAEGLE AND, YOU SEE, I'M A TV PRODUCER.
OOOOOOOH!
WHAT IF MR. SIMPSON WAS TO APPEAR ON A NEW REALITY TV SERIES I'M PRODUCING?
HMMM...YES, IN THIS STATE TIME ON REALITY TV DOES COUNT AS COMMUNITY SERVICE.
THE DEFENDANT IS SENTENCED TO APPEAR ON TELEVISION! AND MAY GOD HAVE MERCY ON YOUR SOUL!
THANK YOU SO MUCH!
NOT AT ALL. AND DON'T WORRY, HOMER IS IN GOOD HANDS WITH ME.
NEXT ON THE DOCKET, THE TRIAL OF LINDSEY NAEGLE FOR CRIMES AGAINST HUMANITY COMMITTED ON HER CANNIBAL REALITY SERIES, "WHAT'S EATING YOU?"
NOW, YOUR HONOR, THAT RUGBY TEAM WAS HAPPY WITH THAT FREE TRIP TO THE ALPS.
MY CLIENT SIMPLY "FORGOT" TO PROVIDE THEM WITH ANY FOOD.

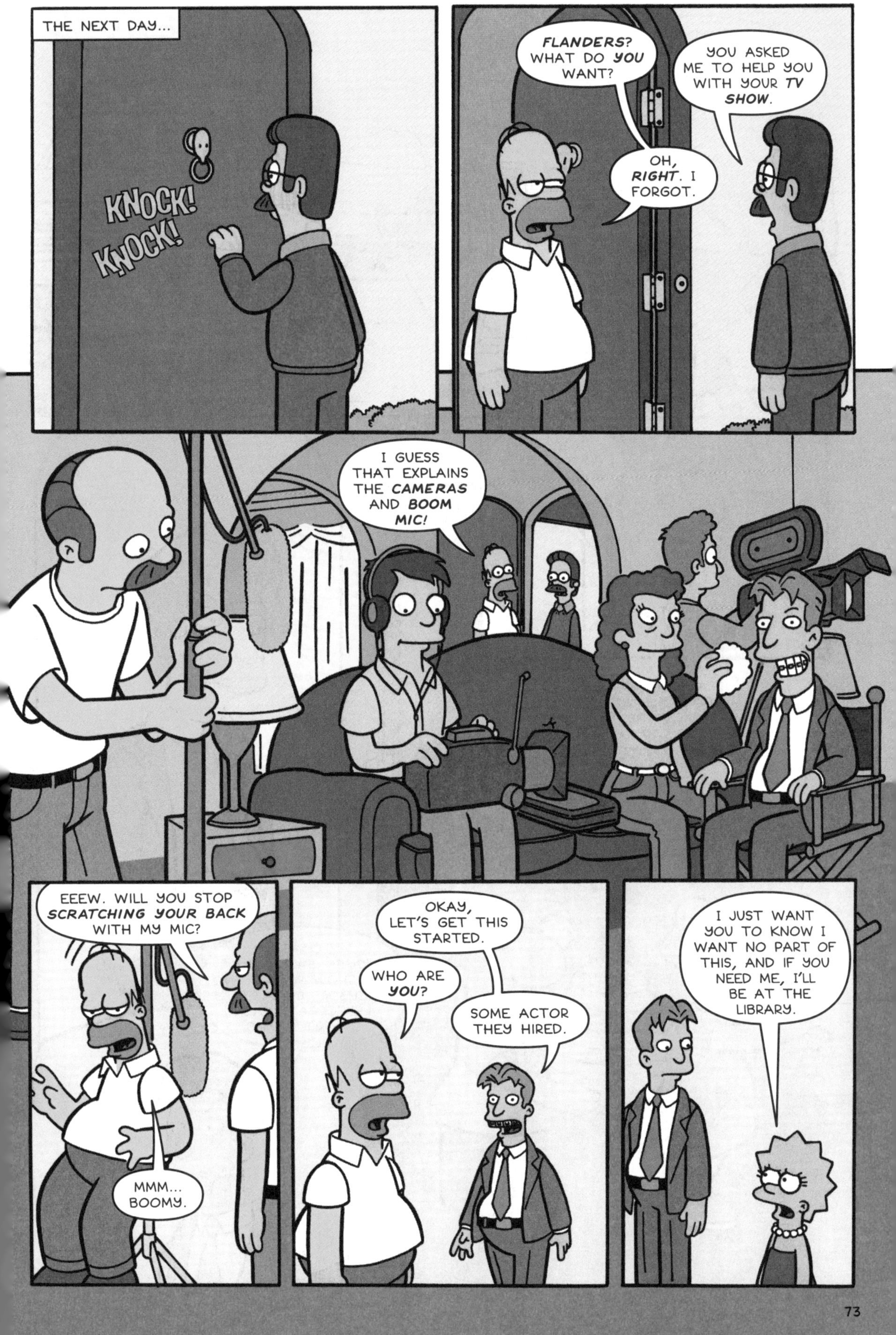
THE NEXT DAY...
KNOCK! KNOCK!
FLANDERS? WHAT DO YOU WANT?
YOU ASKED ME TO HELP YOU WITH YOUR TV SHOW.
OH, RIGHT. I FORGOT.
I GUESS THAT EXPLAINS THE CAMERAS AND BOOM MIC!
EEEW. WILL YOU STOP SCRATCHING YOUR BACK WITH MY MIC?
MMM... BOOMY.
OKAY, LET'S GET THIS STARTED.
WHO ARE YOU?
SOME ACTOR THEY HIRED.
I JUST WANT YOU TO KNOW I WANT NO PART OF THIS, AND IF YOU NEED ME, I'LL BE AT THE LIBRARY.

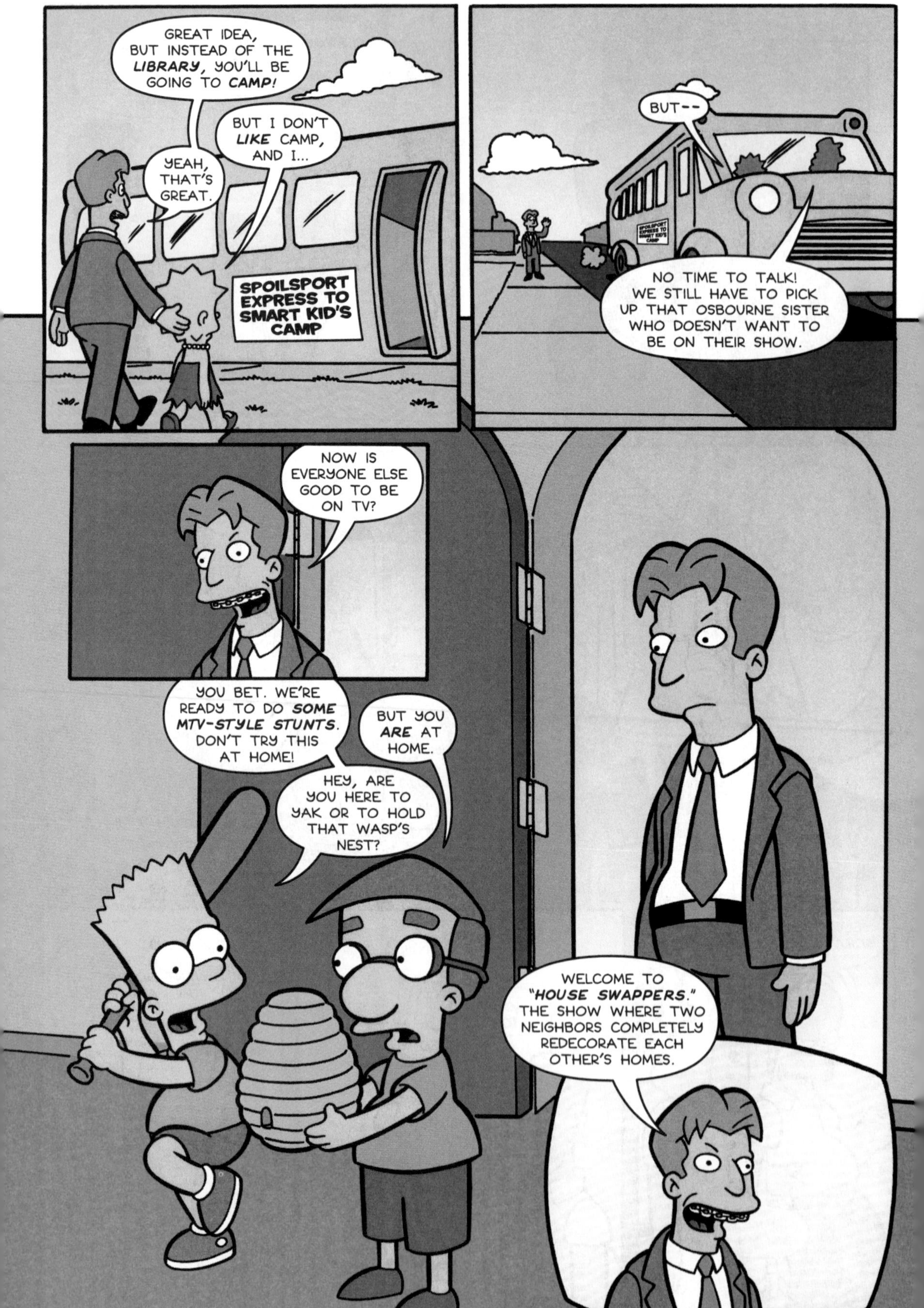
GREAT IDEA, BUT INSTEAD OF THE LIBRARY, YOU'LL BE GOING TO CAMP!
YEAH, THAT'S GREAT.
BUT I DON'T LIKE CAMP, AND I...
SPOILSPORT EXPRESS TO SMART KID'S CAMP
BUT--
NO TIME TO TALK! WE STILL HAVE TO PICK UP THAT OSBOURNE SISTER WHO DOESN'T WANT TO BE ON THEIR SHOW.
NOW IS EVERYONE ELSE GOOD TO BE ON TV?
YOU BET. WE'RE READY TO DO SOME MTV-STYLE STUNTS. DON'T TRY THIS AT HOME!
BUT YOU ARE AT HOME.
HEY, ARE YOU HERE TO YAK OR TO HOLD THAT WASP'S NEST?
WELCOME TO "HOUSE SWAPPERS." THE SHOW WHERE TWO NEIGHBORS COMPLETELY REDECORATE EACH OTHER'S HOMES.

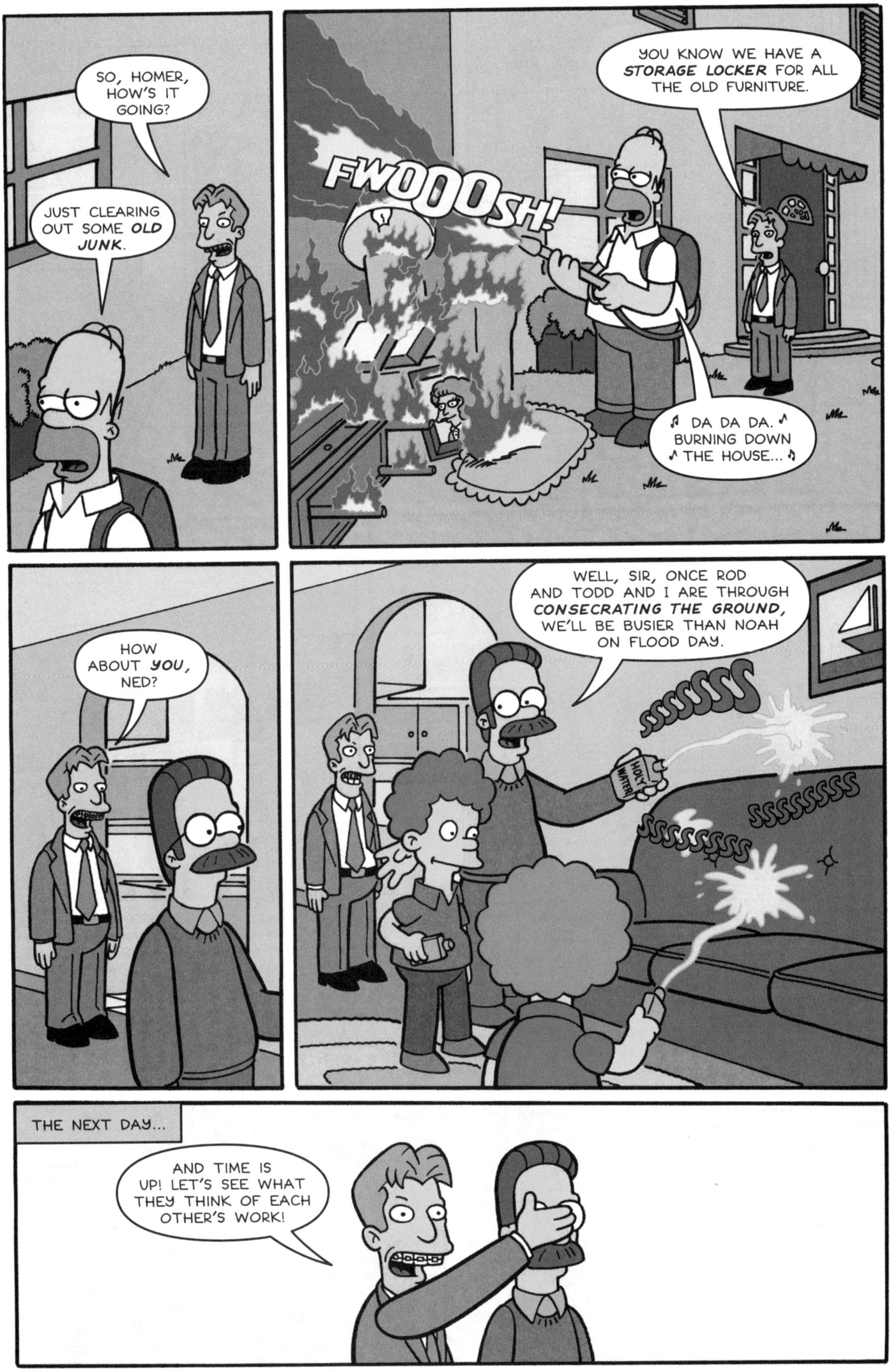
SO, HOMER, HOW'S IT GOING?
JUST CLEARING OUT SOME OLD JUNK.
FWOOOOSH!
YOU KNOW WE HAVE A STORAGE LOCKER FOR ALL THE OLD FURNITURE.
♪ DA DA DA. ♪ BURNING DOWN ♪ THE HOUSE... ♫
HOW ABOUT YOU, NED?
WELL, SIR, ONCE ROD AND TODD AND I ARE THROUGH CONSECRATING THE GROUND, WE'LL BE BUSIER THAN NOAH ON FLOOD DAY.
SSSSSSS
HOLY WATER!
SSSSSSSS
SSSSSSSSS
THE NEXT DAY...
AND TIME IS UP! LET'S SEE WHAT THEY THINK OF EACH OTHER'S WORK!

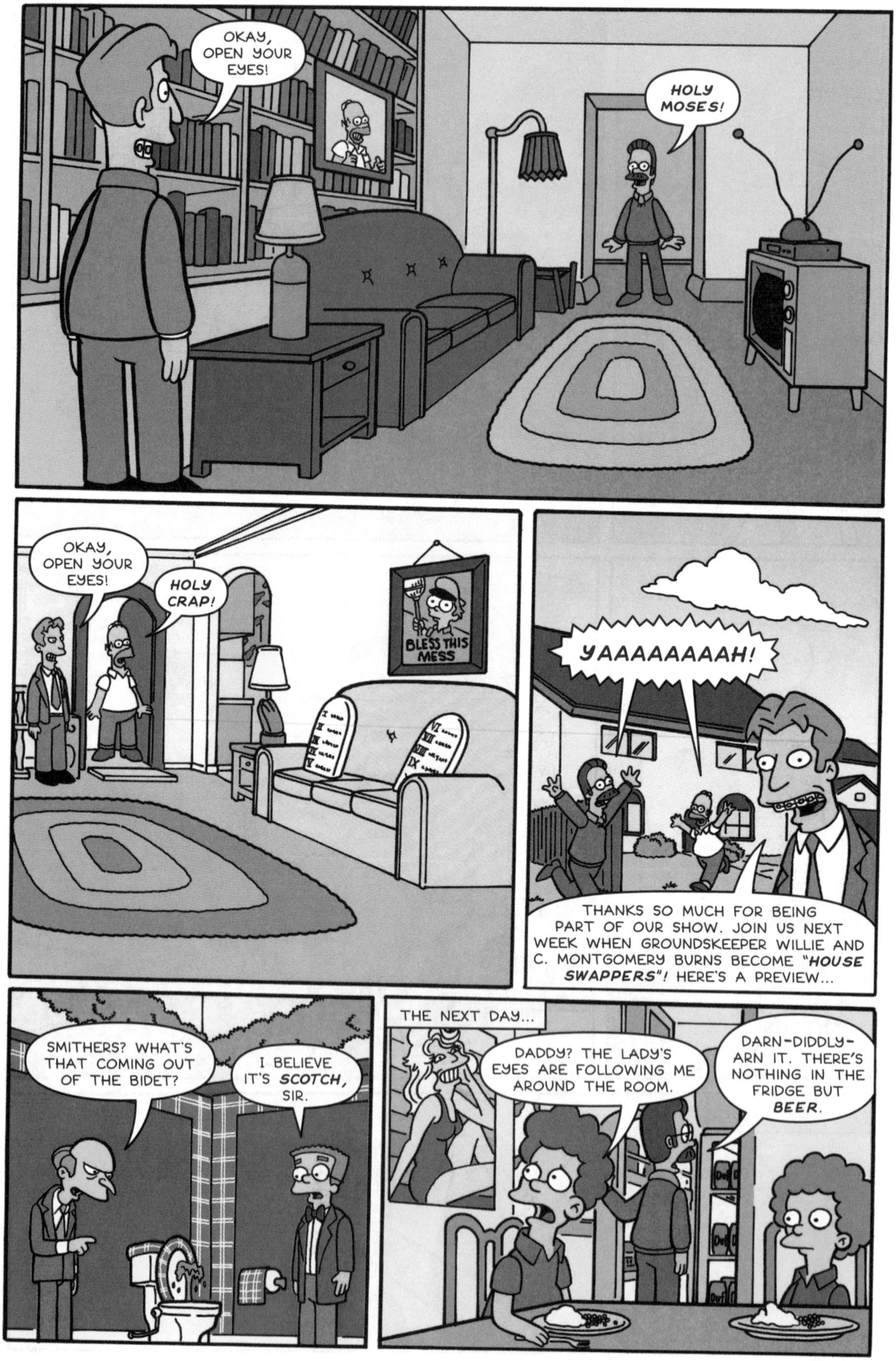
OKAY, OPEN YOUR EYES!
HOLY MOSES!
OKAY, OPEN YOUR EYES!
HOLY CRAP!
BLESS THIS MESS
YAAAAAAAAH!
THANKS SO MUCH FOR BEING PART OF OUR SHOW. JOIN US NEXT WEEK WHEN GROUNDSKEEPER WILLIE AND C. MONTGOMERY BURNS BECOME "HOUSE SWAPPERS"! HERE'S A PREVIEW...
SMITHERS? WHAT'S THAT COMING OUT OF THE BIDET?
I BELIEVE IT'S SCOTCH, SIR.
THE NEXT DAY...
DADDY? THE LADY'S EYES ARE FOLLOWING ME AROUND THE ROOM.
DARN-DIDDLY-ARN IT. THERE'S NOTHING IN THE FRIDGE BUT BEER.

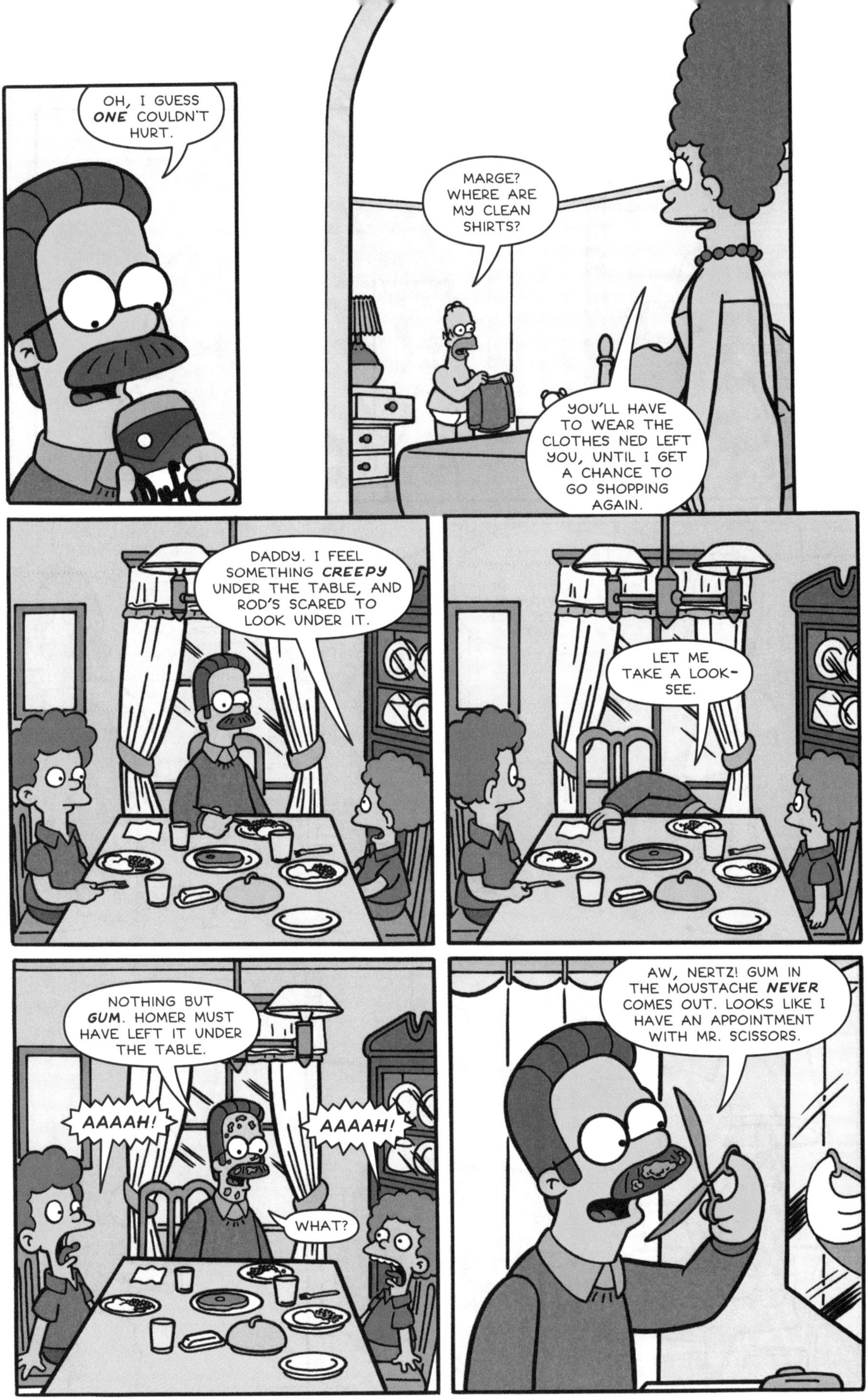
OH, I GUESS ONE COULDN'T HURT.
MARGE? WHERE ARE MY CLEAN SHIRTS?
YOU'LL HAVE TO WEAR THE CLOTHES NED LEFT YOU, UNTIL I GET A CHANCE TO GO SHOPPING AGAIN.
DADDY. I FEEL SOMETHING CREEPY UNDER THE TABLE, AND ROD'S SCARED TO LOOK UNDER IT.
LET ME TAKE A LOOK-SEE.
NOTHING BUT GUM. HOMER MUST HAVE LEFT IT UNDER THE TABLE.
AAAAH!
AAAAH!
WHAT?
AW, NERTZ! GUM IN THE MOUSTACHE NEVER COMES OUT. LOOKS LIKE I HAVE AN APPOINTMENT WITH MR. SCISSORS.

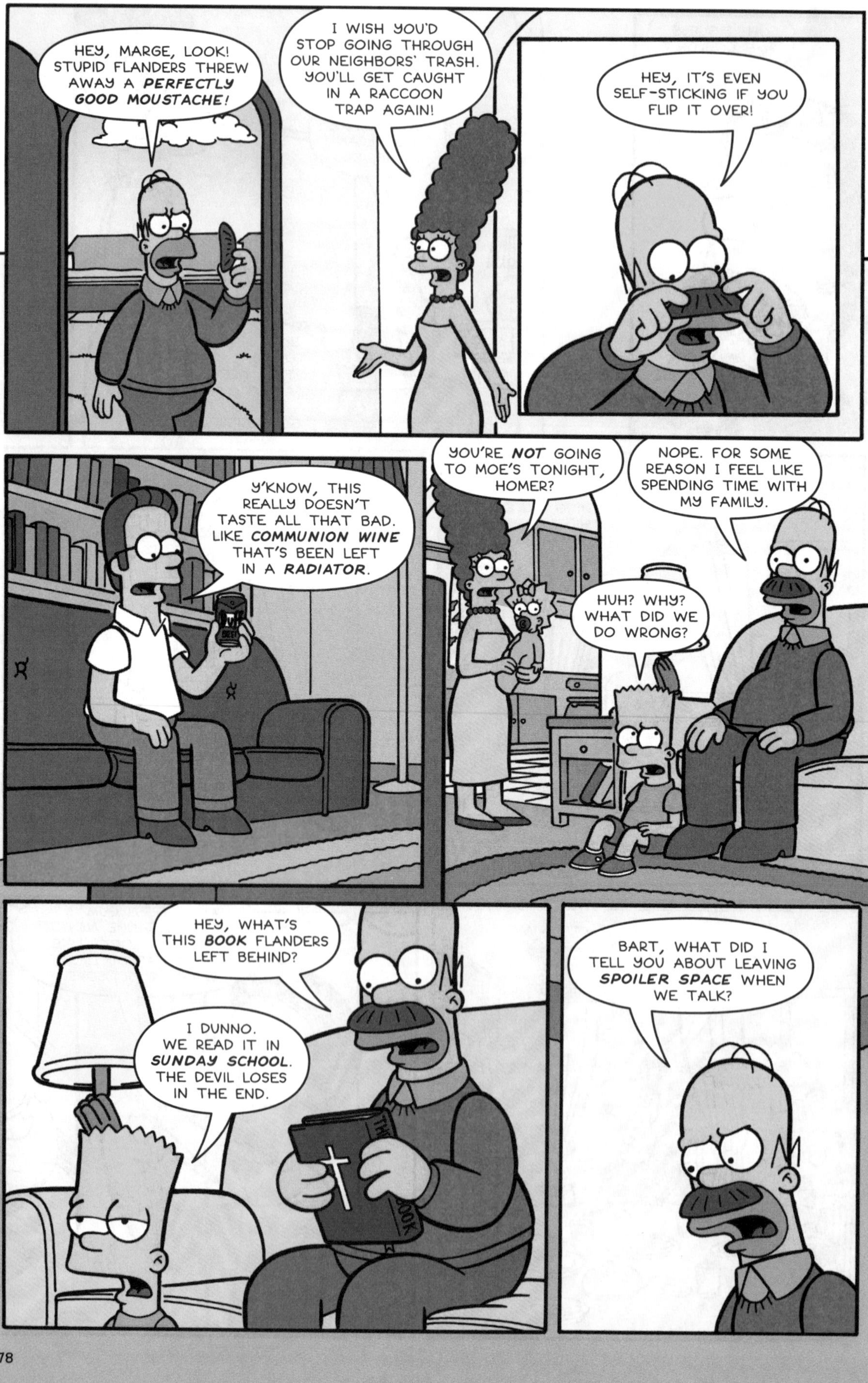
HEY, MARGE, LOOK! STUPID FLANDERS THREW AWAY A **PERFECTLY GOOD MOUSTACHE**!
I WISH YOU'D STOP GOING THROUGH OUR NEIGHBORS' TRASH. YOU'LL GET CAUGHT IN A RACCOON TRAP AGAIN!
HEY, IT'S EVEN SELF-STICKING IF YOU FLIP IT OVER!
Y'KNOW, THIS REALLY DOESN'T TASTE ALL THAT BAD. LIKE **COMMUNION WINE** THAT'S BEEN LEFT IN A **RADIATOR**.
YOU'RE **NOT** GOING TO MOE'S TONIGHT, HOMER?
NOPE. FOR SOME REASON I FEEL LIKE SPENDING TIME WITH MY FAMILY.
HUH? WHY? WHAT DID WE DO WRONG?
HEY, WHAT'S THIS **BOOK** FLANDERS LEFT BEHIND?
I DUNNO. WE READ IT IN **SUNDAY SCHOOL**. THE DEVIL LOSES IN THE END.
BART, WHAT DID I TELL YOU ABOUT LEAVING **SPOILER SPACE** WHEN WE TALK?

WHAT'S THIS BLOCK WITH ALL THE DUST ON IT?

THE *TV REMOTE*, DADDY.

TV? THAT SOUNDS GOOD FOR SOME REASON.

CLICK!

5:00 A.M. THE NEXT MORNING...

HOMER, WHY ARE YOU UP SO EARLY?

HUH?

I THOUGHT I'D SNEAK IN A FEW *EXTRA HOURS* AT WORK.

DADDY, YOU'LL BE LATE FOR WORK!

WORK...¿MOAN?... WHY DON'T YOU KIDS CALL IN AND TELL THE BOSS DADDY'S SICK?

BUT DADDY, YOU'VE ALWAYS TOLD US, "WHEN YOU *LIE*, YOU'RE ONLY LYING TO *YOURSELF*."

ESPECIALLY SINCE YOU'RE YOUR *OWN* BOSS.

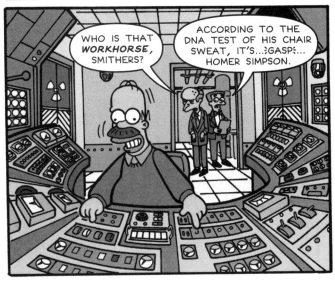

WHO IS THAT *WORKHORSE*, SMITHERS?

ACCORDING TO THE DNA TEST OF HIS CHAIR SWEAT, IT'S...¿GASP?... HOMER SIMPSON.

A MAN WORKING THAT HARD IS UP TO SOMETHING. *FIRE HIM AT ONCE!*

YES, SIR!

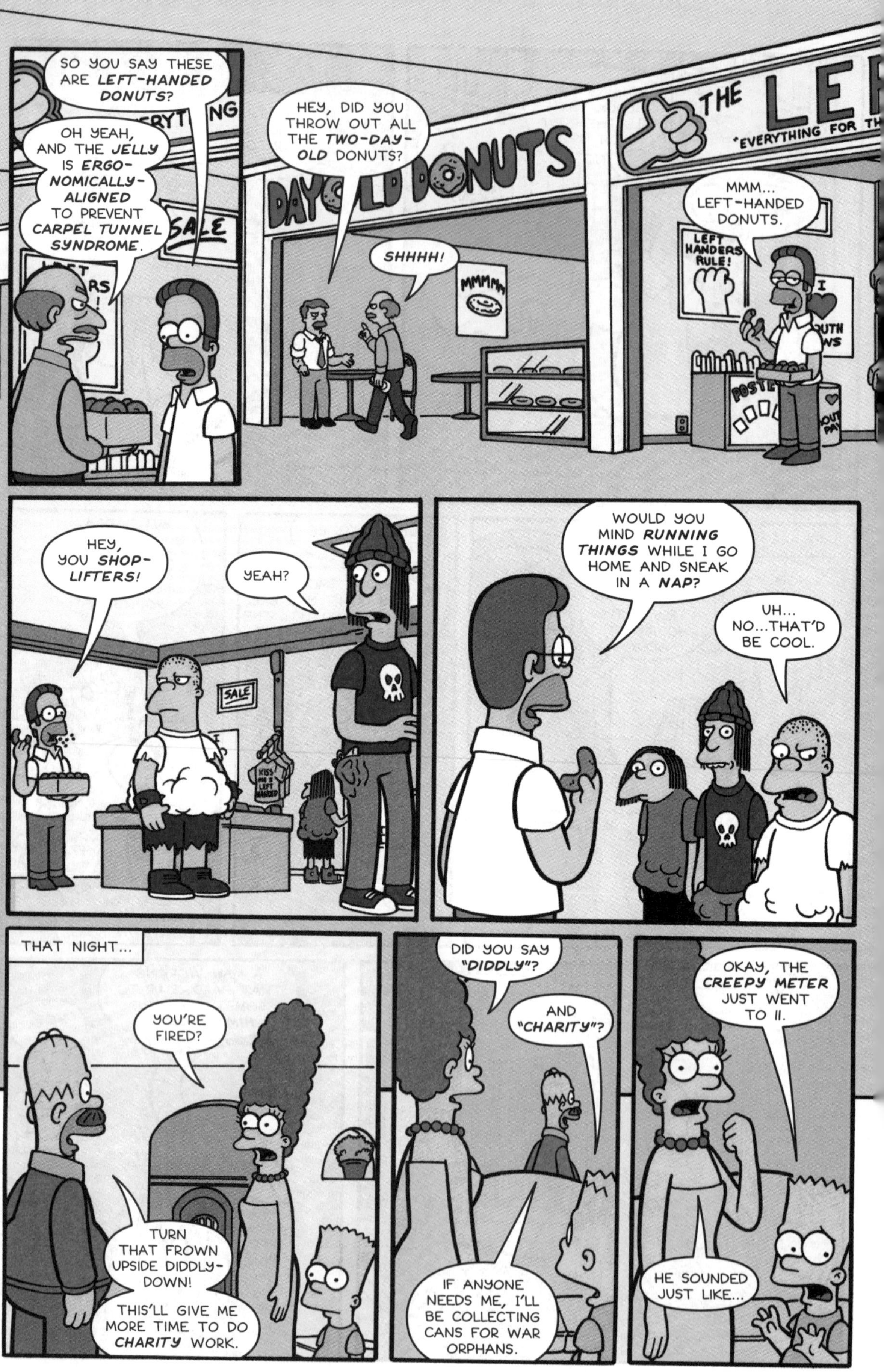
SO YOU SAY THESE ARE LEFT-HANDED DONUTS?
OH YEAH, AND THE JELLY IS ERGO-NOMICALLY-ALIGNED TO PREVENT CARPEL TUNNEL SYNDROME.
SALE
HEY, DID YOU THROW OUT ALL THE TWO-DAY-OLD DONUTS?
SHHHH!
DAY OLD DONUTS
THE LEF
"EVERYTHING FOR TH
MMM... LEFT-HANDED DONUTS.
LEFT HANDERS RULE!
HEY, YOU SHOP-LIFTERS!
YEAH?
SALE
WOULD YOU MIND RUNNING THINGS WHILE I GO HOME AND SNEAK IN A NAP?
UH... NO...THAT'D BE COOL.
THAT NIGHT...
YOU'RE FIRED?
TURN THAT FROWN UPSIDE DIDDLY-DOWN!
THIS'LL GIVE ME MORE TIME TO DO CHARITY WORK.
DID YOU SAY "DIDDLY"?
AND "CHARITY"?
IF ANYONE NEEDS ME, I'LL BE COLLECTING CANS FOR WAR ORPHANS.
OKAY, THE CREEPY METER JUST WENT TO 11.
HE SOUNDED JUST LIKE...

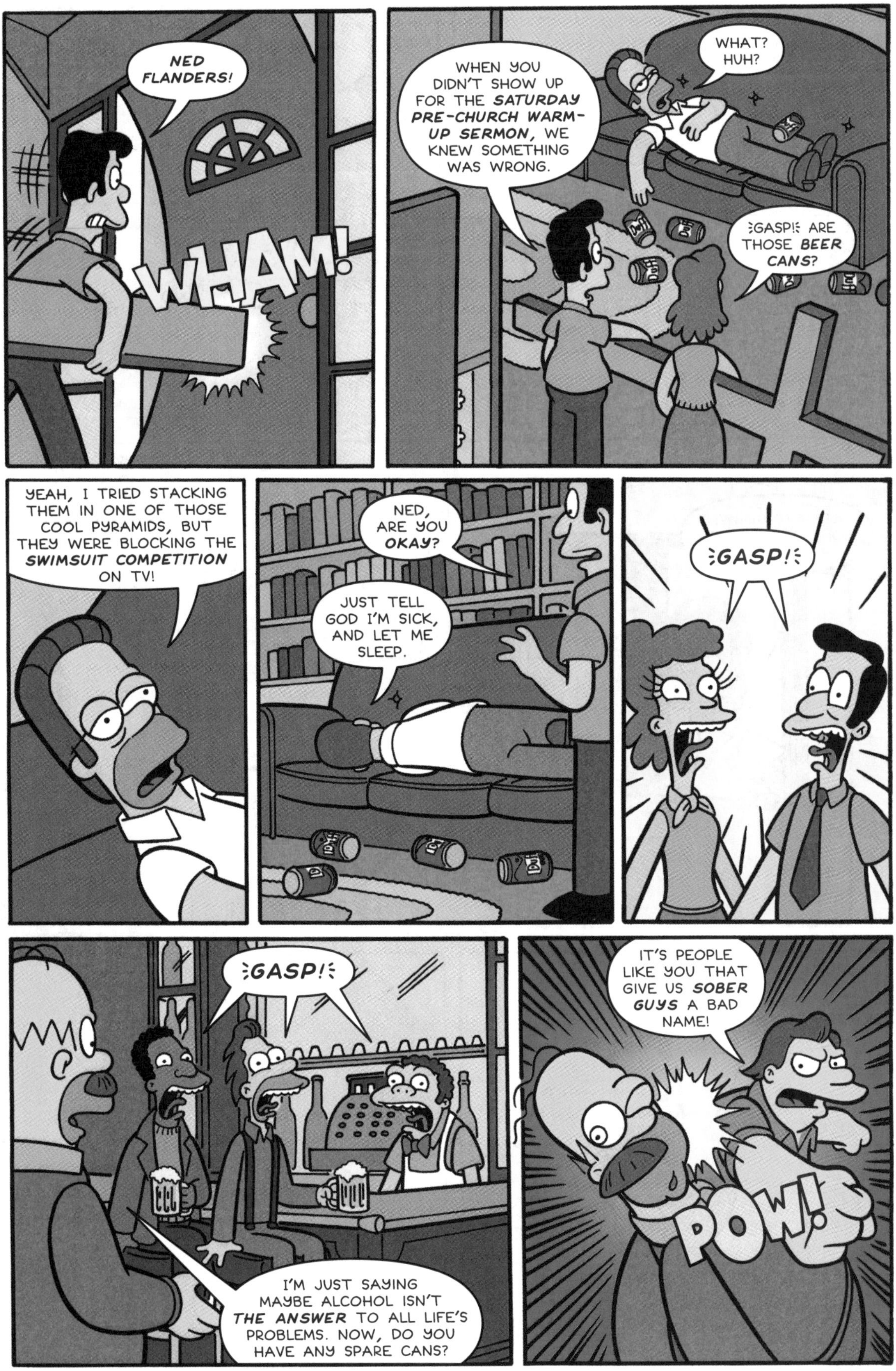
NED FLANDERS!
WHAM!
WHEN YOU DIDN'T SHOW UP FOR THE SATURDAY PRE-CHURCH WARM-UP SERMON, WE KNEW SOMETHING WAS WRONG.
WHAT? HUH?
¡GASP!¡ ARE THOSE BEER CANS?
YEAH, I TRIED STACKING THEM IN ONE OF THOSE COOL PYRAMIDS, BUT THEY WERE BLOCKING THE SWIMSUIT COMPETITION ON TV!
NED, ARE YOU OKAY?
JUST TELL GOD I'M SICK, AND LET ME SLEEP.
GASP!
GASP!
I'M JUST SAYING MAYBE ALCOHOL ISN'T THE ANSWER TO ALL LIFE'S PROBLEMS. NOW, DO YOU HAVE ANY SPARE CANS?
IT'S PEOPLE LIKE YOU THAT GIVE US SOBER GUYS A BAD NAME!
POW!

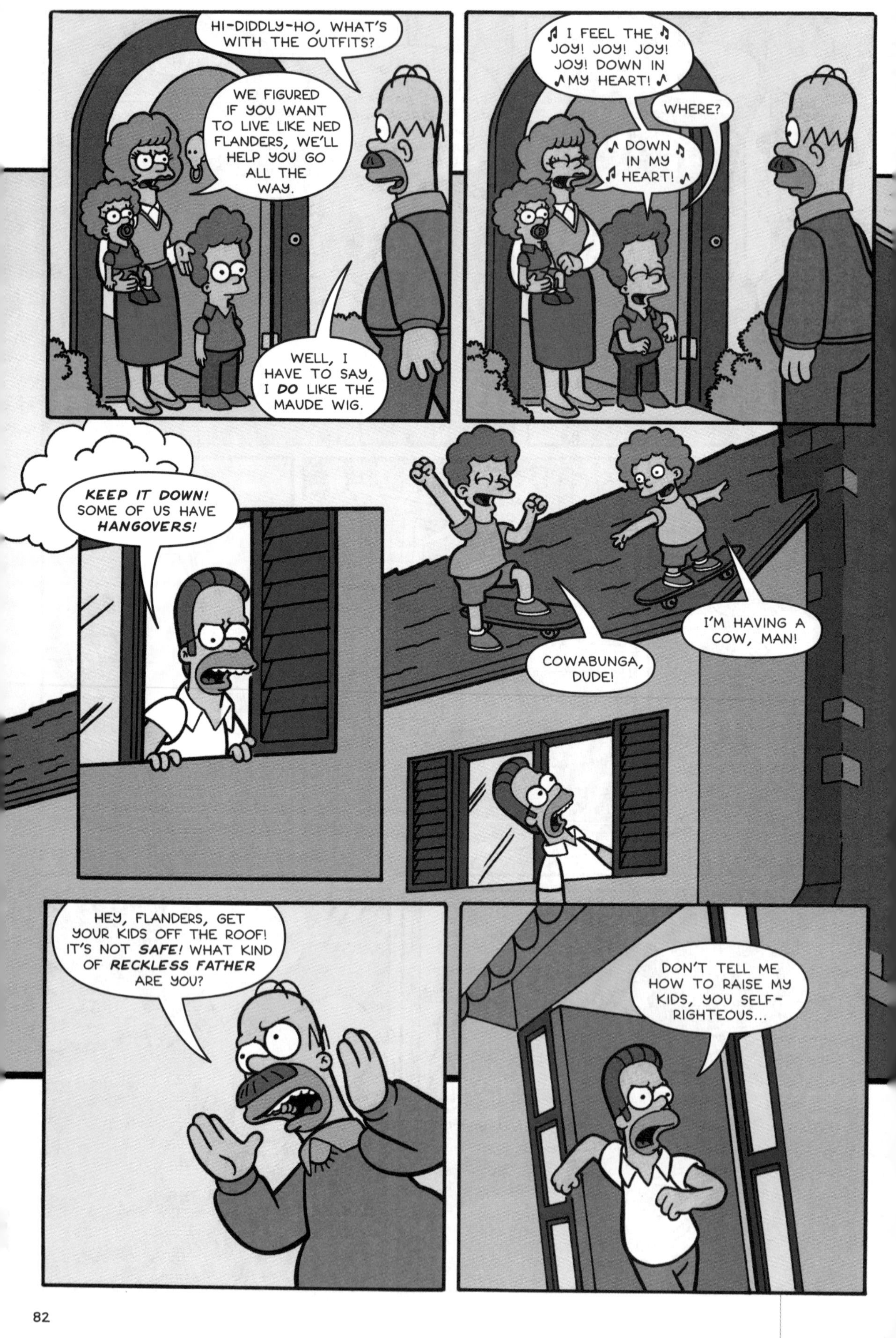
HI-DIDDLY-HO, WHAT'S WITH THE OUTFITS?
WE FIGURED IF YOU WANT TO LIVE LIKE NED FLANDERS, WE'LL HELP YOU GO ALL THE WAY.
WELL, I HAVE TO SAY, I ***DO*** LIKE THE MAUDE WIG.
♫ I FEEL THE ♫ JOY! JOY! JOY! JOY! DOWN IN ♪ MY HEART! ♪
WHERE?
♪ DOWN ♫ IN MY ♫ HEART! ♪
***KEEP IT DOWN!*** SOME OF US HAVE ***HANGOVERS!***
COWABUNGA, DUDE!
I'M HAVING A COW, MAN!
HEY, FLANDERS, GET YOUR KIDS OFF THE ROOF! IT'S NOT ***SAFE!*** WHAT KIND OF ***RECKLESS FATHER*** ARE YOU?
DON'T TELL ME HOW TO RAISE MY KIDS, YOU SELF-RIGHTEOUS...

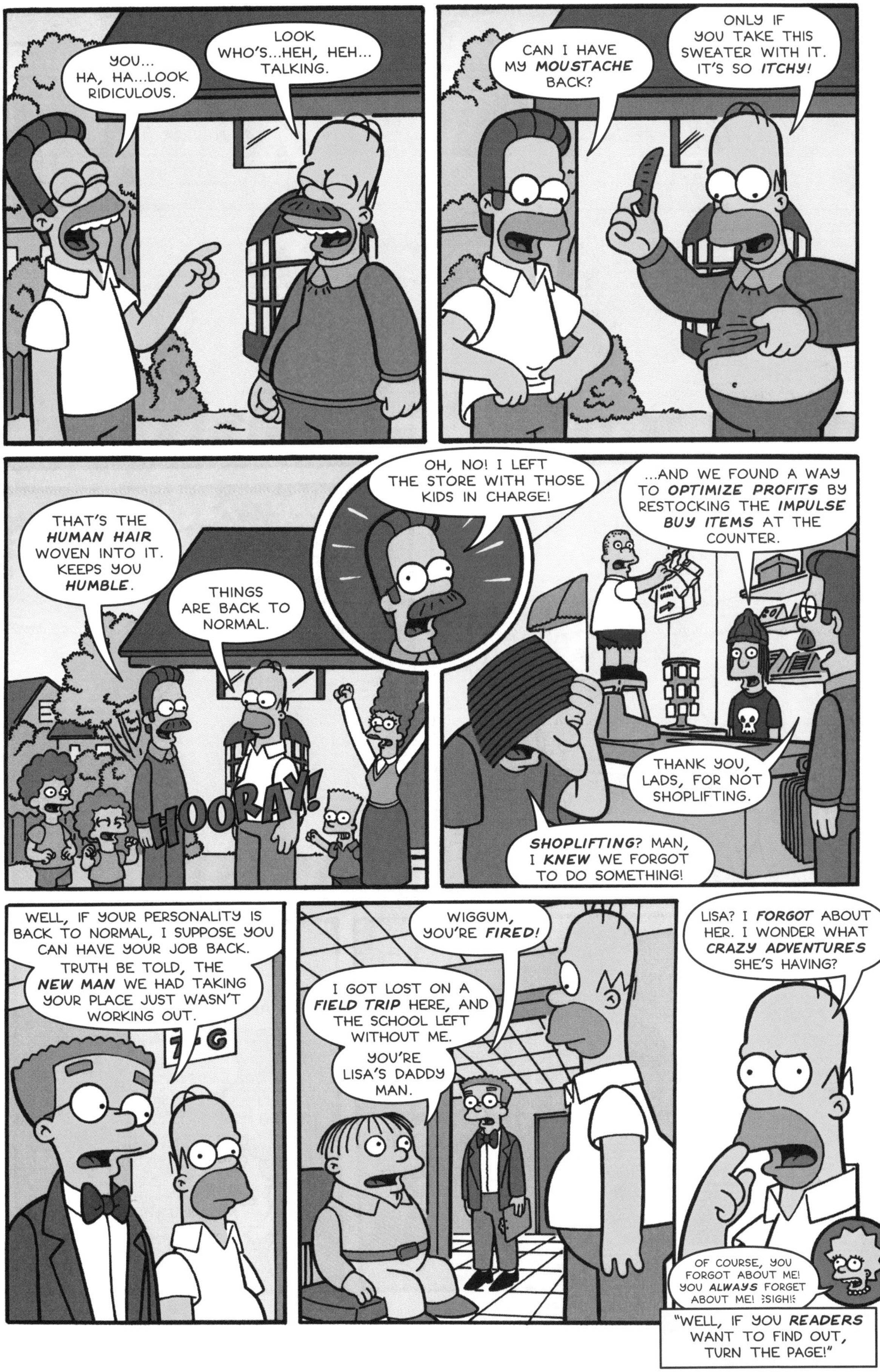
YOU... HA, HA...LOOK RIDICULOUS.
LOOK WHO'S...HEH, HEH... TALKING.
CAN I HAVE MY MOUSTACHE BACK?
ONLY IF YOU TAKE THIS SWEATER WITH IT. IT'S SO ITCHY!
THAT'S THE HUMAN HAIR WOVEN INTO IT. KEEPS YOU HUMBLE.
THINGS ARE BACK TO NORMAL.
HOORAY!
OH, NO! I LEFT THE STORE WITH THOSE KIDS IN CHARGE!
...AND WE FOUND A WAY TO OPTIMIZE PROFITS BY RESTOCKING THE IMPULSE BUY ITEMS AT THE COUNTER.
THANK YOU, LADS, FOR NOT SHOPLIFTING.
SHOPLIFTING? MAN, I KNEW WE FORGOT TO DO SOMETHING!
WELL, IF YOUR PERSONALITY IS BACK TO NORMAL, I SUPPOSE YOU CAN HAVE YOUR JOB BACK.
TRUTH BE TOLD, THE NEW MAN WE HAD TAKING YOUR PLACE JUST WASN'T WORKING OUT.
WIGGUM, YOU'RE FIRED!
I GOT LOST ON A FIELD TRIP HERE, AND THE SCHOOL LEFT WITHOUT ME.
YOU'RE LISA'S DADDY MAN.
LISA? I FORGOT ABOUT HER. I WONDER WHAT CRAZY ADVENTURES SHE'S HAVING?
OF COURSE, YOU FORGOT ABOUT ME! YOU ALWAYS FORGET ABOUT ME! SIGH!
"WELL, IF YOU READERS WANT TO FIND OUT, TURN THE PAGE!"

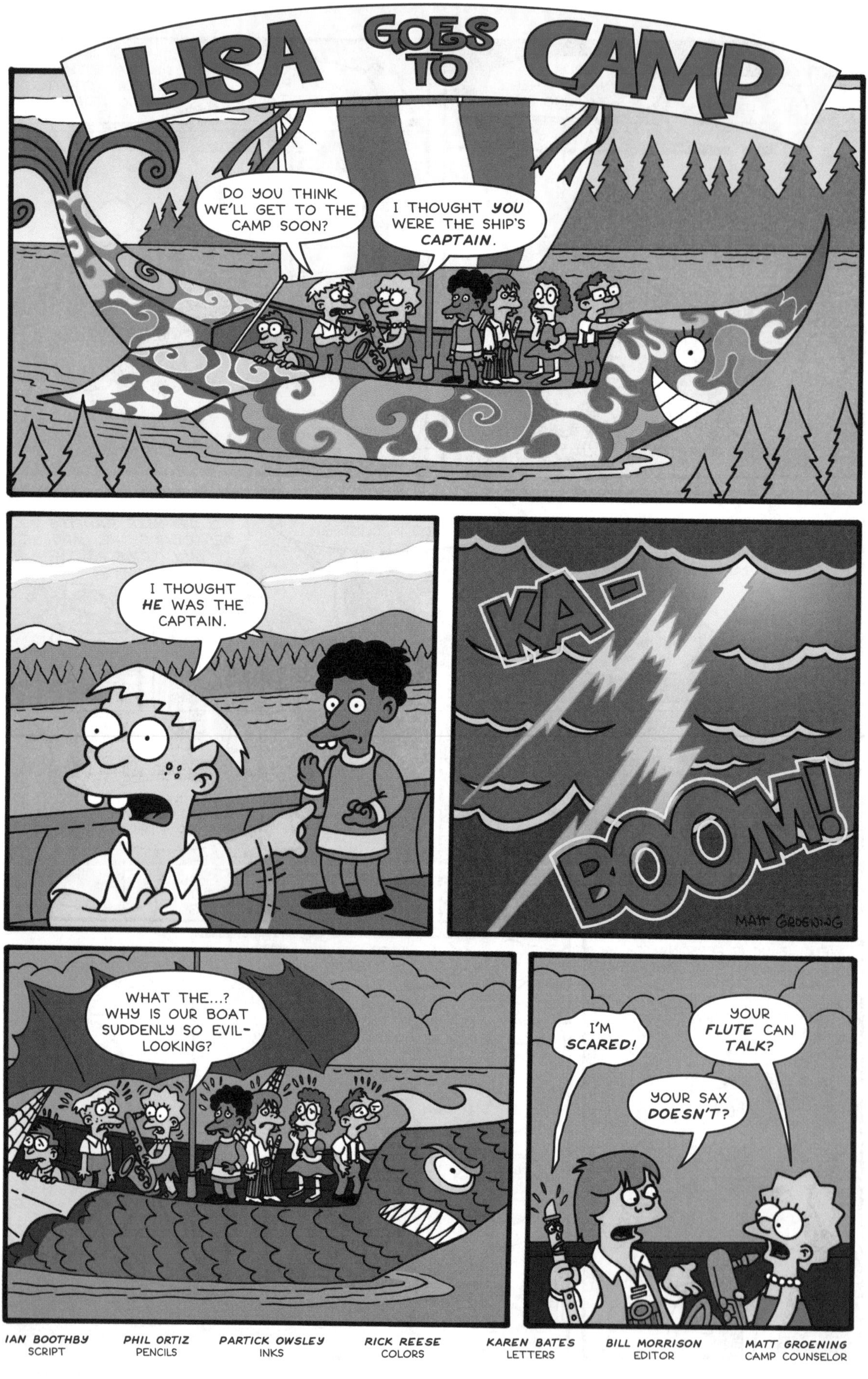
LISA GOES TO CAMP
DO YOU THINK WE'LL GET TO THE CAMP SOON?
I THOUGHT *YOU* WERE THE SHIP'S *CAPTAIN*.
I THOUGHT *HE* WAS THE CAPTAIN.
KA-BOOM!
MATT GROENING
WHAT THE...? WHY IS OUR BOAT SUDDENLY SO EVIL-LOOKING?
I'M *SCARED!*
YOUR *FLUTE* CAN *TALK?*
YOUR SAX *DOESN'T?*

***IAN BOOTHBY*** SCRIPT | ***PHIL ORTIZ*** PENCILS | ***PARTICK OWSLEY*** INKS | ***RICK REESE*** COLORS | ***KAREN BATES*** LETTERS | ***BILL MORRISON*** EDITOR | ***MATT GROENING*** CAMP COUNSELOR

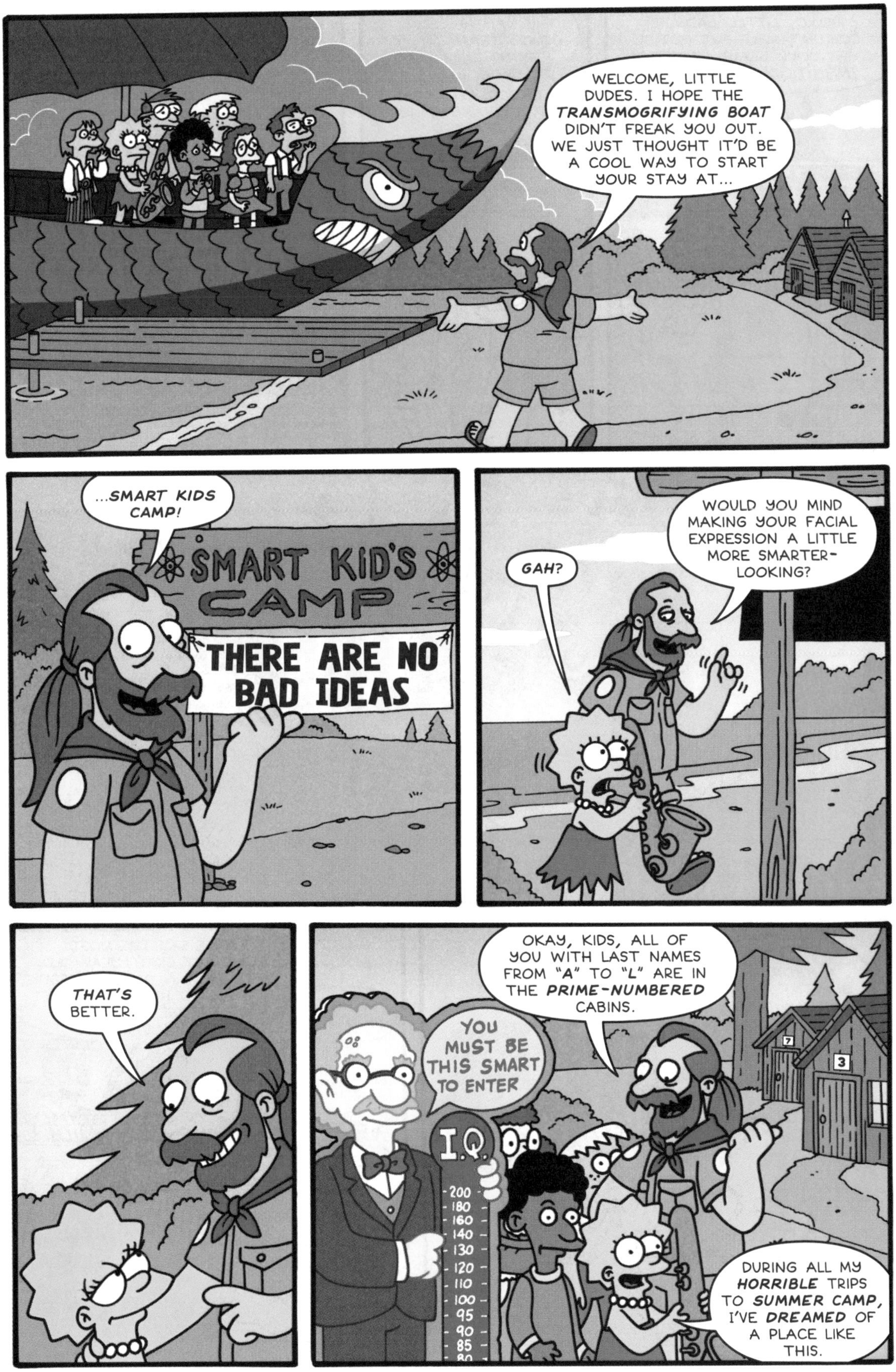
WELCOME, LITTLE DUDES. I HOPE THE TRANSMOGRIFYING BOAT DIDN'T FREAK YOU OUT. WE JUST THOUGHT IT'D BE A COOL WAY TO START YOUR STAY AT...
...SMART KIDS CAMP!
SMART KID'S CAMP
THERE ARE NO BAD IDEAS
WOULD YOU MIND MAKING YOUR FACIAL EXPRESSION A LITTLE MORE SMARTER-LOOKING?
GAH?
THAT'S BETTER.
OKAY, KIDS, ALL OF YOU WITH LAST NAMES FROM "A" TO "L" ARE IN THE PRIME-NUMBERED CABINS.
YOU MUST BE THIS SMART TO ENTER
I.Q.
200
180
160
140
130
120
110
100
95
90
85
7
3
DURING ALL MY HORRIBLE TRIPS TO SUMMER CAMP, I'VE DREAMED OF A PLACE LIKE THIS.

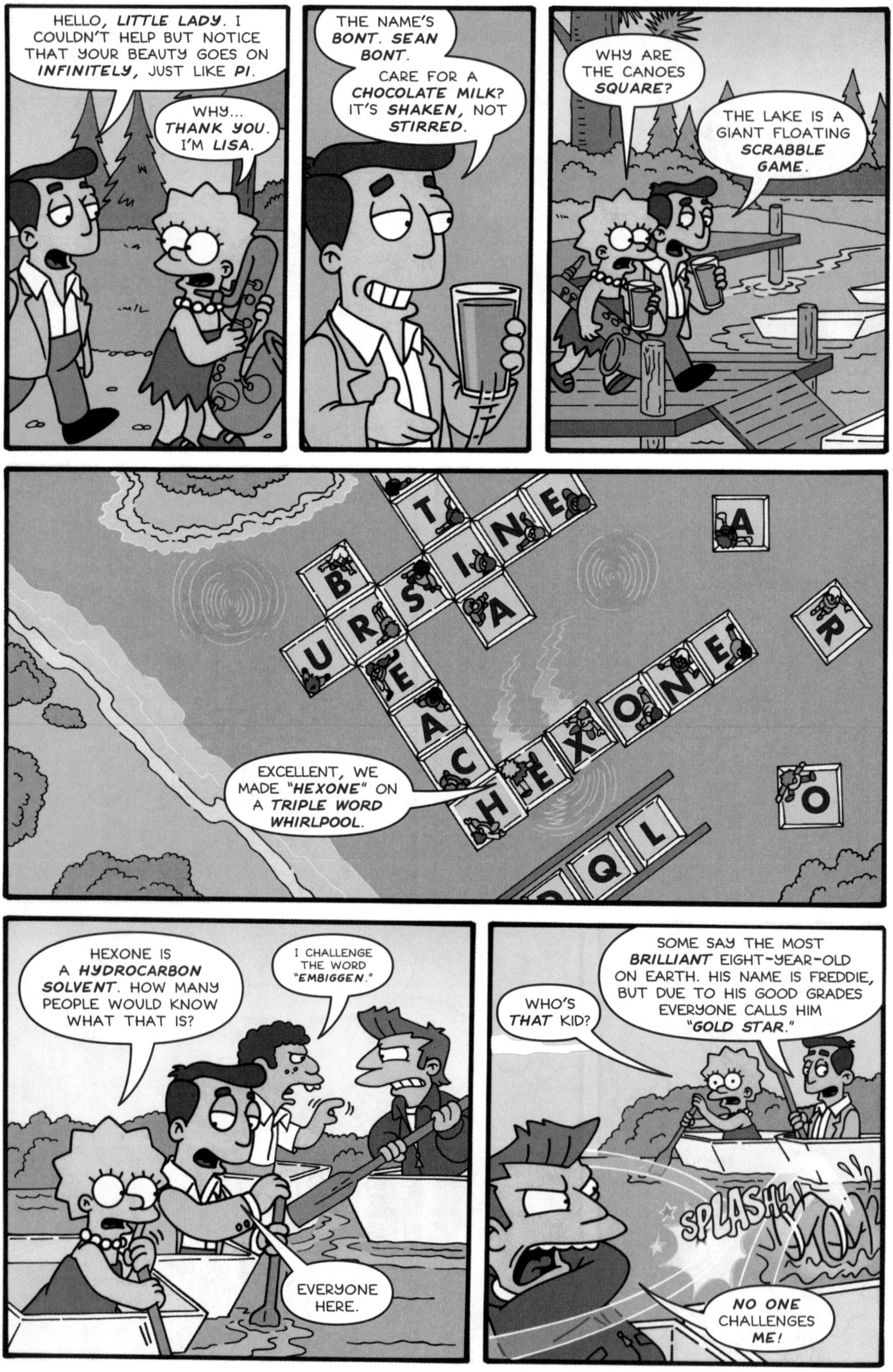
HELLO, LITTLE LADY. I COULDN'T HELP BUT NOTICE THAT YOUR BEAUTY GOES ON INFINITELY, JUST LIKE PI.
WHY... THANK YOU. I'M LISA.
THE NAME'S BONT. SEAN BONT.
CARE FOR A CHOCOLATE MILK? IT'S SHAKEN, NOT STIRRED.
WHY ARE THE CANOES SQUARE?
THE LAKE IS A GIANT FLOATING SCRABBLE GAME.
EXCELLENT, WE MADE "HEXONE" ON A TRIPLE WORD WHIRLPOOL.
HEXONE IS A HYDROCARBON SOLVENT. HOW MANY PEOPLE WOULD KNOW WHAT THAT IS?
I CHALLENGE THE WORD "EMBIGGEN."
EVERYONE HERE.
WHO'S THAT KID?
SOME SAY THE MOST BRILLIANT EIGHT-YEAR-OLD ON EARTH. HIS NAME IS FREDDIE, BUT DUE TO HIS GOOD GRADES EVERYONE CALLS HIM "GOLD STAR."
SPLASH!
NO ONE CHALLENGES ME!

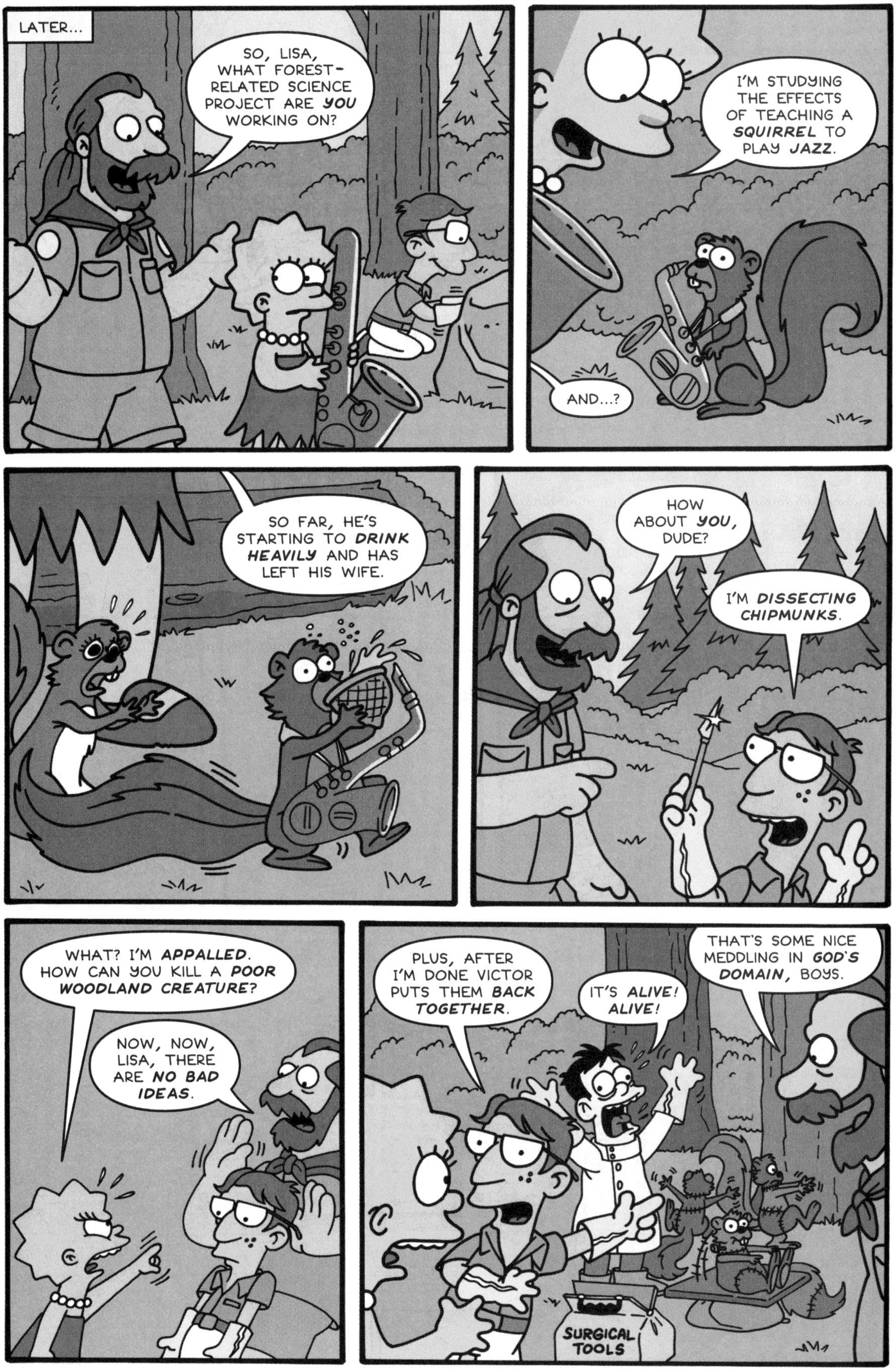
LATER...
SO, LISA, WHAT FOREST-RELATED SCIENCE PROJECT ARE YOU WORKING ON?
I'M STUDYING THE EFFECTS OF TEACHING A SQUIRREL TO PLAY JAZZ.
AND...?
SO FAR, HE'S STARTING TO DRINK HEAVILY AND HAS LEFT HIS WIFE.
HOW ABOUT YOU, DUDE?
I'M DISSECTING CHIPMUNKS.
WHAT? I'M APPALLED. HOW CAN YOU KILL A POOR WOODLAND CREATURE?
NOW, NOW, LISA, THERE ARE NO BAD IDEAS.
PLUS, AFTER I'M DONE VICTOR PUTS THEM BACK TOGETHER.
IT'S ALIVE! ALIVE!
THAT'S SOME NICE MEDDLING IN GOD'S DOMAIN, BOYS.
SURGICAL TOOLS

THAT NIGHT...

...AND THE *MATHEMA-TICIAN* RETURNED HOME TO FIND HER *DEAD HUSBAND* IN THE CELLAR DOING *LONG DIVISION*.

AW, THAT ISN'T SCARY.

HE WAS DIVIDING BY *ZERO*!

AAAAH!

*NO!* THIS *CAN'T* BE A *TRUE* STORY!

OKAY, LITTLE DUDES. TIME FOR 8.3 HOURS OF SHUT EYE. LET THE GOOD R.E.M.S FLOW!

FSSHH!

HMM...I WONDER WHERE SEAN IS?

BWAH-HA-HA!

BWAH-HA...HUH?

*HEY!* WHY DOES GOLD STAR GET HIS OWN *CABIN* AND ALL THOSE *TVS*?

RUSSIA · GERMANY · CHINA · POLAND · UGANDA · UNITED STATES · FRANCE · CANADA · SINGAPORE · AUSTRALIA · BRITAIN · SOUTH AMERICA

GREETINGS, WORLD REPRESENTATIVES! IT IS I, *GOLD STAR*!

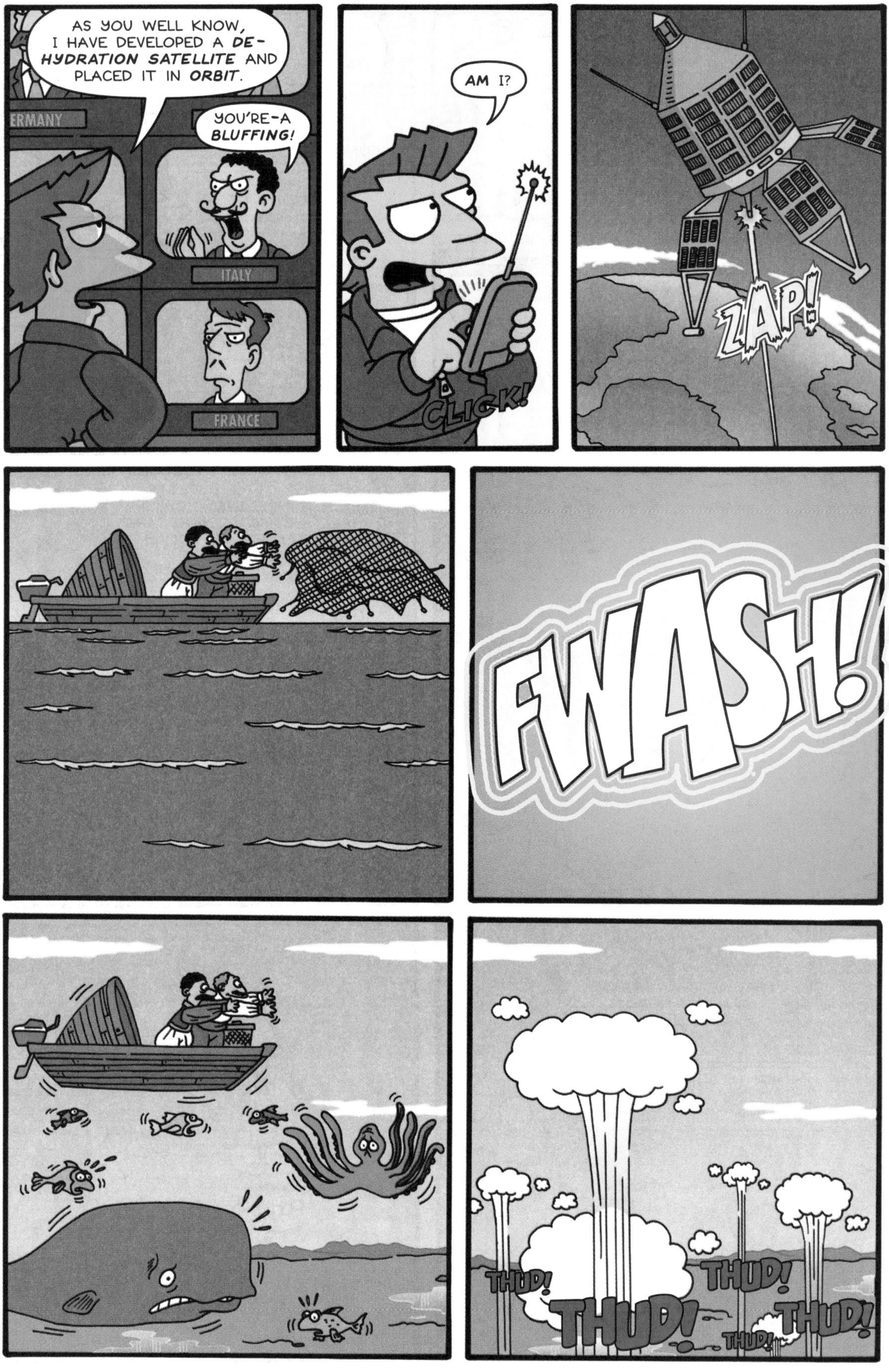

AS YOU WELL KNOW, I HAVE DEVELOPED A DE-HYDRATION SATELLITE AND PLACED IT IN ORBIT.
ERMANY
YOU'RE-A BLUFFING!
ITALY
FRANCE
AM I?
CLICK!
ZAP!
FWASH!
THUD!
THUD!
THUD!
THUD!
THUD!

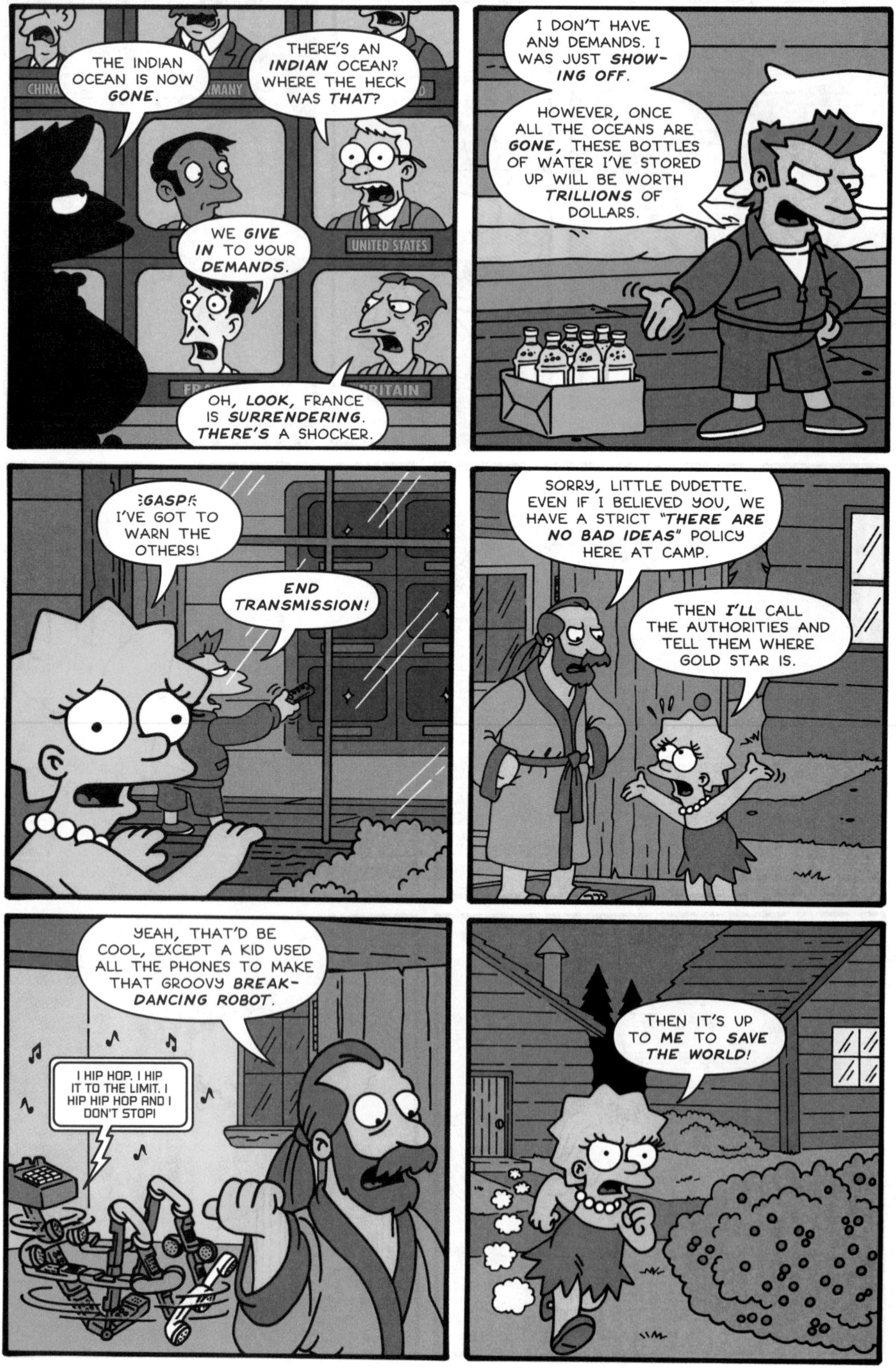

CHINA
GERMANY
THE INDIAN OCEAN IS NOW GONE.
THERE'S AN INDIAN OCEAN? WHERE THE HECK WAS THAT?
UNITED STATES
WE GIVE IN TO YOUR DEMANDS.
BRITAIN
OH, LOOK, FRANCE IS SURRENDERING. THERE'S A SHOCKER.
I DON'T HAVE ANY DEMANDS. I WAS JUST SHOWING OFF.
HOWEVER, ONCE ALL THE OCEANS ARE GONE, THESE BOTTLES OF WATER I'VE STORED UP WILL BE WORTH TRILLIONS OF DOLLARS.
GASP! I'VE GOT TO WARN THE OTHERS!
END TRANSMISSION!
SORRY, LITTLE DUDETTE. EVEN IF I BELIEVED YOU, WE HAVE A STRICT "THERE ARE NO BAD IDEAS" POLICY HERE AT CAMP.
THEN I'LL CALL THE AUTHORITIES AND TELL THEM WHERE GOLD STAR IS.
YEAH, THAT'D BE COOL, EXCEPT A KID USED ALL THE PHONES TO MAKE THAT GROOVY BREAK-DANCING ROBOT.
I HIP HOP. I HIP IT TO THE LIMIT. I HIP HIP HOP AND I DON'T STOP!
THEN IT'S UP TO ME TO SAVE THE WORLD!

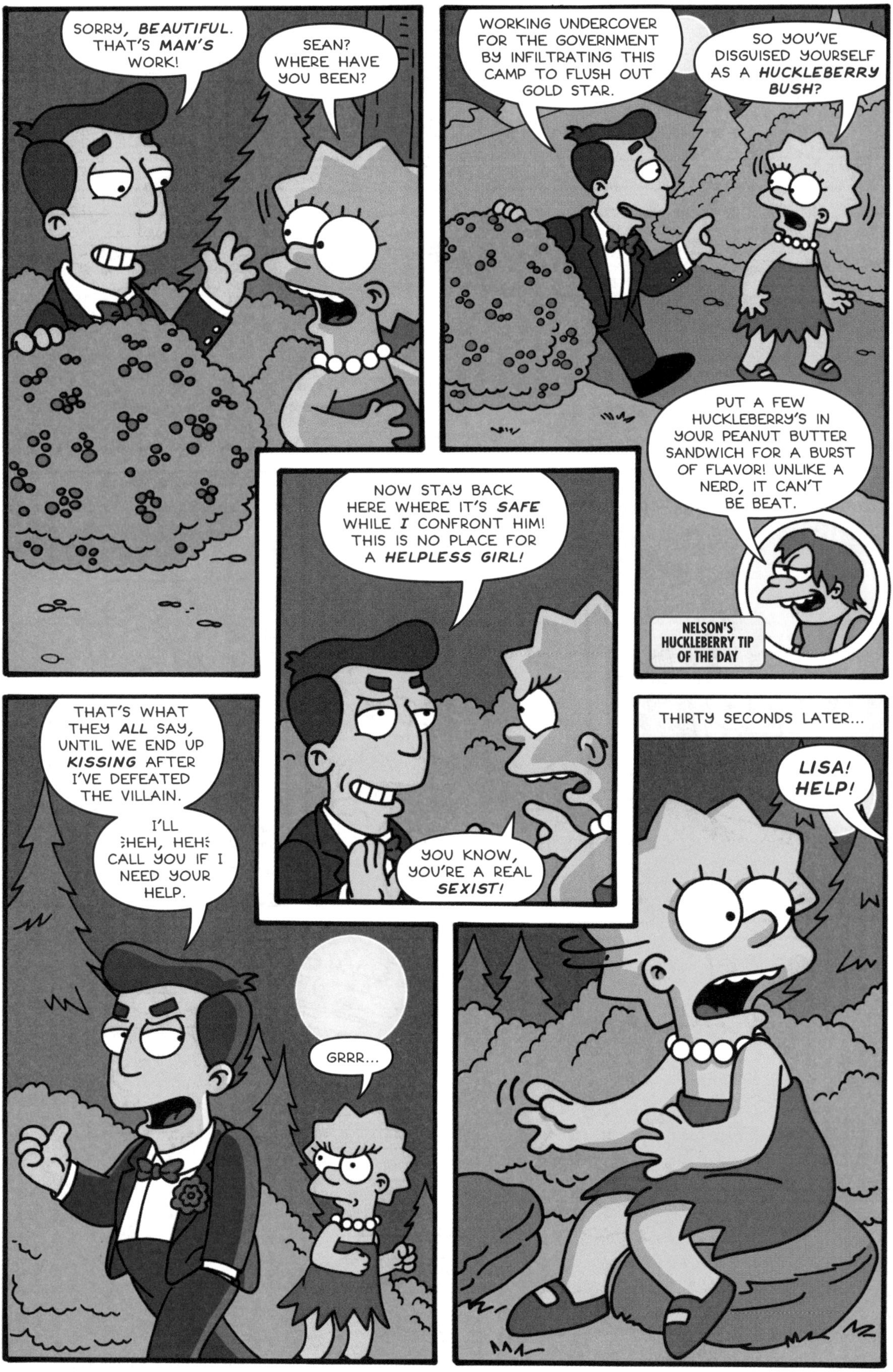
SORRY, BEAUTIFUL. THAT'S MAN'S WORK!
SEAN? WHERE HAVE YOU BEEN?
WORKING UNDERCOVER FOR THE GOVERNMENT BY INFILTRATING THIS CAMP TO FLUSH OUT GOLD STAR.
SO YOU'VE DISGUISED YOURSELF AS A HUCKLEBERRY BUSH?
PUT A FEW HUCKLEBERRY'S IN YOUR PEANUT BUTTER SANDWICH FOR A BURST OF FLAVOR! UNLIKE A NERD, IT CAN'T BE BEAT.
NELSON'S HUCKLEBERRY TIP OF THE DAY
NOW STAY BACK HERE WHERE IT'S SAFE WHILE I CONFRONT HIM! THIS IS NO PLACE FOR A HELPLESS GIRL!
YOU KNOW, YOU'RE A REAL SEXIST!
THAT'S WHAT THEY ALL SAY, UNTIL WE END UP KISSING AFTER I'VE DEFEATED THE VILLAIN.
I'LL ⁝HEH, HEH⁝ CALL YOU IF I NEED YOUR HELP.
GRRR...
THIRTY SECONDS LATER...
LISA! HELP!

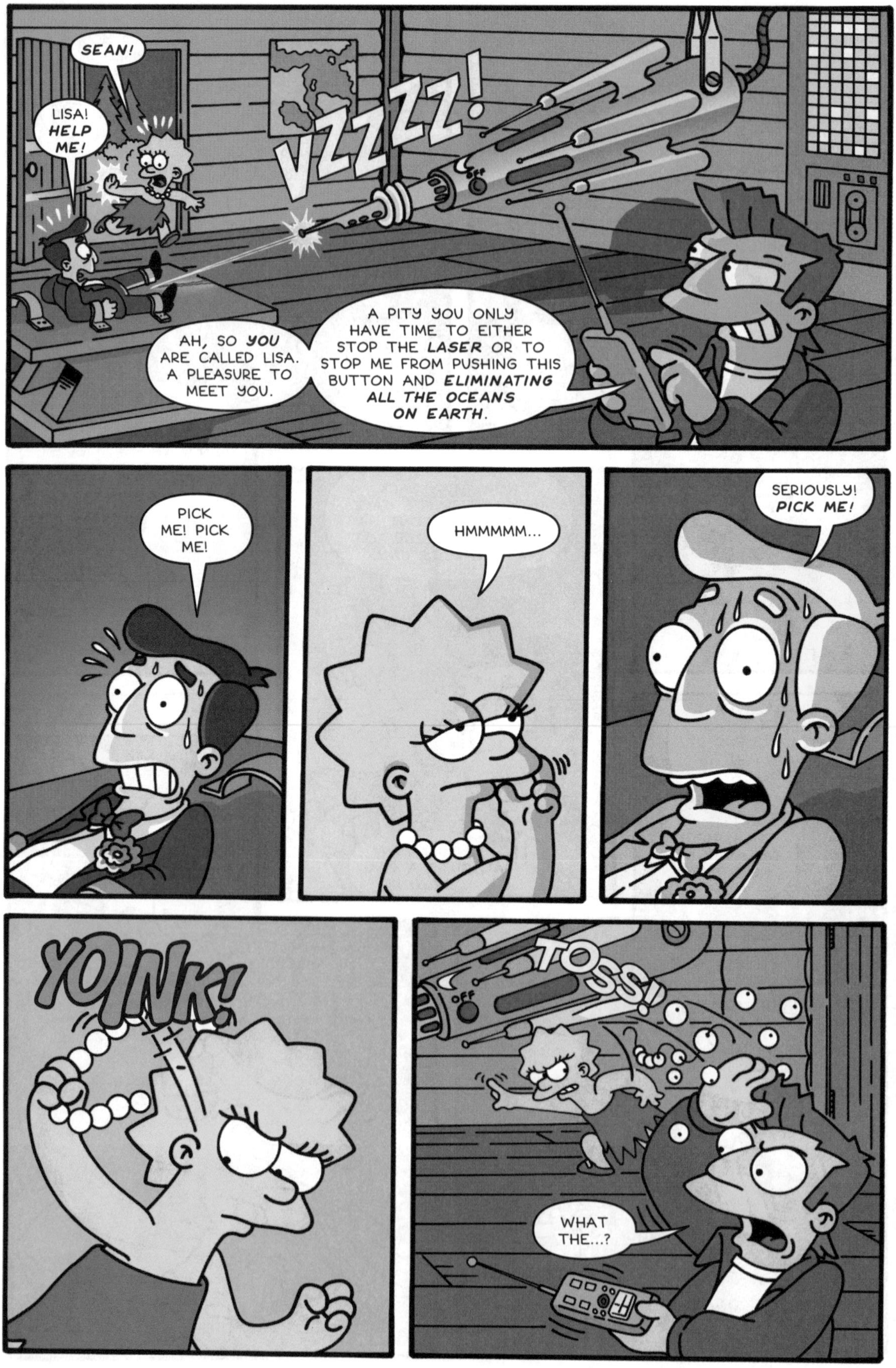
SEAN!
LISA! HELP ME!
VZZZZ!
AH, SO YOU ARE CALLED LISA. A PLEASURE TO MEET YOU.
A PITY YOU ONLY HAVE TIME TO EITHER STOP THE LASER OR TO STOP ME FROM PUSHING THIS BUTTON AND ELIMINATING ALL THE OCEANS ON EARTH.
PICK ME! PICK ME!
HMMMMM...
SERIOUSLY! PICK ME!
YOINK!
TOSS!
OFF
WHAT THE...?

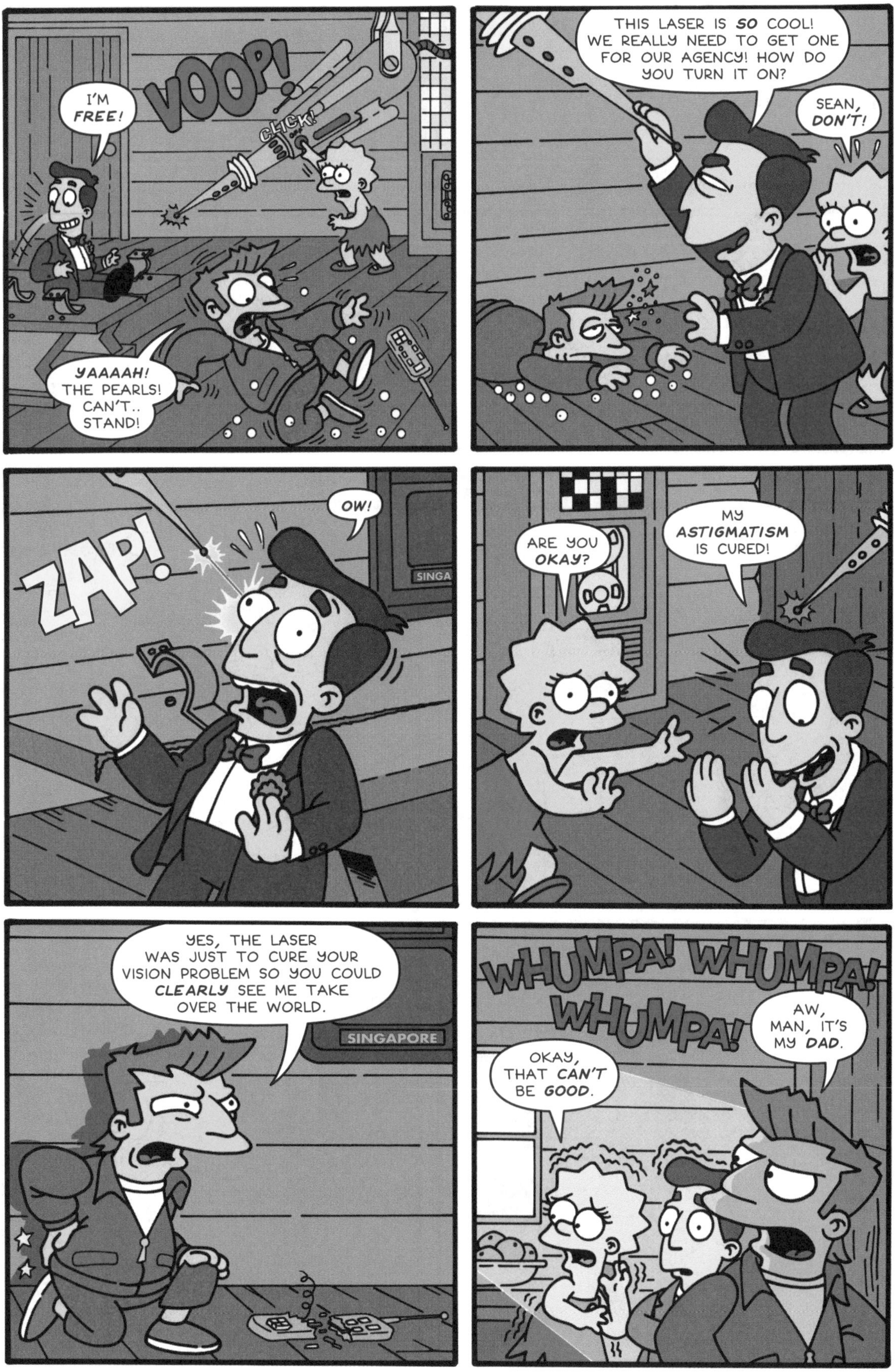
VOOP!
CLICK!
I'M FREE!
YAAAAH! THE PEARLS! CAN'T.. STAND!
THIS LASER IS SO COOL! WE REALLY NEED TO GET ONE FOR OUR AGENCY! HOW DO YOU TURN IT ON?
SEAN, DON'T!
ZAP!
OW!
ARE YOU OKAY?
MY ASTIGMATISM IS CURED!
YES, THE LASER WAS JUST TO CURE YOUR VISION PROBLEM SO YOU COULD CLEARLY SEE ME TAKE OVER THE WORLD.
SINGAPORE
WHUMPA! WHUMPA! WHUMPA!
OKAY, THAT CAN'T BE GOOD.
AW, MAN, IT'S MY DAD.

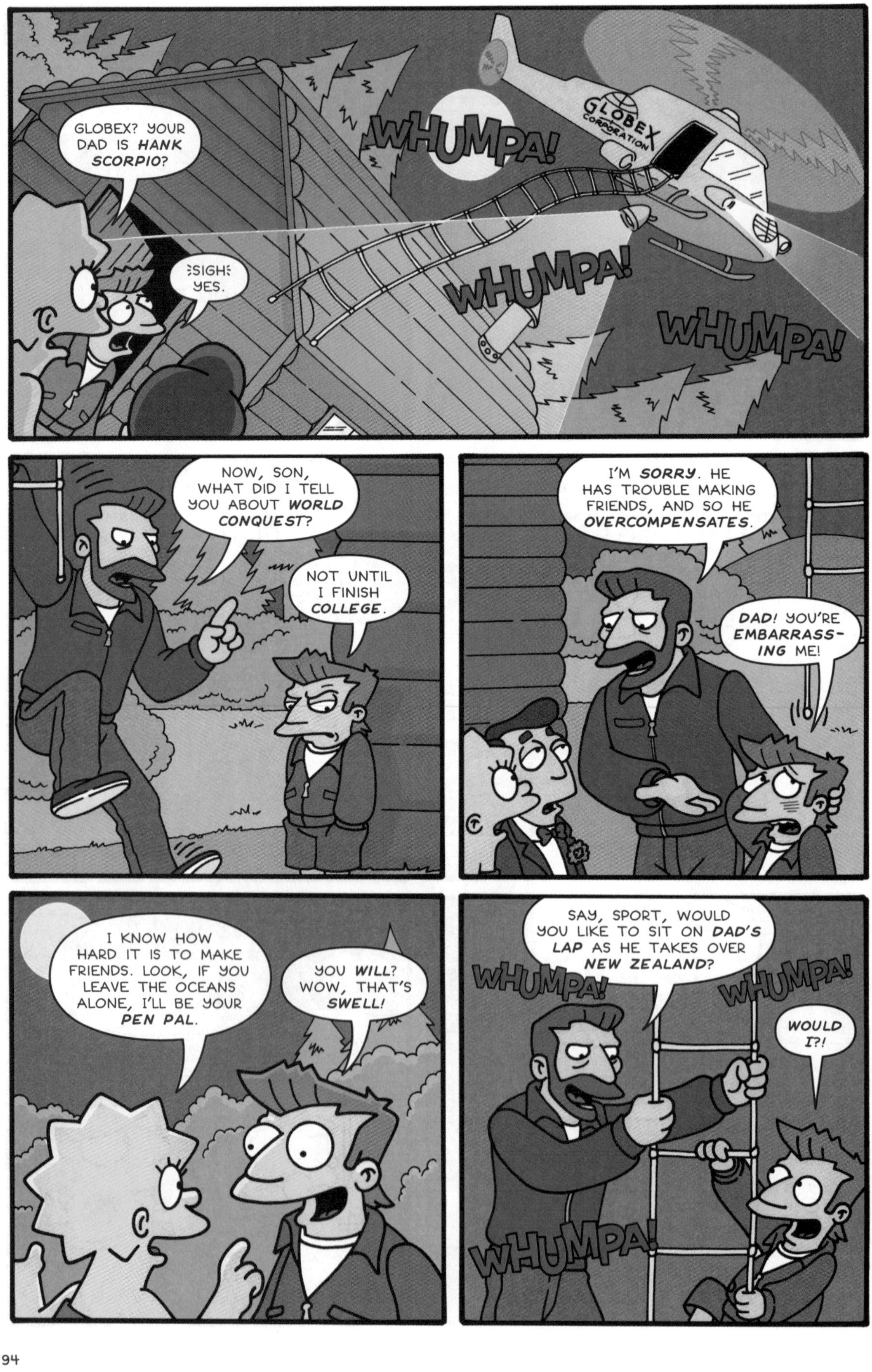
GLOBEX? YOUR DAD IS HANK SCORPIO?
WHUMPA!
GLOBEX CORPORATION
SIGH YES.
WHUMPA!
WHUMPA!
NOW, SON, WHAT DID I TELL YOU ABOUT WORLD CONQUEST?
NOT UNTIL I FINISH COLLEGE.
I'M SORRY. HE HAS TROUBLE MAKING FRIENDS, AND SO HE OVERCOMPENSATES.
DAD! YOU'RE EMBARRASSING ME!
I KNOW HOW HARD IT IS TO MAKE FRIENDS. LOOK, IF YOU LEAVE THE OCEANS ALONE, I'LL BE YOUR PEN PAL.
YOU WILL? WOW, THAT'S SWELL!
SAY, SPORT, WOULD YOU LIKE TO SIT ON DAD'S LAP AS HE TAKES OVER NEW ZEALAND?
WHUMPA!
WHUMPA!
WOULD I?!
WHUMPA!

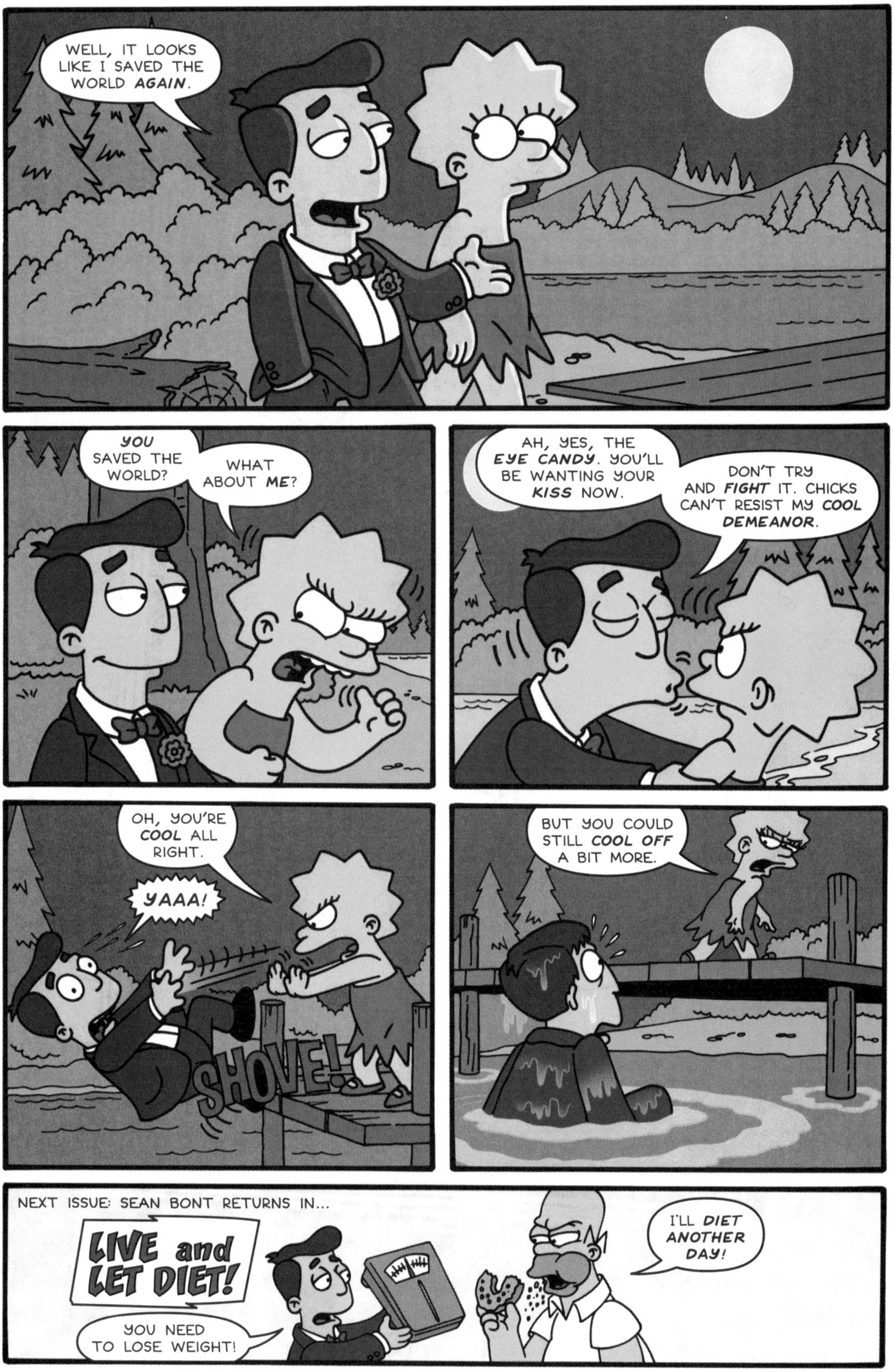
WELL, IT LOOKS LIKE I SAVED THE WORLD AGAIN.
YOU SAVED THE WORLD?
WHAT ABOUT ME?
AH, YES, THE EYE CANDY. YOU'LL BE WANTING YOUR KISS NOW.
DON'T TRY AND FIGHT IT. CHICKS CAN'T RESIST MY COOL DEMEANOR.
OH, YOU'RE COOL ALL RIGHT.
YAAA!
SHOVE!
BUT YOU COULD STILL COOL OFF A BIT MORE.
NEXT ISSUE: SEAN BONT RETURNS IN...
LIVE and LET DIET!
YOU NEED TO LOSE WEIGHT!
I'LL DIET ANOTHER DAY!

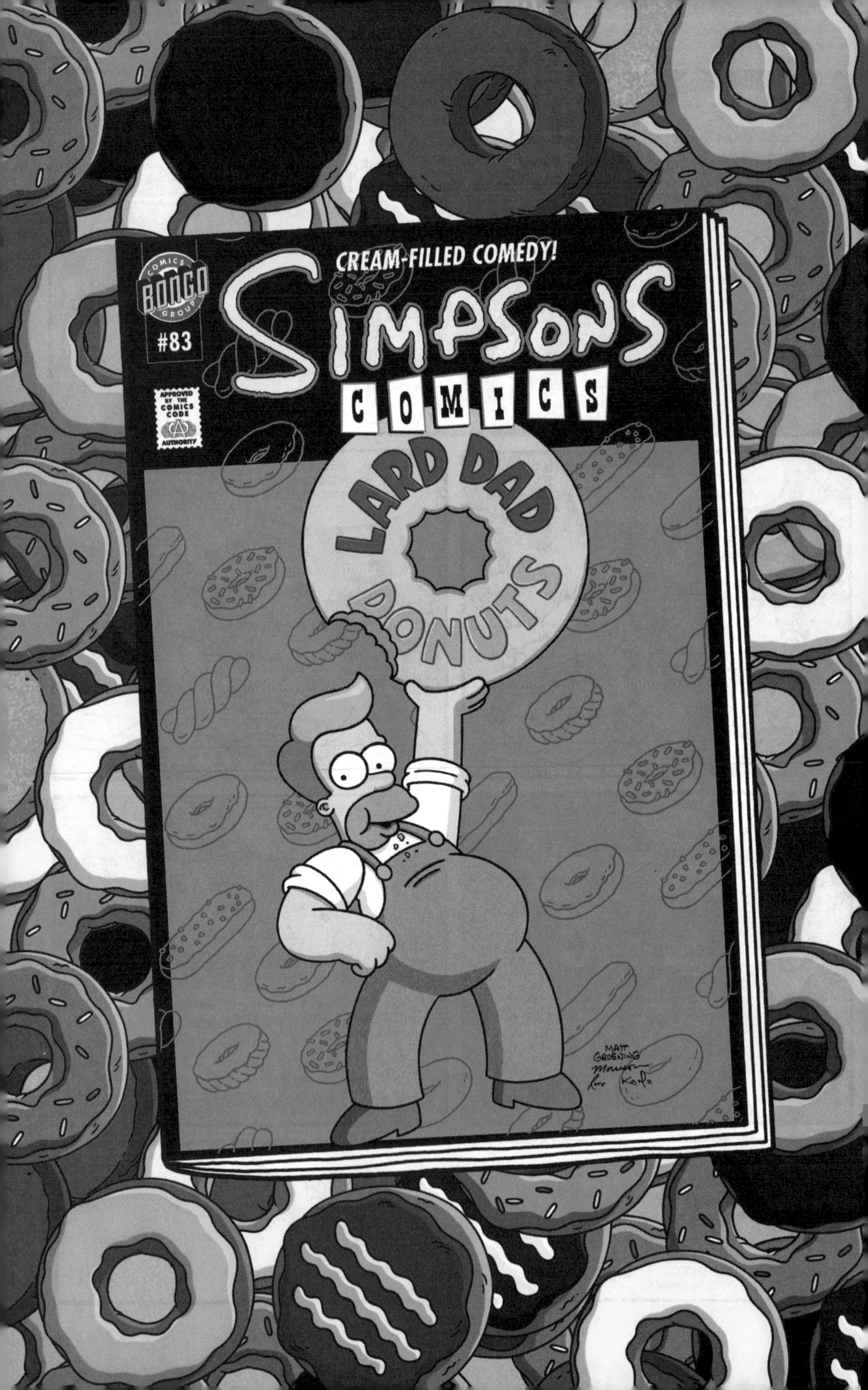

BONGO COMICS GROUP
#83
CREAM-FILLED COMEDY!
SIMPSONS COMICS
APPROVED BY THE COMICS CODE AUTHORITY
LARD DAD DONUTS
MATT GROENING

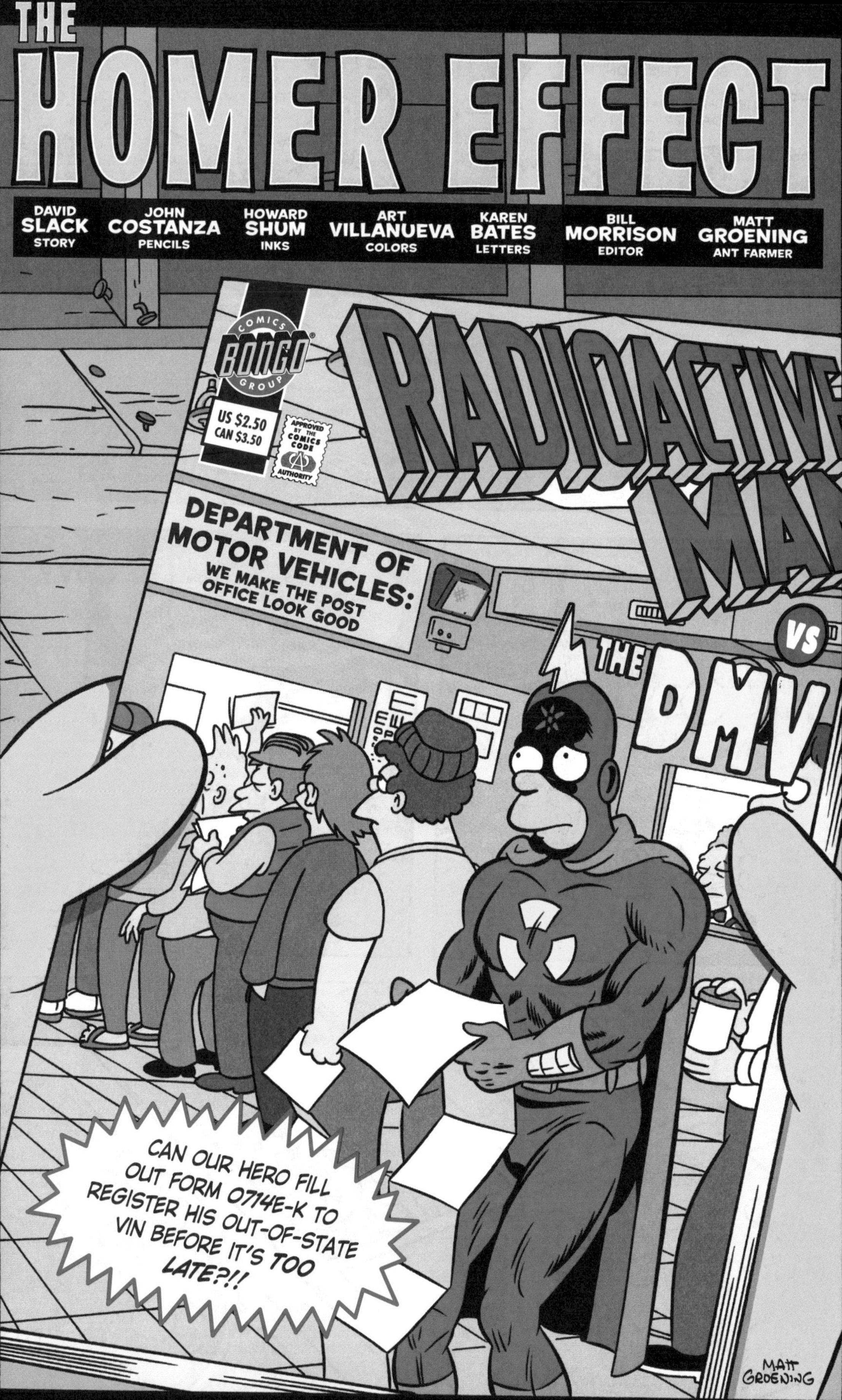
THE HOMER EFFECT
DAVID SLACK STORY
JOHN COSTANZA PENCILS
HOWARD SHUM INKS
ART VILLANUEVA COLORS
KAREN BATES LETTERS
BILL MORRISON EDITOR
MATT GROENING ANT FARMER
COMICS BONGO GROUP
US $2.50
CAN $3.50
APPROVED BY THE COMICS CODE AUTHORITY
RADIOACTIVE MA
VS
THE DMV
DEPARTMENT OF MOTOR VEHICLES:
WE MAKE THE POST OFFICE LOOK GOOD
CAN OUR HERO FILL OUT FORM 0714E-K TO REGISTER HIS OUT-OF-STATE VIN BEFORE IT'S TOO LATE?!!
MATT GROENING

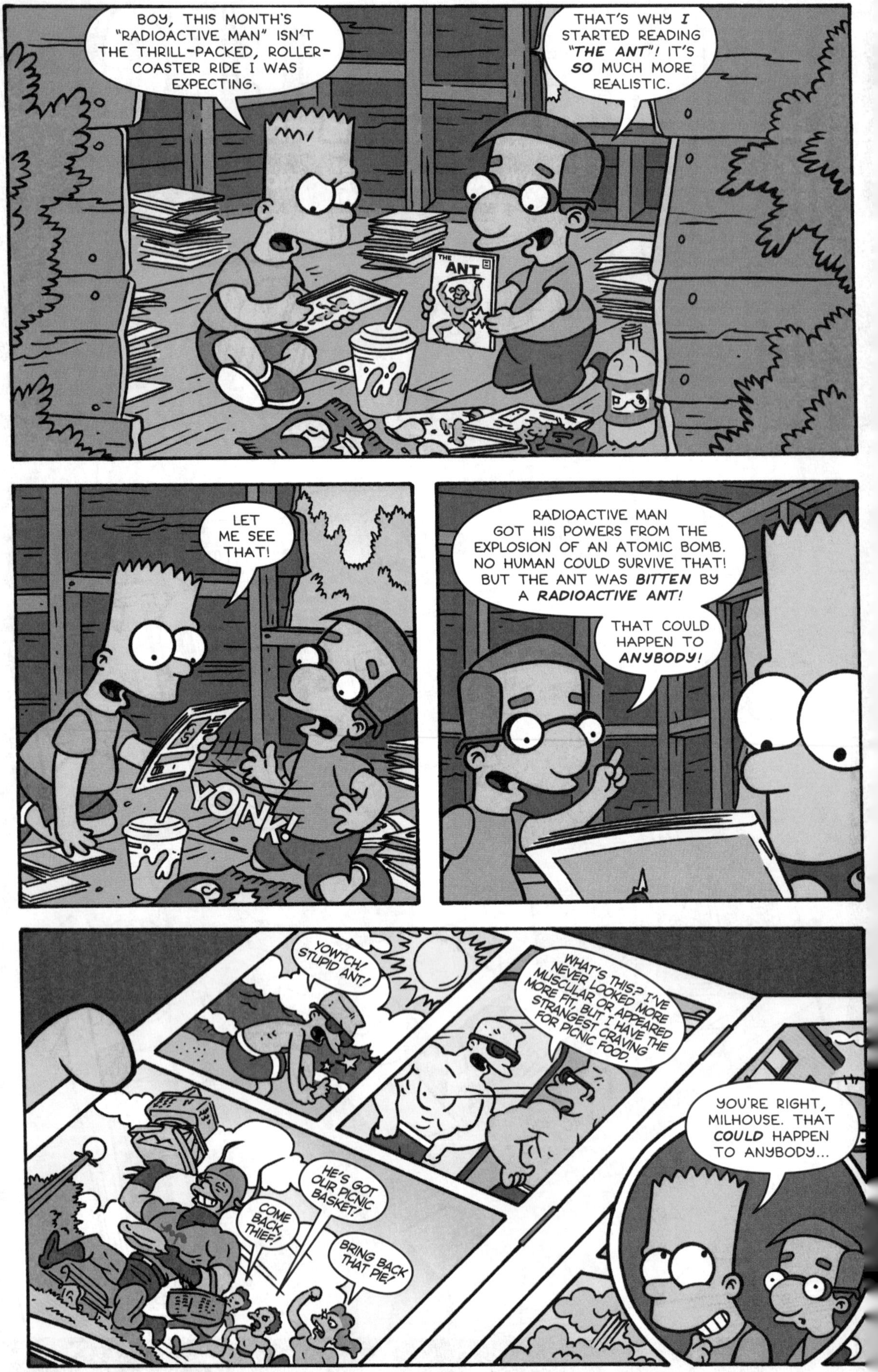
BOY, THIS MONTH'S "RADIOACTIVE MAN" ISN'T THE THRILL-PACKED, ROLLER-COASTER RIDE I WAS EXPECTING.
THAT'S WHY I STARTED READING "THE ANT"! IT'S SO MUCH MORE REALISTIC.
THE ANT
LET ME SEE THAT!
YOINK!
RADIOACTIVE MAN GOT HIS POWERS FROM THE EXPLOSION OF AN ATOMIC BOMB. NO HUMAN COULD SURVIVE THAT! BUT THE ANT WAS BITTEN BY A RADIOACTIVE ANT!
THAT COULD HAPPEN TO ANYBODY!
YOWTCH! STUPID ANT!
WHAT'S THIS? I'VE NEVER LOOKED MORE MUSCULAR OR APPEARED MORE FIT, BUT I HAVE THE STRANGEST CRAVING FOR PICNIC FOOD.
HE'S GOT OUR PICNIC BASKET!
COME BACK, THIEF!
BRING BACK THAT PIE!
YOU'RE RIGHT, MILHOUSE. THAT COULD HAPPEN TO ANYBODY...

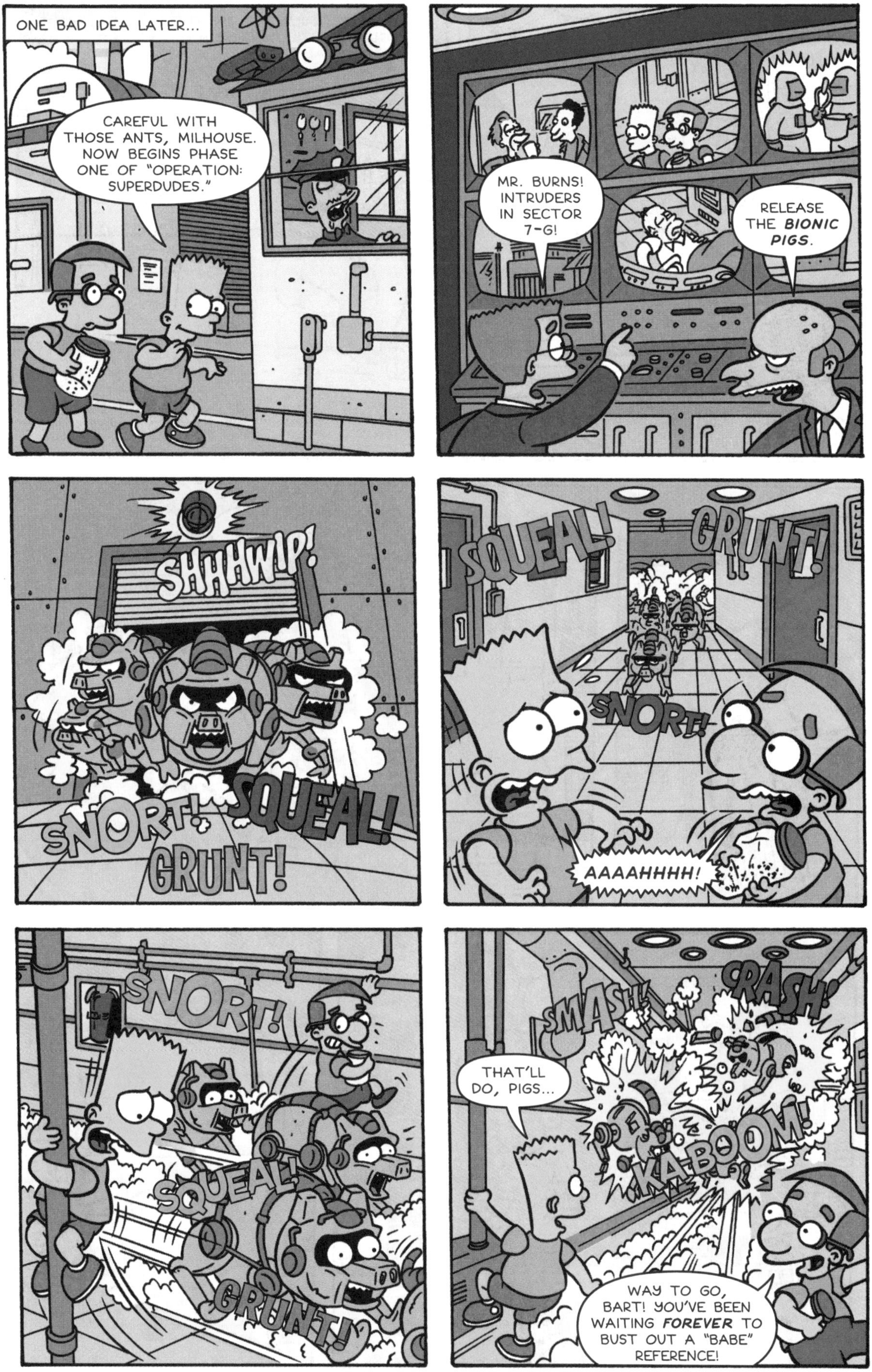
ONE BAD IDEA LATER...
CAREFUL WITH THOSE ANTS, MILHOUSE. NOW BEGINS PHASE ONE OF "OPERATION: SUPERDUDES."
MR. BURNS! INTRUDERS IN SECTOR 7-G!
RELEASE THE *BIONIC PIGS*.
SHHHWIP!
SNORT!
SQUEAL!
GRUNT!
SQUEAL!
GRUNT!
SNORT!
AAAAHHHH!
SNORT!
SQUEAL!
GRUNT!
SMASH!
CRASH!
THAT'LL DO, PIGS...
KA-BOOM!
WAY TO GO, BART! YOU'VE BEEN WAITING *FOREVER* TO BUST OUT A "BABE" REFERENCE!

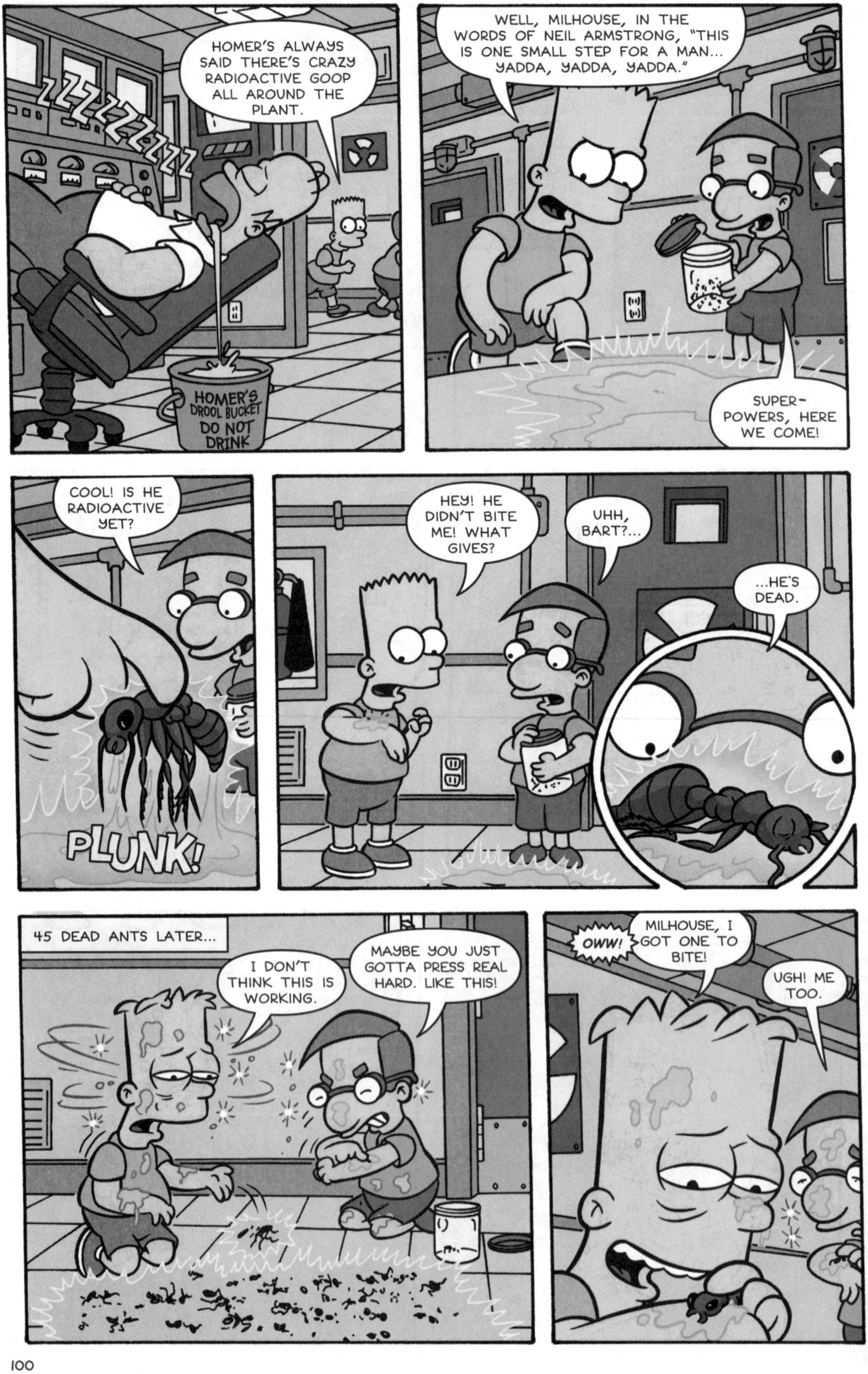
HOMER'S ALWAYS SAID THERE'S CRAZY RADIOACTIVE GOOP ALL AROUND THE PLANT.
ZZZZZZZZZZ
HOMER'S DROOL BUCKET DO NOT DRINK
WELL, MILHOUSE, IN THE WORDS OF NEIL ARMSTRONG, "THIS IS ONE SMALL STEP FOR A MAN... YADDA, YADDA, YADDA."
SUPER-POWERS, HERE WE COME!
COOL! IS HE RADIOACTIVE YET?
PLUNK!
HEY! HE DIDN'T BITE ME! WHAT GIVES?
UHH, BART?...
...HE'S DEAD.
45 DEAD ANTS LATER...
I DON'T THINK THIS IS WORKING.
MAYBE YOU JUST GOTTA PRESS REAL HARD. LIKE THIS!
OWW!
MILHOUSE, I GOT ONE TO BITE!
UGH! ME TOO.

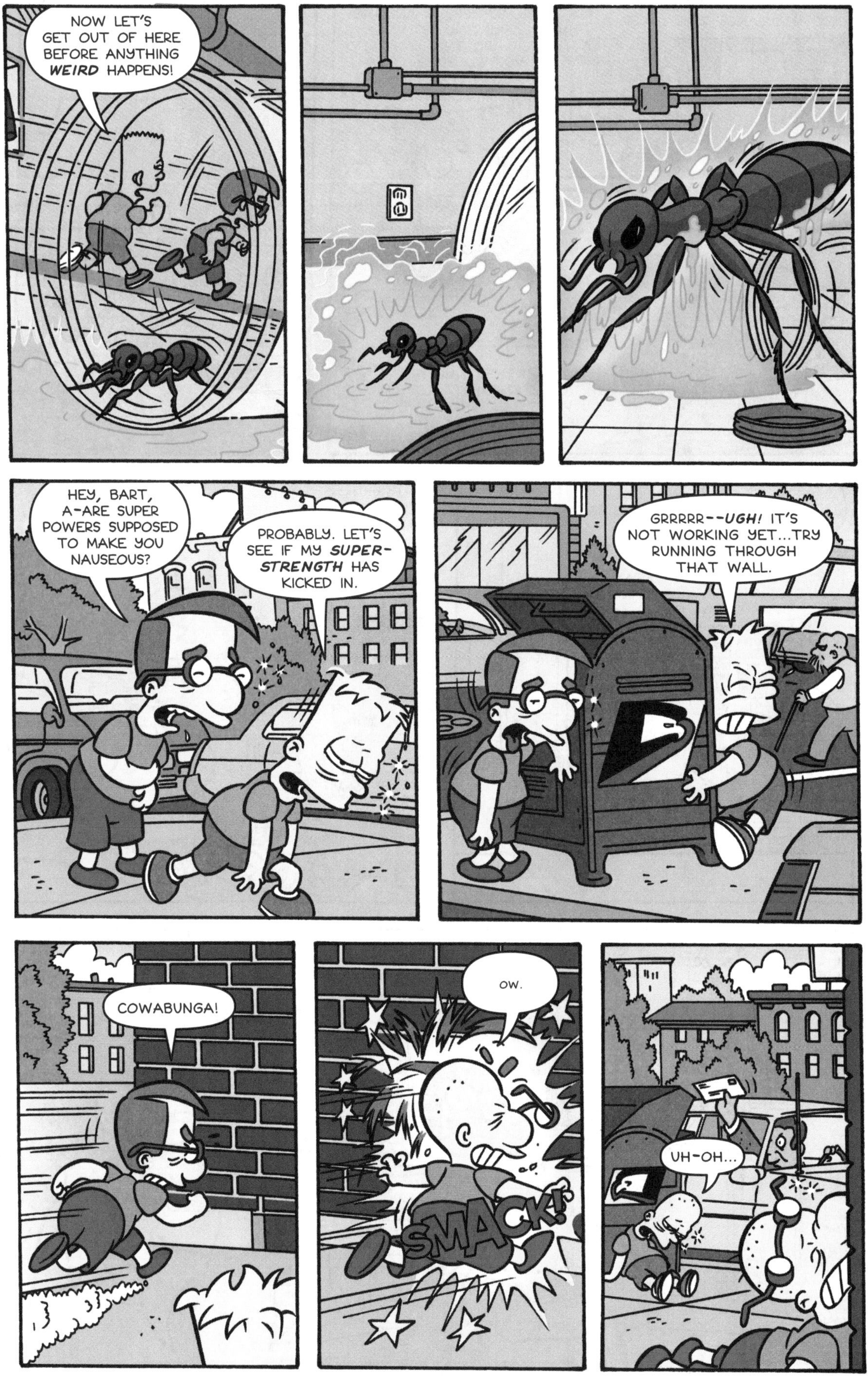
NOW LET'S GET OUT OF HERE BEFORE ANYTHING WEIRD HAPPENS!
HEY, BART, A-ARE SUPER POWERS SUPPOSED TO MAKE YOU NAUSEOUS?
PROBABLY. LET'S SEE IF MY SUPER-STRENGTH HAS KICKED IN.
GRRRRR--UGH! IT'S NOT WORKING YET...TRY RUNNING THROUGH THAT WALL.
COWABUNGA!
OW.
SMACK!
UH-OH...

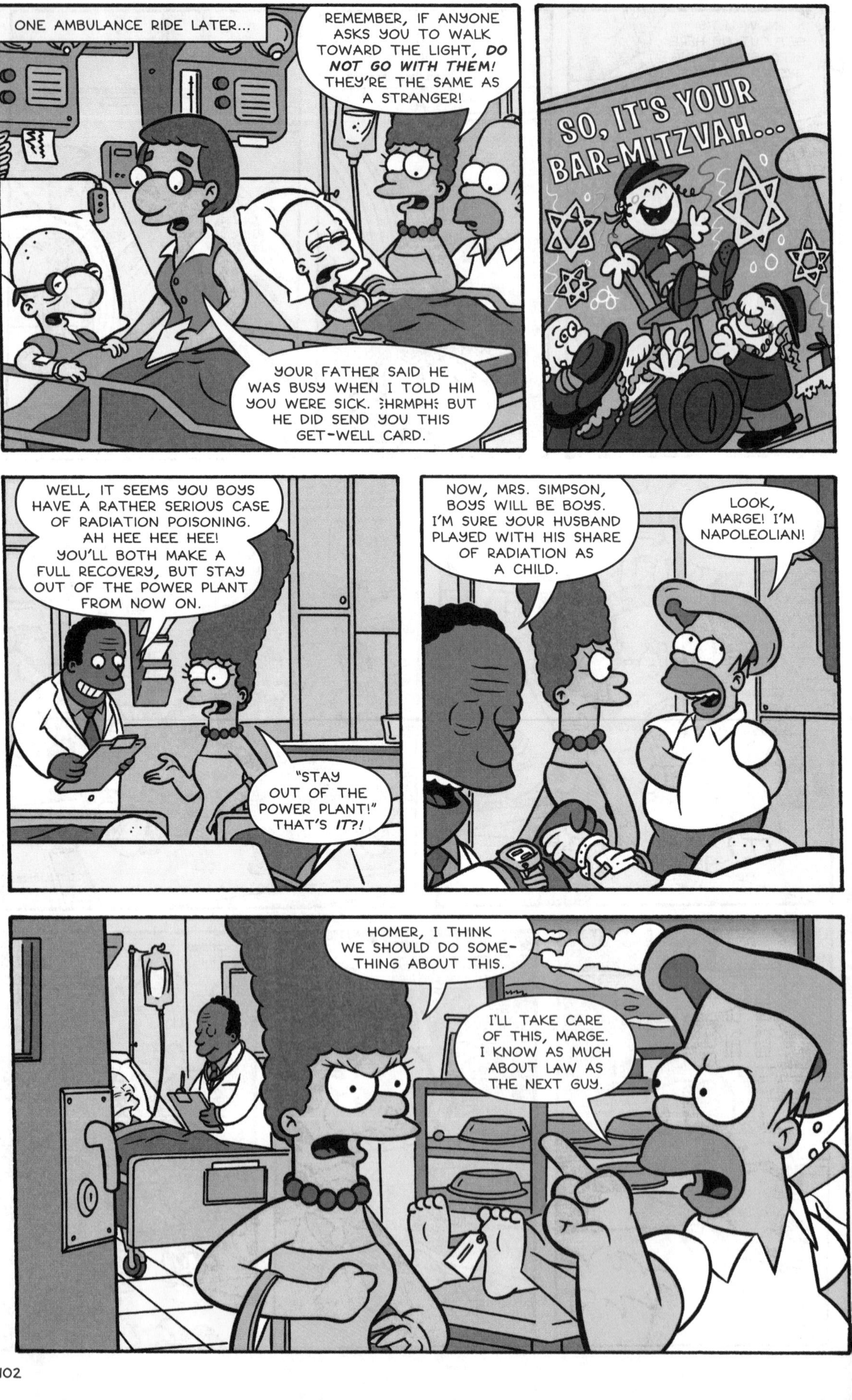
ONE AMBULANCE RIDE LATER...
REMEMBER, IF ANYONE ASKS YOU TO WALK TOWARD THE LIGHT, ***DO NOT GO WITH THEM!*** THEY'RE THE SAME AS A STRANGER!
YOUR FATHER SAID HE WAS BUSY WHEN I TOLD HIM YOU WERE SICK. ƐHRMPHƎ BUT HE DID SEND YOU THIS GET-WELL CARD.
SO, IT'S YOUR BAR-MITZVAH...
WELL, IT SEEMS YOU BOYS HAVE A RATHER SERIOUS CASE OF RADIATION POISONING. AH HEE HEE HEE! YOU'LL BOTH MAKE A FULL RECOVERY, BUT STAY OUT OF THE POWER PLANT FROM NOW ON.
"STAY OUT OF THE POWER PLANT!" THAT'S *IT?!*
NOW, MRS. SIMPSON, BOYS WILL BE BOYS. I'M SURE YOUR HUSBAND PLAYED WITH HIS SHARE OF RADIATION AS A CHILD.
LOOK, MARGE! I'M NAPOLEOLIAN!
HOMER, I THINK WE SHOULD DO SOME-THING ABOUT THIS.
I'LL TAKE CARE OF THIS, MARGE. I KNOW AS MUCH ABOUT LAW AS THE NEXT GUY.

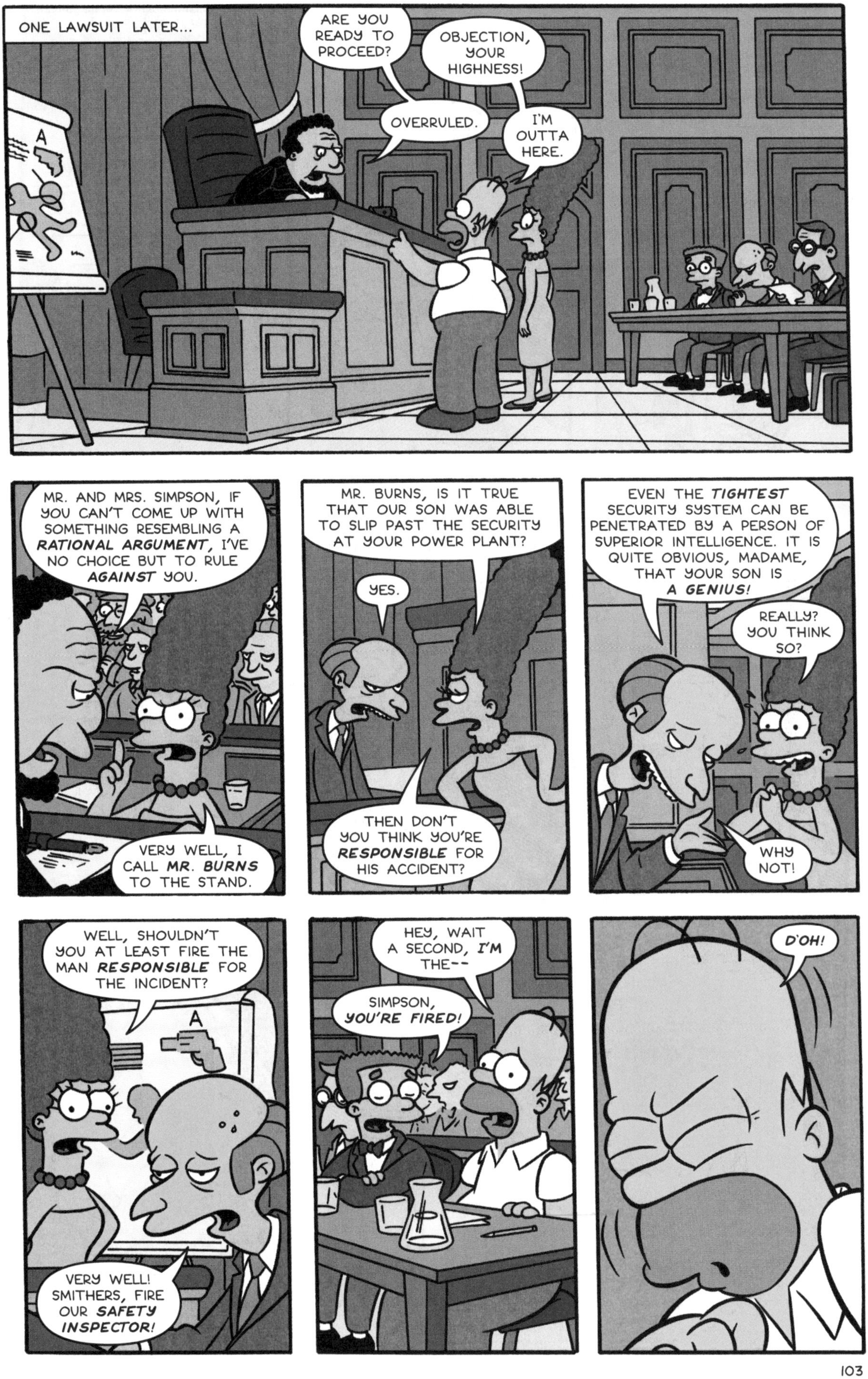
ONE LAWSUIT LATER...
ARE YOU READY TO PROCEED?
OBJECTION, YOUR HIGHNESS!
OVERRULED.
I'M OUTTA HERE.
MR. AND MRS. SIMPSON, IF YOU CAN'T COME UP WITH SOMETHING RESEMBLING A RATIONAL ARGUMENT, I'VE NO CHOICE BUT TO RULE AGAINST YOU.
VERY WELL, I CALL MR. BURNS TO THE STAND.
MR. BURNS, IS IT TRUE THAT OUR SON WAS ABLE TO SLIP PAST THE SECURITY AT YOUR POWER PLANT?
YES.
THEN DON'T YOU THINK YOU'RE RESPONSIBLE FOR HIS ACCIDENT?
EVEN THE TIGHTEST SECURITY SYSTEM CAN BE PENETRATED BY A PERSON OF SUPERIOR INTELLIGENCE. IT IS QUITE OBVIOUS, MADAME, THAT YOUR SON IS A GENIUS!
REALLY? YOU THINK SO?
WHY NOT!
WELL, SHOULDN'T YOU AT LEAST FIRE THE MAN RESPONSIBLE FOR THE INCIDENT?
VERY WELL! SMITHERS, FIRE OUR SAFETY INSPECTOR!
HEY, WAIT A SECOND, I'M THE--
SIMPSON, YOU'RE FIRED!
D'OH!

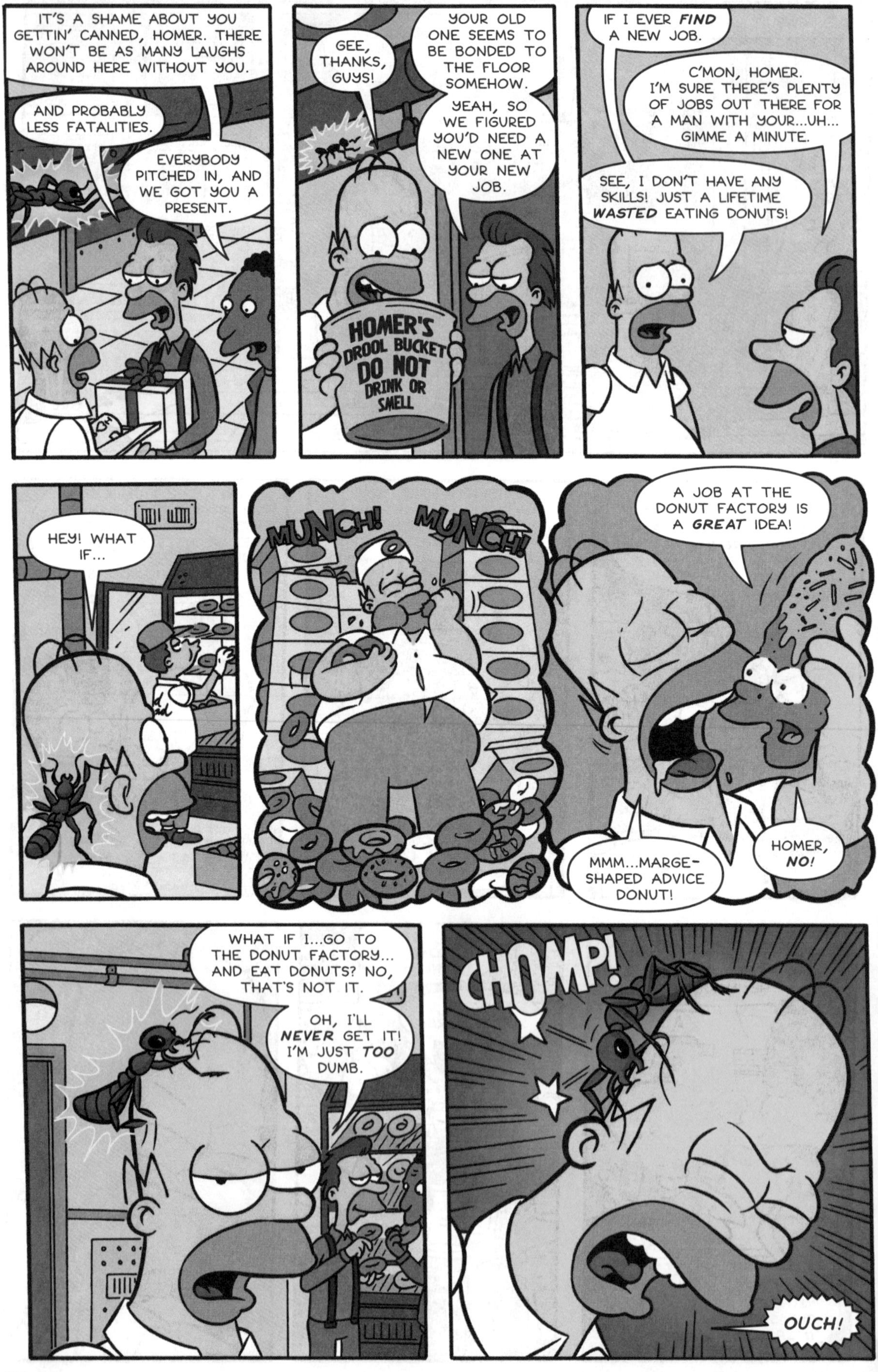
IT'S A SHAME ABOUT YOU GETTIN' CANNED, HOMER. THERE WON'T BE AS MANY LAUGHS AROUND HERE WITHOUT YOU.
AND PROBABLY LESS FATALITIES.
EVERYBODY PITCHED IN, AND WE GOT YOU A PRESENT.
GEE, THANKS, GUYS!
YOUR OLD ONE SEEMS TO BE BONDED TO THE FLOOR SOMEHOW.
YEAH, SO WE FIGURED YOU'D NEED A NEW ONE AT YOUR NEW JOB.
HOMER'S DROOL BUCKET DO NOT DRINK OR SMELL
IF I EVER FIND A NEW JOB.
C'MON, HOMER. I'M SURE THERE'S PLENTY OF JOBS OUT THERE FOR A MAN WITH YOUR...UH... GIMME A MINUTE.
SEE, I DON'T HAVE ANY SKILLS! JUST A LIFETIME WASTED EATING DONUTS!
HEY! WHAT IF...
MUNCH! MUNCH!
A JOB AT THE DONUT FACTORY IS A GREAT IDEA!
MMM...MARGE-SHAPED ADVICE DONUT!
HOMER, NO!
WHAT IF I...GO TO THE DONUT FACTORY... AND EAT DONUTS? NO, THAT'S NOT IT.
OH, I'LL NEVER GET IT! I'M JUST TOO DUMB.
CHOMP!
OUCH!

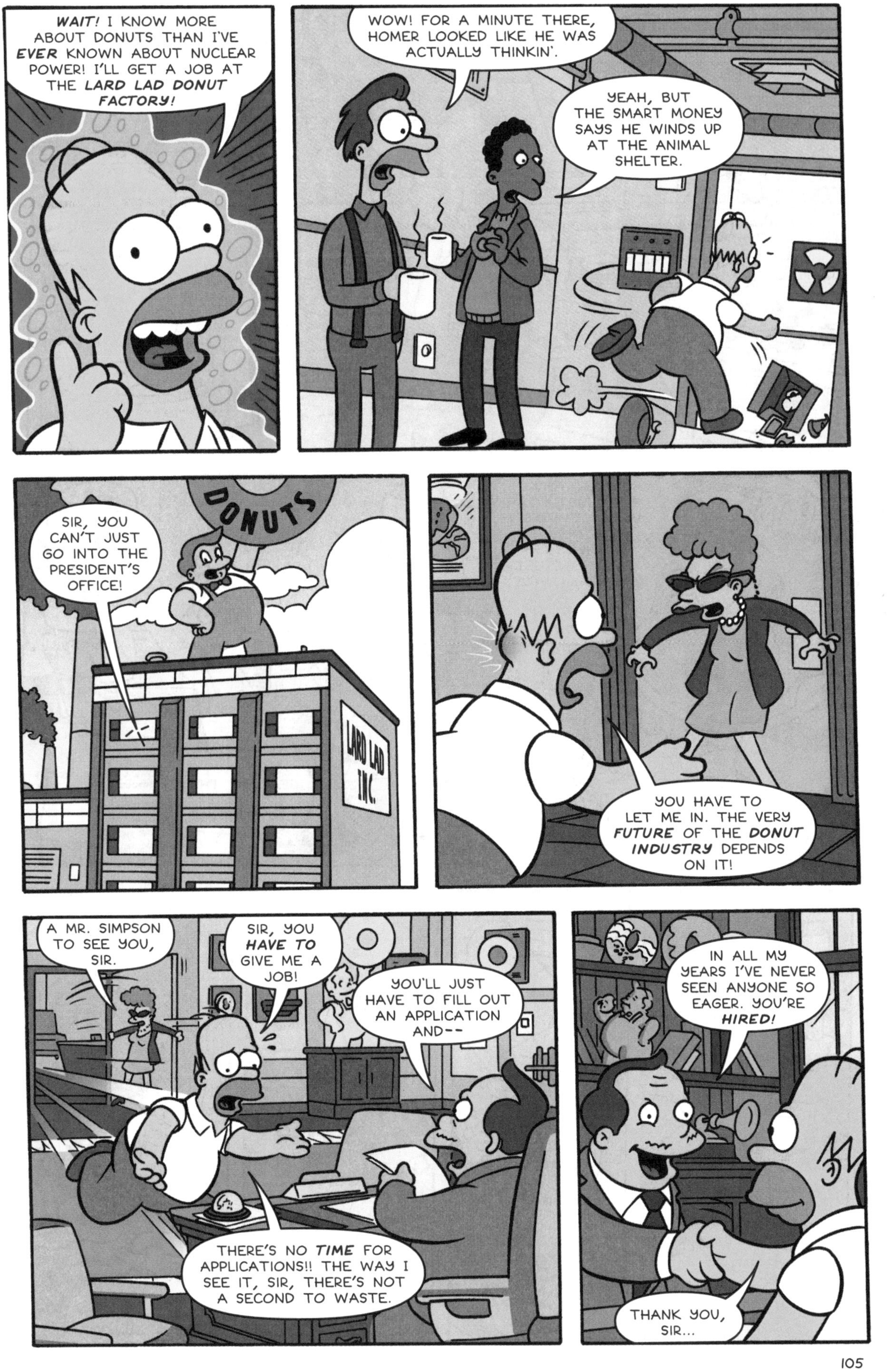
WAIT! I KNOW MORE ABOUT DONUTS THAN I'VE EVER KNOWN ABOUT NUCLEAR POWER! I'LL GET A JOB AT THE LARD LAD DONUT FACTORY!
WOW! FOR A MINUTE THERE, HOMER LOOKED LIKE HE WAS ACTUALLY THINKIN'.
YEAH, BUT THE SMART MONEY SAYS HE WINDS UP AT THE ANIMAL SHELTER.
DONUTS
SIR, YOU CAN'T JUST GO INTO THE PRESIDENT'S OFFICE!
LARD LAD INC.
YOU HAVE TO LET ME IN. THE VERY FUTURE OF THE DONUT INDUSTRY DEPENDS ON IT!
A MR. SIMPSON TO SEE YOU, SIR.
SIR, YOU HAVE TO GIVE ME A JOB!
YOU'LL JUST HAVE TO FILL OUT AN APPLICATION AND--
THERE'S NO TIME FOR APPLICATIONS!! THE WAY I SEE IT, SIR, THERE'S NOT A SECOND TO WASTE.
IN ALL MY YEARS I'VE NEVER SEEN ANYONE SO EAGER. YOU'RE HIRED!
THANK YOU, SIR...

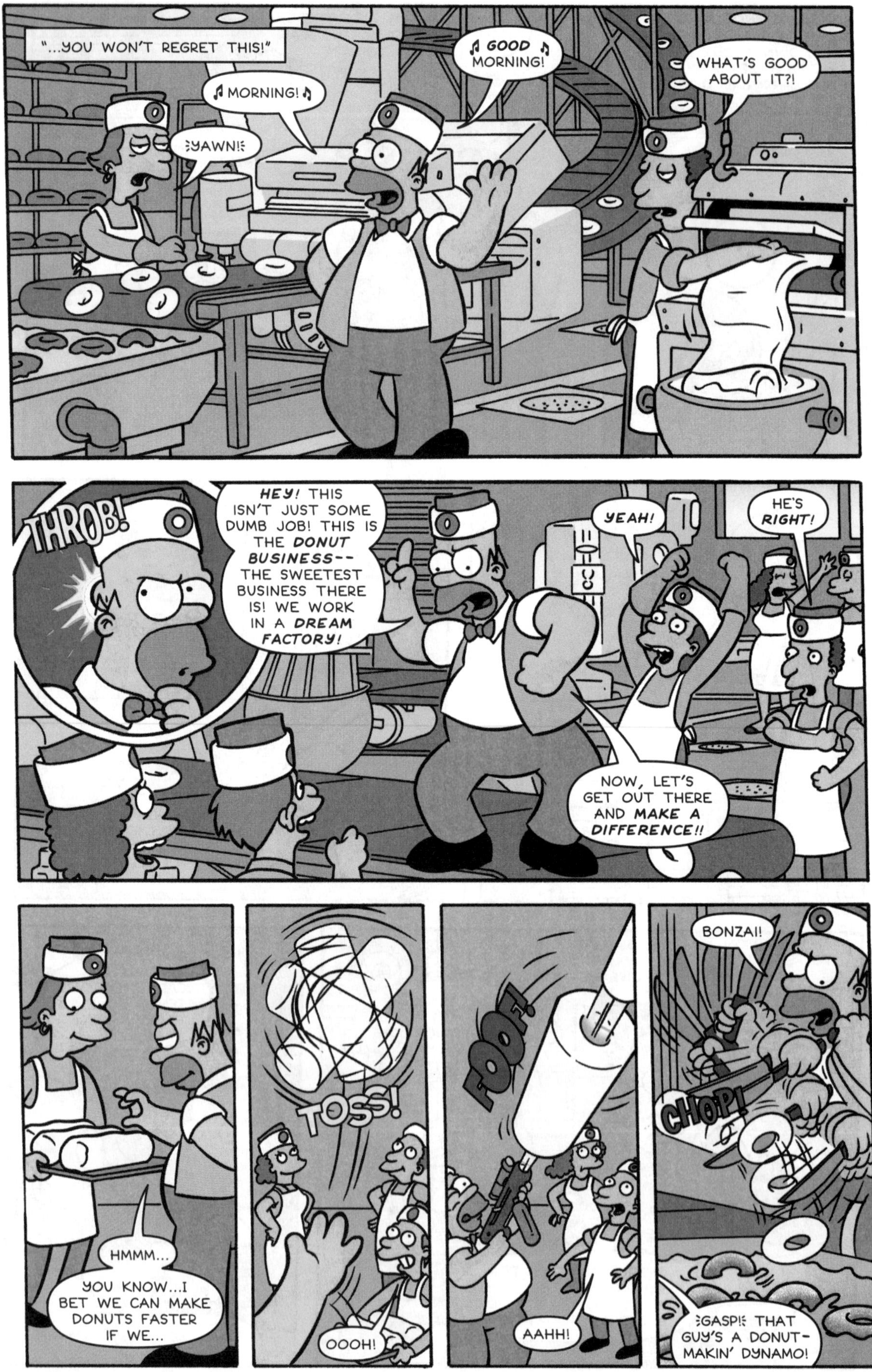
"...YOU WON'T REGRET THIS!"
♫ MORNING! ♫
ƎYAWN!Ǝ
♫ GOOD ♫ MORNING!
WHAT'S GOOD ABOUT IT?!
THROB!
HEY! THIS ISN'T JUST SOME DUMB JOB! THIS IS THE DONUT BUSINESS-- THE SWEETEST BUSINESS THERE IS! WE WORK IN A DREAM FACTORY!
YEAH!
HE'S RIGHT!
NOW, LET'S GET OUT THERE AND MAKE A DIFFERENCE!!
HMMM...
YOU KNOW...I BET WE CAN MAKE DONUTS FASTER IF WE...
TOSS!
OOOH!
FOOF!
AAHH!
BONZAI!
CHOP!
ƎGASP!Ǝ THAT GUY'S A DONUT-MAKIN' DYNAMO!

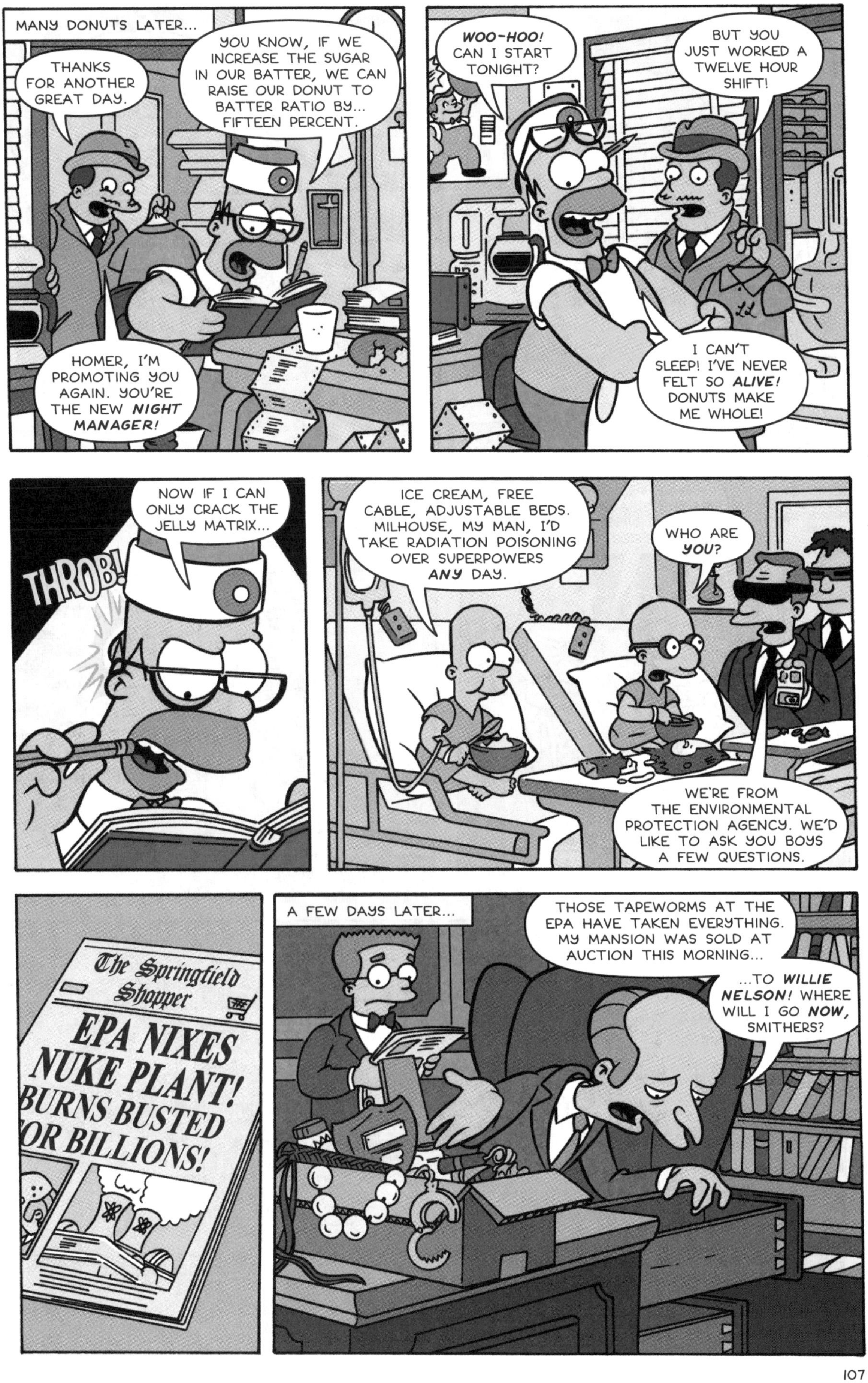
MANY DONUTS LATER...
THANKS FOR ANOTHER GREAT DAY.
YOU KNOW, IF WE INCREASE THE SUGAR IN OUR BATTER, WE CAN RAISE OUR DONUT TO BATTER RATIO BY... FIFTEEN PERCENT.
HOMER, I'M PROMOTING YOU AGAIN. YOU'RE THE NEW NIGHT MANAGER!
WOO-HOO! CAN I START TONIGHT?
BUT YOU JUST WORKED A TWELVE HOUR SHIFT!
I CAN'T SLEEP! I'VE NEVER FELT SO ALIVE! DONUTS MAKE ME WHOLE!
NOW IF I CAN ONLY CRACK THE JELLY MATRIX...
THROB!
ICE CREAM, FREE CABLE, ADJUSTABLE BEDS. MILHOUSE, MY MAN, I'D TAKE RADIATION POISONING OVER SUPERPOWERS ANY DAY.
WHO ARE YOU?
WE'RE FROM THE ENVIRONMENTAL PROTECTION AGENCY. WE'D LIKE TO ASK YOU BOYS A FEW QUESTIONS.
The Springfield Shopper
EPA NIXES NUKE PLANT!
BURNS BUSTED
OR BILLIONS!
A FEW DAYS LATER...
THOSE TAPEWORMS AT THE EPA HAVE TAKEN EVERYTHING. MY MANSION WAS SOLD AT AUCTION THIS MORNING...
...TO WILLIE NELSON! WHERE WILL I GO NOW, SMITHERS?

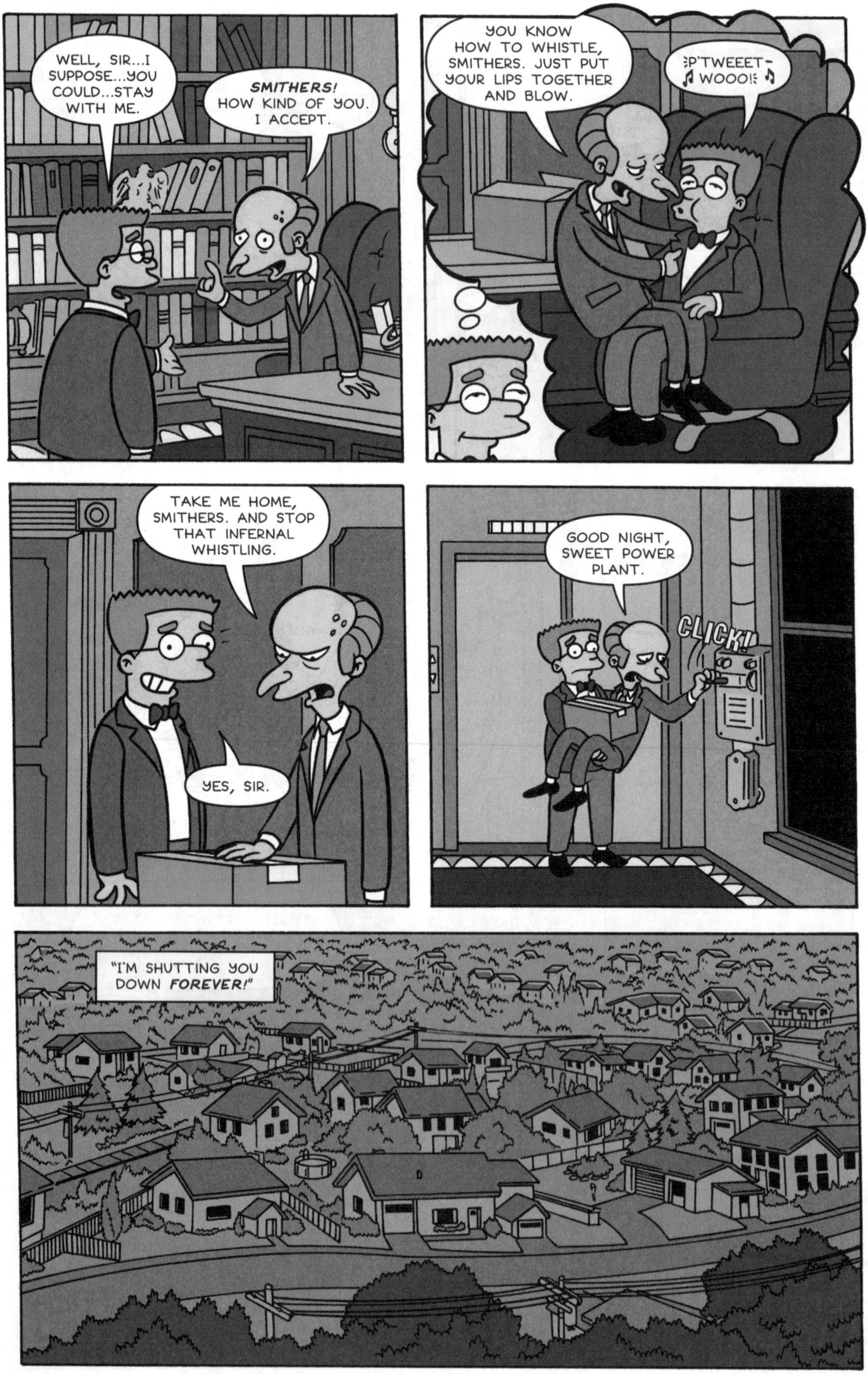
WELL, SIR...I SUPPOSE...YOU COULD...STAY WITH ME.
**SMITHERS!** HOW KIND OF YOU. I ACCEPT.
YOU KNOW HOW TO WHISTLE, SMITHERS. JUST PUT YOUR LIPS TOGETHER AND BLOW.
P'TWEEET- WOOO!
TAKE ME HOME, SMITHERS. AND STOP THAT INFERNAL WHISTLING.
YES, SIR.
GOOD NIGHT, SWEET POWER PLANT.
CLICK!
"I'M SHUTTING YOU DOWN ***FOREVER!***"

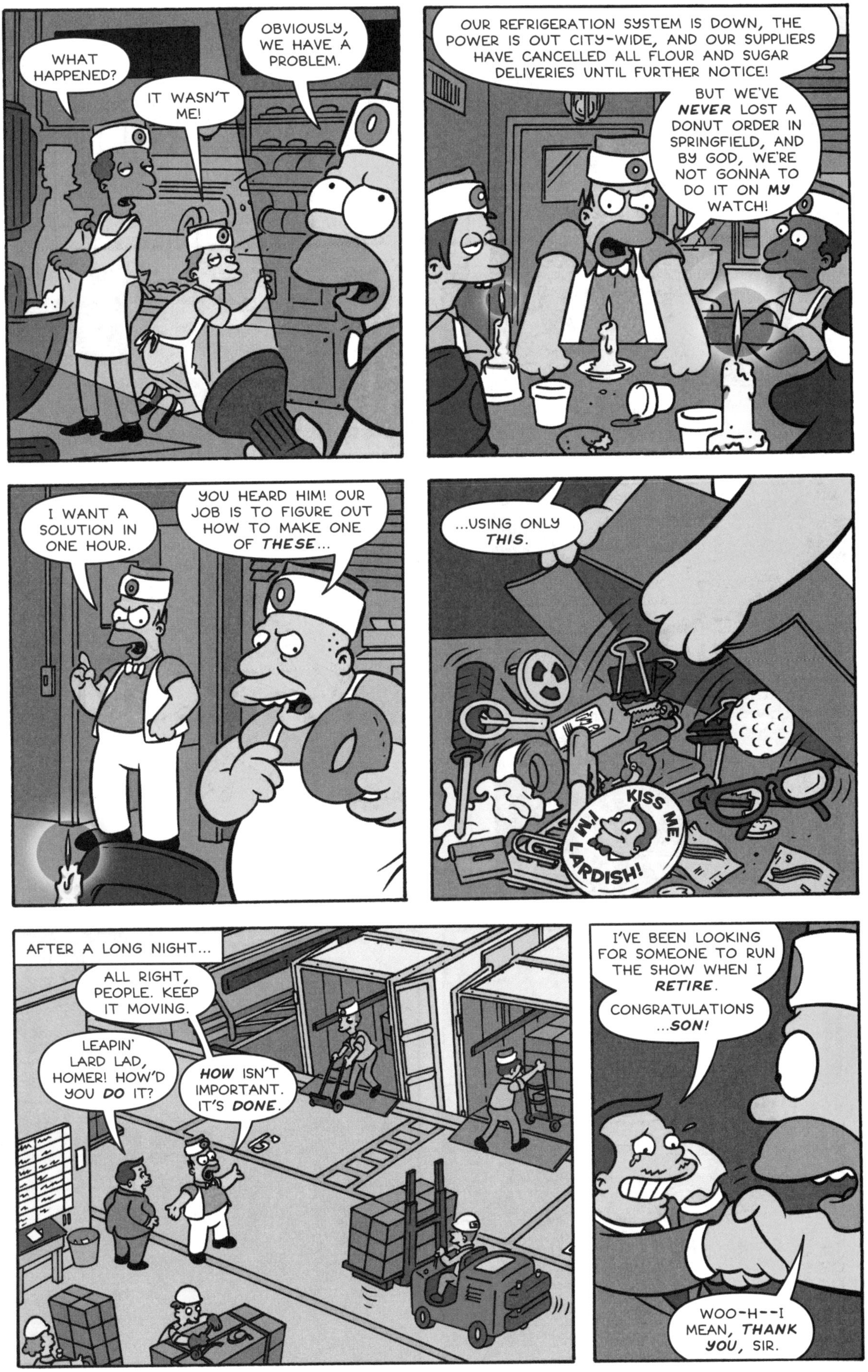
WHAT HAPPENED?
IT WASN'T ME!
OBVIOUSLY, WE HAVE A PROBLEM.
OUR REFRIGERATION SYSTEM IS DOWN, THE POWER IS OUT CITY-WIDE, AND OUR SUPPLIERS HAVE CANCELLED ALL FLOUR AND SUGAR DELIVERIES UNTIL FURTHER NOTICE!
BUT WE'VE NEVER LOST A DONUT ORDER IN SPRINGFIELD, AND BY GOD, WE'RE NOT GONNA TO DO IT ON MY WATCH!
I WANT A SOLUTION IN ONE HOUR.
YOU HEARD HIM! OUR JOB IS TO FIGURE OUT HOW TO MAKE ONE OF THESE...
...USING ONLY THIS.
KISS ME, I'M LARDISH!
AFTER A LONG NIGHT...
ALL RIGHT, PEOPLE. KEEP IT MOVING.
LEAPIN' LARD LAD, HOMER! HOW'D YOU DO IT?
HOW ISN'T IMPORTANT. IT'S DONE.
I'VE BEEN LOOKING FOR SOMEONE TO RUN THE SHOW WHEN I RETIRE.
CONGRATULATIONS ...SON!
WOO-H--I MEAN, THANK YOU, SIR.

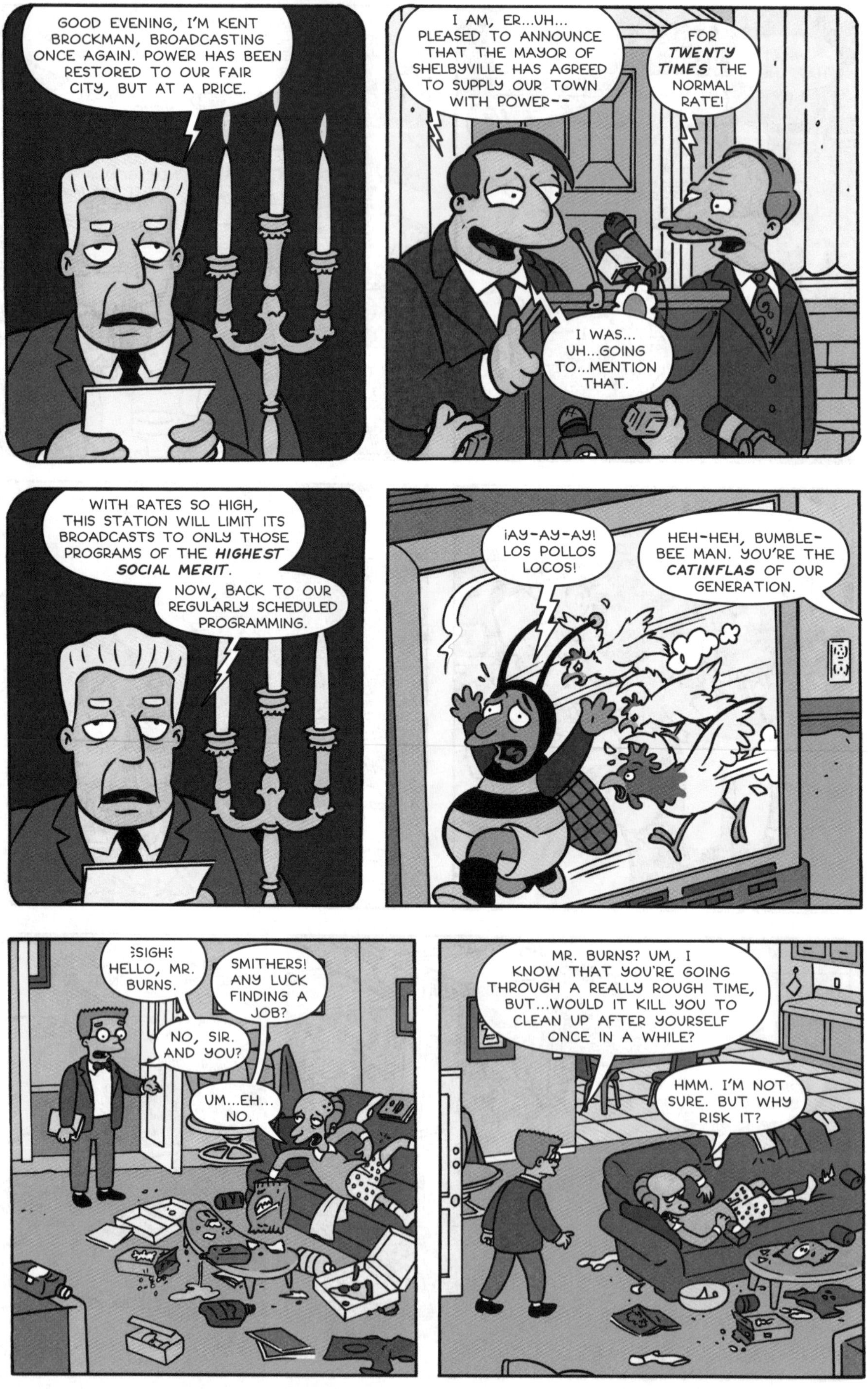

GOOD EVENING, I'M KENT BROCKMAN, BROADCASTING ONCE AGAIN. POWER HAS BEEN RESTORED TO OUR FAIR CITY, BUT AT A PRICE.
I AM, ER...UH... PLEASED TO ANNOUNCE THAT THE MAYOR OF SHELBYVILLE HAS AGREED TO SUPPLY OUR TOWN WITH POWER--
FOR TWENTY TIMES THE NORMAL RATE!
I WAS... UH...GOING TO...MENTION THAT.
WITH RATES SO HIGH, THIS STATION WILL LIMIT ITS BROADCASTS TO ONLY THOSE PROGRAMS OF THE HIGHEST SOCIAL MERIT.
NOW, BACK TO OUR REGULARLY SCHEDULED PROGRAMMING.
¡AY-AY-AY! LOS POLLOS LOCOS!
HEH-HEH, BUMBLE-BEE MAN. YOU'RE THE CATINFLAS OF OUR GENERATION.
:SIGH: HELLO, MR. BURNS.
SMITHERS! ANY LUCK FINDING A JOB?
NO, SIR. AND YOU?
UM...EH... NO.
MR. BURNS? UM, I KNOW THAT YOU'RE GOING THROUGH A REALLY ROUGH TIME, BUT...WOULD IT KILL YOU TO CLEAN UP AFTER YOURSELF ONCE IN A WHILE?
HMM. I'M NOT SURE. BUT WHY RISK IT?

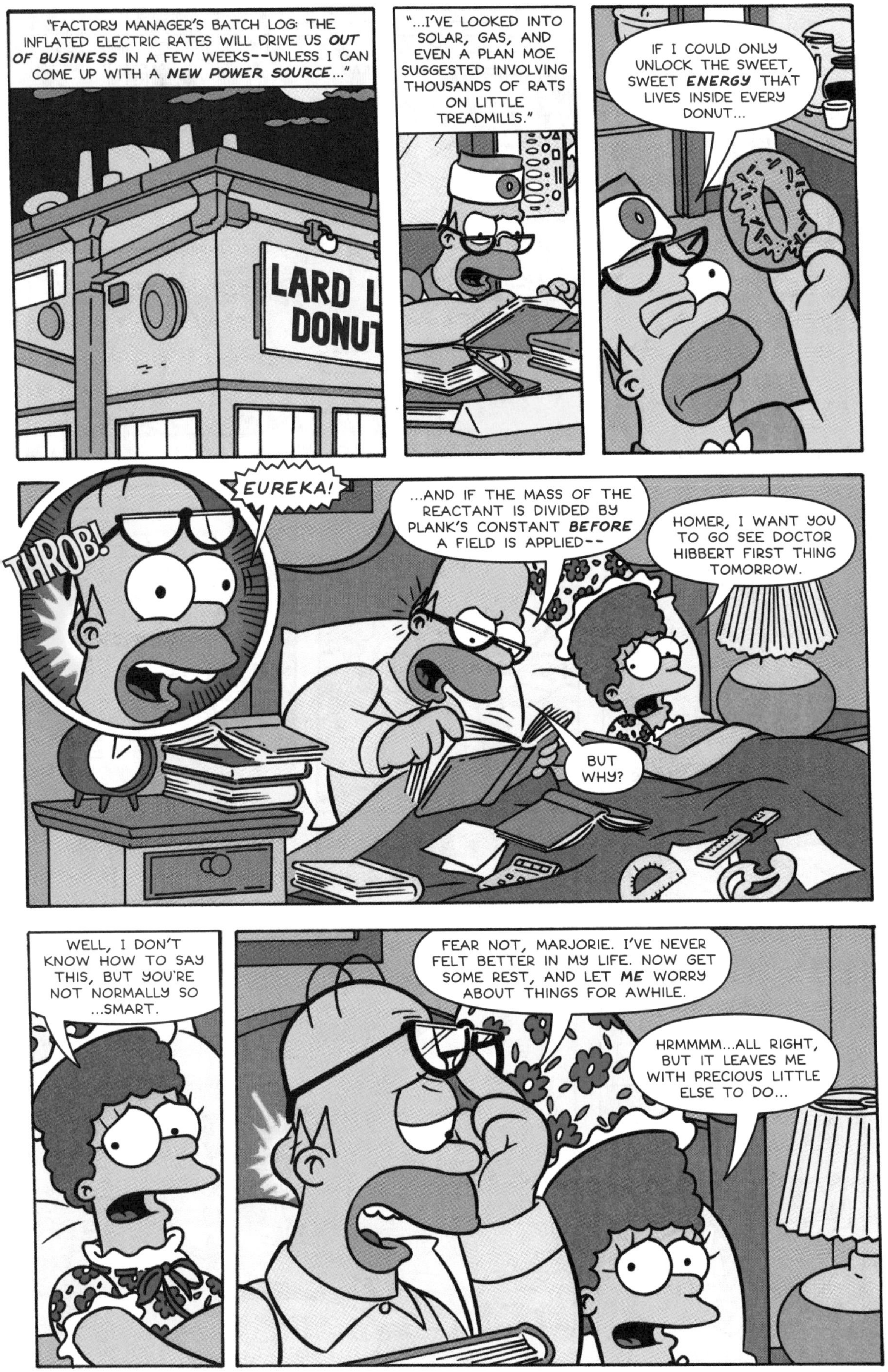

"FACTORY MANAGER'S BATCH LOG: THE INFLATED ELECTRIC RATES WILL DRIVE US OUT OF BUSINESS IN A FEW WEEKS--UNLESS I CAN COME UP WITH A NEW POWER SOURCE..."
LARD L DONUT
"...I'VE LOOKED INTO SOLAR, GAS, AND EVEN A PLAN MOE SUGGESTED INVOLVING THOUSANDS OF RATS ON LITTLE TREADMILLS."
IF I COULD ONLY UNLOCK THE SWEET, SWEET ENERGY THAT LIVES INSIDE EVERY DONUT...
THROB!
EUREKA!
...AND IF THE MASS OF THE REACTANT IS DIVIDED BY PLANK'S CONSTANT BEFORE A FIELD IS APPLIED--
HOMER, I WANT YOU TO GO SEE DOCTOR HIBBERT FIRST THING TOMORROW.
BUT WHY?
WELL, I DON'T KNOW HOW TO SAY THIS, BUT YOU'RE NOT NORMALLY SO ...SMART.
FEAR NOT, MARJORIE. I'VE NEVER FELT BETTER IN MY LIFE. NOW GET SOME REST, AND LET ME WORRY ABOUT THINGS FOR AWHILE.
HRMMMM...ALL RIGHT, BUT IT LEAVES ME WITH PRECIOUS LITTLE ELSE TO DO...

WELL, MR. SIMPSON. OTHER THAN YOUR **WEAK HEART** AND **PERILOUS OBESITY,** YOU'RE FIT AS A FIDDLE! AH HEE HEE HEE!

BUT I FEEL **DIFFERENT.** I CAN LEARN THINGS THAT I NEVER COULD BEFORE, I HAVE BOUNDLESS ENERGY, AND... WATCH THIS.

WHAP!

HMMM...

WELL, I'M SURE THAT'S NORMAL FOR A MAN YOUR AGE.

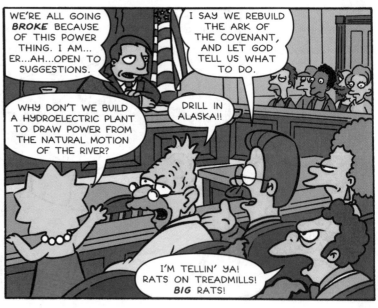

WE'RE ALL GOING **BROKE** BECAUSE OF THIS POWER THING. I AM... ER...AH...OPEN TO SUGGESTIONS.

I SAY WE REBUILD THE ARK OF THE COVENANT, AND LET GOD TELL US WHAT TO DO.

WHY DON'T WE BUILD A HYDROELECTRIC PLANT TO DRAW POWER FROM THE NATURAL MOTION OF THE RIVER?

DRILL IN ALASKA!!

I'M TELLIN' YA! RATS ON TREADMILLS! **BIG** RATS!

HOLD EVERYTHING! I'VE FOUND A WAY TO POWER THE ENTIRE TOWN...

...BY HARNESSING THE POWER OF *DONUTS!*

USING THESE BLUEPRINTS AND THROUGH A *GENEROUS* GRANT GIVEN BY LARD LAD DONUTS, WE CAN *TRANSFORM* THE ABANDONED NUCLEAR PLANT AND *SAVE OUR CITY!*

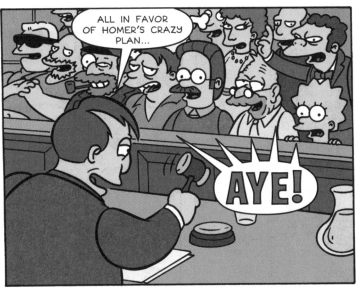

ALL IN FAVOR OF HOMER'S CRAZY PLAN...

AYE!

SMITHERS! WE'RE OUT OF COOKIE-DOUGH!

CAN'T TALK NOW, MONTY. MR. SIMPSON IS EXPECTING ME AT THE POWER PLANT.

POWER PLANT? *SIMPSON*?! WHAT THE DEVIL'S GOING ON? WHERE ARE YOU GOING?

I'VE GOT A *NEW JOB!* HOMER SIMPSON IS LEADING US INTO A NEW ERA IN POWER CONSUMPTION! AND *I'LL* BE THERE BY HIS SIDE, TENDING TO HIS EVERY NEED!

SMITHERS!? COME BACK!

WAIT A MOMENT, THIS MAY BE JUST THE KICK IN THE PROSTATE I'VE NEEDED.

REVENGE IS AN *EXCELLENT* MOTIVATOR.

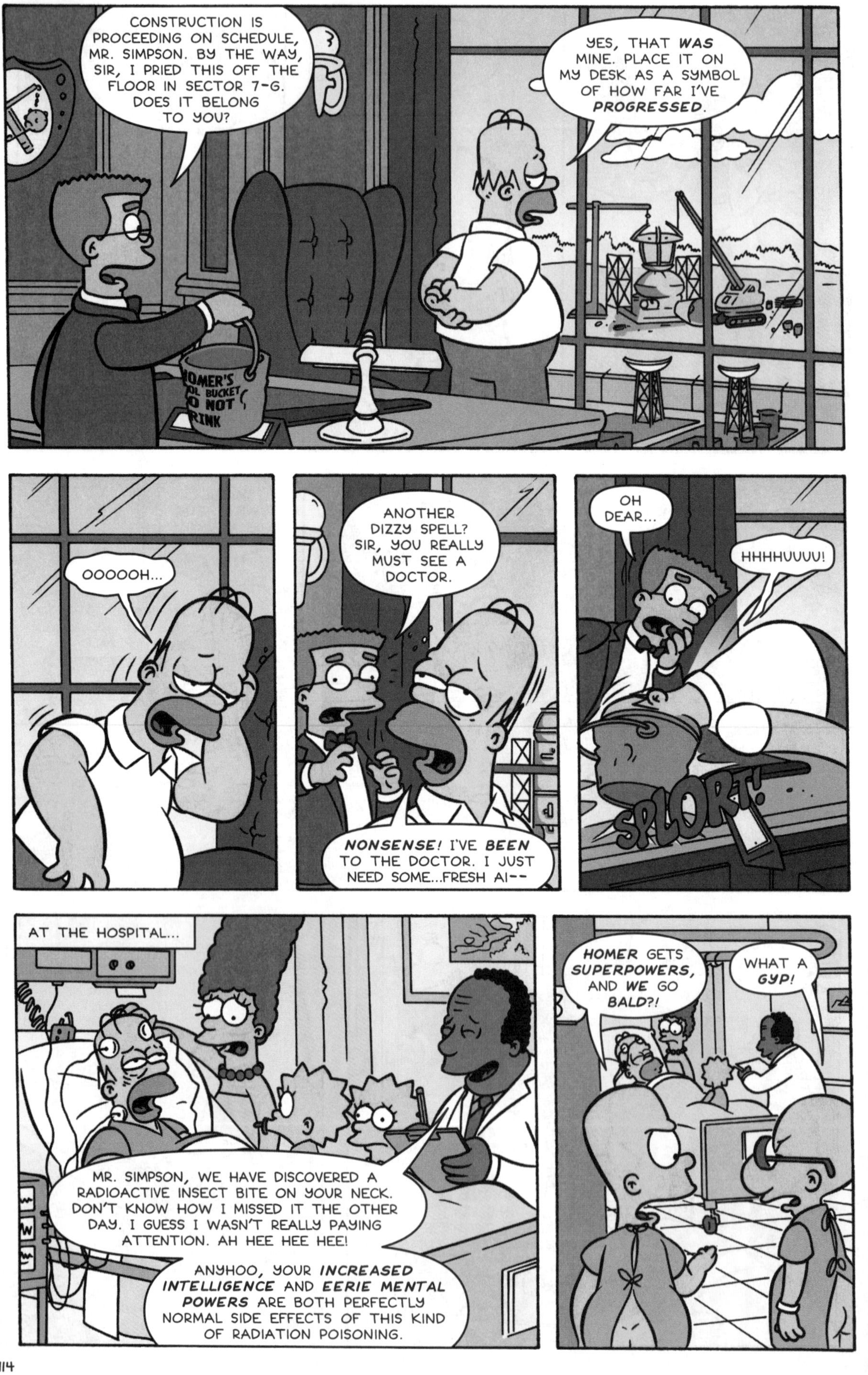

CONSTRUCTION IS PROCEEDING ON SCHEDULE, MR. SIMPSON. BY THE WAY, SIR, I PRIED THIS OFF THE FLOOR IN SECTOR 7-G. DOES IT BELONG TO YOU?
YES, THAT **WAS** MINE. PLACE IT ON MY DESK AS A SYMBOL OF HOW FAR I'VE **PROGRESSED**.
OOOOOH...
ANOTHER DIZZY SPELL? SIR, YOU REALLY MUST SEE A DOCTOR.
**NONSENSE!** I'VE **BEEN** TO THE DOCTOR. I JUST NEED SOME...FRESH AI--
OH DEAR...
HHHHUUUU!
SPLORT!
AT THE HOSPITAL...
MR. SIMPSON, WE HAVE DISCOVERED A RADIOACTIVE INSECT BITE ON YOUR NECK. DON'T KNOW HOW I MISSED IT THE OTHER DAY. I GUESS I WASN'T REALLY PAYING ATTENTION. AH HEE HEE HEE!
ANYHOO, YOUR **INCREASED INTELLIGENCE** AND **EERIE MENTAL POWERS** ARE BOTH PERFECTLY NORMAL SIDE EFFECTS OF THIS KIND OF RADIATION POISONING.
**HOMER** GETS **SUPERPOWERS,** AND **WE** GO **BALD?!**
WHAT A **GYP!**

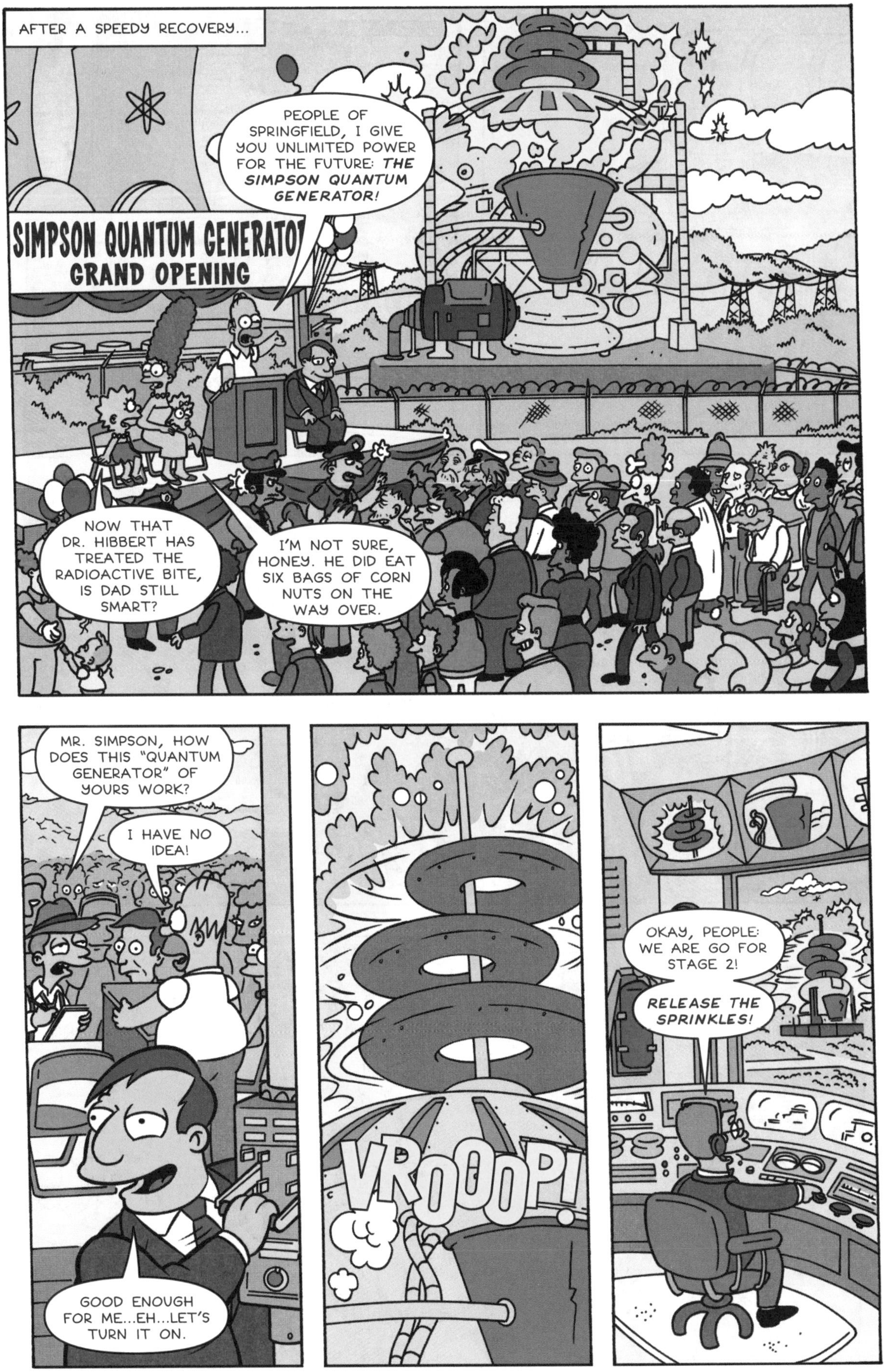
AFTER A SPEEDY RECOVERY...
PEOPLE OF SPRINGFIELD, I GIVE YOU UNLIMITED POWER FOR THE FUTURE: THE SIMPSON QUANTUM GENERATOR!
SIMPSON QUANTUM GENERATO
GRAND OPENING
NOW THAT DR. HIBBERT HAS TREATED THE RADIOACTIVE BITE, IS DAD STILL SMART?
I'M NOT SURE, HONEY. HE DID EAT SIX BAGS OF CORN NUTS ON THE WAY OVER.
MR. SIMPSON, HOW DOES THIS "QUANTUM GENERATOR" OF YOURS WORK?
I HAVE NO IDEA!
GOOD ENOUGH FOR ME...EH...LET'S TURN IT ON.
VROOOP!
OKAY, PEOPLE: WE ARE GO FOR STAGE 2!
RELEASE THE SPRINKLES!

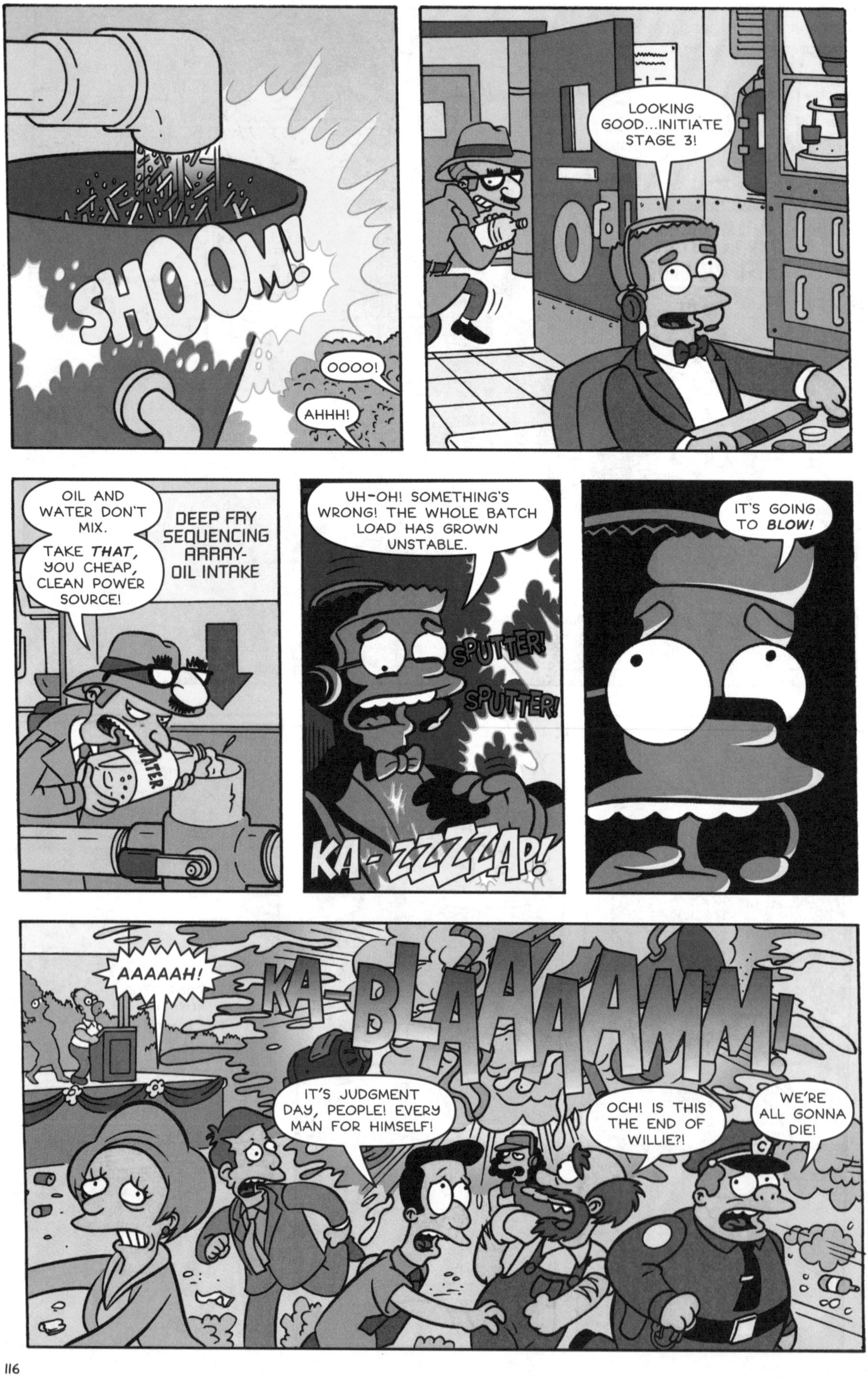
SHOOM!
OOOO!
AHHH!
LOOKING GOOD...INITIATE STAGE 3!
OIL AND WATER DON'T MIX.
TAKE THAT, YOU CHEAP, CLEAN POWER SOURCE!
DEEP FRY SEQUENCING ARRAY- OIL INTAKE
WATER
UH-OH! SOMETHING'S WRONG! THE WHOLE BATCH LOAD HAS GROWN UNSTABLE.
SPUTTER!
SPUTTER!
KA-ZZZZAP!
IT'S GOING TO BLOW!
AAAAAH!
KA-BLAAAAMM!
IT'S JUDGMENT DAY, PEOPLE! EVERY MAN FOR HIMSELF!
OCH! IS THIS THE END OF WILLIE?!
WE'RE ALL GONNA DIE!

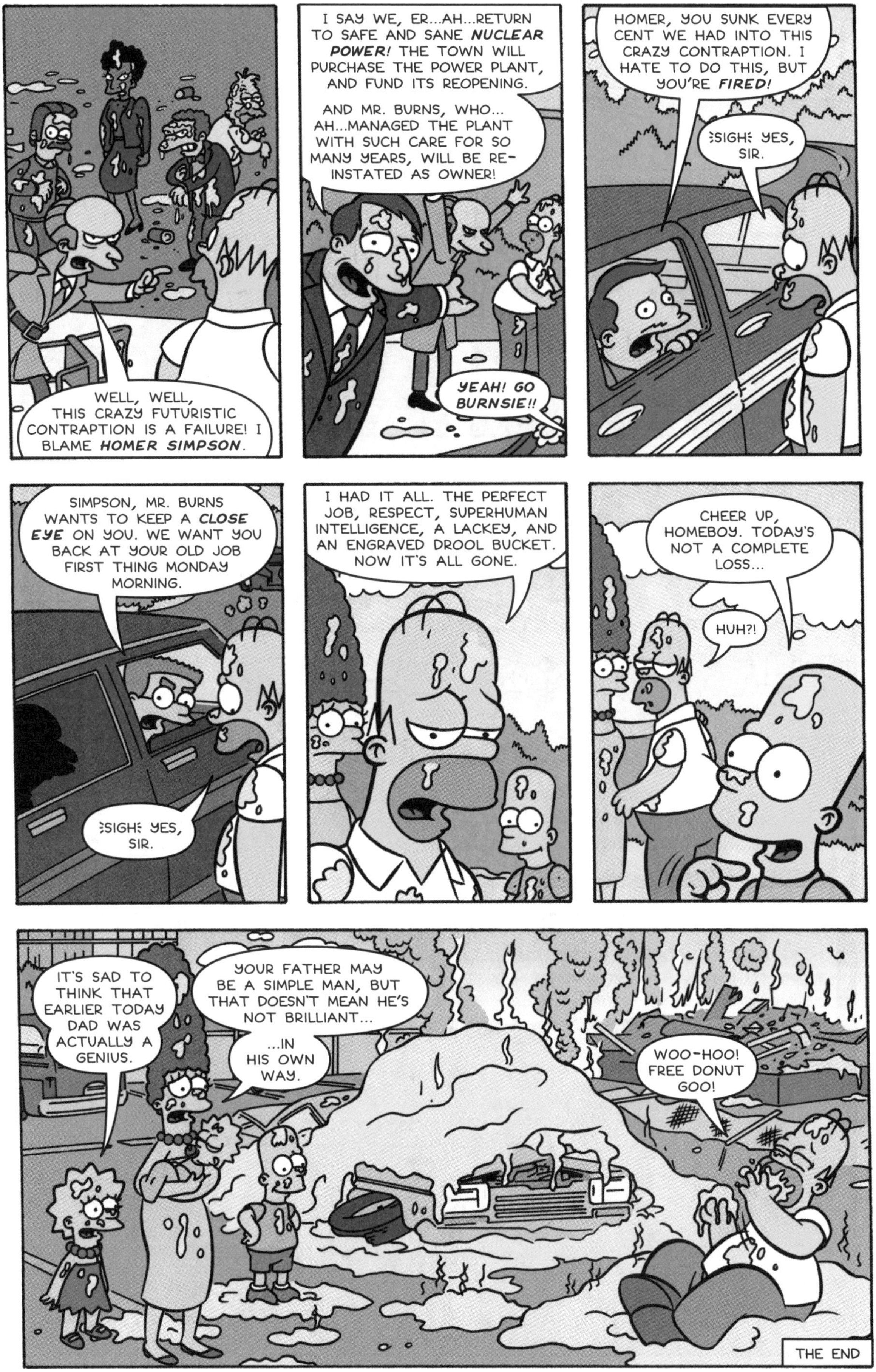
WELL, WELL, THIS CRAZY FUTURISTIC CONTRAPTION IS A FAILURE! I BLAME HOMER SIMPSON.
I SAY WE, ER...AH...RETURN TO SAFE AND SANE NUCLEAR POWER! THE TOWN WILL PURCHASE THE POWER PLANT, AND FUND ITS REOPENING.
AND MR. BURNS, WHO... AH...MANAGED THE PLANT WITH SUCH CARE FOR SO MANY YEARS, WILL BE RE-INSTATED AS OWNER!
YEAH! GO BURNSIE!!
HOMER, YOU SUNK EVERY CENT WE HAD INTO THIS CRAZY CONTRAPTION. I HATE TO DO THIS, BUT YOU'RE FIRED!
:SIGH: YES, SIR.
SIMPSON, MR. BURNS WANTS TO KEEP A CLOSE EYE ON YOU. WE WANT YOU BACK AT YOUR OLD JOB FIRST THING MONDAY MORNING.
:SIGH: YES, SIR.
I HAD IT ALL. THE PERFECT JOB, RESPECT, SUPERHUMAN INTELLIGENCE, A LACKEY, AND AN ENGRAVED DROOL BUCKET. NOW IT'S ALL GONE.
CHEER UP, HOMEBOY. TODAY'S NOT A COMPLETE LOSS...
HUH?!
IT'S SAD TO THINK THAT EARLIER TODAY DAD WAS ACTUALLY A GENIUS.
YOUR FATHER MAY BE A SIMPLE MAN, BUT THAT DOESN'T MEAN HE'S NOT BRILLIANT...
...IN HIS OWN WAY.
WOO-HOO! FREE DONUT GOO!
THE END

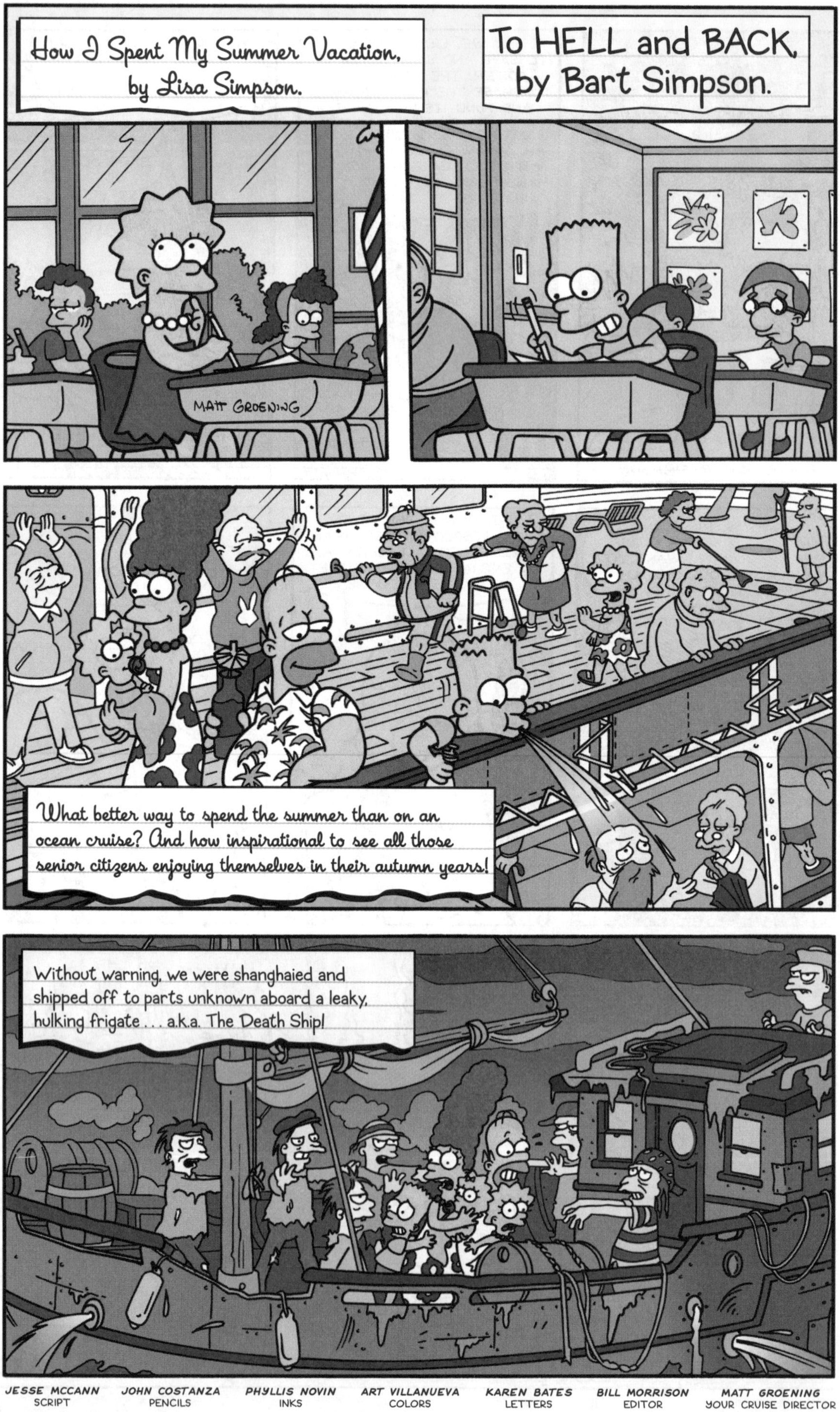
How I Spent My Summer Vacation, by Lisa Simpson.
To HELL and BACK by Bart Simpson.
MATT GROENING
What better way to spend the summer than on an ocean cruise? And how inspirational to see all those senior citizens enjoying themselves in their autumn years!
Without warning, we were shanghaied and shipped off to parts unknown aboard a leaky, hulking frigate . . . a.k.a. The Death Ship!

**JESSE MCCANN** SCRIPT | **JOHN COSTANZA** PENCILS | **PHYLLIS NOVIN** INKS | **ART VILLANUEVA** COLORS | **KAREN BATES** LETTERS | **BILL MORRISON** EDITOR | **MATT GROENING** YOUR CRUISE DIRECTOR

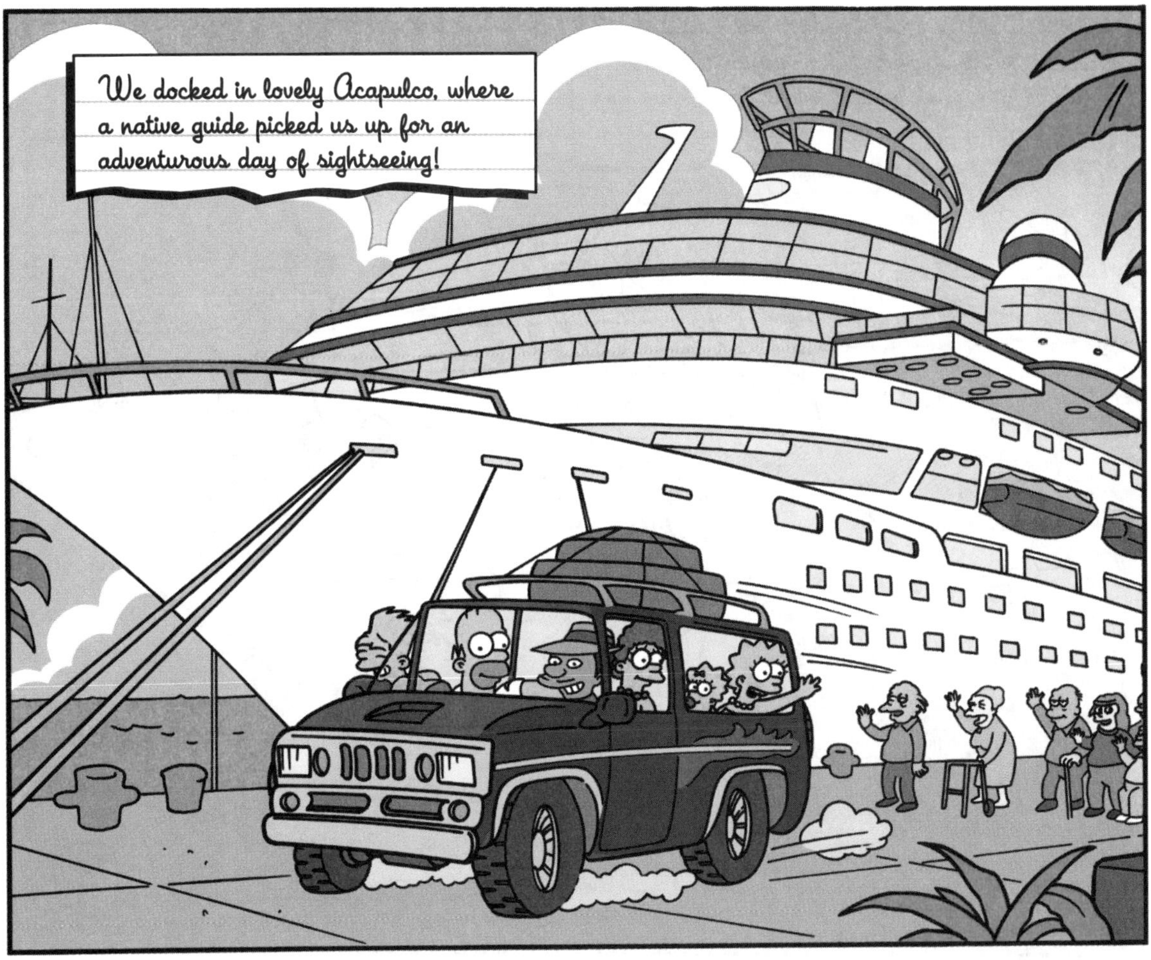
We docked in lovely Acapulco, where a native guide picked us up for an adventurous day of sightseeing!

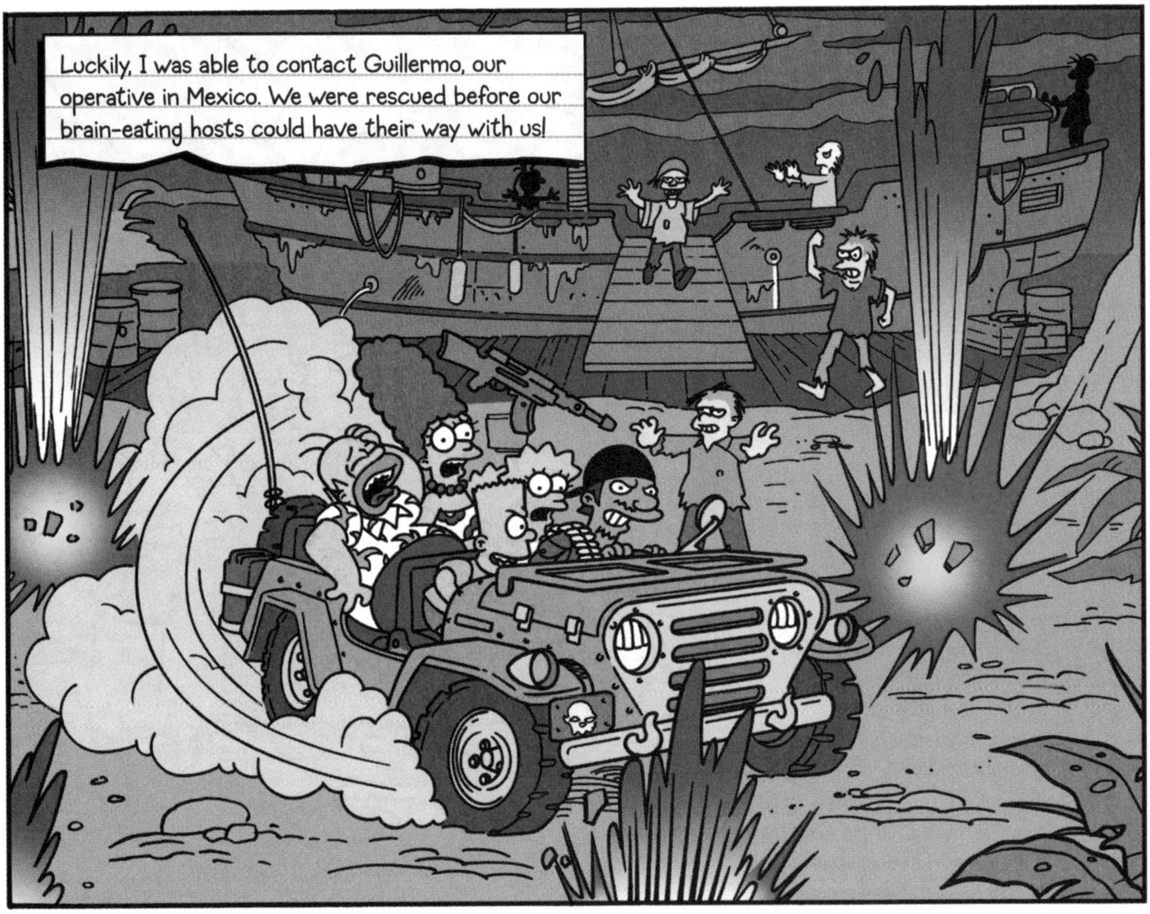
Luckily, I was able to contact Guillermo, our operative in Mexico. We were rescued before our brain-eating hosts could have their way with us!

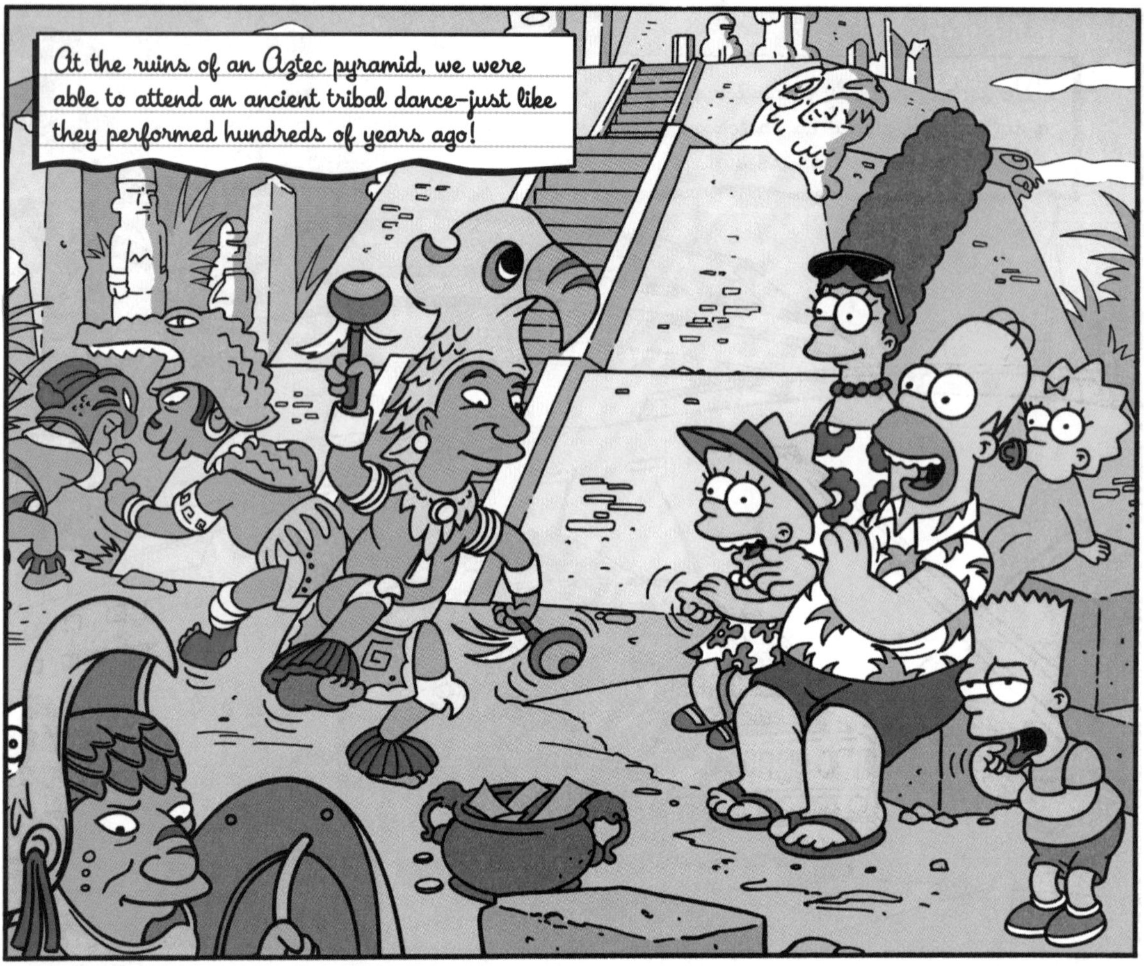
At the ruins of an Aztec pyramid, we were able to attend an ancient tribal dance—just like they performed hundreds of years ago!

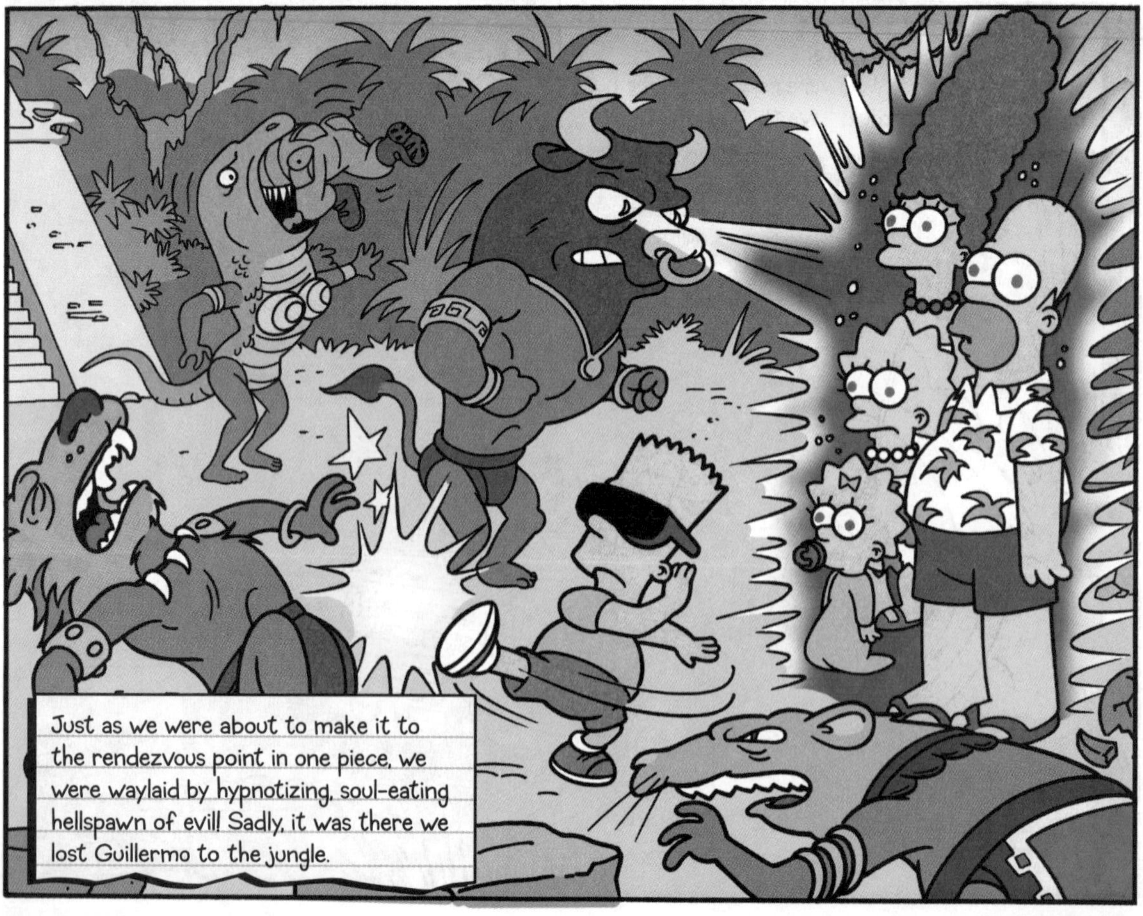
Just as we were about to make it to the rendezvous point in one piece, we were waylaid by hypnotizing, soul-eating hellspawn of evil! Sadly, it was there we lost Guillermo to the jungle.

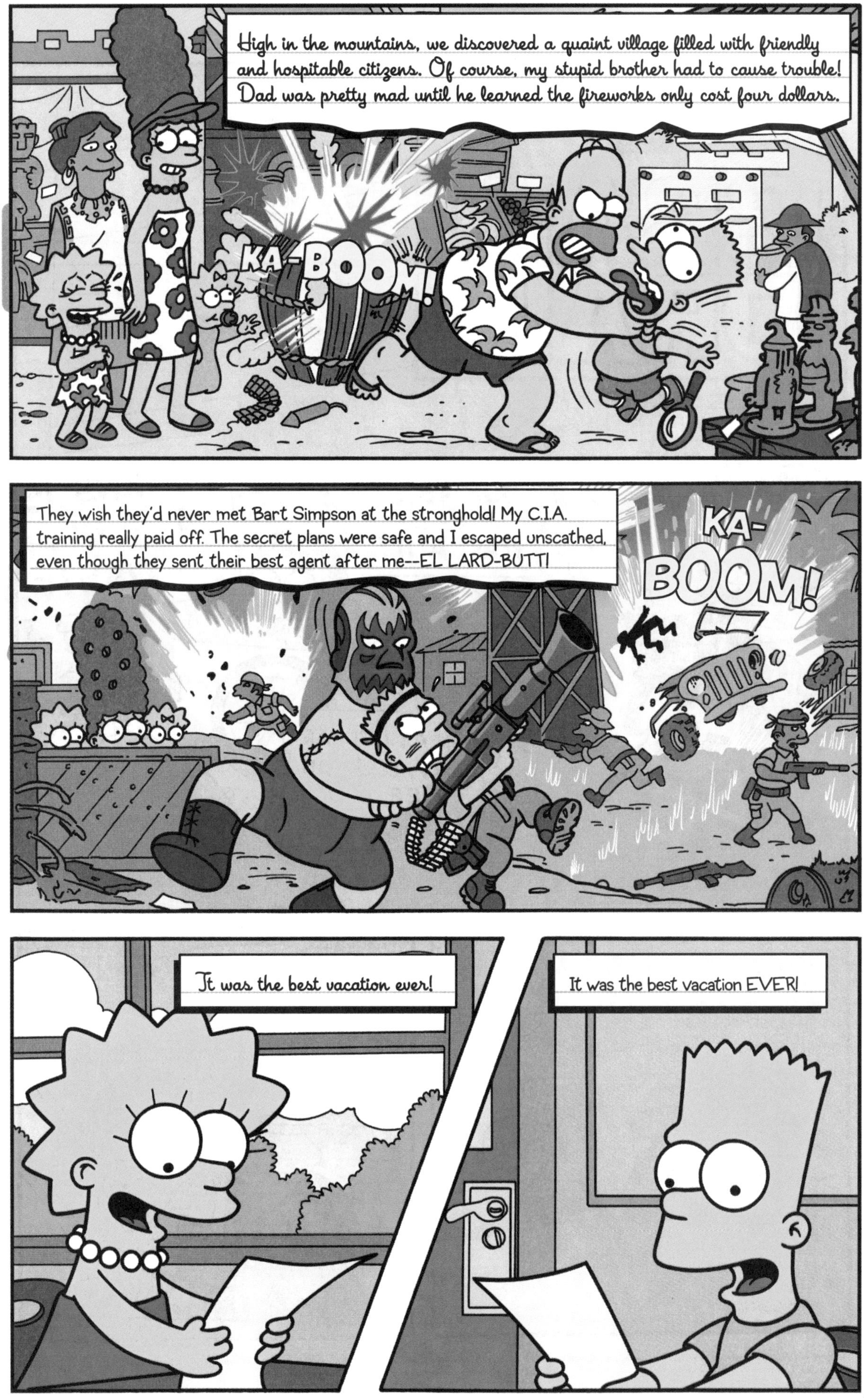
High in the mountains, we discovered a quaint village filled with friendly and hospitable citizens. Of course, my stupid brother had to cause trouble! Dad was pretty mad until he learned the fireworks only cost four dollars.
KA-BOOM!
They wish they'd never met Bart Simpson at the stronghold! My C.I.A. training really paid off. The secret plans were safe and I escaped unscathed, even though they sent their best agent after me--EL LARD-BUTT!
KA-BOOM!
It was the best vacation ever!
It was the best vacation EVER!

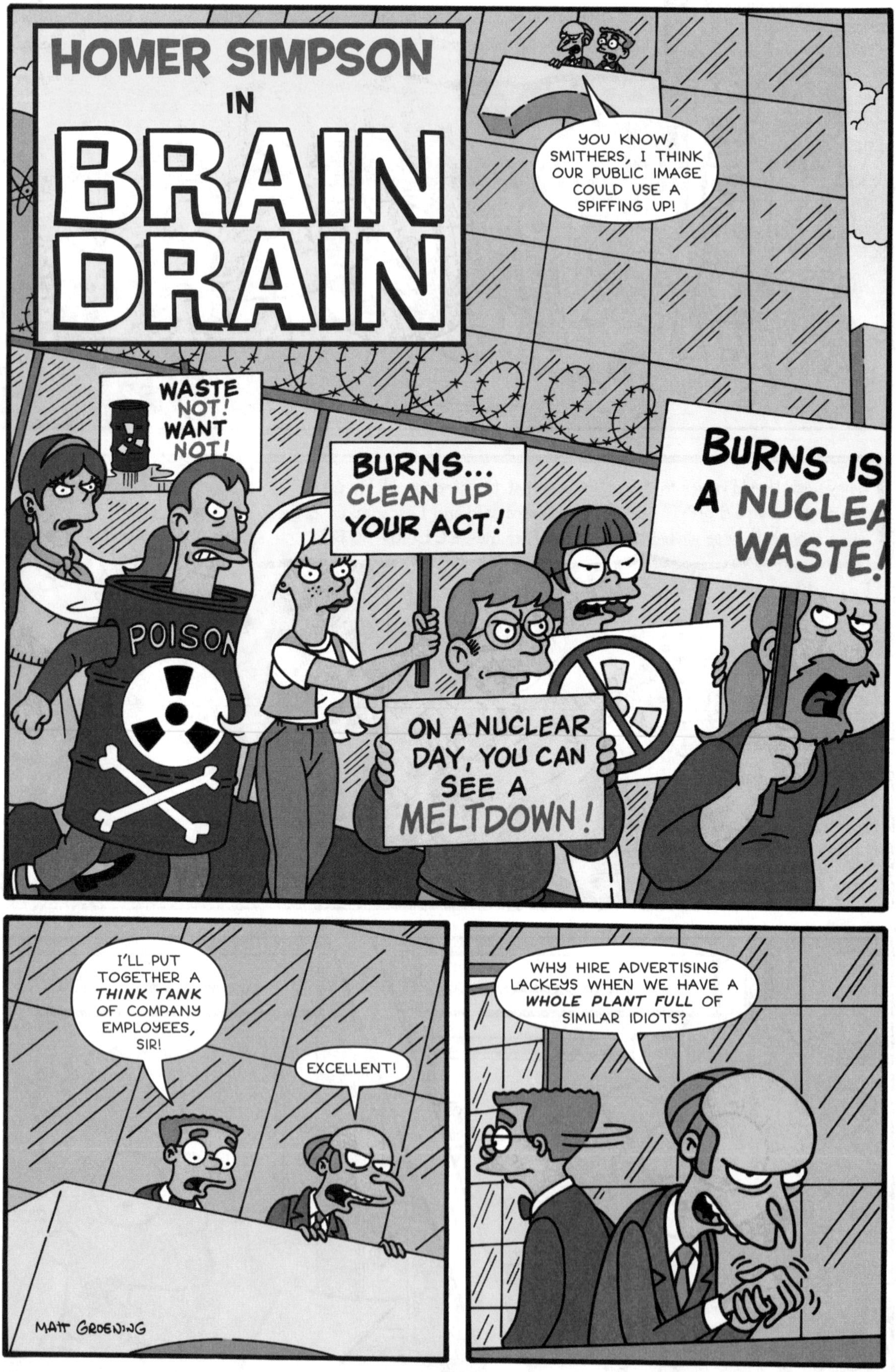
HOMER SIMPSON
IN
BRAIN DRAIN
YOU KNOW, SMITHERS, I THINK OUR PUBLIC IMAGE COULD USE A SPIFFING UP!
WASTE NOT! WANT NOT!
BURNS... CLEAN UP YOUR ACT!
BURNS IS A NUCLEA WASTE!
POISON
ON A NUCLEAR DAY, YOU CAN SEE A MELTDOWN!
I'LL PUT TOGETHER A THINK TANK OF COMPANY EMPLOYEES, SIR!
EXCELLENT!
MATT GROENING
WHY HIRE ADVERTISING LACKEYS WHEN WE HAVE A WHOLE PLANT FULL OF SIMILAR IDIOTS?

*EARL KRESS* SCRIPT | *PHIL ORTIZ* PENCILS | *PATRICK OWSLEY* INKS | *ART VILLANUEVA* COLORS | *KAREN BATES* LETTERS | *BILL MORRISON* EDITOR | *MATT GROENING* PUBLIC RELATIONS

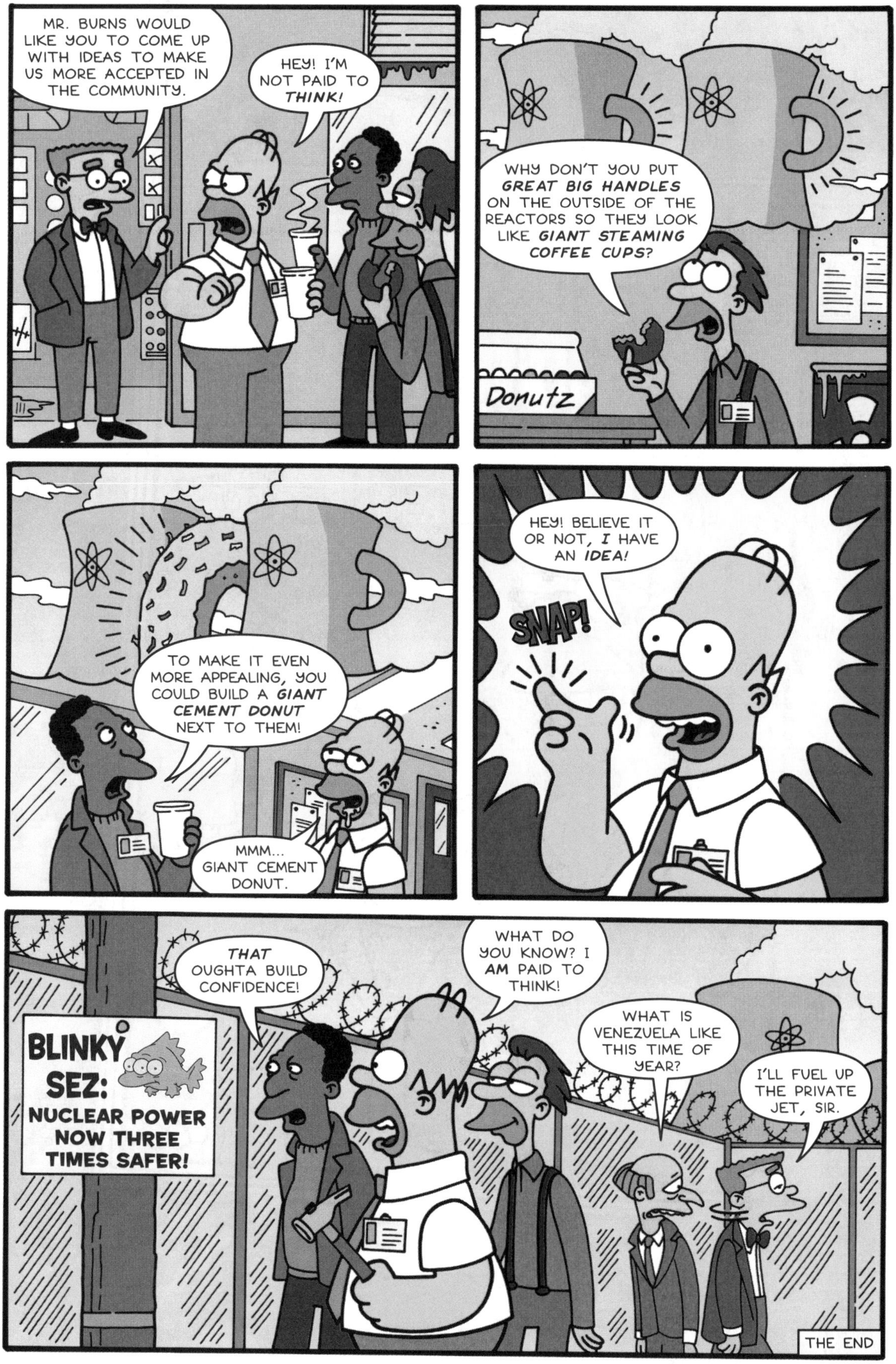
MR. BURNS WOULD LIKE YOU TO COME UP WITH IDEAS TO MAKE US MORE ACCEPTED IN THE COMMUNITY.
HEY! I'M NOT PAID TO *THINK!*
WHY DON'T YOU PUT **GREAT BIG HANDLES** ON THE OUTSIDE OF THE REACTORS SO THEY LOOK LIKE **GIANT STEAMING COFFEE CUPS?**
Donutz
TO MAKE IT EVEN MORE APPEALING, YOU COULD BUILD A **GIANT CEMENT DONUT** NEXT TO THEM!
MMM... GIANT CEMENT DONUT.
HEY! BELIEVE IT OR NOT, *I* HAVE AN *IDEA!*
SNAP!
*THAT* OUGHTA BUILD CONFIDENCE!
WHAT DO YOU KNOW? I **AM** PAID TO THINK!
BLINKY SEZ: NUCLEAR POWER NOW THREE TIMES SAFER!
WHAT IS VENEZUELA LIKE THIS TIME OF YEAR?
I'LL FUEL UP THE PRIVATE JET, SIR.
THE END

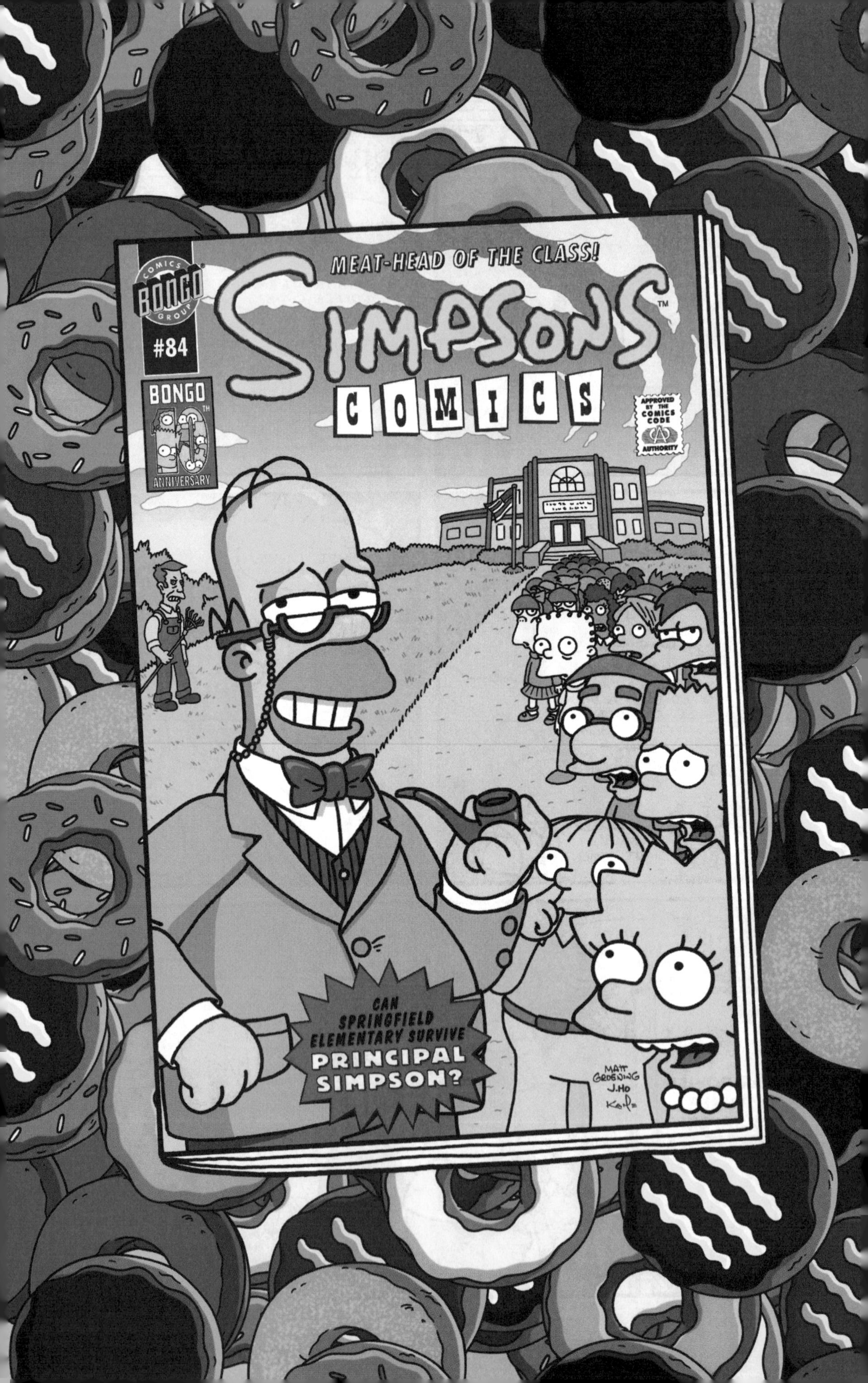
MEAT-HEAD OF THE CLASS!
BONGO COMICS GROUP
#84
SIMPSONS COMICS
BONGO 10TH ANNIVERSARY
APPROVED BY THE COMICS CODE AUTHORITY
CAN SPRINGFIELD ELEMENTARY SURVIVE
PRINCIPAL SIMPSON?
MATT GROENING

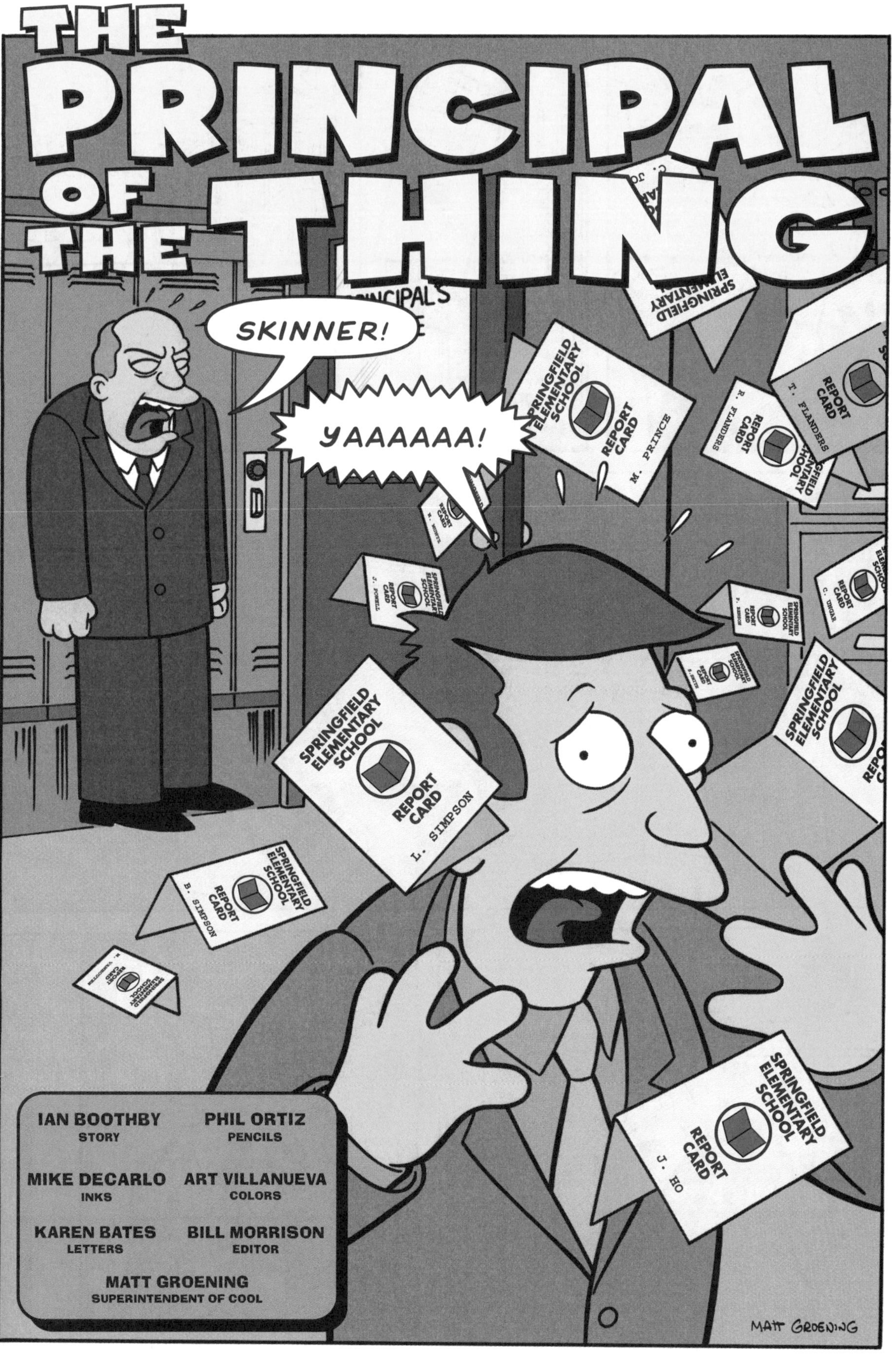
THE PRINCIPAL OF THE THING
SKINNER!
YAAAAAA!
SPRINGFIELD ELEMENTARY SCHOOL REPORT CARD L. SIMPSON
SPRINGFIELD ELEMENTARY SCHOOL REPORT CARD B. SIMPSON
SPRINGFIELD ELEMENTARY SCHOOL REPORT CARD M. PRINCE
SPRINGFIELD ELEMENTARY SCHOOL REPORT CARD J. HO
IAN BOOTHBY STORY
PHIL ORTIZ PENCILS
MIKE DECARLO INKS
ART VILLANUEVA COLORS
KAREN BATES LETTERS
BILL MORRISON EDITOR
MATT GROENING SUPERINTENDENT OF COOL
MATT GROENING

MY REPORT CARDS!

SPRINGFIELD ELEMENTARY SCHOOL

REPORT CARD

K. BATES

SUPERDUDE THE SECOND

MOREY HAMSTERDAM

DAVID HAMSTERHOFF

CLICK!

THE HAMSTERS!

SQUEAK!

REPORT CARD

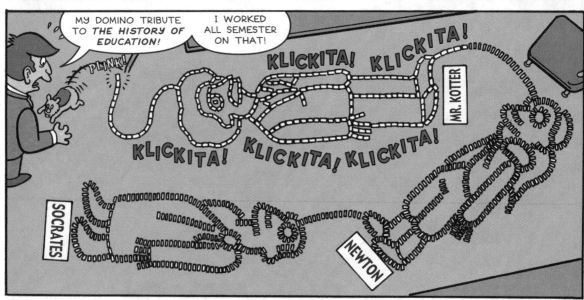

MY DOMINO TRIBUTE TO *THE HISTORY OF EDUCATION!*

I WORKED ALL SEMESTER ON THAT!

PLINK!

KLICKITA! KLICKITA!

KLICKITA! KLICKITA! KLICKITA!

MR. KOTTER

SOCRATES

NEWTON

WHAT WAS SO IMPORTANT, SUPERINTENDENT CHALMERS?

NOTHING. IT'D JUST BEEN *THREE DAYS* SINCE I YELLED AT YOU. I WANTED TO STAY IN PRACTICE!

WITH ALL DUE RESPECT, I REALLY THINK YOU MIGHT BE LETTING YOUR POWER GO TO YOUR...

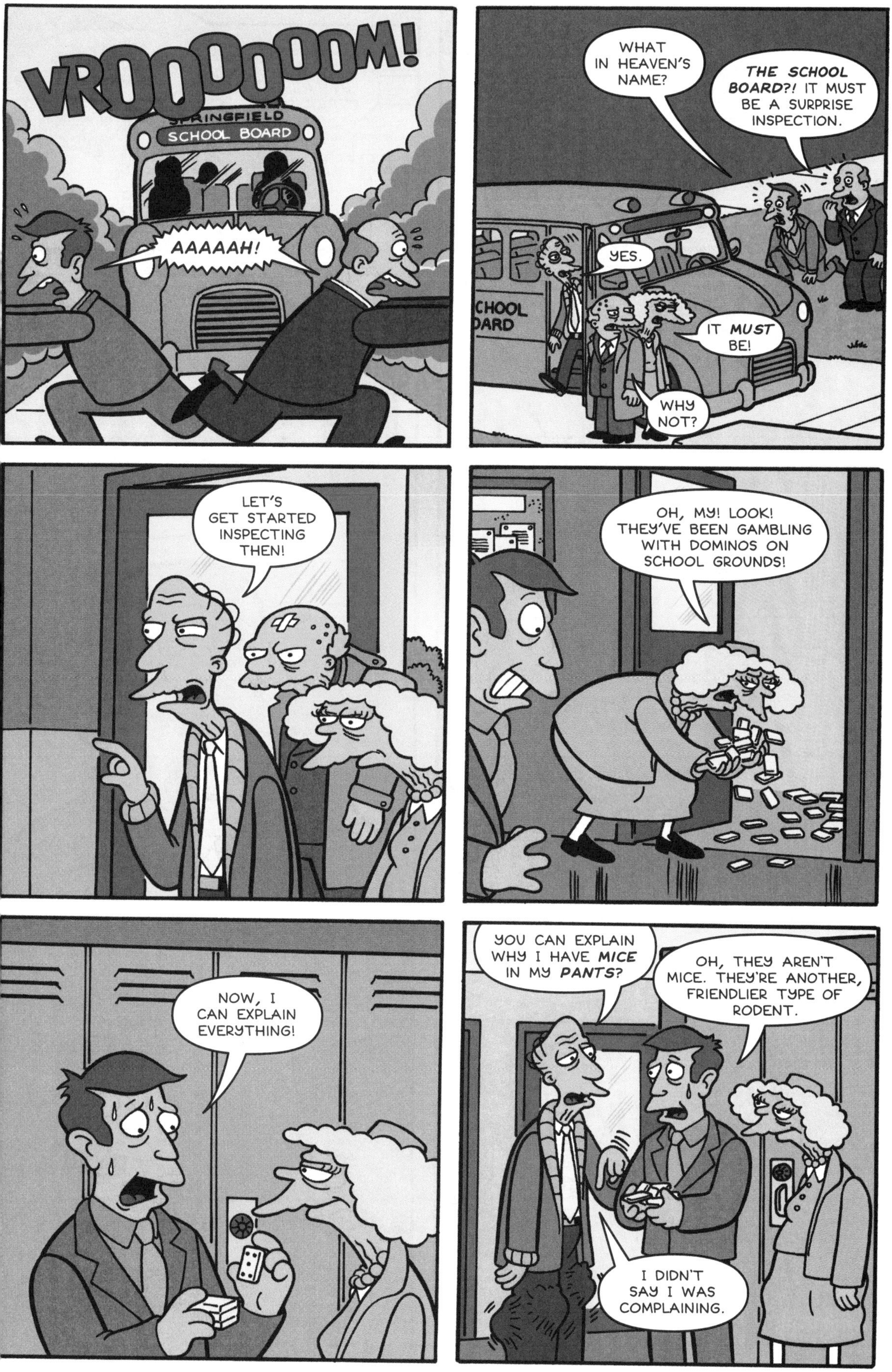
VROOOOOOOM!
SPRINGFIELD
SCHOOL BOARD
AAAAAH!
WHAT IN HEAVEN'S NAME?
*THE SCHOOL BOARD?!* IT MUST BE A SURPRISE INSPECTION.
SCHOOL
BOARD
YES.
IT *MUST* BE!
WHY NOT?
LET'S GET STARTED INSPECTING THEN!
OH, MY! LOOK! THEY'VE BEEN GAMBLING WITH DOMINOS ON SCHOOL GROUNDS!
NOW, I CAN EXPLAIN EVERYTHING!
YOU CAN EXPLAIN WHY I HAVE *MICE* IN MY *PANTS*?
OH, THEY AREN'T MICE. THEY'RE ANOTHER, FRIENDLIER TYPE OF RODENT.
I DIDN'T SAY I WAS COMPLAINING.

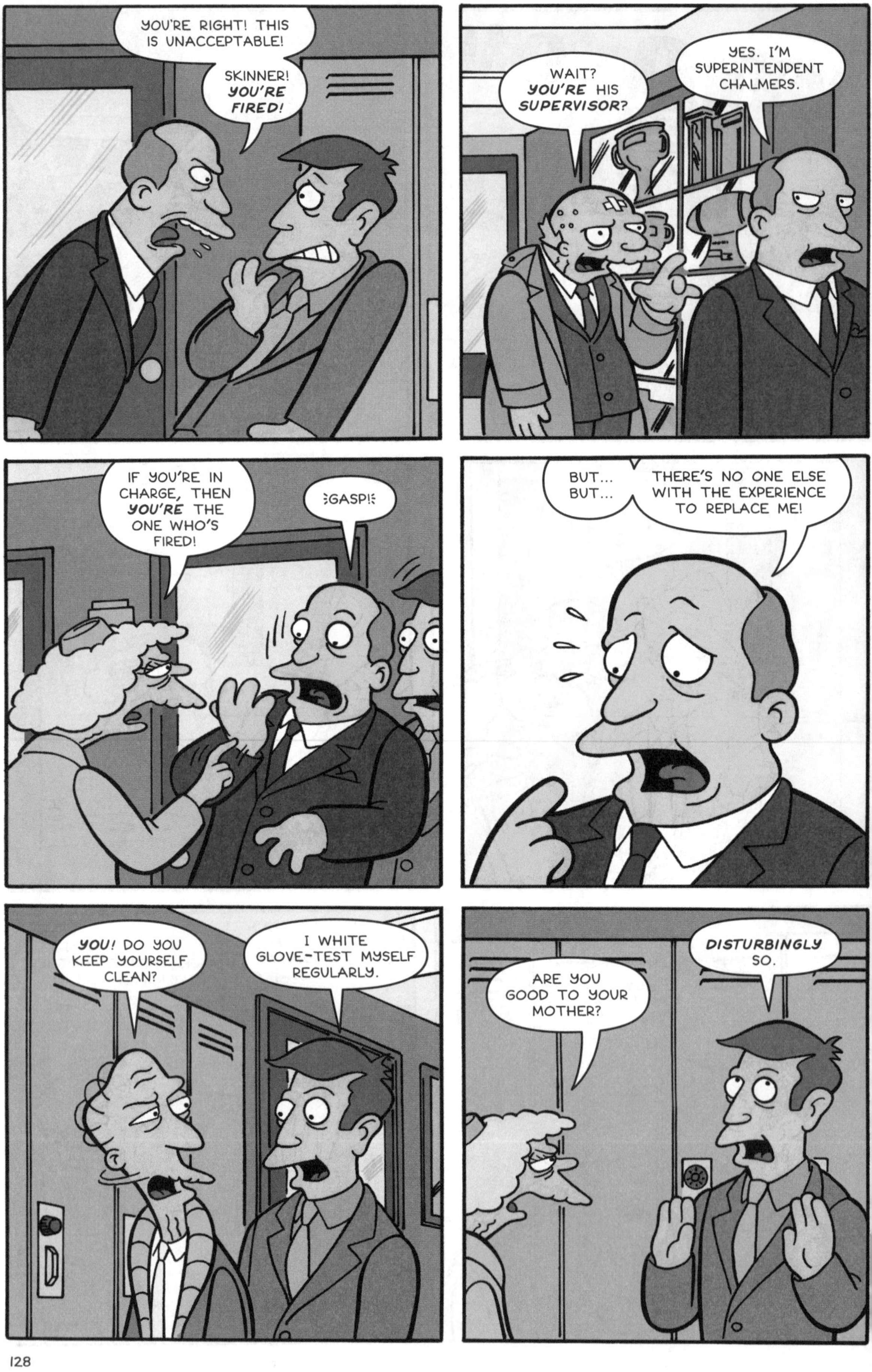
YOU'RE RIGHT! THIS IS UNACCEPTABLE!
SKINNER! **YOU'RE FIRED!**
WAIT? **YOU'RE** HIS **SUPERVISOR**?
YES. I'M SUPERINTENDENT CHALMERS.
IF YOU'RE IN CHARGE, THEN **YOU'RE** THE ONE WHO'S FIRED!
GASP!
BUT... BUT...
THERE'S NO ONE ELSE WITH THE EXPERIENCE TO REPLACE ME!
**YOU!** DO YOU KEEP YOURSELF CLEAN?
I WHITE GLOVE-TEST MYSELF REGULARLY.
ARE YOU GOOD TO YOUR MOTHER?
**DISTURBINGLY** SO.

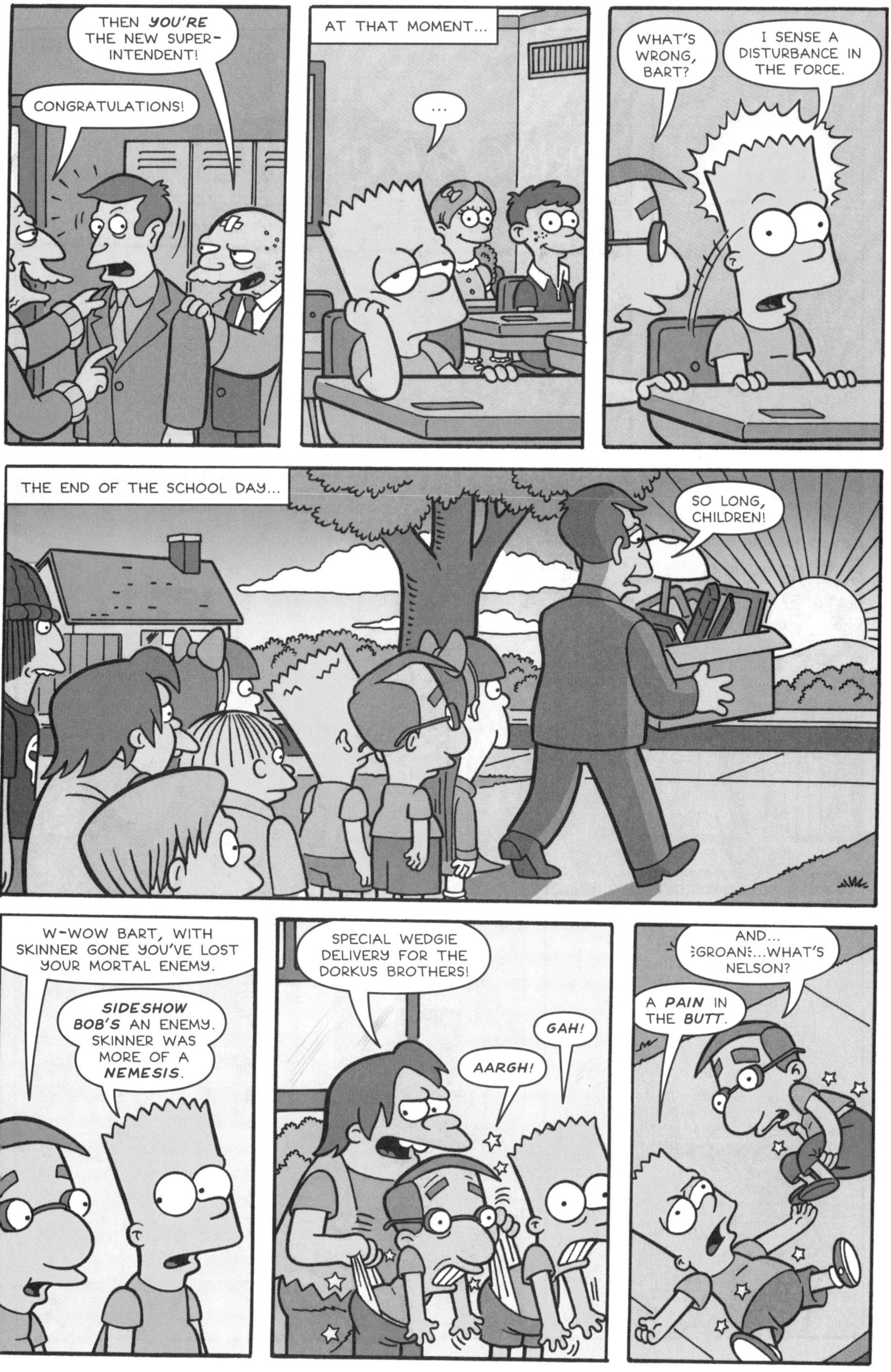

THEN YOU'RE THE NEW SUPER-INTENDENT!
CONGRATULATIONS!
AT THAT MOMENT...
...
WHAT'S WRONG, BART?
I SENSE A DISTURBANCE IN THE FORCE.
THE END OF THE SCHOOL DAY...
SO LONG, CHILDREN!
W-WOW BART, WITH SKINNER GONE YOU'VE LOST YOUR MORTAL ENEMY.
SIDESHOW BOB'S AN ENEMY. SKINNER WAS MORE OF A NEMESIS.
SPECIAL WEDGIE DELIVERY FOR THE DORKUS BROTHERS!
GAH!
AARGH!
AND... GROAN ...WHAT'S NELSON?
A PAIN IN THE BUTT.

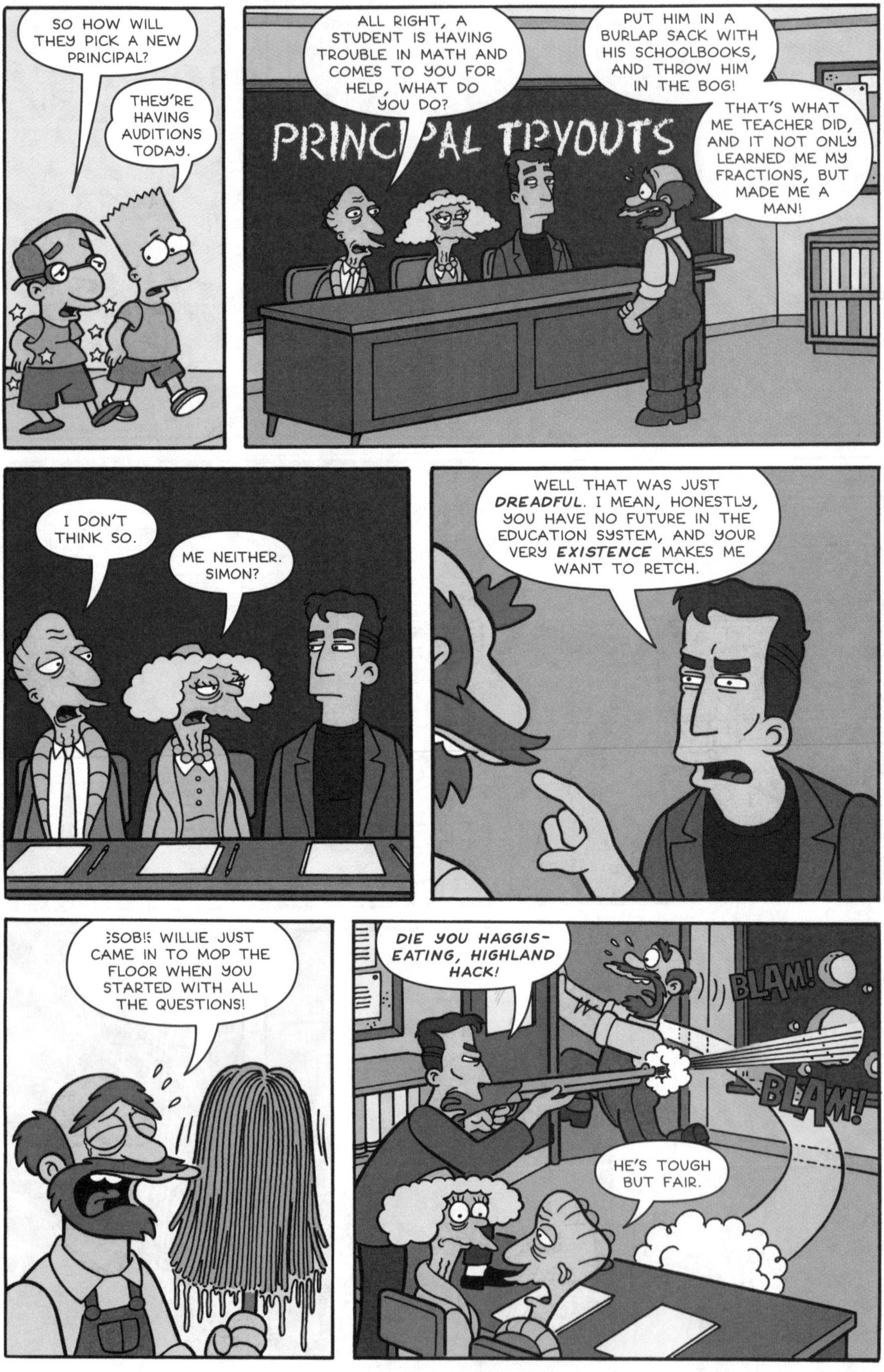
SO HOW WILL THEY PICK A NEW PRINCIPAL?
THEY'RE HAVING AUDITIONS TODAY.
PRINCIPAL TRYOUTS
ALL RIGHT, A STUDENT IS HAVING TROUBLE IN MATH AND COMES TO YOU FOR HELP, WHAT DO YOU DO?
PUT HIM IN A BURLAP SACK WITH HIS SCHOOLBOOKS, AND THROW HIM IN THE BOG!
THAT'S WHAT ME TEACHER DID, AND IT NOT ONLY LEARNED ME MY FRACTIONS, BUT MADE ME A MAN!
I DON'T THINK SO.
ME NEITHER. SIMON?
WELL THAT WAS JUST DREADFUL. I MEAN, HONESTLY, YOU HAVE NO FUTURE IN THE EDUCATION SYSTEM, AND YOUR VERY EXISTENCE MAKES ME WANT TO RETCH.
SOB! WILLIE JUST CAME IN TO MOP THE FLOOR WHEN YOU STARTED WITH ALL THE QUESTIONS!
DIE YOU HAGGIS-EATING, HIGHLAND HACK!
BLAM!
BLAM!
HE'S TOUGH BUT FAIR.

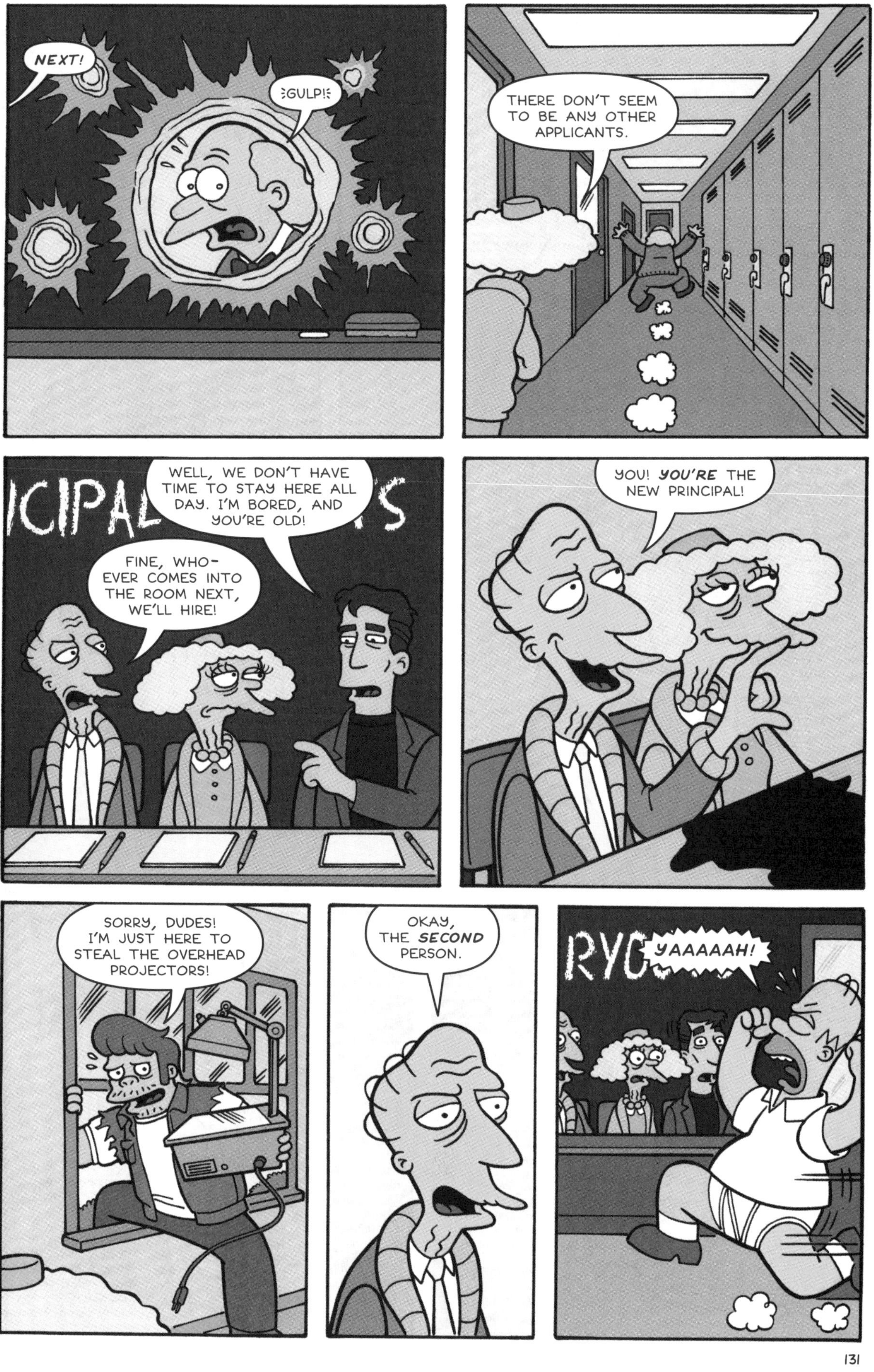

NEXT!
GULP!
THERE DON'T SEEM TO BE ANY OTHER APPLICANTS.
WELL, WE DON'T HAVE TIME TO STAY HERE ALL DAY. I'M BORED, AND YOU'RE OLD!
FINE, WHO-EVER COMES INTO THE ROOM NEXT, WE'LL HIRE!
YOU! YOU'RE THE NEW PRINCIPAL!
SORRY, DUDES! I'M JUST HERE TO STEAL THE OVERHEAD PROJECTORS!
OKAY, THE SECOND PERSON.
YAAAAAH!

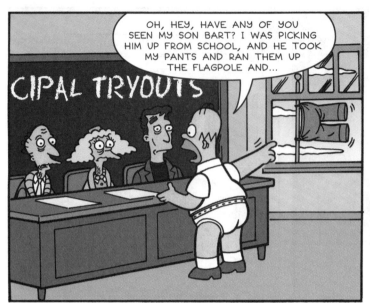
OH, HEY, HAVE ANY OF YOU SEEN MY SON BART? I WAS PICKING HIM UP FROM SCHOOL, AND HE TOOK MY PANTS AND RAN THEM UP THE FLAGPOLE AND...

CIPAL TRYOUTS

I *LIKE* HIM!

AL TRYOUTS

I THINK WE LOST HIM! LET'S HIDE IN HERE!

UH... BART...

WHY YOU LITTLE...

I LIKE HIS HANDS-ON APPROACH!

PRINCIF

ACK!?

AND SO... TRYOUTS

YOU WANT *ME* TO BE PRINCIPAL?

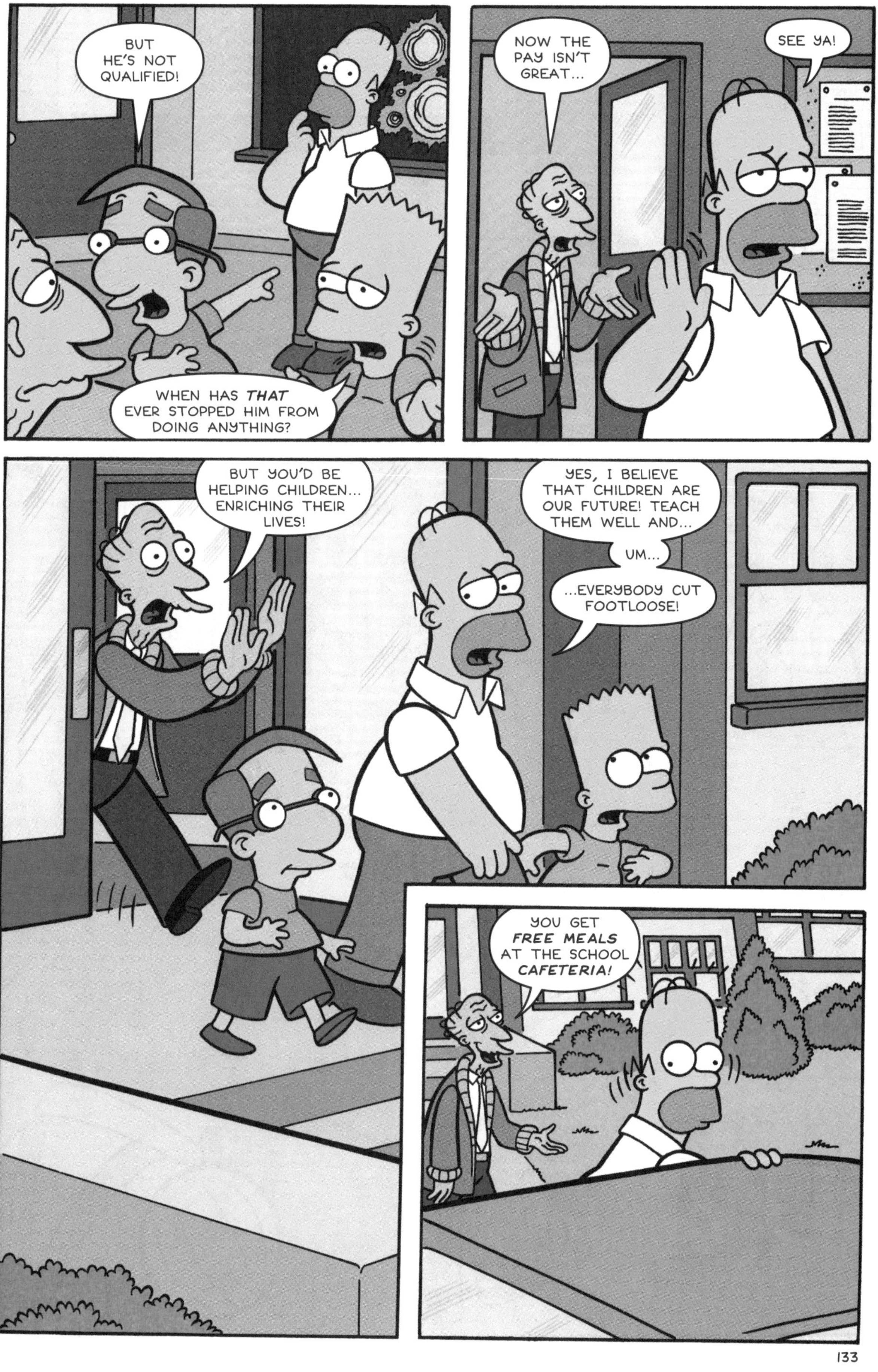
BUT HE'S NOT QUALIFIED!
WHEN HAS *THAT* EVER STOPPED HIM FROM DOING ANYTHING?
NOW THE PAY ISN'T GREAT...
SEE YA!
BUT YOU'D BE HELPING CHILDREN... ENRICHING THEIR LIVES!
YES, I BELIEVE THAT CHILDREN ARE OUR FUTURE! TEACH THEM WELL AND...
UM...
...EVERYBODY CUT FOOTLOOSE!
YOU GET ***FREE MEALS*** AT THE SCHOOL ***CAFETERIA!***

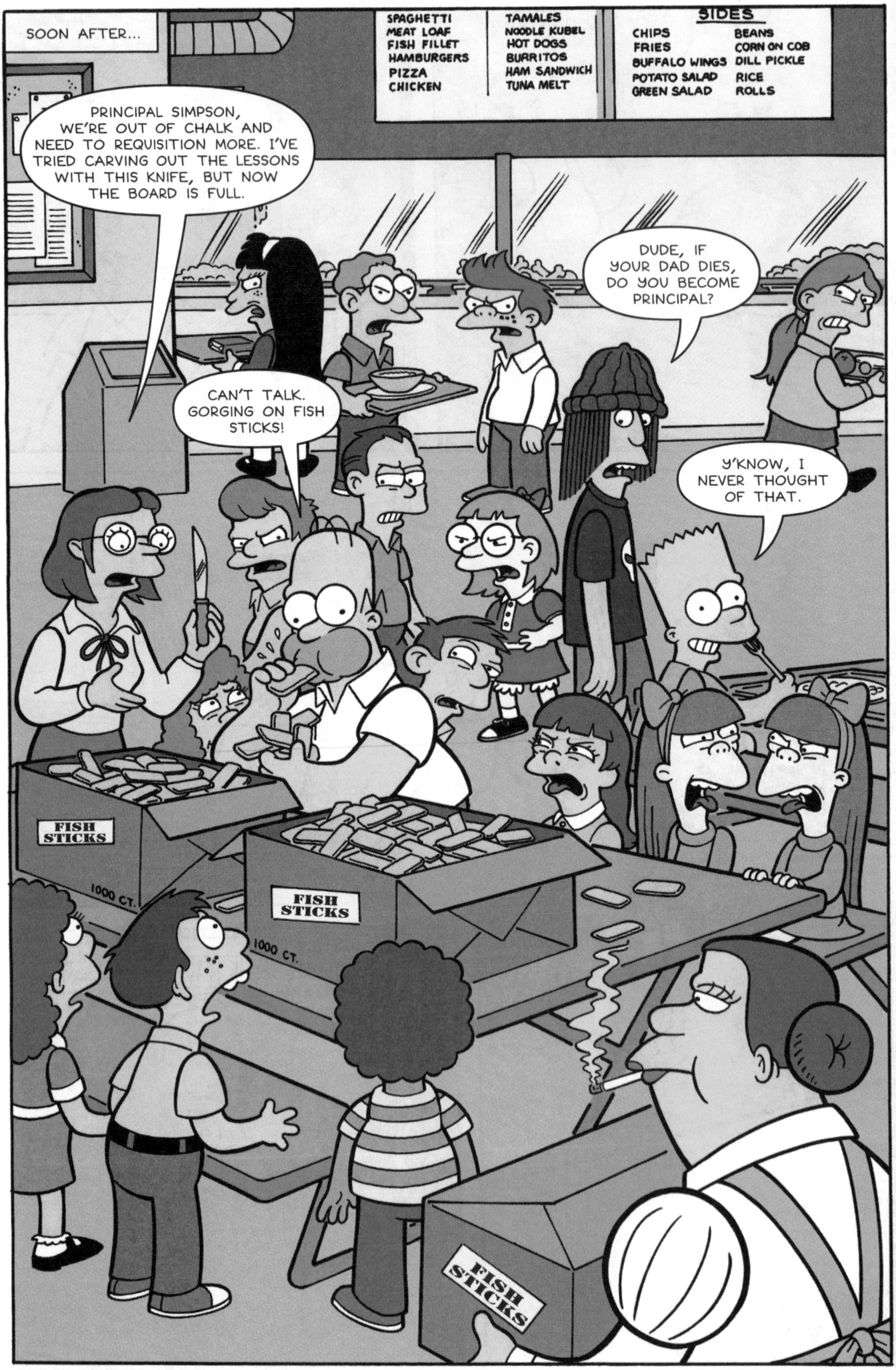

SOON AFTER...
SPAGHETTI
MEAT LOAF
FISH FILLET
HAMBURGERS
PIZZA
CHICKEN
TAMALES
NOODLE KUBEL
HOT DOGS
BURRITOS
HAM SANDWICH
TUNA MELT
SIDES
CHIPS
FRIES
BUFFALO WINGS
POTATO SALAD
GREEN SALAD
BEANS
CORN ON COB
DILL PICKLE
RICE
ROLLS
PRINCIPAL SIMPSON, WE'RE OUT OF CHALK AND NEED TO REQUISITION MORE. I'VE TRIED CARVING OUT THE LESSONS WITH THIS KNIFE, BUT NOW THE BOARD IS FULL.
CAN'T TALK. GORGING ON FISH STICKS!
DUDE, IF YOUR DAD DIES, DO YOU BECOME PRINCIPAL?
Y'KNOW, I NEVER THOUGHT OF THAT.
FISH STICKS
1000 CT.
FISH STICKS
1000 CT.
FISH STICKS

MEANWHILE... OH, SORRY, I DIDN'T THINK YOU'D BE HERE YET.

SUPERINTENDENT CHALMERS

SUPERINTENDENT ...I MEAN, *MR.* CHALMERS!

I JUST WANTED TO PICK UP THE REST OF MY THINGS.

HERE'S YOUR DART-BOARD.

YOU KNOW, I NEVER WANTED THIS TO HAPPEN.

I KNOW. JUST TAKE CARE OF EVERYTHING, AND DON'T SCREW UP *TOO* BADLY, SEYMOUR.

SUPERINTENDENT CHALMERS

I MEAN... *SUPERINTENDENT SKINNER.*

WHAT'LL YOU DO NOW?

Y'KNOW, I HAVEN'T GIVEN IT MUCH THOUGHT.

I'M SURE *SOMETHING'LL* COME TO ME.

SUPERINTENDENT CHALMERS

TWO DAYS LATER...

...AND IN AN AMAZING TURN OF EVENTS, A NON-PARTISAN CANDIDATE HAS BECOME A U.S. SENATOR IN A NON-ELECTION YEAR!

KENT

THAT'S ENOUGH TV! TIME FOR DINNER!

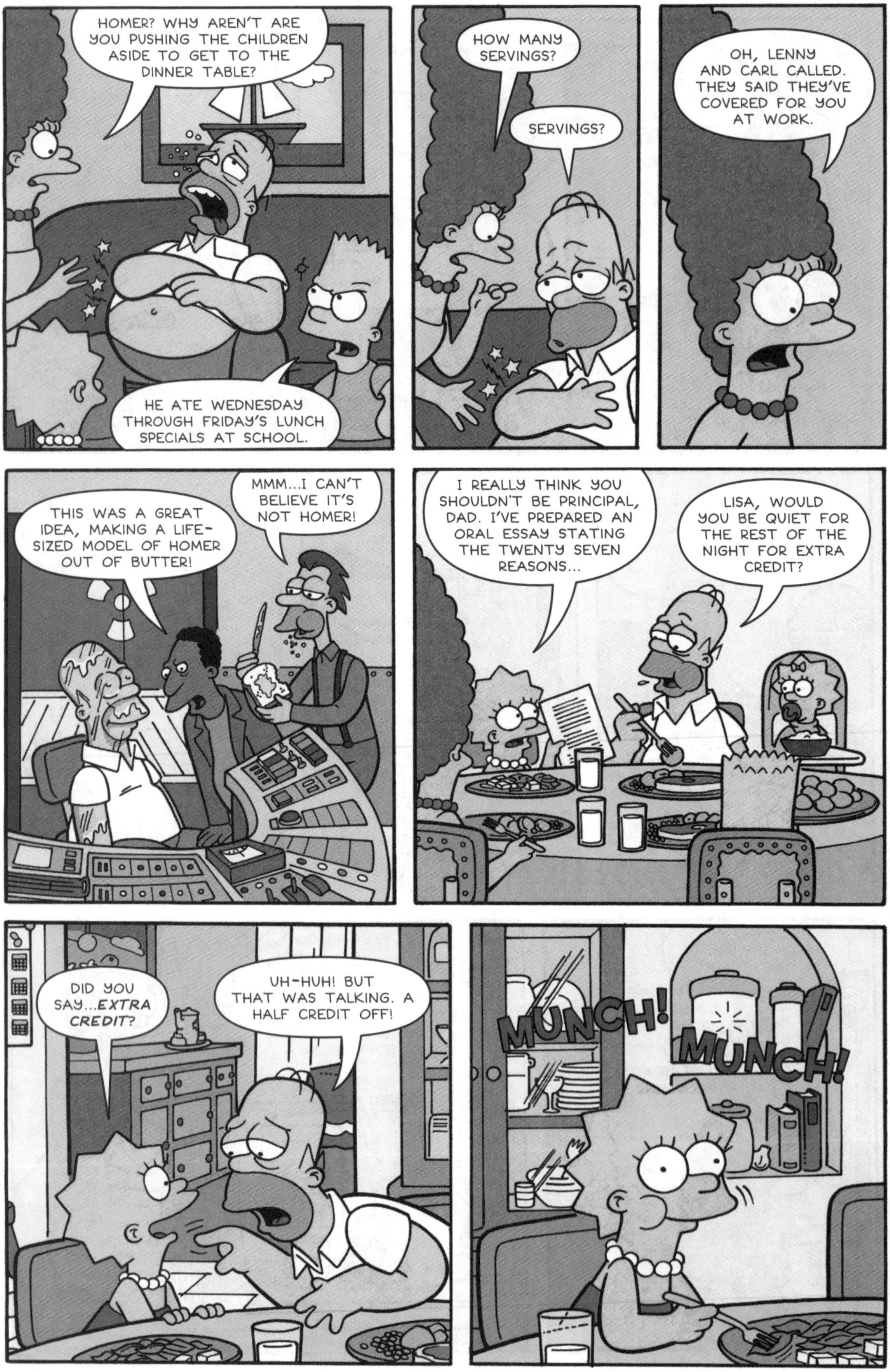
HOMER? WHY AREN'T ARE YOU PUSHING THE CHILDREN ASIDE TO GET TO THE DINNER TABLE?
HE ATE WEDNESDAY THROUGH FRIDAY'S LUNCH SPECIALS AT SCHOOL.
HOW MANY SERVINGS?
SERVINGS?
OH, LENNY AND CARL CALLED. THEY SAID THEY'VE COVERED FOR YOU AT WORK.
THIS WAS A GREAT IDEA, MAKING A LIFE-SIZED MODEL OF HOMER OUT OF BUTTER!
MMM...I CAN'T BELIEVE IT'S NOT HOMER!
I REALLY THINK YOU SHOULDN'T BE PRINCIPAL, DAD. I'VE PREPARED AN ORAL ESSAY STATING THE TWENTY SEVEN REASONS...
LISA, WOULD YOU BE QUIET FOR THE REST OF THE NIGHT FOR EXTRA CREDIT?
DID YOU SAY...EXTRA CREDIT?
UH-HUH! BUT THAT WAS TALKING. A HALF CREDIT OFF!
MUNCH!
MUNCH!

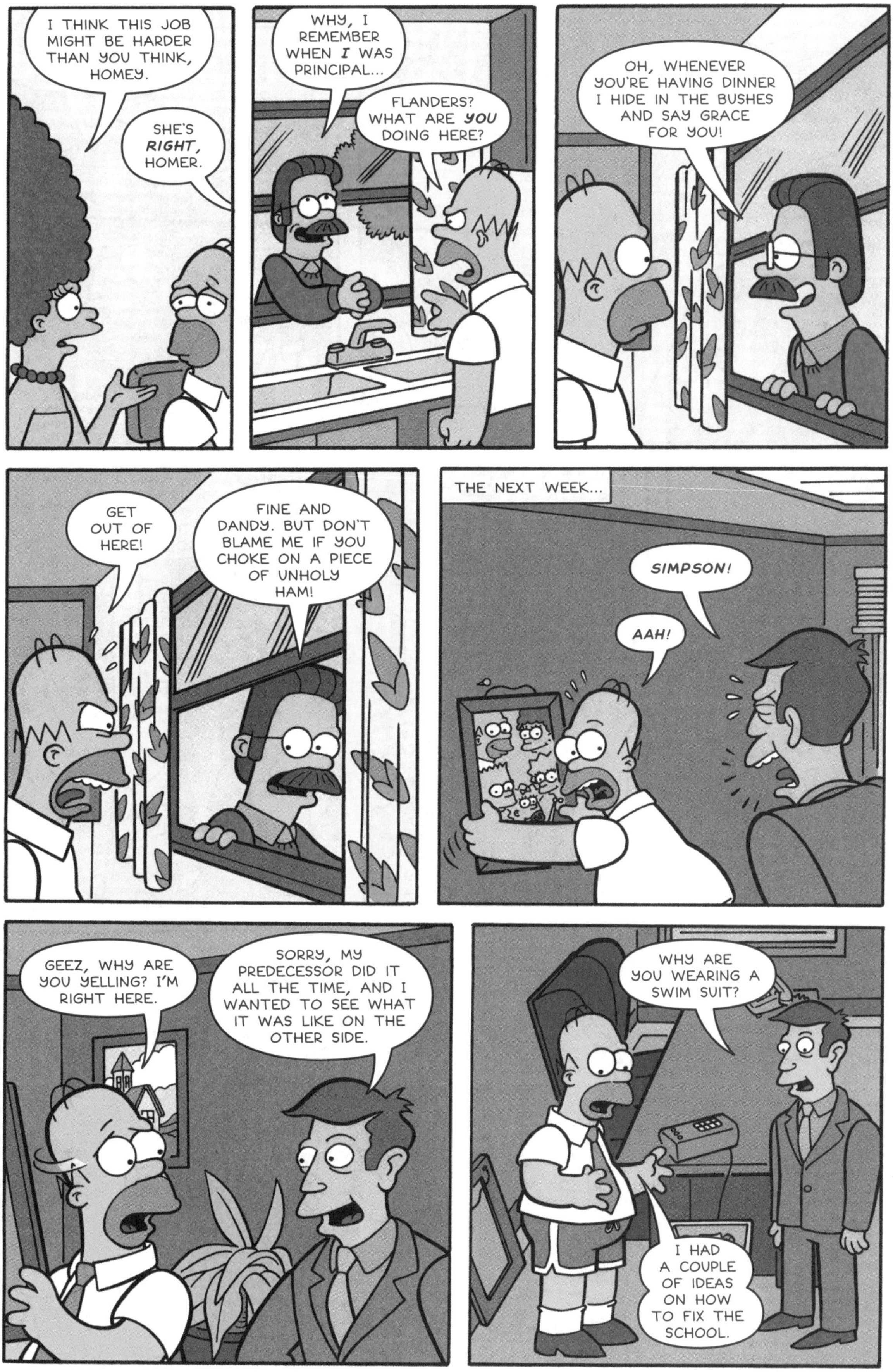
I THINK THIS JOB MIGHT BE HARDER THAN YOU THINK, HOMEY.
SHE'S *RIGHT*, HOMER.
WHY, I REMEMBER WHEN *I* WAS PRINCIPAL...
FLANDERS? WHAT ARE *YOU* DOING HERE?
OH, WHENEVER YOU'RE HAVING DINNER I HIDE IN THE BUSHES AND SAY GRACE FOR YOU!
GET OUT OF HERE!
FINE AND DANDY. BUT DON'T BLAME ME IF YOU CHOKE ON A PIECE OF UNHOLY HAM!
THE NEXT WEEK...
*SIMPSON!*
*AAH!*
GEEZ, WHY ARE YOU YELLING? I'M RIGHT HERE.
SORRY, MY PREDECESSOR DID IT ALL THE TIME, AND I WANTED TO SEE WHAT IT WAS LIKE ON THE OTHER SIDE.
WHY ARE YOU WEARING A SWIM SUIT?
I HAD A COUPLE OF IDEAS ON HOW TO FIX THE SCHOOL.

WHEEEEE!

WATER-SLIDES?!!!

YEAH, NOW THE KIDS ALWAYS GET TO CLASS ON TIME.

PLUS THE SPILLED WATER HELPS WASH AWAY THE RODENTS AND SCOTSMEN!

*OCH!* WILLIE'D BE INSULTED AND ANGRY IF THIS WASN'T SO REFRESHING!

OW!

PLUNK!

*SIMPSON!* WHY IS THERE A *BANANA* IN MY EAR?

*WAIT!* I KNOW THIS JOKE! BECAUSE THE WATERMELON WOULDN'T FIT?

MULTIPLICATION TABLES

OH, THAT WOULD BE THE NEW SUBSTITUTE TEACHER, MR. KONGO.

THAT'S A *MOUNTAIN GORILLA!*

WHAT DOES HE TEACH?

WwXx

7x9=63    2x5=10
          5x5=25
2x8=16    3x4=12
9x10=90

OH WAIT! I KNOW *THIS* ONE, TOO! WHATEVER HE *WANTS* TO!

WE GOT HIM WHEN THE CITY ZOO DOWNSIZED. NOW ALL THE KIDS PAY ATTENTION. WE WRITE THE DAY'S ASSIGNMENT ON HIS DIAPER!

GRRRR!

AAAAH!

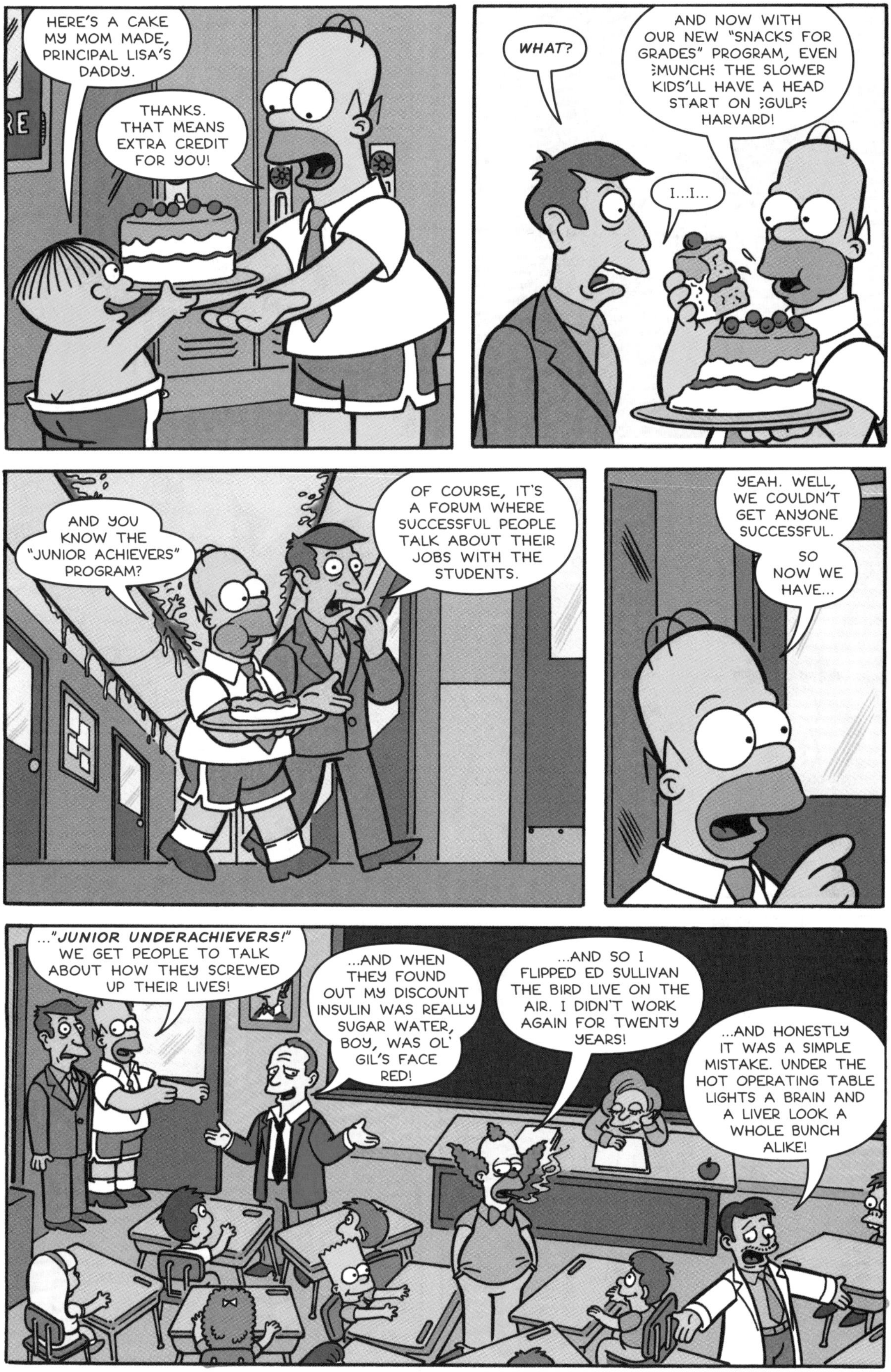
HERE'S A CAKE MY MOM MADE, PRINCIPAL LISA'S DADDY.
THANKS. THAT MEANS EXTRA CREDIT FOR YOU!
WHAT?
AND NOW WITH OUR NEW "SNACKS FOR GRADES" PROGRAM, EVEN ⁝MUNCH⁝ THE SLOWER KIDS'LL HAVE A HEAD START ON ⁝GULP⁝ HARVARD!
I...I...
AND YOU KNOW THE "JUNIOR ACHIEVERS" PROGRAM?
OF COURSE, IT'S A FORUM WHERE SUCCESSFUL PEOPLE TALK ABOUT THEIR JOBS WITH THE STUDENTS.
YEAH. WELL, WE COULDN'T GET ANYONE SUCCESSFUL.
SO NOW WE HAVE...
..."JUNIOR UNDERACHIEVERS!" WE GET PEOPLE TO TALK ABOUT HOW THEY SCREWED UP THEIR LIVES!
...AND WHEN THEY FOUND OUT MY DISCOUNT INSULIN WAS REALLY SUGAR WATER, BOY, WAS OL' GIL'S FACE RED!
...AND SO I FLIPPED ED SULLIVAN THE BIRD LIVE ON THE AIR. I DIDN'T WORK AGAIN FOR TWENTY YEARS!
...AND HONESTLY IT WAS A SIMPLE MISTAKE. UNDER THE HOT OPERATING TABLE LIGHTS A BRAIN AND A LIVER LOOK A WHOLE BUNCH ALIKE!

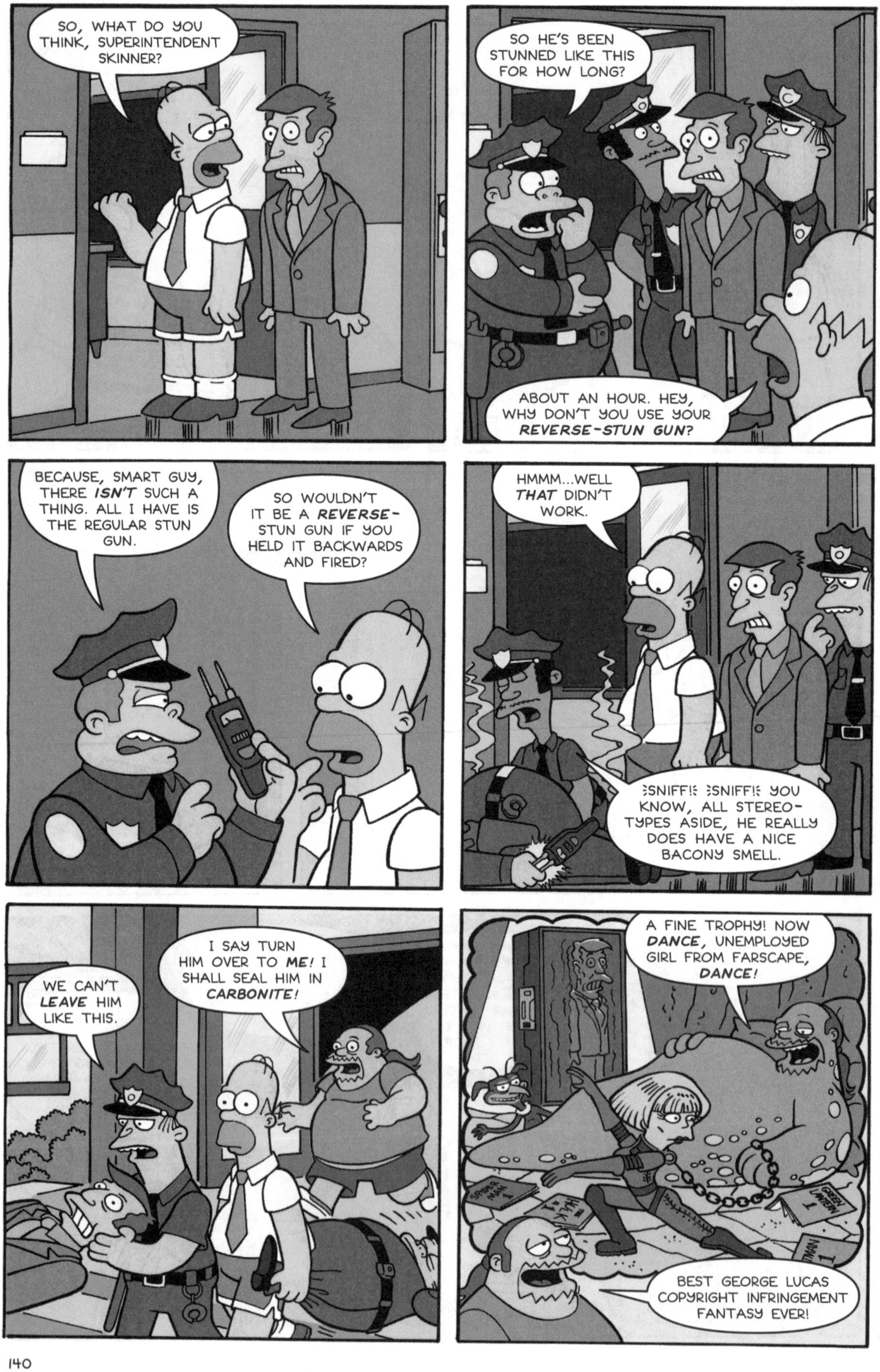

SO, WHAT DO YOU THINK, SUPERINTENDENT SKINNER?
SO HE'S BEEN STUNNED LIKE THIS FOR HOW LONG?
ABOUT AN HOUR. HEY, WHY DON'T YOU USE YOUR ***REVERSE-STUN GUN***?
BECAUSE, SMART GUY, THERE ***ISN'T*** SUCH A THING. ALL I HAVE IS THE REGULAR STUN GUN.
SO WOULDN'T IT BE A ***REVERSE-*** STUN GUN IF YOU HELD IT BACKWARDS AND FIRED?
HMMM...WELL ***THAT*** DIDN'T WORK.
SNIFF! SNIFF! YOU KNOW, ALL STEREO-TYPES ASIDE, HE REALLY DOES HAVE A NICE BACONY SMELL.
WE CAN'T ***LEAVE*** HIM LIKE THIS.
I SAY TURN HIM OVER TO ***ME!*** I SHALL SEAL HIM IN ***CARBONITE!***
A FINE TROPHY! NOW ***DANCE,*** UNEMPLOYED GIRL FROM FARSCAPE, ***DANCE!***
GREEN LANTERN 1
BEST GEORGE LUCAS COPYRIGHT INFRINGEMENT FANTASY EVER!

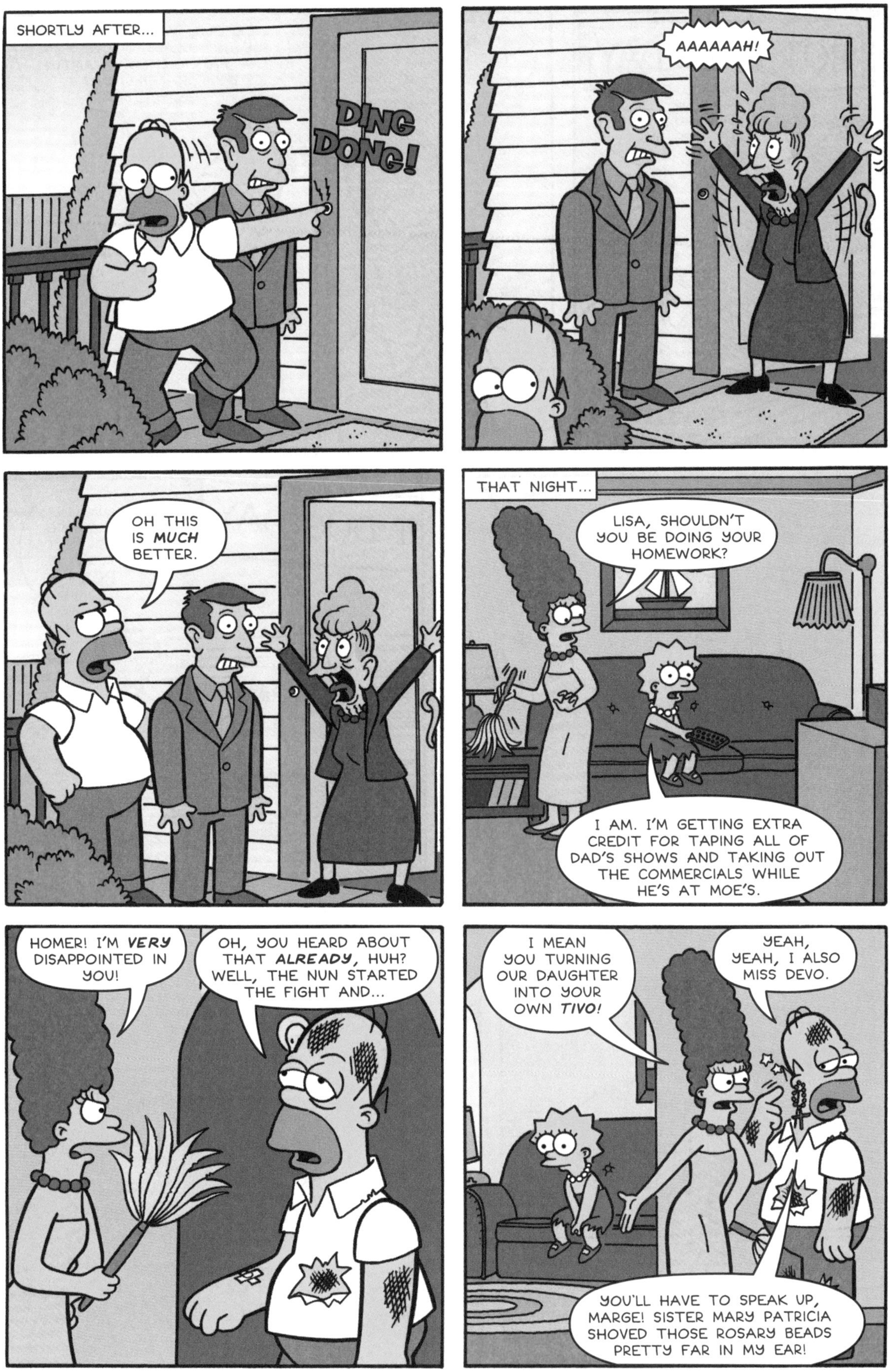

SHORTLY AFTER...
DING DONG!
AAAAAAH!
OH THIS IS MUCH BETTER.
THAT NIGHT...
LISA, SHOULDN'T YOU BE DOING YOUR HOMEWORK?
I AM. I'M GETTING EXTRA CREDIT FOR TAPING ALL OF DAD'S SHOWS AND TAKING OUT THE COMMERCIALS WHILE HE'S AT MOE'S.
HOMER! I'M VERY DISAPPOINTED IN YOU!
OH, YOU HEARD ABOUT THAT ALREADY, HUH? WELL, THE NUN STARTED THE FIGHT AND...
I MEAN YOU TURNING OUR DAUGHTER INTO YOUR OWN TIVO!
YEAH, YEAH, I ALSO MISS DEVO.
YOU'LL HAVE TO SPEAK UP, MARGE! SISTER MARY PATRICIA SHOVED THOSE ROSARY BEADS PRETTY FAR IN MY EAR!

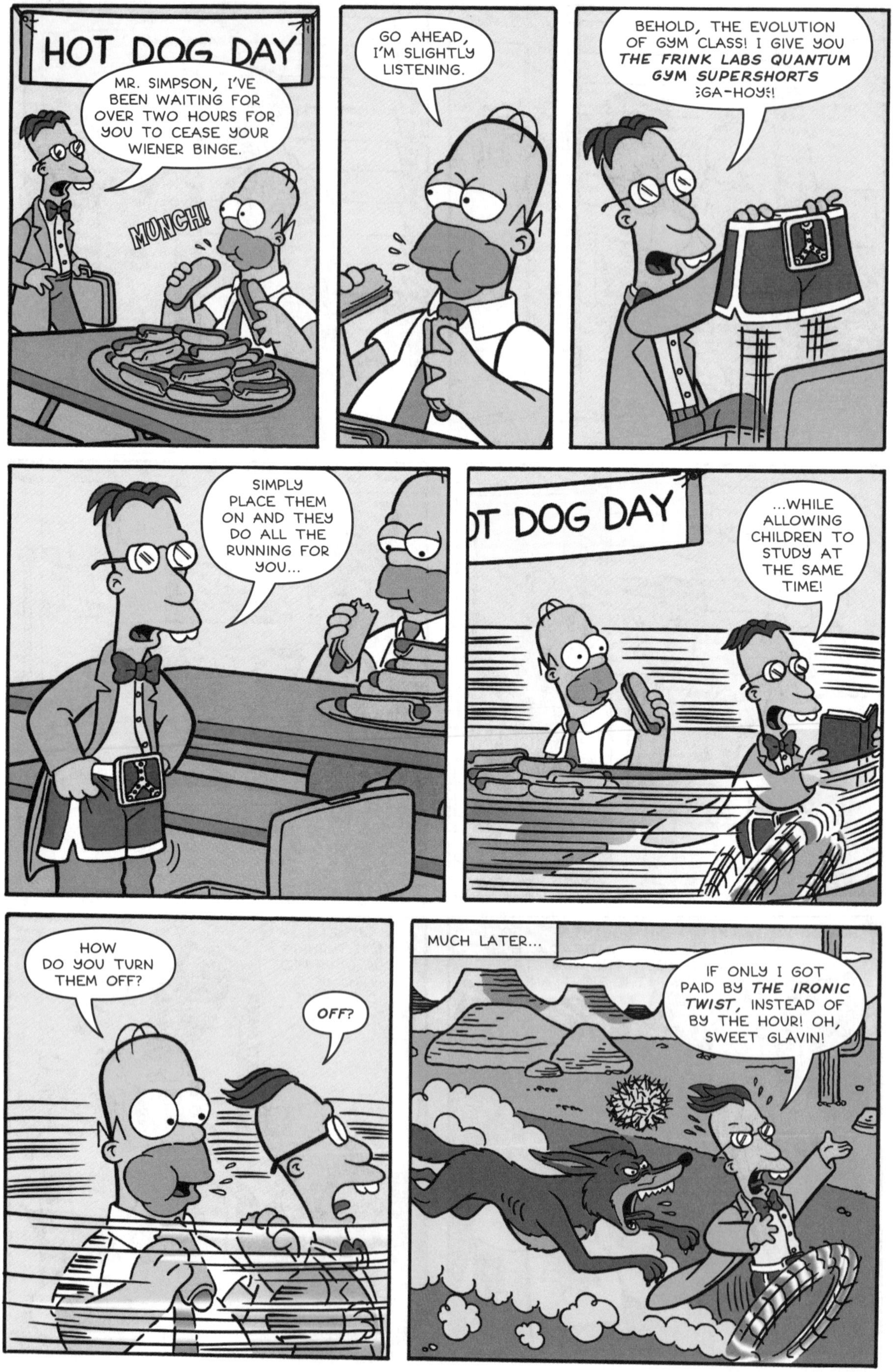
HOT DOG DAY
MR. SIMPSON, I'VE BEEN WAITING FOR OVER TWO HOURS FOR YOU TO CEASE YOUR WIENER BINGE.
MUNCH!
GO AHEAD, I'M SLIGHTLY LISTENING.
BEHOLD, THE EVOLUTION OF GYM CLASS! I GIVE YOU ***THE FRINK LABS QUANTUM GYM SUPERSHORTS*** GA-HOY!
SIMPLY PLACE THEM ON AND THEY DO ALL THE RUNNING FOR YOU...
OT DOG DAY
...WHILE ALLOWING CHILDREN TO STUDY AT THE SAME TIME!
HOW DO YOU TURN THEM OFF?
***OFF?***
MUCH LATER...
IF ONLY I GOT PAID BY ***THE IRONIC TWIST,*** INSTEAD OF BY THE HOUR! OH, SWEET GLAVIN!

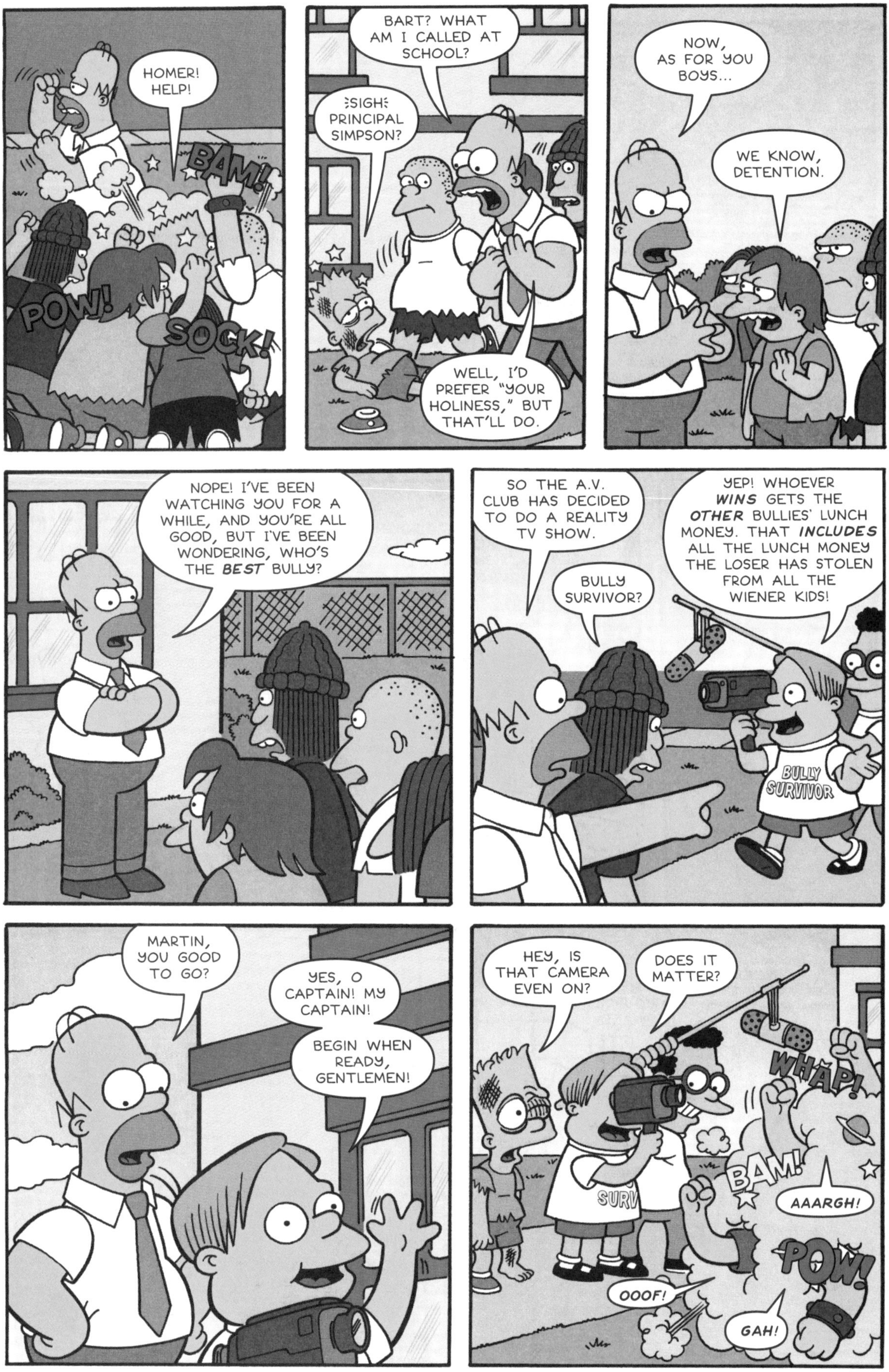
HOMER! HELP!
BAM!
POW!
SOCK!
BART? WHAT AM I CALLED AT SCHOOL?
SIGH PRINCIPAL SIMPSON?
WELL, I'D PREFER "YOUR HOLINESS," BUT THAT'LL DO.
NOW, AS FOR YOU BOYS...
WE KNOW, DETENTION.
NOPE! I'VE BEEN WATCHING YOU FOR A WHILE, AND YOU'RE ALL GOOD, BUT I'VE BEEN WONDERING, WHO'S THE BEST BULLY?
SO THE A.V. CLUB HAS DECIDED TO DO A REALITY TV SHOW.
BULLY SURVIVOR?
YEP! WHOEVER WINS GETS THE OTHER BULLIES' LUNCH MONEY. THAT INCLUDES ALL THE LUNCH MONEY THE LOSER HAS STOLEN FROM ALL THE WIENER KIDS!
BULLY SURVIVOR
MARTIN, YOU GOOD TO GO?
YES, O CAPTAIN! MY CAPTAIN!
BEGIN WHEN READY, GENTLEMEN!
HEY, IS THAT CAMERA EVEN ON?
DOES IT MATTER?
WHAP!
BAM!
AAARGH!
POW!
OOOF!
GAH!

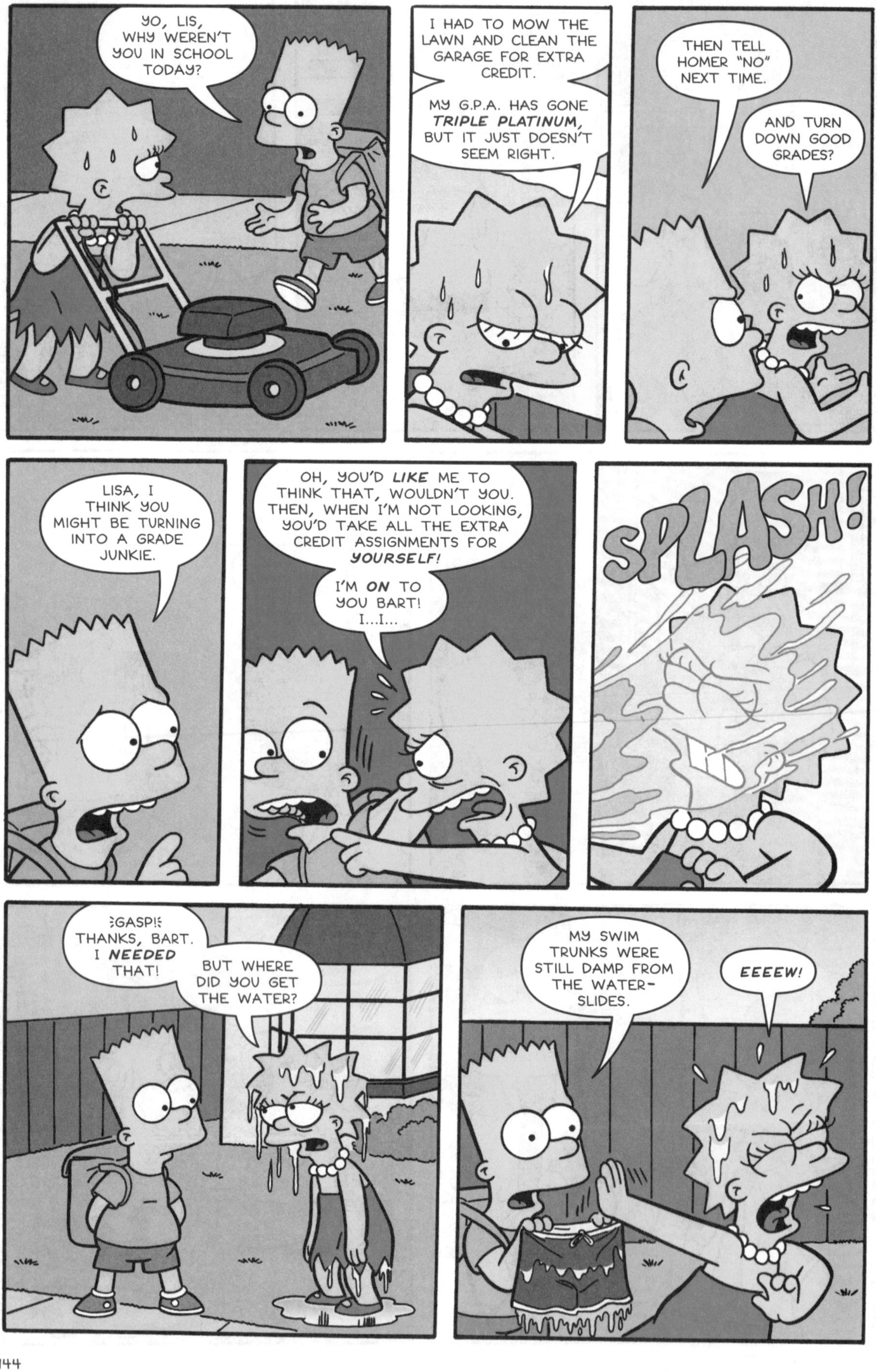
YO, LIS, WHY WEREN'T YOU IN SCHOOL TODAY?
I HAD TO MOW THE LAWN AND CLEAN THE GARAGE FOR EXTRA CREDIT.
MY G.P.A. HAS GONE TRIPLE PLATINUM, BUT IT JUST DOESN'T SEEM RIGHT.
THEN TELL HOMER "NO" NEXT TIME.
AND TURN DOWN GOOD GRADES?
LISA, I THINK YOU MIGHT BE TURNING INTO A GRADE JUNKIE.
OH, YOU'D LIKE ME TO THINK THAT, WOULDN'T YOU. THEN, WHEN I'M NOT LOOKING, YOU'D TAKE ALL THE EXTRA CREDIT ASSIGNMENTS FOR YOURSELF!
I'M ON TO YOU BART! I...I...
SPLASH!
GASP! THANKS, BART. I NEEDED THAT!
BUT WHERE DID YOU GET THE WATER?
MY SWIM TRUNKS WERE STILL DAMP FROM THE WATER-SLIDES.
EEEEW!

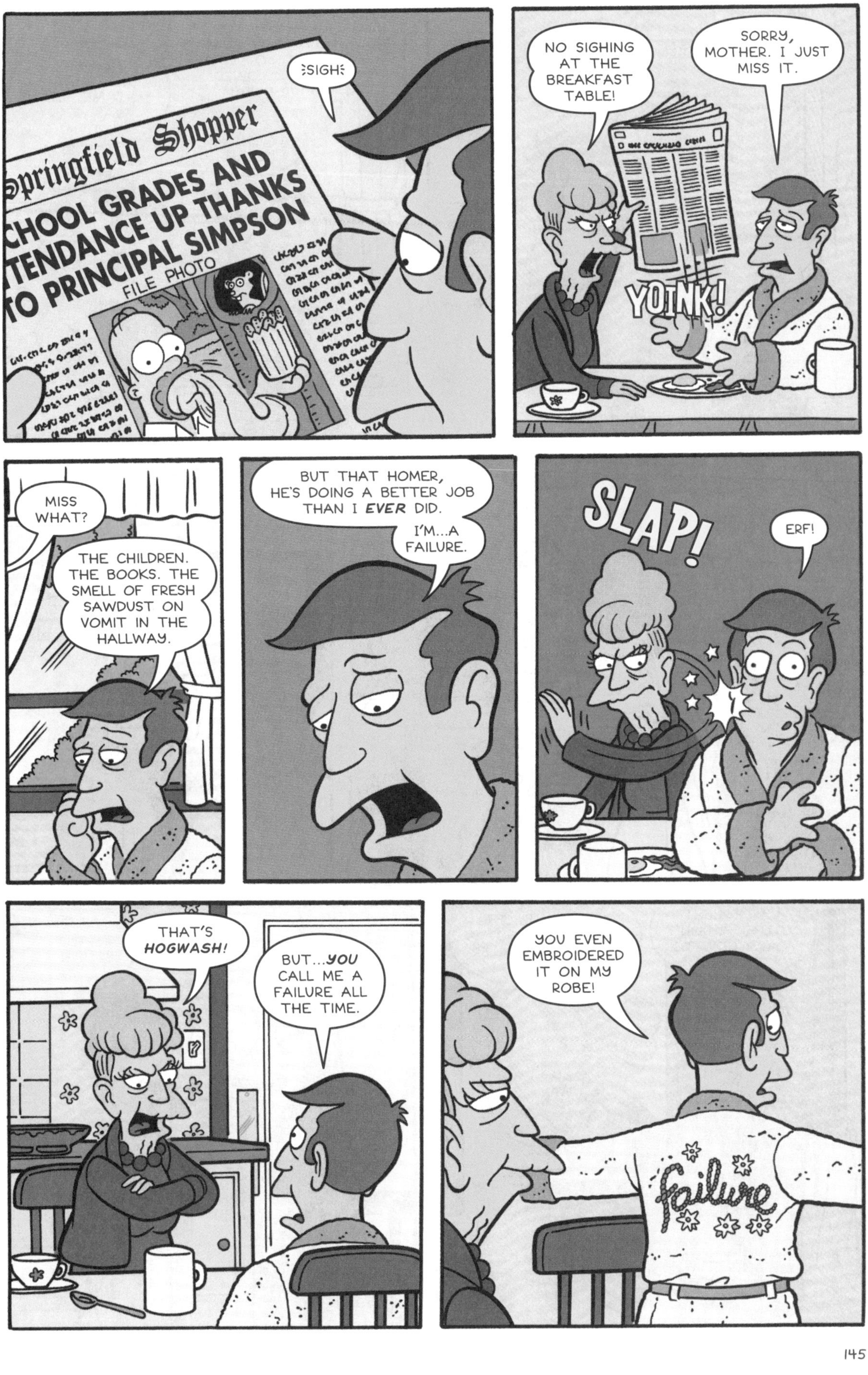
Springfield Shopper
CHOOL GRADES AND
TENDANCE UP THANKS
TO PRINCIPAL SIMPSON
FILE PHOTO
SIGH
NO SIGHING AT THE BREAKFAST TABLE!
SORRY, MOTHER. I JUST MISS IT.
YOINK!
MISS WHAT?
THE CHILDREN. THE BOOKS. THE SMELL OF FRESH SAWDUST ON VOMIT IN THE HALLWAY.
BUT THAT HOMER, HE'S DOING A BETTER JOB THAN I EVER DID.
I'M...A FAILURE.
SLAP!
ERF!
THAT'S HOGWASH!
BUT...YOU CALL ME A FAILURE ALL THE TIME.
YOU EVEN EMBROIDERED IT ON MY ROBE!
failure

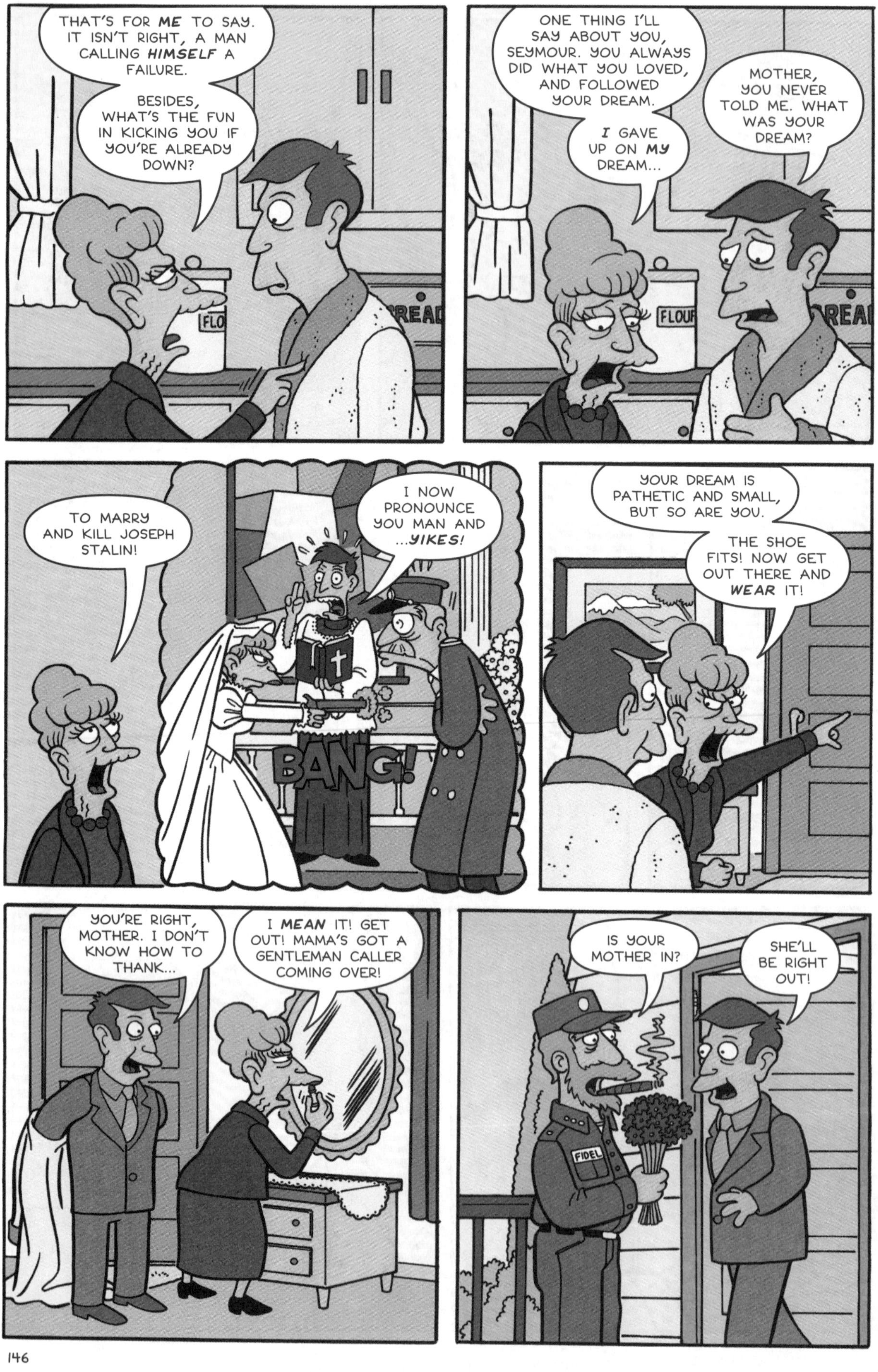
THAT'S FOR ME TO SAY. IT ISN'T RIGHT, A MAN CALLING HIMSELF A FAILURE.
BESIDES, WHAT'S THE FUN IN KICKING YOU IF YOU'RE ALREADY DOWN?
FLO
READ
ONE THING I'LL SAY ABOUT YOU, SEYMOUR. YOU ALWAYS DID WHAT YOU LOVED, AND FOLLOWED YOUR DREAM.
I GAVE UP ON MY DREAM...
MOTHER, YOU NEVER TOLD ME. WHAT WAS YOUR DREAM?
FLOUR
READ
TO MARRY AND KILL JOSEPH STALIN!
I NOW PRONOUNCE YOU MAN AND ...YIKES!
BANG!
YOUR DREAM IS PATHETIC AND SMALL, BUT SO ARE YOU.
THE SHOE FITS! NOW GET OUT THERE AND WEAR IT!
YOU'RE RIGHT, MOTHER. I DON'T KNOW HOW TO THANK...
I MEAN IT! GET OUT! MAMA'S GOT A GENTLEMAN CALLER COMING OVER!
IS YOUR MOTHER IN?
SHE'LL BE RIGHT OUT!
FIDEL

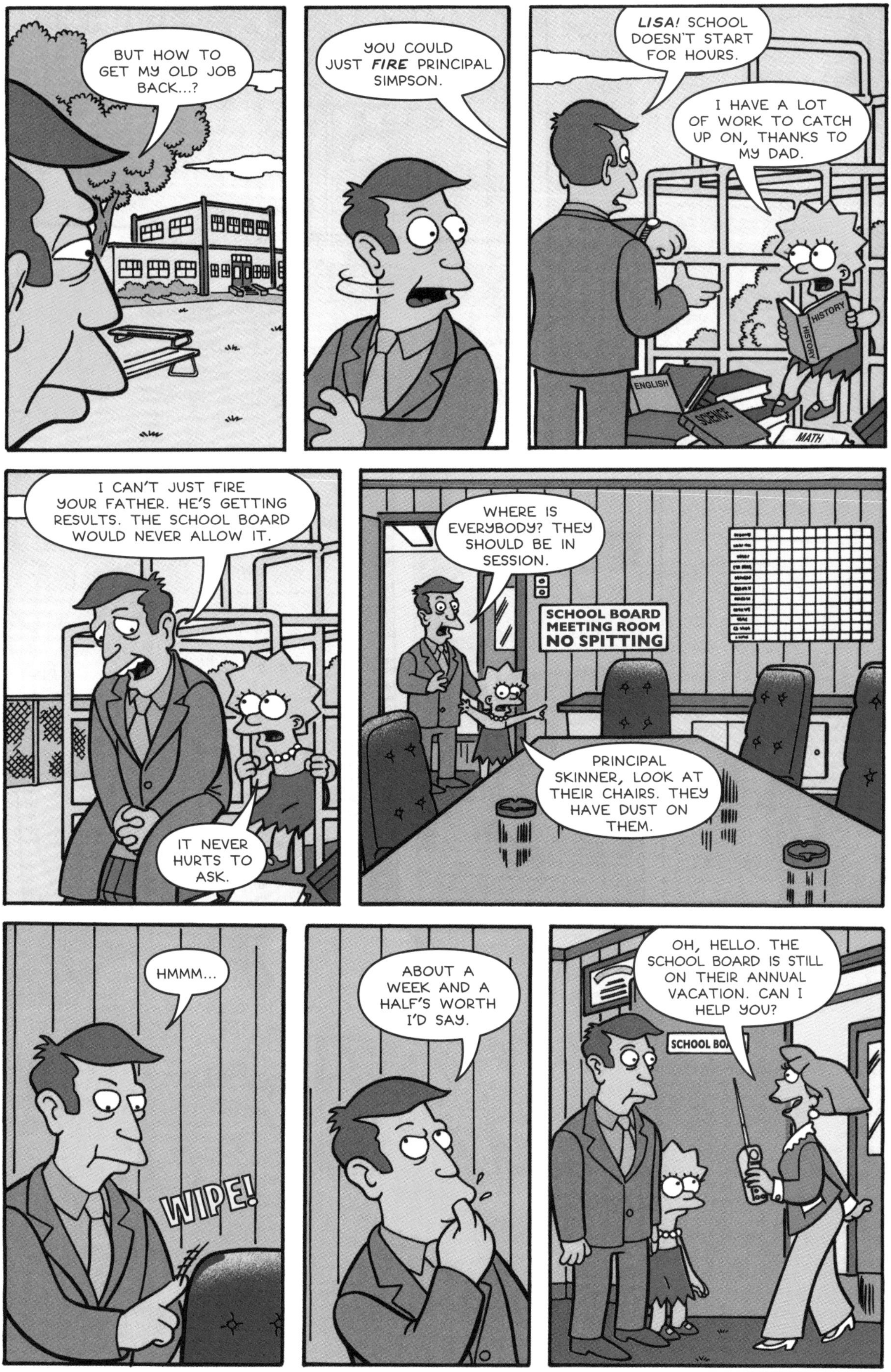
BUT HOW TO GET MY OLD JOB BACK...?
YOU COULD JUST FIRE PRINCIPAL SIMPSON.
LISA! SCHOOL DOESN'T START FOR HOURS.
I HAVE A LOT OF WORK TO CATCH UP ON, THANKS TO MY DAD.
HISTORY
ENGLISH
SCIENCE
MATH
I CAN'T JUST FIRE YOUR FATHER. HE'S GETTING RESULTS. THE SCHOOL BOARD WOULD NEVER ALLOW IT.
IT NEVER HURTS TO ASK.
WHERE IS EVERYBODY? THEY SHOULD BE IN SESSION.
SCHOOL BOARD MEETING ROOM NO SPITTING
PRINCIPAL SKINNER, LOOK AT THEIR CHAIRS. THEY HAVE DUST ON THEM.
HMMM...
WIPE!
ABOUT A WEEK AND A HALF'S WORTH I'D SAY.
OH, HELLO. THE SCHOOL BOARD IS STILL ON THEIR ANNUAL VACATION. CAN I HELP YOU?
SCHOOL BO

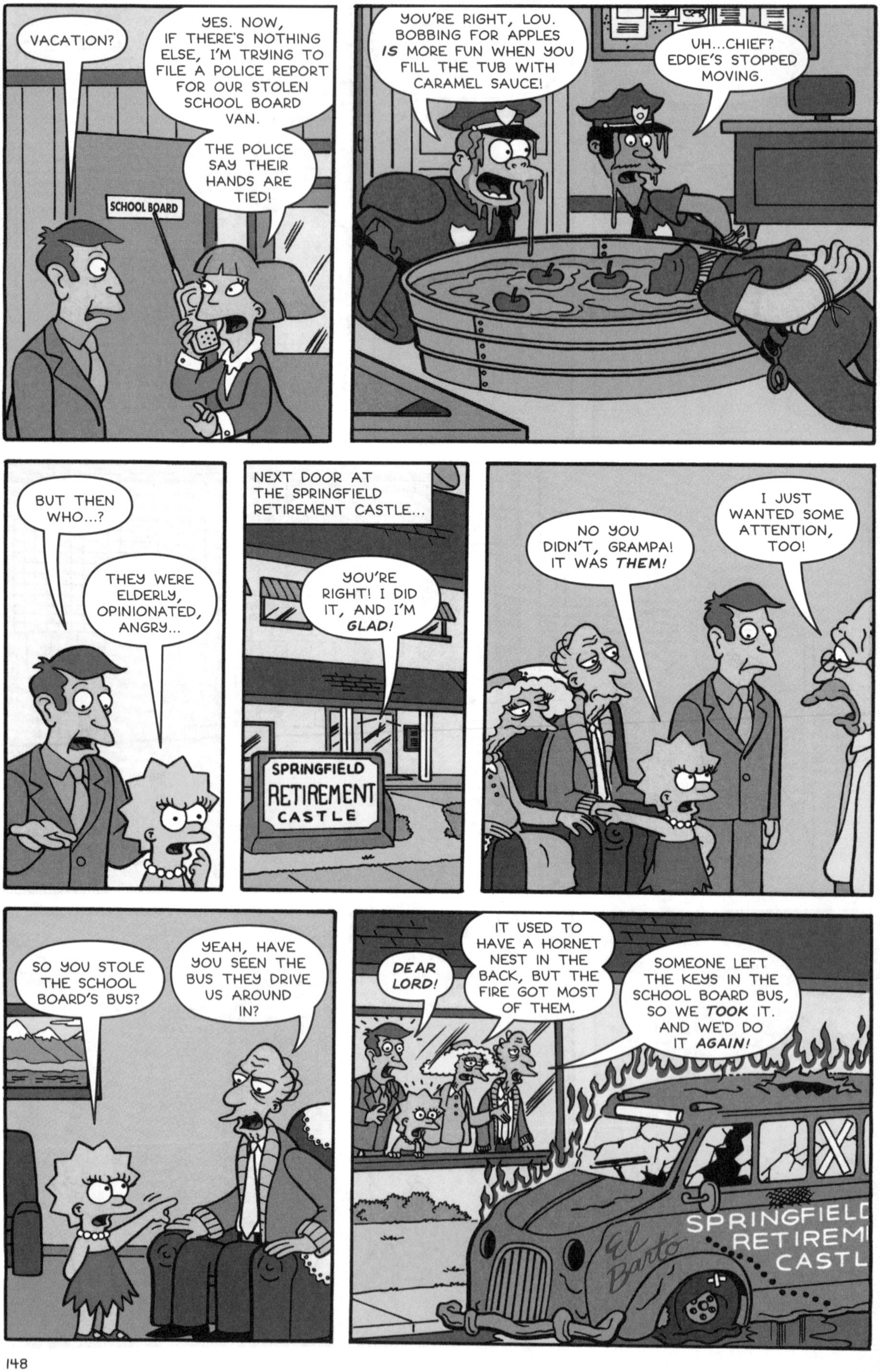
VACATION?
YES. NOW, IF THERE'S NOTHING ELSE, I'M TRYING TO FILE A POLICE REPORT FOR OUR STOLEN SCHOOL BOARD VAN.
THE POLICE SAY THEIR HANDS ARE TIED!
SCHOOL BOARD
YOU'RE RIGHT, LOU. BOBBING FOR APPLES *IS* MORE FUN WHEN YOU FILL THE TUB WITH CARAMEL SAUCE!
UH...CHIEF? EDDIE'S STOPPED MOVING.
BUT THEN WHO...?
THEY WERE ELDERLY, OPINIONATED, ANGRY...
NEXT DOOR AT THE SPRINGFIELD RETIREMENT CASTLE...
YOU'RE RIGHT! I DID IT, AND I'M *GLAD!*
SPRINGFIELD RETIREMENT CASTLE
NO YOU DIDN'T, GRAMPA! IT WAS *THEM!*
I JUST WANTED SOME ATTENTION, TOO!
SO YOU STOLE THE SCHOOL BOARD'S BUS?
YEAH, HAVE YOU SEEN THE BUS THEY DRIVE US AROUND IN?
*DEAR LORD!*
IT USED TO HAVE A HORNET NEST IN THE BACK, BUT THE FIRE GOT MOST OF THEM.
SOMEONE LEFT THE KEYS IN THE SCHOOL BOARD BUS, SO WE *TOOK* IT. AND WE'D DO IT *AGAIN!*
El Barto
SPRINGFIELD RETIREM CASTL

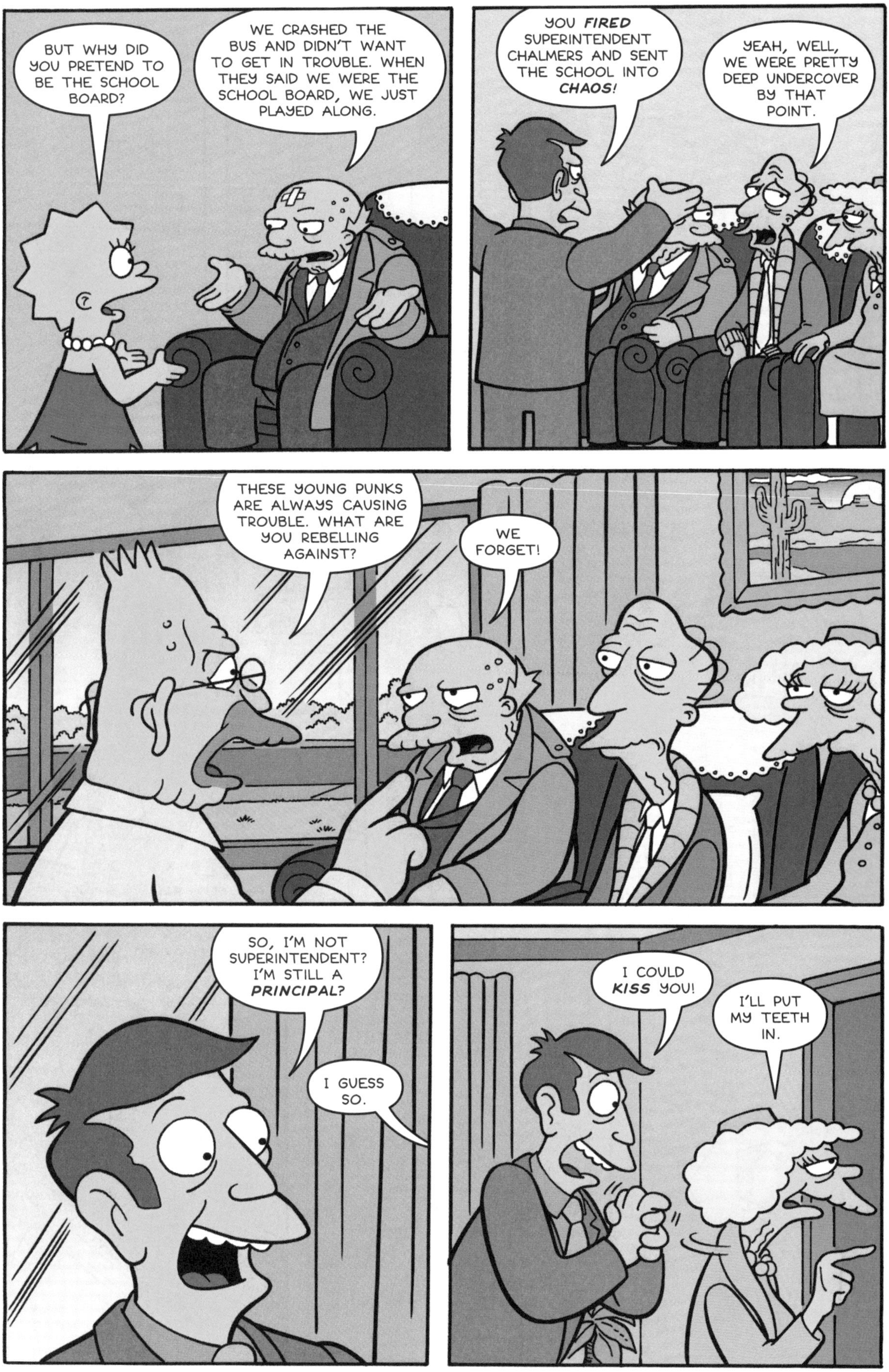
BUT WHY DID YOU PRETEND TO BE THE SCHOOL BOARD?
WE CRASHED THE BUS AND DIDN'T WANT TO GET IN TROUBLE. WHEN THEY SAID WE WERE THE SCHOOL BOARD, WE JUST PLAYED ALONG.
YOU **FIRED** SUPERINTENDENT CHALMERS AND SENT THE SCHOOL INTO **CHAOS**!
YEAH, WELL, WE WERE PRETTY DEEP UNDERCOVER BY THAT POINT.
THESE YOUNG PUNKS ARE ALWAYS CAUSING TROUBLE. WHAT ARE YOU REBELLING AGAINST?
WE FORGET!
SO, I'M NOT SUPERINTENDENT? I'M STILL A **PRINCIPAL**?
I GUESS SO.
I COULD **KISS** YOU!
I'LL PUT MY TEETH IN.

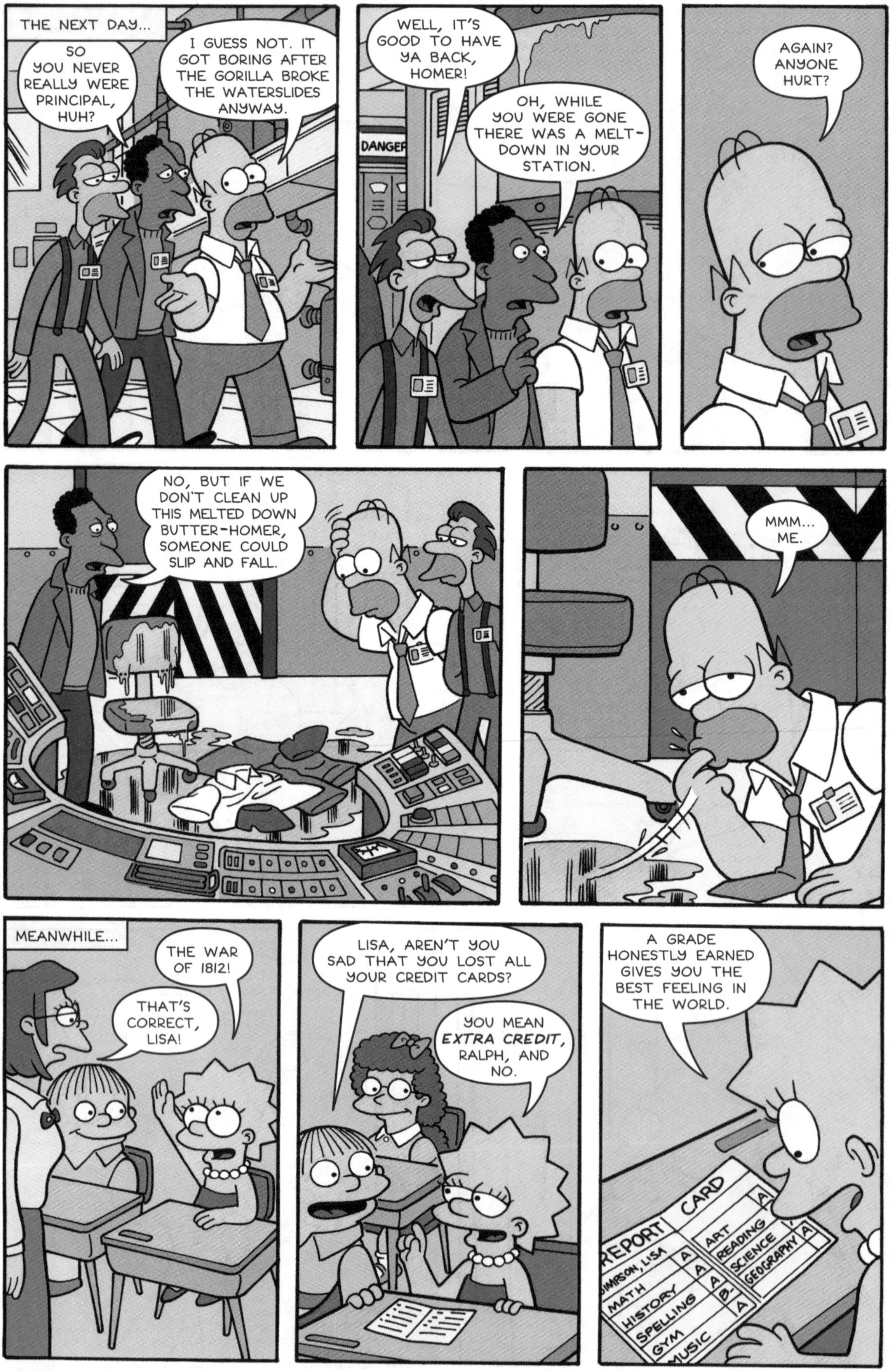
THE NEXT DAY...
SO YOU NEVER REALLY WERE PRINCIPAL, HUH?
I GUESS NOT. IT GOT BORING AFTER THE GORILLA BROKE THE WATERSLIDES ANYWAY.
WELL, IT'S GOOD TO HAVE YA BACK, HOMER!
DANGER
OH, WHILE YOU WERE GONE THERE WAS A MELT-DOWN IN YOUR STATION.
AGAIN? ANYONE HURT?
NO, BUT IF WE DON'T CLEAN UP THIS MELTED DOWN BUTTER-HOMER, SOMEONE COULD SLIP AND FALL.
MMM... ME.
MEANWHILE...
THE WAR OF 1812!
THAT'S CORRECT, LISA!
LISA, AREN'T YOU SAD THAT YOU LOST ALL YOUR CREDIT CARDS?
YOU MEAN ***EXTRA CREDIT***, RALPH, AND NO.
A GRADE HONESTLY EARNED GIVES YOU THE BEST FEELING IN THE WORLD.
REPORT CARD
SIMPSON, LISA
MATH A
HISTORY A
SPELLING A
GYM B-
MUSIC A
ART A
READING
SCIENCE
GEOGRAPHY A

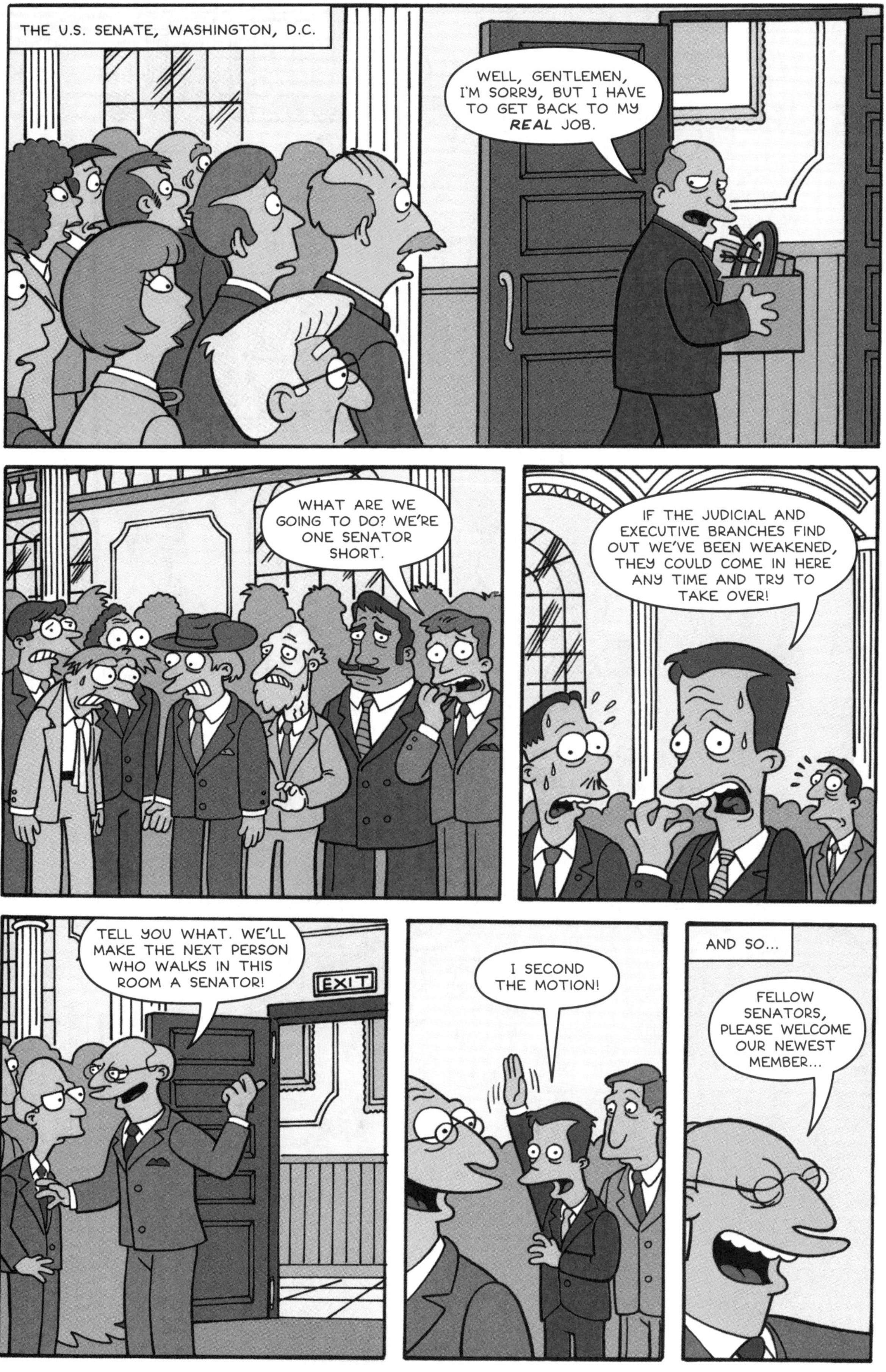
THE U.S. SENATE, WASHINGTON, D.C.
WELL, GENTLEMEN, I'M SORRY, BUT I HAVE TO GET BACK TO MY **REAL** JOB.
WHAT ARE WE GOING TO DO? WE'RE ONE SENATOR SHORT.
IF THE JUDICIAL AND EXECUTIVE BRANCHES FIND OUT WE'VE BEEN WEAKENED, THEY COULD COME IN HERE ANY TIME AND TRY TO TAKE OVER!
TELL YOU WHAT. WE'LL MAKE THE NEXT PERSON WHO WALKS IN THIS ROOM A SENATOR!
EXIT
I SECOND THE MOTION!
AND SO...
FELLOW SENATORS, PLEASE WELCOME OUR NEWEST MEMBER...

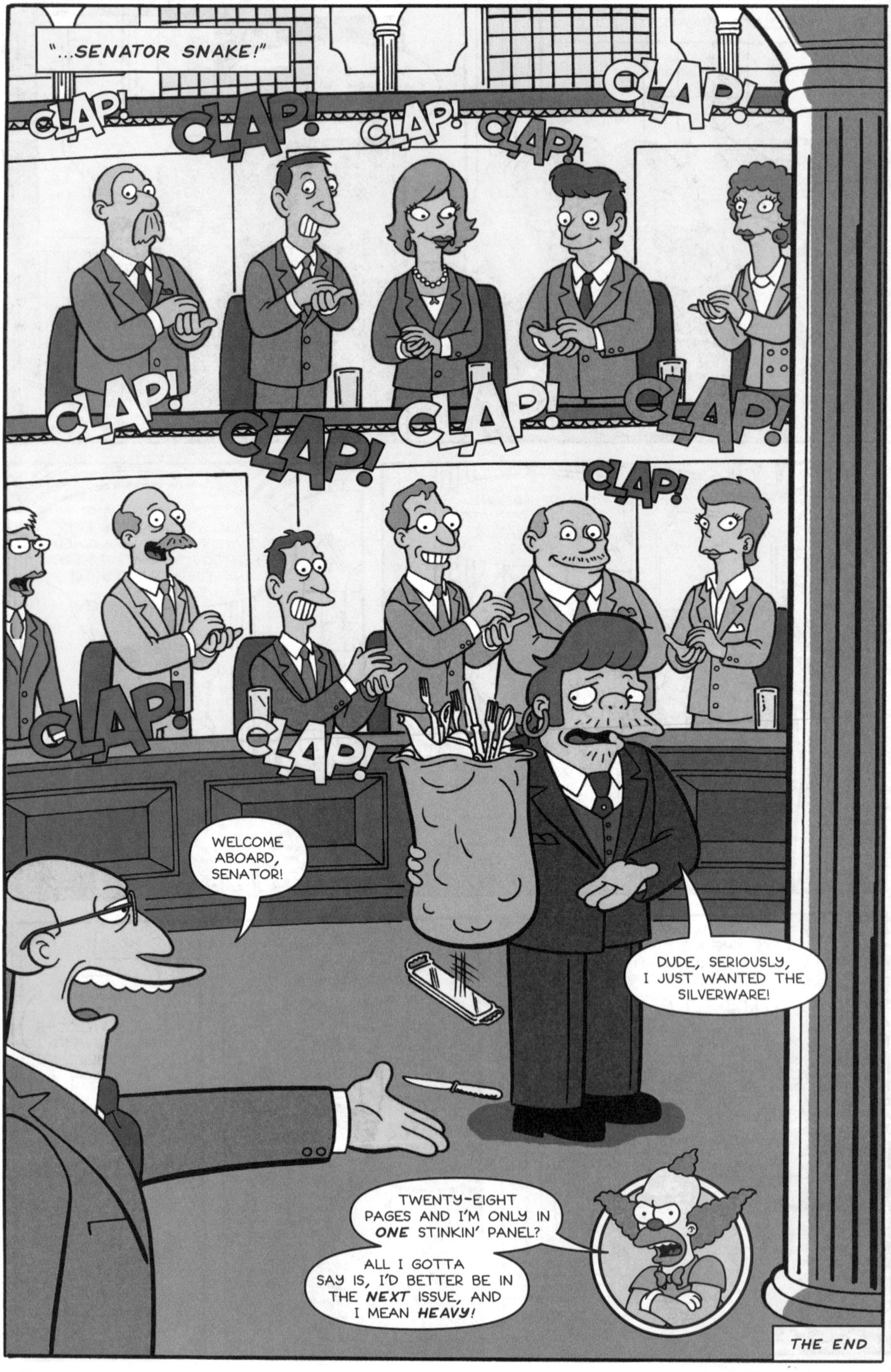
"...SENATOR SNAKE!"
CLAP!
CLAP!
CLAP!
CLAP!
CLAP!
CLAP!
CLAP!
CLAP!
CLAP!
CLAP!
CLAP!
CLAP!
WELCOME ABOARD, SENATOR!
DUDE, SERIOUSLY, I JUST WANTED THE SILVERWARE!
TWENTY-EIGHT PAGES AND I'M ONLY IN ONE STINKIN' PANEL?
ALL I GOTTA SAY IS, I'D BETTER BE IN THE NEXT ISSUE, AND I MEAN HEAVY!
THE END

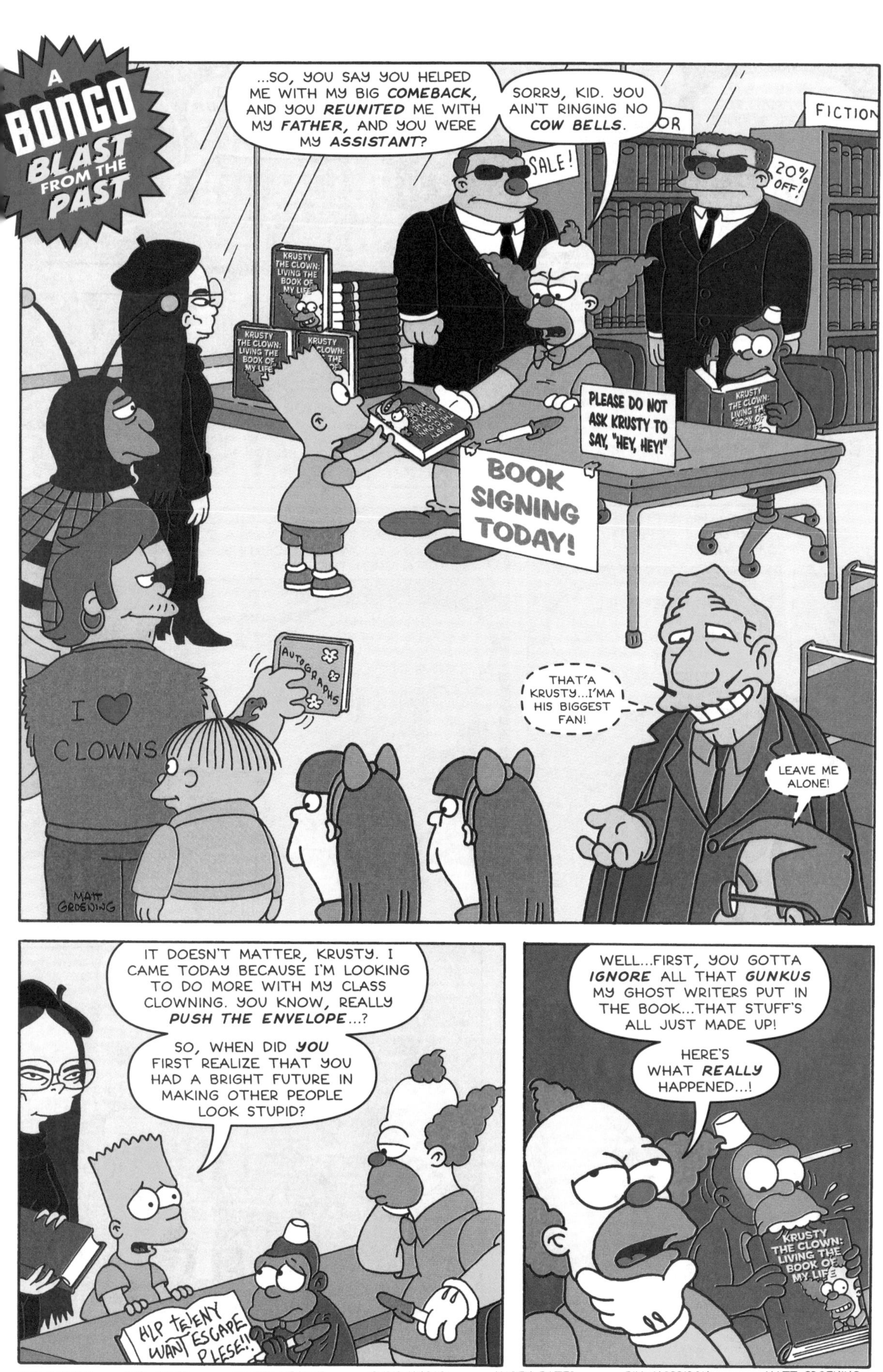
A BONGO BLAST FROM THE PAST
...SO, YOU SAY YOU HELPED ME WITH MY BIG COMEBACK, AND YOU REUNITED ME WITH MY FATHER, AND YOU WERE MY ASSISTANT?
SORRY, KID. YOU AIN'T RINGING NO COW BELLS.
FICTION
SALE!
20% OFF!
KRUSTY THE CLOWN: LIVING THE BOOK OF MY LIFE
PLEASE DO NOT ASK KRUSTY TO SAY, "HEY, HEY!"
BOOK SIGNING TODAY!
AUTOGRAPHS
I ♥ CLOWNS
THAT'A KRUSTY...I'MA HIS BIGGEST FAN!
LEAVE ME ALONE!
MATT GROENING
IT DOESN'T MATTER, KRUSTY. I CAME TODAY BECAUSE I'M LOOKING TO DO MORE WITH MY CLASS CLOWNING. YOU KNOW, REALLY PUSH THE ENVELOPE...?
SO, WHEN DID YOU FIRST REALIZE THAT YOU HAD A BRIGHT FUTURE IN MAKING OTHER PEOPLE LOOK STUPID?
HLP TEENY WANT ESCAPE PLESE!!
WELL...FIRST, YOU GOTTA IGNORE ALL THAT GUNKUS MY GHOST WRITERS PUT IN THE BOOK...THAT STUFF'S ALL JUST MADE UP!
HERE'S WHAT REALLY HAPPENED...!
KRUSTY THE CLOWN: LIVING THE BOOK OF MY LIFE

GAIL SIMONE SCRIPT | PHIL ORTIZ PENCILS | SCOTT MCCRAE INKS | CHRIS UNGAR COLORS | KAREN BATES LETTERS | BILL MORRISON EDITOR | MATT GROENING BAD APPLE

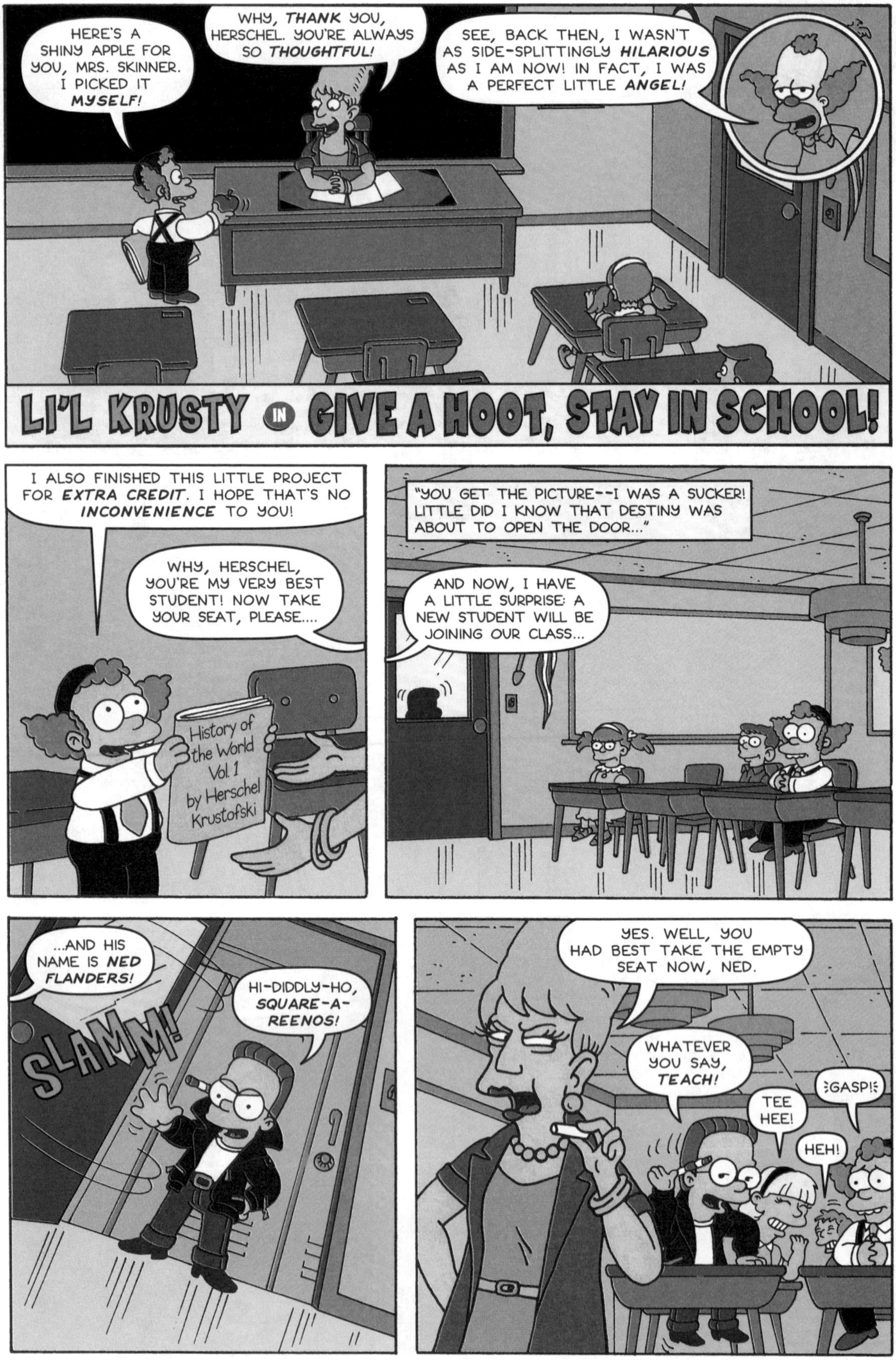
HERE'S A SHINY APPLE FOR YOU, MRS. SKINNER. I PICKED IT MYSELF!
WHY, THANK YOU, HERSCHEL. YOU'RE ALWAYS SO THOUGHTFUL!
SEE, BACK THEN, I WASN'T AS SIDE-SPLITTINGLY HILARIOUS AS I AM NOW! IN FACT, I WAS A PERFECT LITTLE ANGEL!
LI'L KRUSTY IN GIVE A HOOT, STAY IN SCHOOL!
I ALSO FINISHED THIS LITTLE PROJECT FOR EXTRA CREDIT. I HOPE THAT'S NO INCONVENIENCE TO YOU!
WHY, HERSCHEL, YOU'RE MY VERY BEST STUDENT! NOW TAKE YOUR SEAT, PLEASE....
History of the World Vol. 1 by Herschel Krustofski
"YOU GET THE PICTURE--I WAS A SUCKER! LITTLE DID I KNOW THAT DESTINY WAS ABOUT TO OPEN THE DOOR..."
AND NOW, I HAVE A LITTLE SURPRISE: A NEW STUDENT WILL BE JOINING OUR CLASS...
...AND HIS NAME IS NED FLANDERS!
SLAMM!
HI-DIDDLY-HO, SQUARE-A-REENOS!
YES. WELL, YOU HAD BEST TAKE THE EMPTY SEAT NOW, NED.
WHATEVER YOU SAY, TEACH!
TEE HEE!
GASP!
HEH!

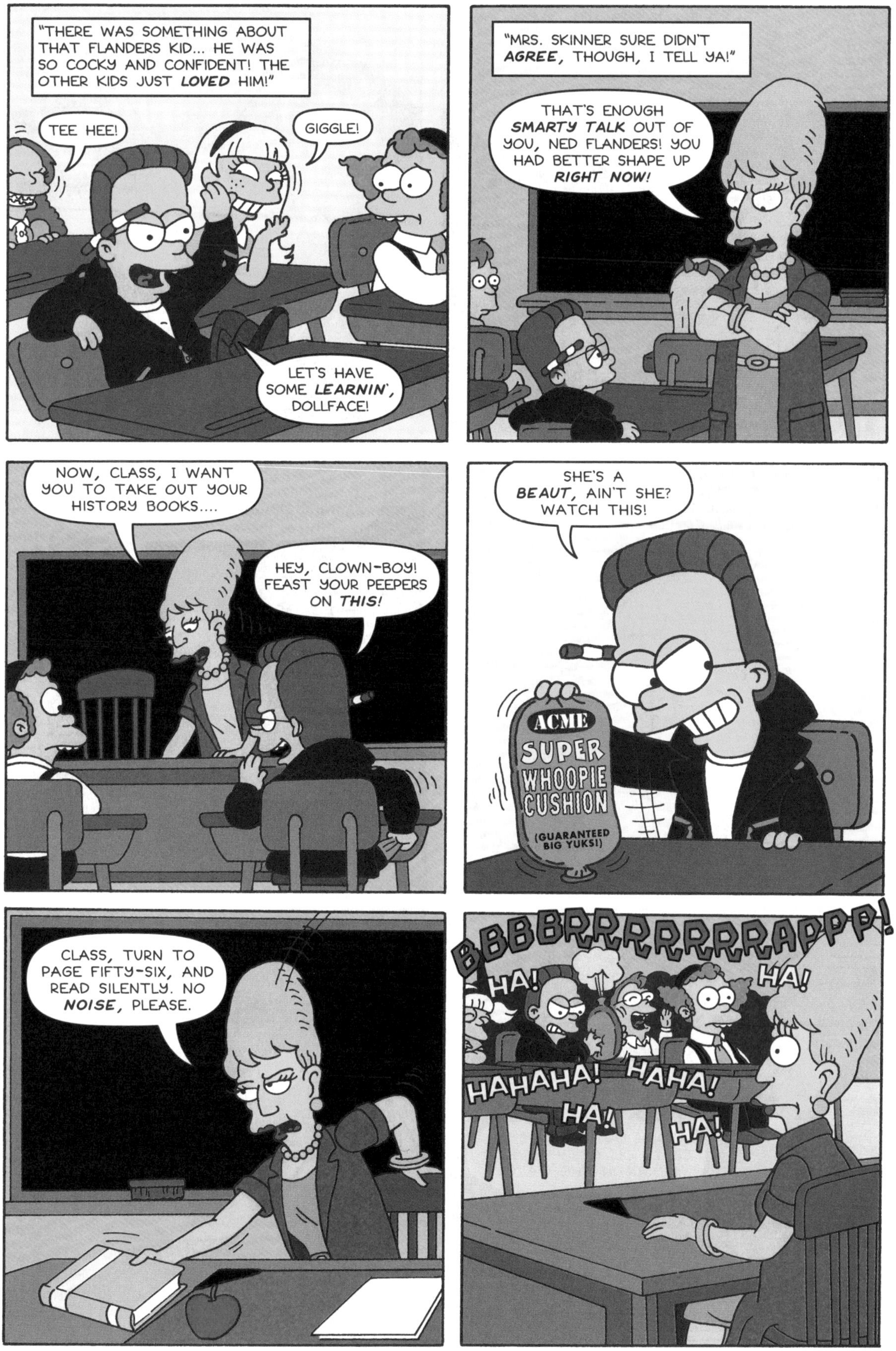
"THERE WAS SOMETHING ABOUT THAT FLANDERS KID... HE WAS SO COCKY AND CONFIDENT! THE OTHER KIDS JUST LOVED HIM!"
TEE HEE!
GIGGLE!
LET'S HAVE SOME LEARNIN', DOLLFACE!
"MRS. SKINNER SURE DIDN'T AGREE, THOUGH, I TELL YA!"
THAT'S ENOUGH SMARTY TALK OUT OF YOU, NED FLANDERS! YOU HAD BETTER SHAPE UP RIGHT NOW!
NOW, CLASS, I WANT YOU TO TAKE OUT YOUR HISTORY BOOKS....
HEY, CLOWN-BOY! FEAST YOUR PEEPERS ON THIS!
SHE'S A BEAUT, AIN'T SHE? WATCH THIS!
ACME
SUPER WHOOPIE CUSHION
(GUARANTEED BIG YUKS!)
CLASS, TURN TO PAGE FIFTY-SIX, AND READ SILENTLY. NO NOISE, PLEASE.
BBBBRRRRRRRRRAPPPP!
HA!
HA!
HAHAHA!
HAHA!
HA!
HA!

NED FLANDERS! DID YOU JUST MAKE THAT OBSCENE NOISE?!?!

QUICK! HIDE THIS!

WHA...?

PEEEEEEEYEW, MRS. SKINNER! YOU MUSTA HAD BEANS FOR BREAKFAST!

GIGGLE!

HAHA!

SNORT!

HA!

HA!

THAT'S MY LAST WARNING, NED. YOU TRY ONE MORE FUNNY STUNT IN MY CLASSROOM, AND I'LL MAKE SURE YOU'RE EXPELLED FOR GOOD!

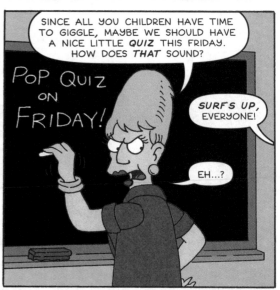

SINCE ALL YOU CHILDREN HAVE TIME TO GIGGLE, MAYBE WE SHOULD HAVE A NICE LITTLE QUIZ THIS FRIDAY. HOW DOES THAT SOUND?

POP QUIZ ON FRIDAY!

SURF'S UP, EVERYONE!

EH...?

HA! HA! HA! HA!

WE LOVE YOU, NED!

LOOK OUT! THERE'S A CRAZY OL' GREY-HAIRED SHARK IN THE WATER!

OH, MY LORD!

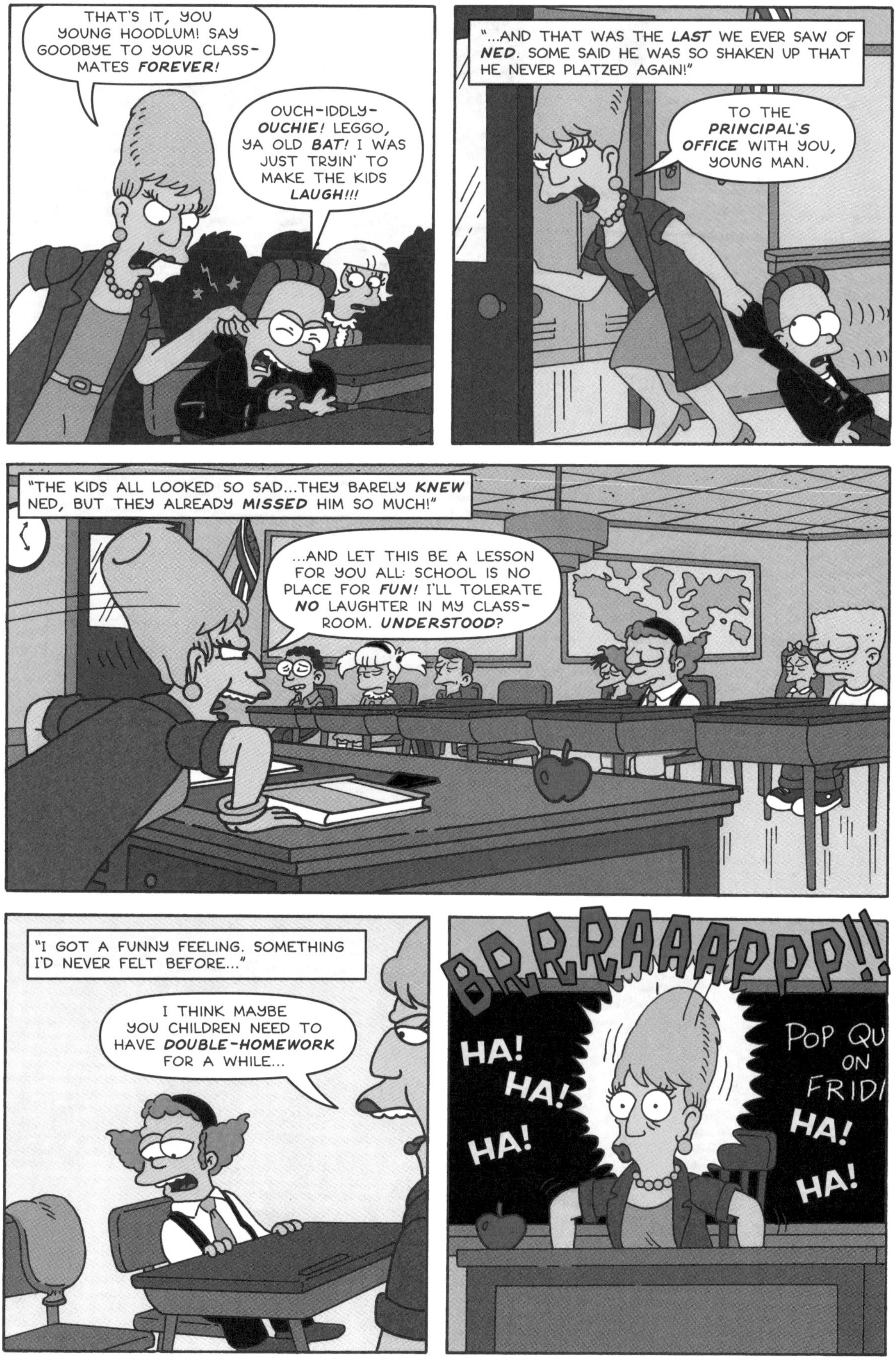

THAT'S IT, YOU YOUNG HOODLUM! SAY GOODBYE TO YOUR CLASS-MATES FOREVER!
OUCH-IDDLY-OUCHIE! LEGGO, YA OLD BAT! I WAS JUST TRYIN' TO MAKE THE KIDS LAUGH!!!
"...AND THAT WAS THE LAST WE EVER SAW OF NED. SOME SAID HE WAS SO SHAKEN UP THAT HE NEVER PLATZED AGAIN!"
TO THE PRINCIPAL'S OFFICE WITH YOU, YOUNG MAN.
"THE KIDS ALL LOOKED SO SAD...THEY BARELY KNEW NED, BUT THEY ALREADY MISSED HIM SO MUCH!"
...AND LET THIS BE A LESSON FOR YOU ALL: SCHOOL IS NO PLACE FOR FUN! I'LL TOLERATE NO LAUGHTER IN MY CLASS-ROOM. UNDERSTOOD?
"I GOT A FUNNY FEELING. SOMETHING I'D NEVER FELT BEFORE..."
I THINK MAYBE YOU CHILDREN NEED TO HAVE DOUBLE-HOMEWORK FOR A WHILE...
BRRRRAAAAPPPP!!
HA! HA! HA!
POP QU ON FRID
HA! HA!

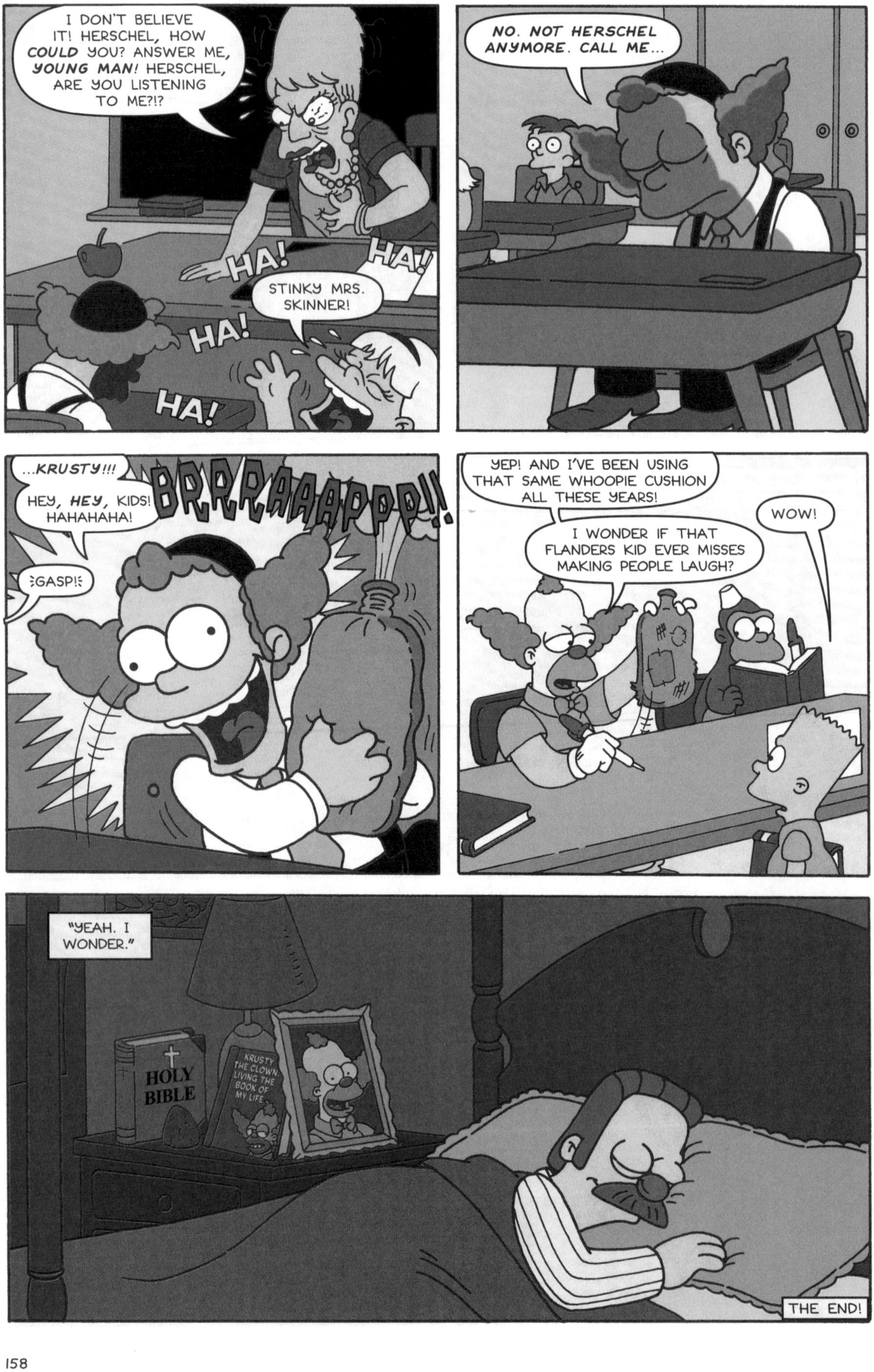
I DON'T BELIEVE IT! HERSCHEL, HOW COULD YOU? ANSWER ME, YOUNG MAN! HERSCHEL, ARE YOU LISTENING TO ME?!?
HA!
HA!
STINKY MRS. SKINNER!
HA!
HA!
NO. NOT HERSCHEL ANYMORE. CALL ME...
...KRUSTY!!!
HEY, HEY, KIDS! HAHAHAHA!
BRRRAAAAPPP!!
GASP!
YEP! AND I'VE BEEN USING THAT SAME WHOOPIE CUSHION ALL THESE YEARS!
I WONDER IF THAT FLANDERS KID EVER MISSES MAKING PEOPLE LAUGH?
WOW!
"YEAH. I WONDER."
HOLY BIBLE
KRUSTY THE CLOWN: LIVING THE BOOK OF MY LIFE
THE END!

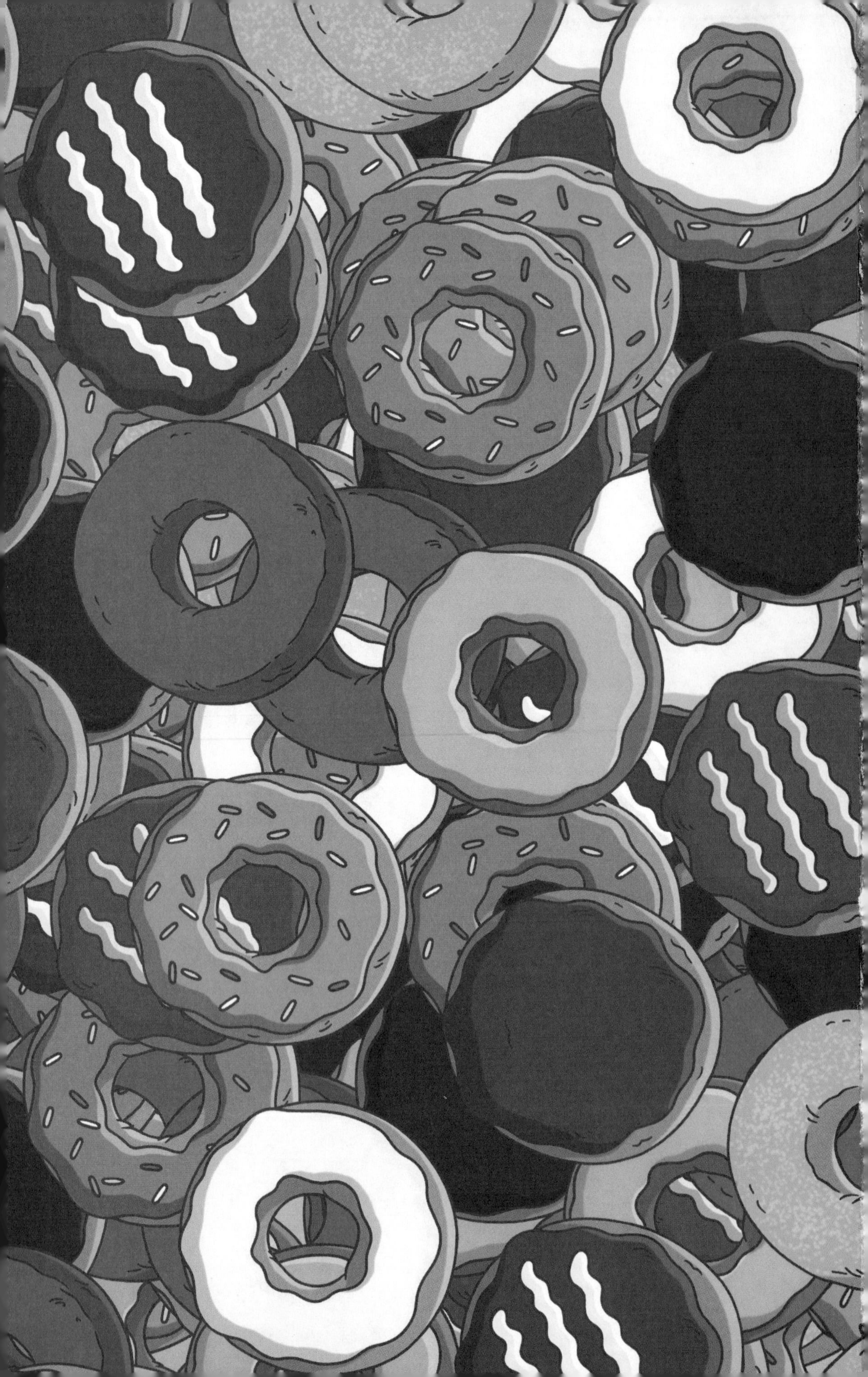